FILLING THE RANKS

CARLETON LIBRARY SERIES

The Carleton Library Series publishes books about Canadian economics, geography, history, politics, public policy, society and culture, and related topics, in the form of leading new scholarship and reprints of classics in these fields. The series is funded by Carleton University, published by McGill-Queen's University Press, and is under the guidance of the Carleton Library Series Editorial Board, which consists of faculty members of Carleton University. Suggestions and proposals for manuscripts and new editions of classic works are welcome and may be directed to the Carleton Library Series Editorial Board c/o the Library, Carleton University, Ottawa K1S 5B6, at cls@carleton.ca, or on the web at www.carleton.ca/cls.

CLS board members: John Clarke, Ross Eaman, Jennifer Henderson, Laura Macdonald, Paul Litt, Stanley Winer, Barry Wright

224 *How Schools Worked*
Public Education in English Canada, 1900–1940
R.D. Gidney and W.P.J. Millar

225 *A Two-Edged Sword*
The Navy as an Instrument of Canadian Foreign Policy
Nicholas Tracy

226 *The Illustrated History of Canada*
25th Anniversary Edition
Edited by Craig Brown

227 *In Duty Bound*
Men, Women, and the State in Upper Canada, 1783–1841
J.K. Johnson

228 *Asleep at the Switch*
The Political Economy of Federal Research and Development Policy since 1960
Bruce Smardon

229 *And We Go On*
Will R. Bird
Introduction and Afterword by David Williams

230 *The Great War as I Saw It*
Frederick George Scott
Introduction by Mark G. McGowan

231 *The Canadian Oral History Reader*
Edited by Kristina R. Llewellyn, Alexander Freund, and Nolan Reilly

232 *Lives in Transition*
Longitudinal Analysis from Historical Sources
Edited by Peter Baskerville and Kris Inwood

233 *W.A. Mackintosh*
The Life of a Canadian Economist
Hugh Grant

234 *Green-lite*
Complexity in Fifty Years of Canadian Environmental Policy, Governance, and Democracy
G. Bruce Doern, Graeme Auld, and Christopher Stoney

235 *Canadian Expeditionary Force, 1914–1919*
Official History of the Canadian Army in the First World War
G.W.L. Nicholson
Introduction by Mark Osborne Humphries

236 *Trade, Industrial Policy, and International Competition, Second Edition*
Richard G. Harris
Introduction by David A. Wolfe

237 *An Undisciplined Economist*
Robert G. Evans on Health Economics, Health Care Policy, and Population Health
Edited by Morris L. Barer, Greg L. Stoddart, Kimberlyn M. McGrail, and Chris B. McLeod

238 *Wildlife, Land, and People*
A Century of Change in Prairie Canada
Donald G. Wetherell

239 *Filling the Ranks*
Manpower in the Canadian Expeditionary Force, 1914–1918
Richard Holt

Filling the Ranks

Manpower in the Canadian Expeditionary Force, 1914–1918

RICHARD HOLT

Carleton Library Series 239

McGill-Queen's University Press
Montreal & Kingston · London · Chicago

© McGill-Queen's University Press 2017

ISBN 978-0-7735-4877-0 (cloth)
ISBN 978-0-7735-4910-4 (ePDF)
ISBN 978-0-7735-4911-1 (ePUB)

Legal deposit first quarter 2017
Bibliothèque nationale du Québec

Printed in Canada on acid-free paper that is 100% ancient forest free (100% post-consumer recycled), processed chlorine free

McGill-Queen's University Press acknowledges the support of the Canada Council for the Arts for our publishing program. We also acknowledge the financial support of the Government of Canada through the Canada Book Fund for our publishing activities.

Library and Archives Canada Cataloguing in Publication

Holt, Richard, 1948 February 21–, author
    Filling the ranks: manpower in the Canadian Expeditionary Force, 1914–1918 / Richard Holt.

(Carleton Library series; 239)
Includes bibliographical references and index.
Issued in print and electronic formats.
ISBN 978-0-7735-4877-0 (hardback). – ISBN 978-0-7735-4910-4 (ePDF). – ISBN 978-0-7735-4911-1 (ePUB)

    1. Canada. Canadian Army. Canadian Expeditionary Force – Personnel management. 2. Canada. Canadian Army. Canadian Expeditionary Force. 3. World War, 1914–1918 – Regimental histories – Canada. 4. World War, 1914–1918. I. Title. II. Series: Carleton library series; 239

UB325.C3H65 2017   355.6'10971   C2016-906554-5
                                       C2016-906555-3

This book was typeset by Marquis Interscript in 10.5/13 Sabon.

Contents

Tables and Figures   vii
Acknowledgments   ix
Foreword   xi
Abbreviations   xv
Illustrations   xvii

Introduction   3
1   Militia Roots   13
2   Regulating Manpower: Government and Military Policies 1914–18   34
3   Enlistment Criteria   55
4   Alternative Sources of Manpower   83
5   The Recruiting Structure 1914–18   104
6   Infantry Training   128
7   Reinforcements: Policy, Management, and Wastage   169
8   Reinforcements: Canada to England   184
9   The Overseas *Via Dolorosa:* Reinforcements in England and France   209
Conclusion   251

Notes   257
Bibliography   329
Index   343

Tables and Figures

TABLES

1.1 District and divisional organization, 31 March 1914   19
2.1 Canadian units outside of Canadian Corps, 11 November 1918   54
3.1 Unfit soldiers, 1914–18   65
3.2 MSA medical board results, 1917: men aged 20–35   81
3.3 Revised manpower pool: men aged 18–45   82
4.1 Medical categories   96
4.2 Sample of foreign-born enlistments   99
6.1 Militia volunteers, August 1914   134
6.2 Training levels of battalions arriving in England, 1917   156
7.1 CEF average draft times   178
7.2 Wastage, other ranks: selected arms and services   179
7.3 Monthly average of non-effectives, August 1916–November 1918   182
8.1 Sample of reinforcements, service in Canada: formed battalions 1916 and drafts 1915   194
8.2 Sample of reinforcements, service in Canada: formed battalions and drafts, 1917   194
8.3 Depot battalions in Canada, April 1918   203
8.4 Infantry arrivals in England, 1917   204
8.5 Infantry arrivals in England, 1918   205
8.6 Comparison sample of infantry reinforcements service before embarkation, 1916–18   207

8.7 Infantry fatalities, Canada's Hundred Days, 8 August–11 November 1918   208
9.1 Reserve battalions: unfit men, April–December 1915   215

FIGURES

7.1 Pre-war British infantry reinforcement structure   172
7.2 British infantry reinforcement structure, July 1915   174
7.3 British reinforcement structure: all arms, September 1917   174
7.4 Simplified organizational control of reinforcements, September 1917   175
9.1 Elements held in CCRC camp, 1918   246
9.2 CCRC elements dispersed in corps area, 1918   246

Acknowledgments

Producing this book was not easy, and I am grateful for the advice and encouragement I have received over the last several years.

Among others, I am grateful to my PhD supervisor, Professor Jonathan Vance of the University of Western Ontario. His patience and tactful guidance were very much appreciated. Thank you.

The staff at Library and Archives Canada, the National Archives at Kew, Directorate of History and Heritage, Archives of Ontario, the Imperial War Museum, Peterborough Centennial Museum and Archives, the Royal Canadian Regiment Museum, Woodstock City Museum, the Elgin Military Museum, the Archives and Research Collections Centre of the University of Western Ontario, and the St Marys Museum all went out of their way to help me. Thanks also to the Reference Room of the Saskatoon Public Library for providing a photocopy of part of Roy McLellan's privately published memoirs from what appears to be the only copy available in Canada. I am also grateful to Jennifer Holland, the reference librarian at the University of Western Ontario Law School, for her assistance in tracking down US legislation relevant to the British-Canadian Recruiting Mission. Thanks also to the ever-helpful staff at the D.B. Weldon Library, in particular Anne Morris, who answered impossible questions, and David Murphy, who was able to finesse seemingly impossible interlibrary loans.

I am particularly grateful to Dr Tim Cook and Professor Emeritus J.L. Granatstein who stepped forward at a difficult moment for me and offered to help steer this book through the publication process. I would also like to thank Philip Cercone and the staff of McGill-Queen's University Press for making this book possible.

Finally, I would like to acknowledge my wife, Victoria, who has been a tremendous help over the years. For everything, thank you.

Foreword

TIM COOK AND J.L. GRANATSTEIN

Attrition defined the Great War. Once the initial hope of a decisive victory disappeared in a hail of shell and machine gun fire, the warring sides turned to wearing out the enemy in preparation for a knock-out blow. The intention was to kill enough of the enemy's soldiers that the demoralized survivors would lay down their arms or retreat. Of course, this also meant that one's own armies would not escape the attritional battles, as all sides engaged in relentless acts of mutually assured destruction.

Yet the armies of millions refused to break, no matter the horrendous casualties or debilitating conditions of the trenches. Even when tens and then hundreds of thousands fell in battle, there seemed always to be more troops to fill the ranks. But there was a finite number of men who could serve in the armies. Not all of the adult male population was suitable for service; although imperfectly enforced, criteria for age, height, and physical and mental fitness excluded many from enlistment. Malnutrition and disease made many more unfit. Even flat feet or bad teeth could keep a man out of uniform, although all countries lessened restrictions as the war dragged on and the bodies piled higher.

The manpower question became crucial to every nation that had been drawn into the vortex of the war. Finding the necessary men to serve in the armed forces was an increasingly complex task, especially in unlimited warfare that demanded that industry feed the fronts with shells, armaments, and other war supplies. Workers were needed for those industries. Nor could farms be denuded of all the young men, lest nations starve. Were scientists, skilled toolmakers, and physicians best used in jobs for which they were trained, or as foot soldiers at the front? There were no easy answers, and as the fighting fronts drew in more and more resources, it became more challenging to raise new units and recruits.

Canada's initial contribution of soldiers to the Allied war effort in 1914 saw an astonishing 31,000 men leave the Dominion in October 1914 to fight for Britain. Most were British-born; all had strong ties to the Empire. Never had Canada sent such a force overseas. By war's end, more than 620,000 Canadians would serve from a nation of fewer than 8 million. Ties of blood and belonging compelled these men to enlist, as did a desire for adventure, the promise of steady pay, or a yearning to be a part of something grander than their narrow existence on a farm or their shrinking job prospects in Canada's cities. As the war dragged on and casualties mounted, especially after the Second Battle of Ypres, more Canadian-born enlisted. Almost all young men felt the call of war. Many were pressured to do their bit and go overseas.

How these recruits were convinced to serve was an important part of Canada's war effort, but so too were the means by which the Canadian military tried to organize this mass of men. The structures in place were insufficient to deal with tens and then hundreds of thousands of enlisted men, and the government and the Department of Militia and Defence underwent a continual process of learning, stumbling, failing, and flailing as they tried to cope with the enormous challenge of raising forces, equipping and training the soldiers, transporting them overseas, and further forging effective and efficient structures to get the soldiers to the fighting units in the front lines. The management of manpower was a challenging and demanding task, and it is this crucial story that historian Dr Richard Holt lays out in this book.

Dr Holt, a long-serving officer in the Canadian Forces with a PhD in History, has delved deeply into all manner of records in the nation's archives, often reading against the grain to pull out crucial numbers and statistics. His study focuses on complex manpower questions and the creation of structures, organizations, and policies. This story is not about heroism and the horror of the trenches of the Western Front; instead, Holt demonstrates clearly that the mustering and allocation of manpower was no less crucial to fighting the war. How nations dealt with questions of grand logistics – arming, feeding, training, and finding men – could be the difference between victory and defeat in battle. In Canada, the war effort was overwhelming in its complexity, and even finding or creating places to train tens of thousands of men, provide boots and uniforms, and train them in the ever-changing tactics was a monumental task. Yet without soldiers and adequate training, the overseas forces would have collapsed from the unending bloodletting at the front. The amateurism of the initial war effort gave way to a new professionalism, and Holt unravels the evolution of manpower politics and their impact on recruiting at the armouries and battalions that sprang up across the country. His discussion of the role of women and how they entered the work force to allow males to enlist offers a valuable contribution to the understanding of the war. The inclusion in the ranks, albeit in small numbers, of First Nations, visible minorities, and recent immigrants similarly provides nuances into our understanding of the men who formed the Canadian Expeditionary Force over its five-year existence.

The recruiting of men by battalions involved multiple strategies and imaginative techniques, all of it driven by desperation, as units clashed with others for the dwindling pool of fit men. Many over-age and under-age soldiers, as well as physically unfit men, were taken on strength; they would later prove to be a burden in England, although some would eventually make it to the front. Holt's work provides new insight into the training of men in Canada and overseas and extends beyond the infantry into the other combat arms. Throughout the process, Holt's impressive research uncovers waste and inefficiency in the ad hoc and at times chaotic recruitment and training structure. Some of that was only to be expected with the massive undertaking of putting more than six hundred thousand men in uniform, but Holt offers a new analysis into the impact of the Canadian structure and system on warfighting at the front and helps explain how Canada's overseas army, with its origins in a peacetime militia, evolved into a well-organized professional force.

Neither of us know Richard Holt very well, although Granatstein, while a visiting professor at the University of Western Ontario, taught him in a graduate course in 2003. Both of us independently read the PhD dissertation on which this book is based; both of us thought it was excellent and added much to what we know of manpower, organization, and administration in Canada and in the Canadian Expeditionary Force during the Great War.

When we learned that Richard was seriously ill, we – again independently – offered to assist him in getting his book through the onerous publication process. It thus made sense for us to co-operate in this task. With the able and generous assistance of Philip Cercone and his staff at McGill-Queen's University Press, we are extremely pleased to see this project come to fruition.

Abbreviations

AAG	Assistant Adjutant-General
ACI	Army Council Instruction
ADMS	Assistant Director of Medical Services
AG	Adjutant-General
AO	Army Order
BAC	Brigade Ammunition Column
BCRM	British Canadian Recruiting Mission
BEF	British Expeditionary Force
CCAC	Canadian Casualty Assembly Centre
CCD	Canadian Command Depot
CCRC	Canadian Corps Reinforcement Camp
CDF	Canadian Defence Force
CEF	Canadian Expeditionary Force
CGBD	Canadian General Base Depot
CGS	Chief of the General Staff
CIBD	Canadian Infantry Base Depot
CMR	Canadian Mounted Rifles
CO	Commanding Officer
CTD	Canadian Training Division
DAC	Divisional Ammunition Column
DMT	Directorate of Military Training
GHQ	General Headquarters
GMC	General Musketry Course
GOC	General Officer Commanding
GSO	General Staff Officer
IGC	Inspector-General of Communications
MD	military district

MSA	*Military Service Act*
NCO	non-commissioned officer
OMFC	Overseas Military Forces of Canada
PF	Permanent Force
PPCLI	Princess Patricia's Canadian Light Infantry
QMG	Quartermaster General
RFC	Royal Flying Corps
SMLE	Short Magazine Lee–Enfield rifle
WOI	War Office Instruction

Sam Hughes, Minister of Militia and Defence 1911–16. His pugnacious and uncompromising character is reflected in this photograph. LAC, C-020240

Camp Petawawa in June 1914. Peacetime training areas across Canada had very little hard infrastructure, and troops undergoing training were housed in bell tents.
LAC, PA-016782

Troops handing in their rifles at Camp Barriefield, a peacetime training area near Kingston, in June 1915. Note the apparent youth of the third soldier from the right.
LAC, PA-016466

Italian reservists living in Canada marching through Toronto after being recalled by their parent country. LAC, PA-091104

Peacetime militia armouries were frequently used by newly mobilized CEF units to facilitate recruiting. In Toronto, recruiting tents were pitched near the University Avenue armoury. LAC, PA-071677

In St Catharines, Ontario, recruits were housed in tents next to the 19th Lincoln Regiment armoury. LAC, PA-071608

Young men from Metcalfe, Ontario, who enlisted in the 77th Battalion in 1915. Most CEF units had no qualms about enlisting young soldiers. LAC, PA-122937

A seventy-three-year-old soldier being repatriated to Canada from the Discharge Depot at Buxton, England. Many units felt free to ignore the regulations and enlist men who were obviously over the age limit. LAC, PA-005134

Lewis gunners at Niagara Camp in June 1916. It seems doubtful that this training would have been of much use in trench warfare. LAC, PA-069844

Cyclists staging an ambush during an exercise in Toronto in April 1916. These tactics bore no relation to the reality of the Western Front. LAC, PA-072585

Captain Mary Plummer (left), commanding officer of the Canadian Field Comforts Commission, and her adjutant, Lieutenant Joan Arnoldi, at Shorncliffe, England c. 1916–17. The Commission was a bona fide unit of the CEF, and both of these women were CEF officers. LAC, PA-005194

8th Battalion bayonet training on Salisbury Plain in 1914. Training was very much an ad hoc business at that time; the bags of hay were a hasty improvisation. Note that the soldiers are not wearing equipment as they would in battle. LAC, PA-004965

1st Reserve Battalion bayonet training in England c. 1916–17. A bayonet gallows is in use, and the men are wearing their equipment. A far cry from 1914. LAC, PA-004847

Given the lack of equipment and suitable ranges, advanced training was simply not possible in Canada. These rifle grenadiers are practising on a range in England c. 1916–17. LAC, PA-004745

A key component in the reinforcement structure was remedial training for men who had recovered from their wounds. These men are doing exercises at the 1st Canadian Command Depot in Shorncliffe, England. LAC, PA-005713

Reinforcements with a Canadian entrenching battalion waiting to go forward in August 1916. LAC, PA-000548

Officers and NCOs of the Canadian Corps Reinforcement Camp in October 1918.
LAC, PA-003241

Lieutenant-General Sir Richard Turner (centre), who was largely responsible for reforming the reinforcement structure in England, with two other officers at Bexhill in October 1918. LAC, PA-005803

Recruiting, particularly in small towns and rural areas, was not always a gala event with crowds of onlookers cheering the recruits. A group of 71st Battalion recruiters with new soldiers on the front steps of the town hall in St Marys, Ontario. Note the soldier holding his dog and the beer bottle on the porch behind the man on the right. St Marys Museum

Extracts from the Kingston Penitentiary inmate history description ledger. Private W.H. Parker, at top, is dressed in uniform. Sentenced on 27 September 1916 to two years' imprisonment, he was re-enlisted in the CEF on 11 December 1916. The third man down, Benson Dickson, was not a deserter but a thief who was sentenced in October 1916 to five years in prison. Nineteen months later, he was released from Kingston Penitentiary in order to join the CEF. He later served with the 38th Battalion in France and Belgium.

FILLING THE RANKS

Introduction

Manpower is the lifeblood of armies, regardless of time or place, and much of Canada's military effort in the First World War was engaged in finding men to sustain the Canadian Expeditionary Force (CEF), mainly in France and Belgium. This was not simply a matter of recruiting: policies, procedures, and organizations had to be developed to process, train, and forward these men as reinforcements to the front in a timely fashion. The ability of the CEF to do so was a tremendous accomplishment that, together with the achievements of the Canadian Corps on the battlefield, marked the transition of Canada's army from an amateur militia-based force to a hard-hitting, well-organized professional army.

This book examines the administrative and organizational changes that fostered efficiency and did much to sustain the CEF: the organization of recruiting, the conduct of entry-level training, and the development of a coherent reinforcement structure. The topic is important. After all, the success of the CEF depended on having a supply of trained soldiers to keep forward units up to strength. During the war, the Canadian Corps became an elite formation within the British Expeditionary Force. This achievement was made possible by a number of factors, not the least of which was Canada's ability to provide enough trained men to fill the ranks.

I became interested in this topic for a variety of reasons. As a boy in Winnipeg in the 1950s and early 1960s, I developed a lifelong interest in the CEF after meeting a number of First World War veterans. One of our neighbours, who took the time to talk with me, had not only served in France with the CEF but had also been a regular soldier and officer with the Royal Garrison Artillery and Royal Canadian Garrison Artillery from 1902 to 1947. Eventually, I too joined the Canadian Forces, serving for thirty-eight years and ending as Commanding Officer of the 4th Battalion, The Royal Canadian Regiment. During this time, I was involved with administration, recruiting, entry-level training, and individual training. As a lowly staff-captain at National Defence Headquarters, I was a member of a subcommittee examining personnel mobilization. After retirement, I elected to study at the University of Western Ontario; when the time came to choose the topic for my dissertation, my long-standing interest in the CEF and my own military experience led me to select manpower.

Most historians of the CEF have focused on operations. Very little has been published about the military aspects of recruiting, entry-level training, and the provision of reinforcements. Faced with this, I elected to take a "Rankean" approach and delve into the archives to discover the details of organizational and administrative developments in Canada's first modern war. The result of this recovery operation is an institutional history with a preliminary analysis. This book is obviously not the last word on the subject; no doubt, other scholars will re-examine the issues using alternative constructs and methodologies.

Armies in war are not simply conjured up. They are based on pre-war forces. In the case of the CEF, this meant the militia. For better or worse, the national headquarters in Ottawa, local command structures, training facilities, and equipment were the mainstay of the CEF and shaped its development. For that reason, chapter 1 deals with the militia on the eve of war.

In war, manpower is a precious commodity. Men are needed to work in essential industries, munitions manufacture, and agriculture, and to serve in the armed forces. Ideally, the national effort should balance these competing requirements. However, as discussed in chapter 2, there were no coherent national manpower policies from 1914 to the war's end in 1918. There was no serious effort to husband manpower, and thousands of Canadians were recruited within Canada, with the government's acquiescence, by allied nations. Units that supported the British army but not the CEF were raised, and a complete infantry division with no discernable operational role was formed in England. God may be on the side with the big battalions, as Napoleon is said to have remarked, but keeping them up to strength depended very much on how the nation managed its manpower.

Not every man was eligible for military service. Chapter 3 provides an estimate of the pool of potential recruits and examines the constraints imposed by recruiting standards as well as efforts to enlarge the pool.

Chapter 4 continues this theme with an examination of alternative sources of manpower, including the employment of women.

Chapter 5 discusses the ways and means of recruiting. These strategies did not evolve sequentially; it often happened that several methods were in use at the same time and place. Recruiting agencies were not local creations, but were instituted and controlled by the military. None of these agencies was entirely satisfactory, and it was not until recruiting functions were centralized in 1917 that an efficient recruitment structure finally emerged.

The war was not won just because men enlisted: they had to be trained to do a job with which, for the most part, they were unfamiliar. Training was a complex matter that involved much more than basic drill. First and foremost was control: directing the training, setting the standards, and implementing administrative procedures. Who would be responsible for this? Doctrine – that is, the subjects covered – was critical. What would the new recruits be taught, and who would decide what that should be?

Chapter 6 is concerned with training, a function that depended on weapons, equipment, and facilities. The shortage of modern weapons in Canada meant that training depended on obsolete equipment and limited training facilities. Troops could be housed in improvised barracks, but central camps that offered tactical manoeuvre areas were tented encampments suitable only for the summertime. Meanwhile, a serious shortage of winter clothing restricted training during the coldest months. All of this produced a state of affairs that made it necessary to retrain men on arrival overseas, thus wasting time and resources and impeding the flow of reinforcements from England to France.

Recruiting and training had but one purpose: to produce well-trained reinforcements for front-line units in a timely manner. This was a complex matter, and chapter 7 sets the stage by considering the doctrine that shaped the reinforcement structure in Canada, England, and France, the means by which the supply of reinforcements was managed, and the wastage that determined the number required. Delivery of these reinforcements was another matter, and chapter 8 examines developments in Canada that culminated in the creation of territorial depot battalions in August 1917 – a rational and efficient means of drafting infantry reinforcements to reserve battalions in England. Chapter 9 continues this theme by considering both the movement of reinforcements to France and the creation of an effective organization in 1917 to hold these men and draft them to forward units when required.

Canadian Forces overseas were treated as an integral part of the British army and were therefore governed by British policies and instructions. To put changes in Canadian policies and organizations into context, parallel developments in the British Expeditionary Force are considered. In a few instances, the Australian Imperial Force is also considered, since it was governed by British instructions as well.

Although manpower has been of interest to British historians, the differences in approach between governments makes it difficult to extrapolate their findings to the Canadian experience. That being said, Keith Grieves's *The Politics of Manpower, 1914–1918* provides useful insights into British responses to competing demands for military and industrial manpower.[1] In *The Commonwealth Armies: Manpower and Organisation in Two World Wars*, Frederick Perry takes a broader perspective, and his discussion concerning the consequences of overexpansion puts Canada's difficulties into context.[2] Similarly, Peter Simkins's comments in *Kitchener's Army: The Raising of the New Armies, 1914–16* on shortfalls of clothing, equipment, weapons, and barrack accommodation are helpful, while Charles Messenger's *Call to Arms: The British Army, 1914–1918* provides a wealth of detail on administrative developments in the British Army.[3] Ian Beckett's survey of manpower in *The Great War* is of particular interest; his point that the British army's "teeth-to-tail" ratio fell throughout the war echoes Perry's arguments about overexpansion.[4] John Osborne has examined the voluntary recruiting movement in Britain from 1914 to 1916, and his conclusion supports Canada's decision in 1917 to adopt conscription: relying solely on volunteers "ignored [the fact] that the requirements of prolonged modern warfare dictated that every man should *not* enlist. Early indiscriminate voluntary recruiting had severely hampered Britain's industrial capacity."[5]

To date, there has been no comprehensive study of military administration in either the Canadian or the British Expeditionary Forces, apart from Ian Brown's ground-breaking study of British logistics in France and Belgium and Michael Ryan's thesis on logistics in the Canadian Corps.[6] However, both were concerned only with transportation and the supply of *matériel* and so did not touch on the matter of reinforcements.

Seldom considered by historians is the development of Canadian staffs as well as the subordination of the military to civil direction. Stephen Harris's *Canadian Brass* provides a good overview and is essential to understanding the functions of the Minister of Militia and Defence, the Militia Council, and Militia Headquarters, although discussion of changes in the Great War are necessarily limited by its wide chronological scope (1860–1939).[7] Richard Walker's dissertation on Canadian military and political relations also provides some useful insights but, because it surveys the period 1898 to 1945, discussion about the CEF is also limited.[8] A more detailed overview is provided by William Stewart's recent biography of Lieutenant-General Sir Richard Turner and the operation of Headquarters, Overseas Military Forces of Canada, from December 1916 onward.[9]

Both official histories are indispensible. The *Official History of the Canadian Forces in the Great War 1914–1919* contains a wealth of information, although the sole volume of the projected eight-volume series stops in September 1915.[10] Colonel Nicholson's more recent *Canadian Expeditionary Force 1914–1919*, on the other hand, deals with matters in Canada, England, France, and Siberia from 1914 to demobilization in 1919.[11] As Nicholson commented, the scope of his work was such that events could be covered "only in broad outline, for the limitations imposed by the covers of a single book have ruled out the inclusion of much detail."[12] There is also a one-volume history of Canadian medical services produced by Sir Andrew Macphail in 1925 that contains some useful detail.[13]

Several divisional histories are helpful, although they focus on operations rather than administration. Andrew Iarocci's *Shoestring Soldiers* deals with the 1st Canadian Division in 1914–15 and is a useful introduction to the issues of individual and collective training in the early stages of the war.[14] Kenneth Radley's *We Lead, Others Follow*, on the other hand, deals with the 1st Division throughout the entire war.[15] Radley is one of the few Canadian historians to acknowledge that the Canadian Corps was but one of a number of corps in the British Expeditionary Force, and he has considered the effects of British policies and instructions. No academic studies of the remaining three divisions in the Corps have been published, although David Campbell produced a dissertation on the 2nd Canadian Division in 2003.[16] His account offers some useful insights on the management of untrained reinforcements in December 1916 and briefly considers the role of base depots.

Desmond Morton has dealt with the CEF at length in *When Your Number's Up: The Canadian Soldier in the First War* and *A Peculiar Kind of Politics: Canada's Overseas Ministry in the First World War*.[17] Both books are authoritative and cannot be overlooked, although the former deals with soldiers' experiences while the latter is as much a political history as it is a military history.

Training depended to a great extent on the evolution of technology in battle. Both Tim Cook's *No Place to Run* and Bill Rawling's *Surviving Trench Warfare* contain useful insights into gas warfare and technology in general and are indispensible.[18] Unfortunately, both deal mainly with the Canadian Corps in France and not the CEF in England and Canada.

The various statistical analyses that have been conducted with regard to recruiting and manpower in the CEF have been of limited use in my approach. The first of these, produced in 1982 by Robert Craig Brown and Donald Loveridge, examined regional variations in recruiting, the role of militia and local organizers, and factors that forced the government to adopt conscription.[19] Although groundbreaking, this work overlooked the fact that recruiting was not always a tidy process. The 135th Battalion, for example, was based in the farm districts of Middlesex County, Ontario, while 54 per cent of the battalion came from the city of London. Was the unit rural, or urban? Battalions also recruited outside of their home province, which makes it difficult to determine regional patterns. The 236th New Brunswick Kilties, to name but one, recruited in New Brunswick, New England, Ontario, and British Columbia.

In 1984, Christopher Sharpe published a regional analysis of enlistments that has been cited by a number of historians.[20] However, as Jonathan Vance of Western University has pointed out, Sharpe's analyses were based on flawed data produced by Hollerith tabulators in the early 1920s.[21] Moreover, the Hollerith tabulators counted enlistments, not people: at least 21,000 men enlisted more than once and are thus double-counted.[22]

This book regards recruiting as a national endeavour, although there is a growing body of literature that examines recruiting at a local level. For example, in *Hometown Horizons: Local Responses to Canada's Great War*, Robert Rutherdale has examined how recruiting responsibilities in Three Rivers (Trois-Rivières), Guelph, and Lethbridge shifted from the national to the local level. Although his approach reflects community feelings, it ignores the role of the military in what was, after all, a military effort.[23] On the other hand, Ian Miller's *Our Glory and Our Grief: Torontonians and the Great War*, based in part on Militia and Defence records, deals not only with the social history of Toronto during the war but also with efforts by military authorities to control the recruiting process.[24] Jim Blanchard's *Winnipeg's Great War: A City Comes of Age* is a fascinating account of the profound effect the war had upon the city and only briefly touches on recruiting.[25] Similarly, James Pitsula's *For All We Have and Are: Regina and the Experience of the Great War* examines the social history of Regina during the war, although there is some discussion of the raising of the 28th Battalion and the end of voluntarism.[26] John Thompson's *The Harvests of War: The Prairie West, 1914–1918* is a regional history that covers the social and economic implications of the war on the prairie provinces.[27] Lastly, Paul Maroney has examined recruiting in Ontario as a cultural phenomenon, but in doing so acknowledges the decentralization of the peacetime militia and the role of military staffs in controlling recruiting.[28]

Very few accounts by individual soldiers appear in this book, largely because of the institutional approach necessary in my archival research. It would be difficult, for example, to find first-hand accounts by private soldiers to illustrate national manpower problems or policies regarding the movement of reinforcements from England to France. This is not to say that their experiences were unimportant. Clearly, they *were* important, and two very good recent examples of Canadian historians' considerable use of memoirs are Tim Cook's *At the Sharp End* and *Shock Troops*.[29]

The CEF was made up of a wide variety of units: cavalry, artillery, engineers, infantry, pioneers, signals, medical, service corps, veterinary, forestry, and railway. With the exception of the last three, each had a unique training program. To keep this book to a manageable length, I have focused on entry-level training in the infantry, the largest corps in the CEF.

As noted in chapter 6, entry-level training changed continually throughout the war, which raises the question of whether such changes were made in response to new tactics at the front. Paddy Griffith, in *Battle Tactics of the Western Front*, has discussed at length the care taken in France to examine battle experiences of front-line units. This was not a meaningless staff exercise: GHQ issued a series of pamphlets dealing with doctrine, tactics, and training that were continually updated.[30] It stands to reason that these publications led to changes in entry-level training, although this is far from certain.

In Britain, training doctrine and syllabi were the purview of the Directorate of Military Training (DMT) at the War Office, while the training of all Empire troops in the British Isles was supervised by Commands that were the British equivalent to Canadian Military Districts. There were also Inspectors-General, charged with monitoring training, who visited training camps and reported directly to the DMT.[31] However, few of the wartime records of the DMT and the Inspectors-General have been preserved, while Command records from 1914 to 1918 no longer exist.

Scattered correspondence can be found in Canadian records, but these records are obviously far from complete. Having said this, the War Office, although it did not create a central coordinating authority for the analysis of information from the front and for doctrine, at least went so far as to distribute *Notes from the Front* to units in Britain. These, describing tactical developments at the front, were produced in France by General Headquarters (GHQ).[32] In Canada, *Notes from the Front* as well as pamphlets on field defences and trench warfare, and others, such as *Notes on Sniping*, *Fire Orders*, *Types of German Machine Gun Emplacements*, and *Some Notes on Meteorological Conditions Which Affect Gunnery* were distributed in Canada by Militia Headquarters (Militia HQ).[33] However, the extent to which these publications affected training in Canada, however, is uncertain in the absence of comments from the units concerned.

The matter of conscription under the *Military Service Act* (MSA) of 1917 has not been considered at length, simply because the processing, training, and handling of reinforcements remained the same regardless of whether the recruit was a volunteer or a draftee. Having said this, some discussion of the MSA is needed to put national and military policies into context.

The first full-length study of conscription – *Broken Promises: A History of Conscription in Canada* by J.L. Granatstein and J.M. Hitsman – was produced in 1977. This work was based on the premise that the conscription crisis was a division between French- and English-speaking Canadians; in short, it arose from a fundamental difference between Quebec and the rest of Canada. But, as Andrew Theobald has commented in *Bitter Harvest of War: New Brunswick and the Conscription Crisis of 1917*, there were divisions in New Brunswick between rural and urban populations, liberals and conservatives, Protestants and Catholics, and francophones and anglophones. More recently, Brock Millman has pointed to other divisions in Canada as a whole.[34] Desmond Morton, in *A Military History of Canada*, has also commented on anti-conscription sentiment outside of Quebec, describing ethnic concerns in Kitchener, Ontario; the ambivalence of the organized labour movement; and farmers in Ontario and western Canada who were unhappy about losing their sons.[35] The division, then, was not simply between French and English.

The khaki election of December 1917 produced further divisions between those at home and those serving overseas with the CEF. Prime Minister Borden campaigned on the need for conscription, and his Union Government was elected by a landslide, winning 153 seats as opposed to 82 for the Liberals, who were opposed to the MSA. Only 20 of the 170 seats outside of Quebec were taken by anti-conscriptionists. Overall, 57 per cent of voters in Canada and 90 per cent of those serving overseas supported the Unionists.

Conscription may have created rifts within Canada, but the country was at war and reinforcements were needed. In a reappraisal of his 1984 article, Chris Sharpe has concluded that conscription had to be imposed because the government raised a force that was too large to be maintained by voluntary enlistment.[36] A.M. Willms, in his 1956 article, "Conscription, 1917: A Brief for the Defence," made a compelling case for the need for reinforcements.[37] J.L. Granatstein has noted that the 24,000 conscripts who arrived in France in 1918 were enough to sustain the Canadian Corps for at least six months of intense combat. It was not just a question of numbers: under-strength battalions and brigades had to do the same job as full-sized units, and "[w]ith fewer men, the casualties increased as the firepower in the offence or defence decreased."[38] Trying to maintain full-strength units without conscription would have meant following the British lead by eliminating three battalions in each division. How this would have affected the combat effectiveness of the Corps is uncertain, although British historian William Philpott has observed that "Dominion divisions, which retained the old 12-battalion structure, proved better able to sustain the demands of intensive battle and won themselves a reputation as elite formations during the final campaign [in 1918]."[39]

Conscription was not simply an issue of finding men to fill the ranks. It was a morale issue in the Canadian Corps, as Lieutenant-General Currie, concerned that conscription might not be enforced, wrote in November 1917:

> [The Corps] would suffer not only by reason of its loss in numbers but in the loss of morale of those remaining. The men who are here now are committed until peace is declared. If no others are sent to help them they can look forward to nothing else but to be killed or permanently maimed.[40]

Finally, a few notes on organization, terminology, and method.

There is some apparent repetition within this book. For example, Headquarters Overseas Military Forces of Canada appears in chapters 6,

8, and 9, but in the varying contexts of training, the reserve organization in England, and the reserve structure in France. The emphasis, then, is on the function rather than the entity.

Before 1916, Canada was divided into six divisional areas and three military districts. To avoid any confusion with overseas divisions, I have used the term "military district" from chapter 2 onward.

In discussing recruiting, training, and the movement of reinforcements, I have made use of a number of samples that are not referred to in the endnotes. Unless stated otherwise, those concerning recruiting have been taken from the attestation forms at the Library and Archives Canada website, *Soldiers of the First World War*. Those concerning training and the movement of reinforcements have been taken from nominal rolls published in the regimental histories of the 2nd and 4th Canadian Mounted Rifles, Princess Patricia's Canadian Light Infantry, and the 4th, 16th, 20th, 72nd, and 85th Battalions as well as the Daily Orders, Part II, of the 18th and 21st Battalions.[41]

Unless otherwise stated, detailed personnel statistics for the CEF in France and Belgium have been taken from monthly returns compiled by the Canadian Section, GHQ 3rd Echelon, from February 1916 to November 1918.[42] Similarly, data concerning units when they sailed to England has been taken from embarkation rolls printed by Militia HQ and distributed with Militia Orders 1914–17.

In developing this book, I deliberately chose a narrow focus: the transformation of Canada's army from an amateur body to a professional force. However, the material presented invites further enquiries of a broader nature: the relationship of the Canadian nation to the imperial war it was fighting, the question of a distinct Canadian identity, and the coordination of forces in Canada and those deployed overseas.

This book contains much that has not appeared in other histories of the CEF. To that extent, it modifies and extends existing scholarship. However, my work would not have been possible without the careful research and writing of so many others. They have my sincere gratitude.

I
Militia Roots

From first to last, the CEF was a product of the peacetime army, and many of its difficulties with training and mobilization had their origins in the pre-war militia. The influence of the peacetime army was significant, and understanding the ramshackle mobilization and ineffective training in Canada therefore requires a brief survey of Canada's military as it existed before the war.

The key elements of the peacetime army that influenced the creation of the CEF were the structure of the force; the functioning of the Militia Council; Militia HQ and district headquarters; the nature of militia units and the militiamen themselves; training, equipment, and clothing; and, lastly, weapons.

Effective command and control at the national level – perhaps the most important factor in the war – was erratic, not only because Sam Hughes, the Minister of Militia and Defence, effectively neutered the Militia Council but also because Militia HQ was too small in relation to its responsibilities. This was not just a bureaucratic issue; the size of the HQ made it difficult, if not impossible, to establish uniform standards across the country. Given the circumstances, decentralization was perhaps the only way of managing the militia, and subordinate headquarters as well as units had considerable autonomy – a practice that continued throughout the war.

The peacetime army was not suited for general mobilization. The Permanent Force, Canada's regular army, was small and for the most part was employed in instructional and administrative duties. Nor was the militia an ideal framework for mobilization. Chronic training problems at the unit level, shortages of equipment and facilities, a lack of manoeuvre areas, and a bewildering variety of obsolete weapons resulted in a low standard of training.

STRUCTURE

In 1914, Canada's army – the militia – was divided into an Active Militia and a Reserve Militia. The former consisted of volunteers between the ages of 18 and 45 and paraded on a part-time basis or was embodied on a full-time basis. The latter was referred to as the Permanent Force (PF). Both the militia and the PF were armed, equipped, and paid. In theory, the militia could be balloted (chosen by lot) for active service in an emergency, but this meant that call-out was based on chance, not fitness. Not surprisingly, the *Military Service Act* of 1917 rejected balloting in favour of selective conscription. The Reserve Militia was the last vestige of the nineteenth-century Sedentary Militia, and consisted of all males between the ages of 18 and 60 who were British subjects and capable of bearing arms in the event of a *levée en masse*. With no arms or equipment, the Reserve Militia was for all intents and purposes defunct by 1914, although a number of units were authorized during the First World War. These received little or no support from the Department of Militia and Defence, but their existence diverted local enthusiasm for the CEF and added to the workload of the small, overstretched staff at Militia HQ. Lastly, there were rifle clubs and associations with weapons and ammunition provided by the Department of Militia and Defence that, in an emergency, could be drafted into the militia. It goes without saying that this was never seriously considered during the war.[1]

The PF was the logical basis for mobilization, but was hampered by its limited size, peacetime role, and makeup. Intended to provide instructors for the militia and garrisons for Halifax, Quebec City, and Esquimalt, the PF comprised only 247 officers and 2,656 men in scattered garrisons across the country on the eve of war. Nor was the force evenly balanced. It consisted of one under-strength infantry battalion, the Royal Canadian Regiment, two small cavalry regiments, the Royal Canadian Dragoons in Toronto and Lord Strathcona's Horse (Royal Canadians) in Winnipeg, two Royal Canadian Horse Artillery batteries in Kingston, and companies of the Royal Canadian Garrison Artillery at Halifax, Quebec City, and Esquimalt – but no field artillery. There were also small detachments of the technical corps in major centres throughout the Dominion.[2] The PF was hampered by a high turnover rate. In 1912, for example, "the percentage of men discharged was greatly in excess of enlistments."[3]

The PF technical corps spent much of their time on housekeeping duties. In the case of the Canadian Engineers, the routine maintenance of works and buildings prevented any training in field engineering, their primary raison d'être in war. The Service Corps had the same problems. More than half of the Service Corps supported the Halifax garrison and was neither trained nor equipped for field operations. The Inspector-General considered individual members to be proficient, but British Army instructors were needed if the Service Corps was to progress beyond a basic level.

Although militia units were responsible for their own training, the PF Instructional Cadre provided assistance and staffed central schools to train officers and non-commissioned officers (NCOs). The Cadre was small, however, and in 1913 only 115 infantry and cavalry NCOs were available for the whole of the militia – that is, there was not even one NCO per unit.[4] Despite this, members of the Cadre could be vital to unit efficiency. In St Catharines, for example, the 7th Field Battery was issued with the new 18-pounder field gun on 3 May 1912, but, thanks to a PF sergeant-instructor, mastered the new equipment in time for an artillery concentration at Petawawa starting 8 June 1912.[5]

There were other problems. The PF was an English-speaking entity with no room for unilingual francophones, and few members of the Instructional Cadre spoke French.[6] As a result, English-speaking NCOs were sometimes detailed to francophone units.[7] The Royal Canadian Regiment maintained eight francophone instructors in Quebec City, but this benefited infantry units in the 5th Divisional Area only and ignored French-speaking units elsewhere in the 4th Divisional Area.[8] The language problem was exacerbated by a lack of training manuals in French.

MILITIA COUNCIL

The Canadian Militia had seen tremendous changes before 1914 in response to the exposure of deficiencies during the Boer War, a need to curb the powers of the General Officer Commanding of the Canadian Militia, a British officer who was frequently at loggerheads with the Canadian government, and a desire to modernize the Militia.[9] The most important of these changes was embodied in a new *Militia Act* introduced in 1904 by Sir Frederick Borden and based on recent reforms in the British Army that had been prompted by Lord Esher's War Office (Reconstitution) Committee. In brief, the British reforms did away with the position of Commander-in-Chief and created a general staff, with four branches headed by the Chief of the Imperial General Staff, the Adjutant-General, the Quartermaster-General, and the Master-General of Ordnance. None of these branches had primacy, although the Chief of the Imperial General

Staff was considered *primus inter pares*. Coordination and general guidance was provided by an Army Council with the Secretary of State for War as chairman, the four branch heads as military members, and two civilian appointees responsible for financial and civil matters.[10]

In Canada, the new *Militia Act* followed suit and created a Militia Council broadly similar to the British Army Council. The Minister of Militia and Defence, Sir Frederick Borden, was President, while the Deputy Minister acted as Vice-President. Civilian members consisted of the Accountant and Paymaster General and the Assistant Deputy Minister. Military members consisted of the Chief of the General Staff (CGS), who was responsible for operations and training; the Adjutant-General (AG), responsible for personnel policies, medical services and cadets; the Quartermaster General, who handled supply and transport; and the Master General of Ordnance, who looked after surveys, engineer services, and infrastructure.[11] Like his British counterpart, the CGS did not have primacy, and each military member was responsible to the Minister for his particular branch. Unlike the Army Council, which had some executive authority, the Militia Council was restricted to providing advice to the minister "on all matters relating to the Militia which are referred to the Council by the Minister."[12]

In principle, the new organization was sound, with the Minister and his staff meeting on a weekly or fortnightly basis. Although the Council was advisory and (in theory at least) restricted to discussing only those issues raised by the Minister, Borden adopted a collegial approach; under his direction, "the Militia Council met often [and] produced serious political-military consultation."[13] However, the success of the system depended entirely on the personality of the Minister and his willingness to meet with his Council.

The collegial atmosphere established by Borden abruptly changed in 1911 when the Conservatives came to power and Sam Hughes, a fifty-eight-year-old newspaper proprietor and long-standing militia officer, was appointed Minister of Militia and Defence. Under Hughes, the Militia Council was reduced to impotence, and after a clash with the CGS, Major-General Colin Mackenzie, Hughes either disregarded the Council or used it simply to implement his orders. The upshot was that staff branches at Militia HQ operated in isolation. There was no effective consideration of problems or coordination of effort, a situation that continued to exist until Hughes resigned his portfolio in November 1916.[14]

Hughes was a controversial figure, although his biographer has described him as "popular, dynamic, progressive and decisive."[15] This may have been true to some extent, but Hughes was also impulsive, eccentric, and ruthless, and did much to bring about chaos, particularly after the war broke out. From first to last, Hughes did not understand the nature of his position. As one historian has commented, "the opportunities for damage were incalculable when the minister of defence happened to be impetuous, imperious, and unable to understand the peculiar complexities of managing armed forces in a democratic polity."[16] After the war, W.A. Griesbach, a former brigade commander, prominent Edmonton lawyer, and Conservative Party organizer, acknowledged Hughes's accomplishments, but added: "He had little or no idea of the proper functioning of the staff and was despotic, if not tyrannical. How the wretched staff at National Defence Headquarters [sic] carried on, I do not know. I suspect that they did not carry on at all."[17]

MILITIA HQ AND DISTRICT HQ

The "wretched staff" at Militia HQ was small in relation to its responsibility for controlling, training, and administering a large and complex organization that stretched from one coast to the other. In March 1914, on the eve of war, there were only thirty-five staff officers at Militia HQ, including the Director of Cadet Services. Most were concerned with administration, while only seven officers in the all-important General Staff Branch handled operations and training for the whole of the militia. Clearly, Militia HQ was understaffed, and it is no surprise that fifty-four staff officers were added during the war, although most were devoted to personnel administration.[18]

Understaffing at Militia HQ had several consequences not only for the militia but also for the CEF. Staff had no choice but to shoulder a workload that would be unthinkable today. The CGS, Major-General Sir Willoughby Gwatkin, normally worked until well after midnight, a routine that brought him to the verge of a nervous breakdown in 1917.[19] Others suffered as well. In 1920, the Adjutant-General wrote to Brigadier-General Gwynne, the Director General of Mobilization who left because of ill-health, to express his regrets "that your unremitting devotion to your duties during the war made it necessary for you to retire."[20] Under the circumstances it is, perhaps, no surprise that the coordination and implementation of specific policies was sometimes fumbled.

Command and control with a small staff was difficult, if not impossible, and responsibility for operations and training had to be delegated to subordinate Headquarters. Militia HQ issued annual instructions outlining the conduct of training, but these were not mandatory and were "merely a guide to officers, in the training of those units under their command."[21] To compensate for this, there was an Inspector-General charged with general supervision, but the sheer number of militia units meant that most of annual inspections had to be carried out by local commanders.[22]

Militia HQ did not exercise command directly, but through divisions and military districts, each with specific boundaries. Divisions, located in the Maritime Provinces, Quebec, and Ontario, were intended to counter an invasion by fielding formed bodies of troops. Each division was divided into brigades and, on paper, had the requisite number of arms units. Districts, on the other hand, were intended to be geographic entities responsible for training and administering units (table 1.1). In practice, both divisions and districts were administrative and not operational entities.

The structure of each Divisional or District HQ was similar to Militia HQ, with a small staff that reflected the emphasis on administration rather than operations and training. HQ 6th Division in Halifax, responsible for the Maritime provinces, was perhaps typical, with three staff officers handling operations and training and eleven others employed in administrative positions. As with Militia HQ, the ability of the 6th Division HQ to plan and conduct operations or training was limited, and the responsibility had to be largely delegated to units. Most of the units in the 6th Division were grouped into three infantry brigades, but the brigade commanders were part-time militia officers, had no staff beyond a part-time brigade-major and, like their subordinate commanding officers, were lieutenant-colonels; depending on the personalities involved, command could be an exercise in tact, diplomacy, and negotiation.[23]

Decentralization of training meant that Divisional and District Commanders enjoyed a considerable degree of autonomy, which in turn was passed on to units. Under the circumstances, this may have been inevitable, but it meant that uniformity was difficult to achieve, particularly since the Inspector-General from Militia HQ could not visit many units in the course of the year. This was not an issue in peacetime, when units operated only within the bounds of their particular division or district, but became a major problem during the war, when units from across Canada arrived in England with varying standards of training.

THE UNITS AND MILITIAMEN

In 1914, there were 235 militia units scattered across the country. The force was dominated by the arms: 163 artillery, cavalry, and infantry

Table 1.1 District and divisional organization, 31 March 1914

Division or district	Headquarters	Province	Remarks
1st Divisional Area	London	Ontario	Southwest Ontario
2nd Divisional Area	Toronto	Ontario	Central and northern Ontario
3rd Divisional Area	Kingston	Ontario	Eastern Ontario, western Quebec counties of Labelle and Pontiac
4th Divisional Area	Montreal	Quebec	Western Quebec
5th Divisional Area	Quebec	Quebec	Eastern Quebec
6th Divisional Area	Halifax	Nova Scotia, New Brunswick, and Prince Edward Island	
Military District 10	Winnipeg	Manitoba and Saskatchewan	Included Districts of Thunder Bay and Rainy River in Ontario
Military District 11	Victoria	British Columbia	Included the Yukon Territory
Military District 13	Edmonton	Alberta	Included the District of Mackenzie and the Northwest Territories

Source: *The Quarterly Militia List of the Dominion of Canada (Corrected to 31st March 1914)* (Ottawa: Kings' Printer, 1914).

units. The remaining 72 units were provided by the Medical Corps, Service Corps, Engineers, and Signal Corps. Units were predominantly English-speaking, and there were only seventeen infantry battalions, one regiment of garrison artillery, and one field battery with French as the working language.[24] But, one and all, they had the same general characteristics.

Most militia units had a high annual turnover, which affected both administration and training. There is an abundance of anecdotal evidence, but statistics are available for only a few units, such as the 7th Fusiliers of London and the 22nd Oxford Rifles of Woodstock, Ontario. In the 7th Fusiliers, which had six companies and an establishment of about 400 all ranks, 1,563 recruits were enrolled between 1899 and 1909 – an average of 142 every year.[25] Similarly, in the 22nd Regiment, with a smaller establishment of only four companies, 301 men joined between 1910 and 1913.[26] In short, each regiment lost about a third of its soldiers every year.

The poor retention rate, together with the pressure on units to attend summer camps with as many men as possible, meant that recruiting was geared to the collective training cycle. In the 7th Fusiliers, there were two distinct annual intakes. The spring draft averaged 108 recruits and was intended to bring the unit up to strength for summer camp, while the fall draft, which averaged 34 men, reinforced the unit for the annual Thanksgiving sham battle. The unit paraded from March to October only, and the two intakes meant that many of the unit's NCOs were permanently assigned to recruit training. As well, recruits enlisted over a two- or three-month period. Those who joined in March were reasonably well trained for the summer camp at the end of June, while those who enlisted in late May or early June were raw recruits when they arrived at camp. Like other units, the 7th spent a disproportionate amount of time and energy on recruiting and basic training at the expense of conducting refresher training for those already in the ranks. More importantly, the large numbers of inexperienced soldiers effectively prevented the unit from conducting advanced training in a meaningful way.

The voluntary nature of the militia called for a considerable degree of consensus on the part of those involved. Commanding officers had substantial powers but were not omnipotent and could be forced to resign if there was no consensus among the officers. Lieutenant-Colonel R.B. Hamilton, for example, was removed from command of the 2nd Regiment (Queen's Own Rifles of Canada) in 1896, largely because he did not enjoy the support of the officers and senior NCOs.[27] In 1915, disagreements arose between Lieutenant-Colonel F.B. Ross and the officers of the 13th Royal Regiment that led Ross to resign, "believing it to be in the best interests of my old regiment."[28] The need for collegiality and consensus within units was generally recognized, and inspection reports frequently commented on this aspect of command. Comments made in 1913 about the 48th Highlanders were typical: "An excellent Esprit de corps prevails throughout all ranks and the Commanding Officer is well supported by his officers in all matters affecting the welfare of the Regiment."[29] But there were drawbacks to this, especially in rural units, as Lieutenant-Colonel A.W. Currie of the 50th Regiment in British Columbia commented in 1913: "Too often the officer fears that insisting on things being done in a regimental way may interfere with his relations with his men in civil life."[30] To what extent this collegiality prevailed in the CEF is difficult to say. Certainly, much of the administrative turmoil within the 141st Battalion at Port Arthur in 1916 that effectively halted training was caused by unit officers protesting Lieutenant-Colonel McKenzie's suspension from duty for alleged financial irregularities and a desire to force an unpopular captain to resign.[31] No doubt there were other instances.

Who were these militiamen? Few memoirs exist, and those that do were written by officers. Archival holdings are scanty, but enough has survived to allow for some general observations. Records of the 22nd Oxford Rifles indicate that 63 per cent of those who joined between 1910 and 1913 were British-born, but this may have been an anomaly.[32] The Commanding Officer of the 7th Fusiliers complained that 75 per cent of the recruits in 1910–11 and 60 per cent of the recruits in 1912 were British-born, but this was at odds with earlier recruiting patterns.[33] In the 7th Fusiliers, 85 per cent of a sample of 157 men enrolled between 1900 and 1902 had been born in Canada, while 4 per cent were born in the United States and 11 per cent in Great Britain. The 13th Royal Regiment of Hamilton had a similar pattern: 79 per cent of those who joined between 1894 and 1909 had been born in Canada, and 18.5 per cent in Britain. There was also a small number from Germany and Russia.[34] The birthplace of recruits in the 7th and 13th is roughly consistent with the 1901 Census, which showed that London was 18 per cent British-born and Hamilton 19.6 per cent British-born. However, the predominance of Canadian-born men in the militia was at odds with the CEF, in which 220,589 were British-born and 299,131 Canadian-born.[35] The disparity begs investigation beyond the scope of this work.

The peacetime militia was a youthful force. The age of recruits in the 13th Royal Regiment between 1894 and 1909 ranged from 13 to 58, with an average of 23.2 years. In the 7th Fusiliers, ages ranged from 16 to 44, with an average of 21.4. However, the 157 Fusilier recruits found in the 1901 Census present a somewhat different picture. Ages varied from 14 to 43, with an average of 20.6 – a marked contrast with the CEF, which had an average age of 26.3. Forty-four of the militia recruits, or 28 per cent, were under the minimum enrolment age of eighteen, a trend that continued during the war.

Regulations specified that recruits had to be eighteen to forty-five, but boys of good character aged fourteen to seventeen (or, in special cases, thirteen) could be enrolled as bandsmen with the consent of their parents or guardian.[36] Although some of these youthful soldiers no doubt had their parents' consent, it seems implausible that the 7th Fusiliers needed forty-four musicians in a three-year period; it is more likely that they simply wanted to fill the ranks.

Why were these boys enrolled? Many must have been quite obviously underage. Neither the unit history nor surviving unit records refer to a shortage of recruits, nor is there any apparent correlation between ages and enrolment dates. The simplest explanation may lie in the fact that units saw no harm in using enthusiastic juveniles, either in or out of uniform. At the Thanksgiving manoeuvres in 1912, for example, Colonel Logie's brigade from Hamilton employed boy scouts as messengers on the battlefield.[37] There was also a contradiction between the minimum enrolment age of eighteen and the school-leaving age, which in Ontario was fourteen.[38] Perhaps recruiting sergeants (and others) felt that if a boy could legally make his own way in the world at fourteen, there was no reason why he could not serve with the militia.

VISIBLE MINORITIES

In light of accounts by various scholars of the racist dimensions of Canadian history,[39] it is interesting to note that the militia enlisted a small number of visible minorities. Some units were open to this, while others were not – a trend that continued during the war. "B. Devisie" from India joined the 13th Royal Regiment in Hamilton in 1905, while the 23rd Alberta Rangers took Privates Chang Soo and Wong Hung to summer camp in 1907 as cooks, and Privates Quan Quam and Lee Sing in 1909.[40] The enrolment of Chinese-Canadians did not violate any regulations or orders. Militia HQ was well aware the men were Chinese, and the only concern was whether they were British subjects who had been properly enrolled.[41] Others from the Middle East served in the 29th Field Battery in Yarmouth, Nova Scotia, the 65th Carabiniers Mont-Royal in Montreal, and the 21st Essex Fusiliers in Windsor, Ontario. Further west, Hamid Mriden, a Palestinian Muslim,* served with the 27th Light Horse in Saskatchewan before going on to enlist in the CEF.

Blacks had been part of the Canadian Militia as early as 1793, when some were enrolled in the Kent County Militia in Ontario. A Coloured Company fought at Queenston Heights in 1812, and the Coloured Corps of the Incorporated Militia was stationed along the Ontario border from 1838 to 1850. In British Columbia, blacks comprised the Colony's first militia unit, the Victoria Pioneer Rifle Corps, in 1860.[42] Although it has been argued that this tradition was not continued after Confederation,

---

* At least twenty-two Muslims served with the CEF, including Private Hasam Amat from Singapore of the 1st Battalion, who was killed during a confused night action near Hill 70 on 20 August 1917. His body was not recovered, and he is fittingly commemorated on Canada's iconic memorial on Vimy Ridge.

blacks served in the militia as individuals in the 7th Fusiliers, 19th Lincoln Regiment, 7th Field Battery in St Catherines, 56th Grenville Regiment, and the Governor General's Body Guard, a prestigious Toronto militia unit. There was at least one black from Antigua in the PF who enlisted in the Royal Canadian Regiment at Three Rivers (Trois-Rivières) in 1913. One unit, the 29th Field Battery in Yarmouth, Nova Scotia, seems to have welcomed blacks. At least fifty-two members of the unit went on to serve with the CEF: thirty-eight were white, thirteen were black, and one was Syrian.[43] Considering that in 1911 blacks made up only 3.5 per cent of the Yarmouth census sub-district, the proportion of blacks in the 29th was exceptional.

In the case of the First Nations, much has been made of a supposed national policy issued in 1914 banning Indians from enlisting in the CEF – a subject that will be examined in chapter 3. However, very little has been said about First Nations military service before the war, a tradition that extended back to the American Revolution. The 37th Haldimand Rifles, in particular, had a very strong Native component, and by 1913 six of the eight companies were recruited exclusively on the Six Nations Reserve.[44] In the 26th Middlesex Light Infantry, four companies were based on Reserves at Moraviantown, Muncey, and Sarnia.[45] Further north, the 32nd Bruce Regiment band was drawn from the Cape Croker Reserve, while C, F, and G Companies recruited at the Cape Croker and Chippewa Hill Reserves.[46] Other units recruited Natives as well. E Company of the 49th Hastings Rifles, based in Tyendinaga, recruited men from Deseronto, while B Company of the 18th Franc Tireurs du Saguenay recruited from the Roberval Reserve.[47]

First Nations militiamen were regarded as good soldiers who took their training seriously. In 1912, the Six Nations companies of the 37th were considered to be very good, while the "White Companies [were] young & not up to the others."[48] Native soldiers were regarded as a valuable commodity, and in Quebec the 18th Francs Tireurs du Saguenay were pressured by the Division Commander to raise at least one company of Montagnais (Innu).[49]

First Nations militiamen were not only soldiers; at least five were commissioned as officers in the 37th Haldimand Rifles.[50] Inspecting Officers considered them to be capable officers, and in 1908 A.G.E. Smith was singled out as a "Clever officer with good judgment & tact, even temper[ed] and self-reliant."[51] Native soldiers were also employed as NCOs and specialists. In the 32nd Bruce Regiment, Color-Sergeant Walter Shawbedees, of the Chippewa Hill Reserve, was responsible for discipline in C Company, while Corporal Alex Johnston of Cape Croker commanded a section in G Company.[52] In the 26th Middlesex Light Infantry, First Nations men were also employed as NCOs, while most, if not all, of the Stretcher Bearer section was native as well.[53] Under the *Indian Act*, all of these men were considered to be wards of the Crown; they were not enfranchised and had to be closely supervised by government-appointed Indian agents, some of whom were militia officers themselves.

TRAINING

Training in the peacetime militia depended on a number of factors, of which the most important was whether a unit was urban or rural. Urban units were concentrated entirely in cities, while rural units were dispersed in small towns, villages, and townships in companies, batteries, or squadrons of about fifty men each.

City corps were able to train throughout the year using dedicated armouries. Some of the rural units, however, had no facilities and were usually able to train only during the annual or biannual twelve-day summer camp. Others had drill halls or offices, but there were some that had to improvise. In Lethbridge, the 25th Independent Field Battery had "no building in which to house the guns, for these were lean years for the Militia. [Major] Stewart [Battery Commander] stowed them in the open behind his house, protected only by muzzle and breech covers. The full establishment of harness he kept in his barn, which thus became the first artillery armoury on the western prairies."[54]

To a great extent, training was dependent on whether the unit was concentrated in a purpose-built armoury and had access to a training area nearby where weekend camps could be held. Most city units had access to armouries but, as Sir John French noted in 1910, only Ottawa and Halifax had a nearby manoeuvre area.[55] Considerable use was therefore made of private property at both the unit and District level. The 30th British Columbia Horse, for example, built a rifle range on private property near Vernon.[56] In the 1st Divisional Area, use was made of "leased ground known as the Attrill Farm near Goderich which lacks area for maneuver notwithstanding the use of 2 farms nearby."[57] Private property was a useful stopgap, but field firing could not be conducted, trenches could not be dug, and the need to avoid damage inhibited training.

Central training camps were limited, and not all provinces had adequate training facilities. In Prince Edward Island, the Charlottetown

Camp Commandant wrote in 1914 that the Prince Edward Island Light Horse had made progress in their training, although "there is not a sufficiently large training area available."[58] Camps at Barriefield, Farnham, Lévis, and Sussex were too small for brigade-level training, while others such as Carling Heights in London and Sarcee near Calgary were being slowly engulfed by development. In 1914, Major-General F.L. Lessard reported that "[t]he restricted area of this training ground [Niagara-on-the-Lake] is well known, and has been fully reported upon in the past. Nevertheless, with the kind co-operation of the inhabitants, and the appointment of a committee of adjustment, it has been found possible to maneuver and practice Field Training within an area of some 20 miles from Niagara-on-the-Lake."[59] Large camps with artillery ranges and manoeuvre areas suitable for brigades existed only at Camp Sewell, Manitoba, and Petawawa, Ontario, although these were tented encampments with no barracks and were usable only in the summer.

Militia training comprised local headquarters training at home (at least for the city corps) and central summer camps. In general, artillery units were authorized to train for sixteen days at summer camps, and all other corps for twelve days. But there were exceptions. In 1913, the 3rd, 4th, and 11th Brigades Canadian Field Artillery, the 3rd Regiment Canadian Garrison Artillery, and the Prince Edward Island Heavy Brigade had to demonstrate their efficiency by training for four days at local headquarters before going to camp for twelve days. City corps could schedule training at local HQ and central camps, provided the total did not exceed sixteen days, but rural units were given only twelve days in total.[60]

In 1913, for example, the 57th Peterborough Rangers trained for eleven days at home and five days at camp.[61] The eleven days spent at Peterborough were not calendar days, but rather evenings, each of which counted for a half day. The unit training schedule was fairly intense, considering that the majority of militiamen worked during the day. In 1914, the 57th recruit course started in April 1914 and ran three nights a week for twenty-two evenings until mid-June, when the Regiment went to a five-day camp at Barriefield, near Kingston. Other units followed a similar routine. In 1904, the 41st Brockville Rifles trained for twenty-four evenings before attending summer camp at Rockcliffe, while in 1912 the 7th Battery in St Catharines recruited in March and April and trained three evenings a week in preparation for summer camp at the end of June.[62]

Spring training for experienced militiamen was intended to cover as much ground as possible to gain the maximum benefit from summer camp collective training; a tall order, considering that many NCOs were committed to training recruits. In the 1st Division, units were told that "[i]n order that the best value may be obtained from the period spent in Camp, efforts should be made to perform some of the preliminary training at Company, Squadron or Regimental Headquarters before June."[63] At Edmonton, Major Griesbach of the 19th Alberta Dragoons wrote that, in 1914, "[a]lthough only twelve days were spent in camp, we endeavored to bring our troops into camp with a good deal of the syllabus of training completed before arrival. Therefore, we were able to get on with maneuvers in the field without loss of time."[64]

But the 19th was fortunate. Rural units were usually unable to train throughout the year, and during their twelve-day stint at summer camp recruits had to be trained, musketry practices fired, and collective skills exercised with a one- or two-day sham fight – an impossible task, considering that the twelve-day camp did not represent twelve training days. Sunday was a day of rest, and travelling time (usually two days) was also included.[65] In the case of city corps, this effectively reduced training to three days or less. In 1912, the Governor General's Foot Guards arrived at Petawawa on Saturday, rested Sunday, trained Monday and Tuesday, and returned to Ottawa on Wednesday.[66] The combination of training in drill and ceremonial at local headquarters and five calendar days at camp, in most cases, did not produce soldiers or units fully trained for modern warfare – a state of affairs that created some difficulties on mobilization in 1914.

Training problems were exacerbated not only by the high proportion of new recruits, but also by a high absentee rate from summer camp. At Barriefield in 1913, only 60 per cent of the militia in Eastern Ontario turned out for camp.[67] The problem existed elsewhere. In 1912, the 5th Division in Eastern Quebec found that only a small proportion of men attended more than one camp, while at Halifax in 1913 the Inspecting Officer despaired of any progress in Number 2 (Montreal) Siege Company: "Given each year a large proportion of green men of but little education it is obviously impossible to make any steady and continuous progress in raising the standard of training to what is required for Siege Artillery."[68]

Absenteeism from summer camp varied between units. The 12th York Rangers historian thought that the turnout in rural units was higher because "the night drilling population and the camp going population are two rather distinct classes."[69] There was some truth in this. At the Nova Scotia camp in 1912, two city corps (63rd and 66th Regiments) paraded 386 all ranks with 708 absent. The remaining fourteen units, all rural, with 2,652 men, had only 369 absentees.[70] In Military District

Number 10, only 283 all ranks from the 52nd Prince Albert Volunteers, a city corps, attended Camp Sewell in 1913 out of an establishment of 540. In Calgary, 2,635 men attended summer camp in 1914 with only 674 absent. It is striking, however, that 466 of the absentees, or 69 per cent, came from two city corps, the 101st Edmonton Fusiliers and the 103rd Calgary Rifles.[71] The strength of militia units tended to vary widely because of personalities and local circumstances, but it appears that city corps, generally considered to be more efficient, had lower attendance rates at summer camps. Since summer camps were intended primarily for unit field training, the general standard of collective training could not have been very high.

City corps tended to emphasize the ceremonial aspects of the military in contrast with less glamorous field work. The 48th Highlanders managed to avoid summer camp altogether in 1913, and a 2nd Division staff officer wrote a damning report, saying that although morale was high there was "a tendency to indulge in too much ceremonial which I hope in time will give place to more Infantry training."[72] The 48th attitude is understandable. With no immediate threat on the horizon, a club-like atmosphere, and a desire for public parades to bolster self-confidence, it was difficult to avoid spending training days on ceremony and drill. This emphasis on drill was reinforced by Sam Hughes, no doubt influenced by many years of peacetime militia training, who directed the Chief of the General Staff in 1913 to notify Divisions and Districts that "Officers will be judged by their bearing on parade, and their powers of command and leadership will be tested by the number of different [drill] movements their units can complete, in rapid succession but without confusion, in a given space of time."[73]

The last annual militia training plan issued in February 1914 was typical: training was to be "systematic and progressive; [with] that at local headquarters leading up to the training in camp, which will be devoted entirely to tactical instruction."[74] The aim was reasonable, but the detailed instructions were not. The local headquarters schedule for infantry battalions was a mixture of individual and collective training and emphasized basic drill from squad to battalion level, with and without arms. For some reason, funeral drill was also included. Units were directed to fire their annual musketry practice before camp, but weapons handling was not included in the schedule. The field portion of the syllabus covered a variety of topics, including scouting, minor tactics, entrenching, and construction of obstacles, all of which demanded a convenient manoeuvre area, which most city corps did not possess. The actual routine likely varied, but most units probably divided their preparatory evenings between drill and lectures on tactical subjects, leaving the actual practice to summer camp. The more experienced and receptive militiamen may have benefited from this training, but not newly enrolled men from remote areas, such as those at Lévis Camp in 1913, who thought newly installed shower baths were latrines.[75]

Training in the peacetime militia may have been spotty and focused on ceremonial, but some conscientious and imaginative units were surprisingly progressive, considering the institutional limitations. Lieutenant-Colonel Gwynne, who commanded the 16th Light Horse in Saskatchewan, not only published his own training manual in 1907, but also attempted to enroll women to ride with the unit to provide first aid on the battlefield – a Canadian version of the British First Aid Nursing Yeomanry.[76]

Some units made a conscious effort to make training as realistic as possible. In 1912, the Composite Cavalry Brigade conducted field firing at Petawawa, "firing 15 rounds per man. Three screens were placed as targets, representing the successive positions taken up by a rear guard retreating, while the cavalry squadrons acted as the advanced guard of a pursuing force."[77] The same year, the 26th Middlesex Light Infantry made a point of marching fifty miles under active service conditions from their Headquarters in Strathroy to the Divisional camp at Goderich, "a march that was reported to have been well conducted."[78] Western units were also innovative, and in 1912 the 22nd Saskatchewan Light Horse suggested a two-day exercise in the field under active service conditions. The plan was promptly approved by Militia Headquarters, although it was specified that the General Staff Officer Western Canada should have a hand in planning the scheme.[79] The following year, in Nova Scotia, the 63rd Halifax Rifles completed eight days' training under canvas, a tactical scheme in October, and "a night's bivouac in July, under service conditions."[80]

Field training sometimes involved considerable ingenuity. During an exercise in 1910 the 10th Royal Grenadiers of Toronto deployed a section of motorcycles (presumably privately owned), while the unit's baggage and camp equipment was transported in a borrowed truck at the amazing speed of seven miles per hour.[81] Two years later, the annual Thanksgiving manoeuvres in the 2nd Division included a machine-gun detachment from the 2nd Queen's Own Rifles in Toronto and wireless detachments from Hamilton.[82]

The 1st Division summer camp in 1914 was both ambitious and imaginative. Rural units were to train at Goderich for eleven days, at the end of which city corps would gather at Lucan. The two forces would then advance and meet in an encounter battle. Both forces were equally balanced in terms of composition, with infantry, artillery, cavalry, medical, and service corps elements. The rural units were to use horse transport, the city corps would employ trucks provided free of charge by the Gramm Motor Truck Company, and the Department of Militia and Defence would pay for wages and fuel. The aim of the exercise was not only to train units in an all-arms setting, but also to demonstrate the superiority of motor transport. Unfortunately, the exercise, scheduled to take place 22–27 August 1914, was overtaken by the outbreak of war and had to be cancelled. Perhaps it was just as well. Gramm trucks taken overseas by the First Contingent in 1914 were later condemned as unserviceable in England.[83]

The question of whether the Canadian Militia was well trained on the eve of war is difficult to answer. Training standards, after all, are relative. However, the value of both local and summer training seems questionable, if basic subjects such as proficiency with firearms are considered. Inexperienced and poorly trained militiamen called out in August 1914 had difficulties handling their weapons, sometimes with tragic consequences: fifteen-year-old Private Gordon Betts of the 5th Regiment, Royal Highlanders of Canada, who was called out for security duties on the Soulanges Canal in Quebec, was accidentally shot and killed by a negligent fellow-sentry.[84] In Ontario, the security picquet at Depot Harbour, furnished by a rural unit, the 23rd Northern Pioneers, was withdrawn by 21 August 1914 after the Chief Commissioner of Police in Ottawa received a complaint that a number of sentries had accidentally fired their weapons and "the lives of the people around the elevator are unsafe."[85]

EQUIPMENT AND CLOTHING

The militia was also hampered by a chronic shortage of equipment. Although the Departmental budget had leapt from $6,909,211 in fiscal year 1910–11 (the last Liberal budget) to $10,988,162 in fiscal year 1913–14 (an increase of 59 per cent), three-quarters of this increase was accounted for by pay, engineer services, and building maintenance. "Warlike stores" more than doubled, from $334,548 to $703,375, but much of this must have been attributable to the purchase of 18-pounder and 60-pounder guns. The budget for construction of some fifty-four armouries, drill halls, and gun sheds increased over the same period by 143 per cent to $1,611,180, but this was offset by the creation of new companies, squadrons, and batteries. The budget for uniforms did not increase in proportion and amounted to $916,991 in fiscal year 1913-14, enough to purchase about 26,000 new and replacement uniforms for the PF, militia, and reserve stocks.[86]

Uniforms may seem like a trivial matter, but they are utilitarian and, as a visible mark of modernity, important for morale. Traditionally, scarlet, green, or blue serge uniforms were worn both in the field and on ceremonial parades. The drawback to these uniforms, highly visible on the battlefield, became evident during the Boer War, and in 1903 Canada adopted khaki uniforms for general wear.[87]

The issue of new uniforms proceeded at a glacial pace, and some units purchased their own. The 13th Royal Regiment in Hamilton was one of the first to do so: in 1903 the regiment adopted khaki because the scarlet uniforms "smacked too much of the parade ground and church parades and not enough of the stern realities of war."[88] The 86th Three Rivers Regiment, on the other hand, expected members to buy their own, although as late as 1913 some holdouts were still wearing the old scarlet.[89]

Most units were content to wait for new uniforms. In Toronto, the 2nd Queen's Own Rifles received their khaki uniforms on the eve of their departure to England to participate in the 1910 British Army manoeuvres.[90] The following year, in Quebec, the 11th Argenteuil Rangers attended summer camp wearing the "new khaki issue."[91] The 52nd Prince Albert Volunteers and the newly organized 60th Rifles of Canada were issued with khaki in 1913, although the 60th asked that the brass buttons on the new uniforms be replaced by rifle-regiment black buttons.[92] The 48th Highlanders in Toronto received khaki in June 1914, just in time for summer camp at Petawawa, but many units that spring went to camp clothed partly in the traditional uniforms.[93] The 4th Chasseurs Canadiens at Lévis had only one company with khaki shirts and trousers, while the Prince Edward Island Light Horse at Charlottetown had squadrons wearing both the old and the new.[94] At Niagara-on-the-Lake, the 2nd Field Company thought "the red serge is very unsuitable for Engineers during training,"[95] while Major-General Lessard, a week after the war broke out, urged "that an early issue be made to those Corps not yet furnished with this clothing. The red and green clothing is obviously quite unsuitable for work in camp."[96] Even after the outbreak of war, old uniforms remained in use. As late as 1915, the 63rd Regiment manning the Halifax defences had men dressed in traditional rifle-green, while CEF recruits from Cobourg, Ontario, appeared at the Artillery Depot in Montreal wearing blue serge.[97]

Financial constraints meant that equipment was in short supply. The six Service Corps Divisional Trains, for example, had a combined establishment of 1,080 vehicles and 1,920 draught horses.[98] The cost of purchasing and housing all of these animals and vehicles would have been prohibitive. A reduced establishment could have been adopted for training purposes, but there is no evidence that this was ever considered. An effort was made in 1903 to create a voluntary reserve of horses, drivers, and wagons, but this plan was never very popular and was abandoned in 1911.[99]

In 1913, Service Corps companies in the Maritimes at the summer camp at Sussex, New Brunswick, lacked vehicles and had to rent forty wagons from local farmers. Water carts were non-existent and had to be improvised with sugar barrels mounted on some of the wagons.[100] At the same time, artillery units were issued with obsolete harness from Divisional stocks: "A number of old pattern head-collars were recently issued to this unit from 6th Division," complained Colonel R.W. Rutherford. "These head-collars are very old, evil-smelling of old manure, and are not fitted to take the bit."[101] Engineer Telegraph Detachments also lacked equipment and, by 1914, each of the eight detachments had two cable wagons for carrying reels of telephone line and one airline wagon for stringing telephone lines in the field, a scale of issue adequate for individual but not collective training.[102]

Wireless Detachments were raised before 1914, although there was a shortage of equipment and enthusiastic militiamen had to purchase equipment out of their own pockets. A communications demonstration staged in November 1910 by the 2nd Engineer Field Company of Toronto, for example, was possible only because a unit enthusiast provided wireless sets.[103] By 1914, "[w]ireless telegraphy stores became an Ordnance supply,"[104] but left unsaid was the actual amount of equipment available. As well, the establishment of a specialist unit or detachment did not necessarily mean that equipment would follow. In 1913, the Quartermaster General did "not approve issuing Signalling Equipment to newly organized units [60th Regiment] – not until they have shown proficiency in other work."[105] In the event, the 60th received the equipment, but only after the Chief of the General Staff intervened.[106]

WEAPONS

The most serious deficiencies were in weapons and associated ancillary stores. The standard weapon after Confederation was the single-shot breech-loading Snider–Enfield rifle. In 1896, it was replaced by the Mark I Lee–Enfield magazine rifle, which in turn was replaced by the Ross rifle in 1905.[107] The reasons for the adoption of the Ross rather than the Lee–Enfield are not clear. Sir Frederick Borden, the Minister of Militia and Defence, claimed that British companies either could not or would not establish a factory in Canada to manufacture Lee–Enfields, but Australia was able to build a Lee–Enfield factory at Lithgow in 1909, after calling for tenders in Britain and the United States.[108]

The Ross was obsolete when it first appeared. Unlike with the British Short Magazine that Lee–Enfield introduced in 1902, chargers* could not be used and the magazine had to be loaded with individual cartridges. The Ross magazine also held five rounds, as opposed to ten with the Lee–Enfield. The small magazine and lack of a charger guide made it impossible to fire fifteen rounds a minute, an important part of the pre-war British musketry course. Significantly, a musketry syllabus submitted to Militia HQ by the 2nd Division in 1913 did not include a rapid-fire practice.[109] A bewildering variety of Ross rifles was issued, but none was designed for charger loading until the Ross Mark III was approved in late 1912.[110]

The issue of modern small arms to the militia proceeded unevenly. Lee–Enfield Mark I rifles were first issued in 1896, but it was eight years before the 59th Stormont and Glengarry Regiment were able to hand in their forty-year-old single-shot Sniders, while the 55th Megantic Light Infantry had to wait until 1906 before they received Lee–Enfields.[111] In the meantime, the Ross was issued to other militia units as early as 1905.

Procurement of all marks of the Ross was painfully slow, and there was no apparent effort to make uniform issues to every unit; as a result, many units held a variety of weapons. A few were lucky: the 56th Grenville Regiment with Lee–Enfields and the 63rd Halifax Rifles with the Ross Mark II had only one type of rifle to contend with.[112] Others were less fortunate. In October 1914, the 91st Canadian Highlanders in Hamilton had 436 Lee–Enfields and 83 Ross Mark II rifles, made obsolete by the introduction of the Mark III in 1913. Similarly, the 48th Highlanders had 200 Lee–Enfields and 230 Ross Mark II rifles. Astonishingly, the 65th Carabiniers Mont-Royal in Montreal in June 1914 was equipped with

---

* Chargers were spring-steel clips holding five cartridges that were inserted into a bridge or charger guide over the breech. The shooter then pressed the cartridges down with his thumb to load the magazine. The procedure took only one or two seconds and was far quicker than loading the magazine with individual rounds.

373 Lee-Enfields, 375 Ross rifles Mark II, and 55 modern Ross rifles Mark III.[113]

The profusion of weapons created serious training problems. In April 1914, Militia HQ directed that musketry training be carried out with the Ross rifle and that special issues should be made to units equipped with Lee-Enfields. However, the supply of Ross rifles was inadequate, and newly organized militia units at Camp Sewell in 1914 had to be equipped with Lee-Enfields.[114] The CEF later had the same problem; most of the training in Canada after October 1914 was a waste of time because of the bewildering variety of obsolete firearms.

SUMMARY

In 1914, the militia was of uneven quality with respect to equipment and training. Many of its characteristics – decentralization, collegiality, regimental identity, pomp and circumstance, initiative, and dedication – would be carried over to the CEF. Not surprisingly, the peacetime influence steadily waned as the war went on, although this took some time. The Militia Council, disregarded by Sam Hughes, for example, did not regain its effectiveness until A.E. Kemp was appointed Minister of Militia and Defence in November 1916. Militia units were engaged with recruiting in 1914–15 and again in 1917, but by mid-1917 it was recognized that modern war demanded centrally controlled generic organizations. Some things could not be changed, and the lack of modern weapons, equipment, and training facilities brought about an acknowledgement that entry-level training had to be carried out in England.

The basic organization and the quality of human material was sound, and without the militia it is difficult to see how the CEF could have been formed. But the militia could not sustain the CEF for long. New recruits had to be found from the national manpower pool, and this called for coherent policies and careful management by the Canadian government. How well the government did this forms the central theme of chapter 2.

2

Regulating Manpower: Government and Military Policies 1914–18

The First World War was Canada's first modern war: that is to say, the whole of society was involved, not just the armed forces. Inevitably, there were competing demands for manpower from agriculture, industry, and, above all, the military. The problem was not unique to Canada. Manpower allocation was perhaps the most difficult economic problem faced by combatant states, all of which found it difficult to strike the right balance between the needs of the military and the production of food and material.[1]

During the war the Canadian government never came to grips with the thorny issue of controlling manpower. No attempt was made to allocate manpower on a rational basis, and no measures were taken to economize manpower. Nor was there any serious consideration of the size and composition of the forces that could be raised and sustained. Instead, national policies and measures focused almost exclusively on allocation, as though the nation's manpower resources were infinite and simply had to be pointed in the right direction.

NATIONAL POLICIES

To be fair, the need for manpower policies was not apparent in 1914. The war was expected to last a few months only, and given the abundant supply of volunteers for the CEF, there was no apparent need to manage manpower. Instead, the government was mainly concerned with offsetting the effects of the 1913–14 recessions. These were particularly severe in western Canada, where the construction industry had collapsed and both the Grand Trunk Pacific and the Canadian Northern Railway had ceased laying track, idling thousands of company workers and contract labourers.[2] In eastern Canada, the outbreak of war and the initial economic slump caused problems. Large employers such as Massey-Harris laid off thousands of workers in Toronto and Brantford because their European markets were effectively closed.[3]

No detailed statistics are available, but one historian has estimated that perhaps 20 per cent of all recruits came from the long-term unemployed.[4] Whatever the actual figure might have been, concerns with unemployment were pervasive. In October 1914, HQ Military District 1 (MD 1) in London asked for instructions in dealing with "cases of hardship caused by volunteers for the first Expeditionary Force giving up their permanent employment and not being accepted. Many of these men find a difficulty at this time of year in securing employment."[5] In reply, Militia HQ reminded MD 1 that another overseas division had just been authorized and presumably would provide jobs for those who chose to volunteer again.[6] In November, the 13th (Militia) Field Artillery Brigade of Toronto assembled a full-strength battery in anticipation of mobilization and requested permission to house the men in the University Avenue Armoury because "[t]he men being out of work are apt to drift off."[7] Further west, in December 1914, HQ MD 10 notified Winnipeg militia units recruiting for the CEF that "the first choice is to be made out of all unemployed members of their corps or other unemployed who present themselves for enlistment. The above are to be enlisted prior to any men who already hold positions or who are in good circumstances."[8]

Despite the recession, skilled tradesmen needed by the CEF were in short supply. Service Corps recruiting in the Maritimes was suspended as of 18 August 1914, but it took until 3 September, after an unprecedented amount had been spent on advertisements, to find almost 500 Mechanical Transport drivers, cleaners, and artificers.[9] In England, the 1st Division was short thirty farriers, saddlers, and shoeing-smiths, and special authority had to be sought from the War Office to recruit these specialists in Britain.[10] The shortages persisted: in April 1915, HQ MD 2 appealed to Militia HQ for advertising funds to attract shoeing-smiths to the 4th Field Artillery Brigade in Toronto.[11]

The economic downturn persisted for much of 1915, particularly in areas with large numbers of transient workers. In Vancouver, thousands of unemployed workers, mostly immigrants, rioted in April 1915 when city officials decided to stop providing relief to non-residents. By the end of the year, however, employment had been restored to normal peacetime levels because of increased employment in munitions plants, enlistments, and a sharp reduction in immigration.[12] But there was still a general surplus of labour, and in Alberta the 63rd Battalion reported in July 1915 that, although recruiting had ceased, the unit was still "over-run with applications for enlistment."[13] In Medicine Hat, there were 250 applicants for 100 positions. Militia HQ directed that these men be enlisted and stated that, if necessary, another battalion would be authorized in the province.[14]

The general slack that persisted for much of 1915 meant that Canada had a surplus of skilled workers. But labour was needed abroad, and more than 3,600 civilians were hired to work in Britain and Russia. The largest group was the Canadian Munitions Workers Unit, mainly machinists and members of allied trades, hired in the spring of 1915 by two Britons – G.N. Barnes, MP, and William Windham of the British Board of Trade – to work in British factories. The Canadian government was actively involved. The actual hiring was done by Barnes and Windham or their agents, but the Department of Labour paid separation allowances to families in Canada, retained copies of the contracts, and provided offices and clerical staff for the recruiters.[15] By January 1917, at least 3,000 Canadian munitions workers had been sent to England. These men were deemed British workers, but the Canadian government retained a vested interest and in 1917 tried to make arrangements for those drafted under the British *Military Service Act* to be transferred to the CEF.[16]

Overseas, in both England and France, efforts were made to comb out Canadian soldiers to work in British munitions plants. The practice started as early as August 1915, when a 4th Battalion soldier who had been evacuated to England was discharged because he was employed as a munitions worker. A year later, Eastern Command (British) directed that all units – Canadian units included – canvass their men for skilled tradesmen willing to work in British factories. Canadian military authorities had no objections, and at least two men from the 9th Reserve Battalion were released to become factory workers. In December 1915, Canadian Corps HQ in France, in response to GHQ instructions, directed that all units canvass their men for munitions workers, adding that "no unit artificers will be accepted and no more than 2% of any unit."[17] However, the response was poor; only eighty-seven volunteers were sent to the Base Depot at Le Havre to be tested for technical proficiency. All were returned to their unit by the end of April 1916. Nonetheless, the scheme continued. By November 1916 more than eighty Canadian soldiers serving in France had been discharged from the CEF to work in British munitions plants.[18]

In addition to munitions workers, at least 600 Canadian track-layers, blacksmiths, locomotive drivers, fitters, and bridge carpenters were hired in September and October 1915 by the British firm of Pauling and Company to help build the Murman Railway in northern Russia.[19] The enterprise was civilian in nature, but had been approved by Andrew Bonar Law, Secretary of State for the Colonies, who encouraged the Canadian government to co-operate.[20] The first group of 500 sailed from New York on 13 October 1915, and the remainder followed shortly thereafter. Difficulties arose in Russia, however, because of poor equipment, harsh conditions, and injudicious decisions by Russian authorities; in March 1916, the group – considered by the Russians as incompetent troublemakers – was sent back to Canada.[21]

Employment picked up in 1916, but by November labour bureaus reported that only 45 per cent of all unskilled positions had been filled, perhaps because the labour force had been diminished by 176,919 enlistments.[22] War contracts continued to flow, and the Bureau of Statistics described 1916 as "a year of almost abnormal activity."[23] Skilled labour was increasingly hard to come by, and in Brantford "it was found very difficult to secure men for war work, so difficult that wages up to $8 and $10 a day were paid to machinists working on munitions."[24] By August 1916, there were complaints from Ontario manufacturers that orders could not be filled because of the lack of skilled workers.[25] Interned aliens were released in April 1916 to reinforce the labour force, and the *Alien Labour Act* was suspended to allow employers to import skilled workers from the United States.[26] The relief was short-lived, however; relatively few aliens had been interned in the first place, and the supply of American labour dried up in April 1917 when the United States entered the war.

The agricultural sector was probably even worse off, given the exodus of workers to urban centres from 1915 onward to take advantage of steady jobs with higher wages. Also, farming was seasonal: temporary workers were needed to assist with seeding and harvesting. Estimates vary, but it was thought that about 42,000 seasonal workers were needed in the spring and 54,500 in the fall.[27] Under ordinary circumstances there would have been an ample supply of workers from eastern Canada, but by 1916–17 many had joined the CEF or found more lucrative jobs in the growing munitions industry.[28] The shortage of workers affected recruiting; in Alberta, the General Officer Commanding (GOC) MD 13 complained in January 1917 that farmers were actively discouraging men from joining the CEF.[29]

The effect of all of this on the CEF is difficult to quantify. Almost certainly, there was no impact on recruiting during the first year of the war. Up until October 1915, when Sam Hughes unexpectedly decided to increase the CEF to 250,000 men, recruiting was slow paced, largely because Militia HQ was reluctant to form new units until existing ones were at full strength. Full employment combined with the expansion of the CEF put a strain on the manpower pool. Nor were matters helped when Prime Minister Borden announced on 1 January 1916 that the strength of the Armed Forces would be maintained at 500,000 men. The effect of these increases on recruiting was neatly summarized by Lieutenant-Colonel Knowles of the 129th Battalion when he complained that "[t]he farmers argue that they are being asked by the Minister of Agriculture to produce, produce, produce, and that if they enlist they cannot produce. The manufacturers, whether engaged in munition work or not, complain every time an employee talks about enlisting. This leaves only the clerks in the stores and labourers available."[30]

Despite the increasing shortage of skilled labour that became more evident over time, the Canadian government made no real effort to regulate manpower or to redirect workers from non-essential industries. Instead, the job was left up to the Department of Militia and Defence. The reasons for this are not clear, but as early as August 1915 Militia HQ directed that skilled mechanics could be enlisted only if their expertise was needed for military purposes.[31] The policy was subsequently expanded, and in November 1915 the Adjutant-General in Ottawa forwarded lists of munitions firms to all districts with instructions to "keep in touch with these firms with a view to ascertaining whether they are in need of skilled labour, in order that all such men offering their services will not be enlisted until it is ascertained whether they can be of use to these manufacturers."[32] To some extent, this had the effect of turning recruiting offices into employment bureaus. Recruiting Officers in Toronto, Hamilton, and St Catharines were directed to "take all possible steps for mechanics offering at your Depot to be placed with the above firms. They are only to be enlisted if unable to be so placed."[33]

Although the Adjutant-General's instructions clearly applied only to potential recruits, employers were under the impression the CEF was a labour pool that could be tapped as needed. In Toronto, HQ MD 2 was deluged with letters from factories looking for skilled workers. HQ staff was sympathetic to these requests, but at the same time was reluctant to lose soldiers. Very few seem to have been released at the request of their former employers, although a handful of men were given furloughs to return to their workbenches. Recruiting officers and commanding officers were understandably reluctant to co-operate, and in January 1916 the Waterous Engine Works Company of Brantford complained that units were refusing to release men: "We propose taking this up with the local corps but at the same time our previous efforts along these lines have not been crowned with any success. The Officers are anxious to get men and they have no inclination, and seem to have no power, to allot the men offering for enlistment, as is indicated in your circular letter of November 29th they should do."[34] Commanding officers elsewhere were equally obstreperous, and in June 1916 a battalion commander in Toronto told the head of a munitions plant that a skilled toolmaker would be released only if the plant provided two recruits to take the man's place.[35]

Further restrictions followed. Recruiting Officers were forbidden to enlist officers, engineers, and wireless operators of the merchant navy. In 1916, cable operators could not be enlisted without authority from Militia HQ; steel and coal employees in Cape Breton could not be recruited without permission from District HQ; recruiting was prohibited in the coal, smelter, and coking areas of southern British Columbia; and, from February 1917 onward, telegraph operators could not enlist without the consent of their employers.[36] Not only manufacturers were concerned with the shortage of skilled workers: in January 1918, the commander of MD 11 in British Columbia recommended that recruiting for the Canadian Forestry Corps and Railway Construction Corps be stopped because of the importance of these industries to the province.[37]

Even with the full co-operation of units, the military's efforts to coordinate manpower could have not succeeded, simply because there were no legislative or regulatory means to force soldiers to return to their former jobs. "This is a free country," remarked the Assistant Adjutant-General (AAG) at MD 2 in April 1916, "and a man cannot be compelled to work on Munitions if he does not so desire."[38] In Kingston, one soldier said flatly that if he were released at the request of the Canadian Locomotive Works he would work elsewhere.[39] Other soldiers were equally intransigent and threatened to re-enlist elsewhere under assumed names, while others were careful not to disclose their true occupation on enrolment. In some cases, men who had been identified as skilled workers by various companies claimed to be common labourers, thus leaving the military in the unenviable position of adjudicating conflicting claims. Not surprisingly, commanding officers sided with their men. In March 1916, for example, the Commanding Officer of the 156th Battalion in Brockville interviewed four men identified by the National

Manufacturing Company as skilled mechanics and reported that "they were not qualified mechanics but simply labourers operating simple machines; and they desired to remain with the 156th Battalion.⁴⁰ The policy was clearly unworkable, a fact recognized in May 1916, when Headquarters MD 2 advised the 129th Battalion that men who refused to return to their former jobs would not be discharged.⁴¹

The only meaningful national manpower policy was the *Military Service Act* (MSA), introduced in the House of Commons in June 1917 by Prime Minister Borden. Although the primary purpose of the Act was to secure reinforcements for the CEF, it also gave lip service to national manpower needs. As Borden explained in the House of Commons, new legislation was needed because the existing *Militia Act* provided only for balloting, which did not allow for "an intelligent consideration of the country's needs and conditions."⁴² The new Act was needed, therefore, to allow men to be called up selectively, with provisions to exempt essential workers. The preamble emphasized the dual purpose of the Act: "[B]y reason of the large number of men who have already left agricultural and industrial pursuits in Canada to join such Expeditionary Force as volunteers, and of the necessity of sustaining under such conditions the productivity of the Dominion, it is expedient to secure the men still required, not by ballot as provided in the *Militia Act*, but by selective draft."⁴³ The twin aims were further emphasized by a Department of Justice manual for dealing with claims for exemption from military service; this document stressed the need for CEF reinforcements but added that local tribunals should consider both the civil and military requirements of the nation in granting exemptions. However, the needs of the nation were complex, local and individual circumstances varied widely, and no detailed guidance could be offered. Instead, local tribunals should consider the importance of the production of food, coal, steel, metal, wood, and other manufactured articles as well as the need for the continued operation of railways and steamships, telegraphs and telephones, light, heat, and power plants, and financial institutions. All were equally important, and tribunals were expected to exercise common sense, "having regard to local conditions and to their general knowledge of the domestic and world situation from the point of view of production, manufacturing and commerce."⁴⁴

In effect, much of the labour force enjoyed some degree of immunity from conscription, particularly since both individuals and employers were allowed to request exemptions, a process that favoured wage-earners but not farmers, labourers, and the self-employed. There may have been some intent to use the MSA as a means of rational allocation of manpower, but it does not appear that this was translated into practice.

The Act was not the only means by which the government tried to deal with the problem of "intelligently utilizing Canada's man and woman power in the prosecution of the war."[45] On 16 January 1918, a national conference was convened with representatives from provincial governments, industry, and unions to consider "ways and means of quick and effective mobilization of Canada's man-power."[46] Unfortunately, the results of the conference were inconclusive. T.H. Auld, Deputy Minister of Agriculture for Saskatchewan, encouraged the use of tractors to reduce the need for labourers, while a special committee recommended that conscripts rejected as medically unfit should be drafted to work on farms. It was also felt that federal labour exchanges should be established and a registration scheme implemented to determine the availability of labour. The Railway War Board wanted members of the Chinese Labour Corps, in transit that month from Victoria to Halifax for service in France, to be detained for essential track-laying, while Ontario and British Columbia farmers wanted to make use of indentured Chinese workers, a startling departure from the peacetime dislike of Asians.[47] However, most of these proposals were rejected by union representatives, who opposed the conscription of labour and the use of Chinese workers, although they grudgingly agreed to national registration and coordination of the labour supply.[48]

Faced with this intransigence, the government backed off, and no attempt was made to emulate the British Ministry of National Service, set up in the fall of 1917 with the power to allocate manpower for both military and civilian purposes.[49] In January 1918, a Cabinet subcommittee was convened to deal with the registration of labour and classification of industries, but the emphasis was on co-operation and not compulsion.[50] A Dominion-Provincial Employment Service was set up, but this was intended only to facilitate the exchange of information between the provinces and the federal government. Sixty-six employment offices were organized by the end of the year, but the Employment Service had an annual budget of only $50,000, which suggests the low priority assigned by the Union Government.[51] A few months later, in June, some five million men and women were registered in order to place workers where they were best suited and to ensure that vital industries had enough labour. Names and addresses were passed to employers and local authorities, but no attempt was made to make use of the information to redirect labour, effectively leaving the MSA as the only control over national manpower.[52]

Whether Canada was in a position to control manpower is moot, since the government was in no position to control the wartime economy. Canada's ambiguous status as a Dominion meant that the British government felt free to place orders in Canada without reference to the Canadian government. As early as 1914, orders were placed by the War Office in Canada and the United States for 1,300,000 uniforms and 900,000 greatcoats with no regard for the needs of the CEF.[53] The contracts were viewed as beneficial, and the *Toronto Globe* felt that "as a result of war contracts which will be placed in Canada from the other side of the Atlantic many important industries throughout the Dominion will be in a position to keep their men in steady employment during the coming winter."[54] In other cases, however, British contracts were an obvious intrusion. In 1914, without consulting the Canadian government, the Admiralty ordered ten H-class submarines from Canadian Vickers of Montreal. American supervisors and technicians were provided by Bethlehem Steel, and local militia units provided security details. Informed of this in January 1915, Prime Minister Sir Robert Borden was livid, especially when he found out that repairs to the Canadian icebreaker *J.D. Hazen* had to be suspended because the shipyard was fully occupied with the submarines.[55]

The largest commitment of Canadian manpower under British control was the Imperial Munitions Board, established in November 1915 to coordinate the purchase of munitions for the British government. Under the direction of Sir Joseph Flavelle, a Toronto businessman, the organization flourished; by 1918 almost 700 Canadian plants with 300,000 workers were producing supplies, not only for Britain but also for the United States Ordnance Department. The Board did not answer to the Canadian government, but to the British Ministry of Munitions.[56] The relationship seems to have been regarded with equanimity by the Canadian government, and by 1918 military work parties were being provided to Imperial Munitions plants in MD 2, MD 3, and MD 6.[57] However, the establishment of the Board meant that "the most significant economic activity generated in Canada by the Great War was not supervised by the Government of Canada."[58]

CONSERVATION OF MANPOWER

Apart from the efficient allocation of manpower was the question of husbanding human resources for the CEF. Sadly, Canada did not do well; reservists were surrendered to their home countries, thousands of men were allowed to enlist with British and allied forces, a disproportionate number of units were provided to rear areas in France, and thousands of men were allocated to various enterprises that offered no direct benefit to the nation.

At the outbreak of war 3,294 British reservists were living in Canada, of whom 2,779 returned home. Of the remainder, 149 were with the Permanent Force (PF), while at least 150 joined the CEF. The War Office made attempts to reclaim these men, but with little success; in March 1915 it was decided that they would not be recalled.[59]

Not all foreign reservists in Canada were British. By January 1917, 18,100 French, Russian, Belgian, Italian, and Dutch reservists living in Canada had been returned to their homelands. This was not unwelcome; the Canadian government assisted where possible, going so far as to commission two French doctors as militia officers in November 1916 for the express purpose of examining French reservists before their departure for France.[60] Not all French reservists returned, and at least twenty-nine joined the 1st Division in 1914. Concerns were expressed about the legal status of these men, some of whom were naturalized British subjects, but after some discussion the British ambassador in Paris reported that French authorities would not press for the return of reservists if they were with the CEF.[61] However, this applied only to the 1st Division, and by January 1917 about 5,000 men had been returned to France.

Approximately 5,000 Russian reservists in Canada were also returned under arrangements made by the Russian Consul General in Montreal, although the trip could not have been easy. The Russian Government initially took the position that Russian subjects were liable for military service regardless of their residence, but this was resisted by both the CEF and the men concerned. In June 1915, therefore, the Russian Government relented, and all Russian subjects domiciled in Canada, including reservists, were allowed to join the CEF.[62] All in all, about 20,900 British and foreign reservists were returned to their parent country.

Apart from reservists, Canadians also served with other forces, principally British, although the number is far from certain. In June 1919, E.H. Scammell of the Department of Soldiers' Civil Re-establishment estimated that about 50,300 Canadians served with British forces.[63] On the other hand, in January 1942 Edwin Pye of the Historical Section claimed a total of 17,498.[64] Neither outlined their methodology or sources. Pye's figure appears to refer only to the British army, while Scammell evidently included all those who served with the British forces.

Scammell estimated that about 2,000 men made their own way to Britain to enlist, while 12,000 others left the CEF overseas to join the

British forces. Neither figure can be confirmed, but there is no doubt that many Canadians managed to join the British Army one way or another. In some cases, men were discharged from the CEF to serve as officers with the British Expeditionary Force, although the number is uncertain. However, the Veterans Affairs Virtual War Memorial commemorates 473 former members of the CEF who died while serving as officers in the British army.[65] With an approximate death rate of 10 per cent, this suggests that almost 5,000 soldiers of the CEF were commissioned in the British army. In many cases, they remained on strength of the CEF while they were undergoing officer training at a British cadet battalion. In other words, the CEF not only provided officers but also paid for their training. Most were discharged from the CEF overseas, although in the case of the University of Toronto Overseas Training Company they were discharged in Canada, "having been accepted as a Candidate for a Commission in the British Army."[66] All of this represented a significant loss to the CEF, not least because of the loss of potential leaders such as Edmund De Wind, a soldier from the 31st Battalion who won the Victoria Cross while serving as an officer with the Royal Irish Rifles.

The largest group of Canadians serving with the British Forces were those in the Royal Flying Corps (RFC), the Royal Naval Air Service, and (after 1 April 1918) the Royal Air Force. Some were seconded from the CEF, but most were enlisted in Canada. The total is far from certain. Some years ago, the Directorate of History of the Department of National Defence compiled a database listing 20,613 Canadian pilots, observers, and mechanics who served with British flying services. On the other hand, a panel in the Memorial Chamber of the Parliament Buildings in Ottawa claims that 22,812 men served with British flying services. An exact total, therefore, is impossible to determine, but it would be reasonable to assume that about 22,000 Canadian officers and men served with the British flying services.[67]

RFC recruiting was done with the agreement of the Canadian government. No quota was imposed, but by October 1918 the drain on the CEF was such that transfers to the Royal Air Force were restricted. Recruiting was initially coordinated by Lieutenant-Colonel E.A. Stanton, the Governor General's private secretary, with the assistance of Militia Headquarters, and successful applicants were sent to England for training. In the case of the Royal Naval Air Service, potential pilots were recruited by Naval Service Headquarters in Ottawa and then trained in Toronto before proceeding overseas. A special holding company of the

Royal Navy Canadian Volunteer Reserve was established at Halifax for potential naval aviators waiting for training.[68]

In December 1916, the War Office decided, without consulting the Canadian government, to establish an RFC training organization in Canada. In the event, the Canadian government had no objections; for the remainder of the war, the Department of Militia and Defence provided administrative and logistical support for RFC Canada, as the new organization became known. The Imperial Munitions Board constructed airfields at Camp Borden, Rathbun, Tyendinaga, Armour Heights, and Leaside (all in Ontario), with ground training facilities at the University of Toronto. Two of these facilities (Camp Borden and Tyendinaga) were established militia training areas, while the remainder were leased or donated to the Department of Militia and Defence for use by RFC Canada.[69] The manpower cost of supporting not only RFC Canada, but British flying services in general, was significant. Although the Canadian contribution directly aided the Empire war effort, the unchecked diversion of manpower was a direct loss to the CEF.

Apart from British flying services, the two largest contingents of expatriate Canadians were those with the Inland Water Transport (Royal Engineers) and the mechanical transport section of the Army Service Corps.

The Inland Water Transport (IWT) grew rapidly from its humble beginnings in 1914, and by 1918 had 10,164 men in France and Mesopotamia as well as 41,940 African and Asian labourers.[70] Many were Canadian. Captain W.W. Murray, a Canadian who served in the Middle East, later wrote: "[J]ust to illustrate Canadian ubiquity during the war, let it be known that a large percentage of the officers and men of those river craft [on the Tigris River between Basra and Baghdad] was made up of British Columbians."[71]

Recruiting for the IWT in Canada started in November 1916, when British Royal Engineer Detachments were established in CEF recruiting offices in Montreal, Toronto, Vancouver, and Fort Frances, Ontario, after Militia HQ instructed districts to facilitate recruiting.[72] From 1916 to 1918, at least 3,108 men were either recruited in Canada by the Royal Engineers or transferred from Canadian units.[73] Recruits had to be skilled mariners; advertisements called for master mariners, marine engineers, bargemen, riveters, and caulkers. Men were paid according to British pay scales (lower than their Canadian counterparts) and medical standards were less stringent, although this seems to have boomeranged in 1917, when the IWT complained that Canadian doctors were passing men with tuberculosis, Bright's disease, chronic heart disease, and rheumatism.[74] Once enlisted, the men were Royal Engineers and not members of the CEF. Nonetheless, they seem to have retained their Canadian identity, and ex-Sergeant-Major R.W. Gornall of Vancouver later claimed the men wore Canada badges on their shoulder straps.[75] Some IWT recruits came directly from the CEF, the 1st Canadian Pioneer Battalion providing twenty-three, including three First Nations men from Alert Bay, British Columbia, who served in Mesopotamia.

Men were also enlisted in Canada for the Mechanical Transport section of the British Army Service Corps. With the agreement of the Canadian government, recruiting started in October 1916 with a hoped-for quota of 2,470 men, although in the event only 1,100 enlisted.[76] Applicants had to be skilled driver-mechanics, wheelers, fitters, electricians, or blacksmiths, and an elaborate system was set up in Canada to test trade proficiency.[77] However, Canadian standards were evidently suspect: further tests at the British Army Service Corps Depot at Grove Park in England weeded out some 500 Canadian volunteers who were unsuitable for one reason or another.[78]

Disposing of unsuitable Canadian volunteers was problematic. Initially, they were sent to the Canadian base at Shorncliffe, where a batch of ninety-eight men, many of whom had been without a bath or change of underclothing for a month, arrived in March 1916 with no warning. The incident provoked an outburst from Major-General Carson, Hughes's representative in London:

> I would think that with the terrific demands that are being made on Canada for the purpose of keeping up the present and future Divisions in the Field, we can use all the men that Canada can give us, without turning over these fine boys to the British Service and then find that they are treated in anything but the proper spirit.[79]

The rejected volunteers were eventually given the opportunity to join the CEF at Shorncliffe, but more than half declined and were returned to Grove Park for repatriation to Canada.[80]

Canadian expatriates also served with other nations. A handful of Canadians are known to have served with the French army, although some may have been pre-war Regulars. Some 2,485 Montenegrin and 8,894 Rumanian recruits were also returned home under arrangements made by the Department of Militia and Defence.[81] Most were probably from the United States, but judging by the Polish Legion – which drew 1.7 per cent of its recruits from Canada – about 193 were Canadians.

The Serbian Army also recruited in Canada. The campaign was headed by Nicola Pavlovich, an agent of the Serbian Legation in Washington, who had been authorized by the CGS in February 1917 "to superintend the recruiting of Serbians resident in Canada, not for the Canadian Expeditionary Force but for the Serbian Army."[82] As with the Jewish Legion, recruiting was done by local committees formed by the Srpska Narodna Odbrana, or Serbian National Defence League. Recruits were interviewed, provided with identity cards, and quartered at the nearest Militia District HQ before proceeding to the Serbian Mobilization Camp, originally at Sussex in New Brunswick, and then at Lévis, Quebec.[83]

The number of Serbs recruited in Canada and the United States is not certain, although returns submitted by the Commandant of the Serbian Mobilization Camp at Lévis from March 1917 to November 1918 show that 6,203 Serbs were sent overseas.[84] If the proportion of Canadians was similar to that in the Polish Legion, it is probable that approximately 106 were Canadian.

In some cases, armies were raised by nations that did not exist. Czechoslovakia, part of the Austro-Hungarian Empire, was recognized by the Allies as a nation in August 1917 – but it did not have an army, even though Czech units were serving on both sides with the Russian, French, Italian, and Austro-Hungarian armies.[85] There is no evidence that Czech legions actively recruited in Canada, although it would be surprising if some of the 3,000 Czechs recruited in the United States were not Canadians.

Although Poland had not existed as an independent state since 1792, the ideal of a Polish nation persisted into the twentieth century. In the United States, Polish nationalism was fostered by paramilitary groups such as the Polish Falcon Alliance, which conducted military training from 1913 onward. With the outbreak of war and the possibility of Polish independence, the Falcons actively searched for a sponsor for a national army. In October 1916, Vincent Skarzynski, a member of the Falcons, and Andrzej Malkowski, an associate of Joseph Pilsudski, the Polish nationalist who devoted much of his life to Polish independence, were introduced to Sam Hughes and suggested that Canada take steps to train recruits for a Polish army. Hughes took their proposal seriously. After some discussions with London, the Department of Militia and Defence agreed to train Polish officers, and the first batch of twenty-three arrived at the University of Toronto on 3 January 1917.[86]

However, facilities at the University of Toronto were inadequate. After spending the summer at Camp Borden, the Polish School of Infantry moved to Niagara-on-the-Lake in October 1917, where a Polish Army Camp had been established by a Canadian officer, Lieutenant-Colonel A.D. LePan. Recruiting, at least in the United States, was initially brisk, Niagara Camp very quickly became overcrowded, and at the end of November 1917 the 1st Depot Battalion under CEF Major Madill was moved to PF barracks at St John's (St-Jean-sur-Richelieu), Quebec. Additional quarters were also made available by the United States Army at Fort George, New York, leaving LePan with the unenviable job of coordinating Polish Army activities with two nations and two Canadian military districts.

Between October 1917 and March 1919, the three camps handled 22,395 Polish recruits, of whom 20,720 were sent overseas. The majority of these men were Americans; only 384 claimed Canada as their home.[87] Financial costs were borne by the French government, but Canada had to provide the physical infrastructure, equipment, and uniforms (some were issued with peacetime scarlet uniforms). Twenty-five officers and several hundred NCOs and soldiers were attached to the Polish army, many of whom could have been employed elsewhere by the CEF.[88]

Polish recruiting centres were opened in Winnipeg, Toronto, and Montreal in October 1917 with the approval of Militia HQ.[89] But there were few recruits and the Poles turned to the CEF. In Winnipeg, the Polish Recruiting Centre made arrangements in March 1918 with the 1st Depot Battalion, Manitoba Regiment, to discharge Polish conscripts if they agreed to join the Polish Legion.[90] In Montreal, Number 44 Polish Army Recruiting Centre also sought recruits from the CEF, and in May 1918 was able to persuade MD 3 to hand over twenty-one soldiers from Polish settlements at Wilno and Barry's Bay in Ontario. The majority were Canadian-born and presumably agreed to their discharge from the CEF and enlistment in the Polish Legion, although this is far from clear.[91]

In all, Canada provided about 61,956 men to other armies. Not all of these men could have been enlisted by the CEF; it would have been impossible, for example, to stop 20,879 British and Allied reservists from returning to their home country. Nor was there any mechanism to prevent an estimated 2,000 Canadians from making their way to Britain in order to join the BEF. It is also difficult to argue against the number who served with British flying services. After all, the RFC and Royal Air Force supported the Canadian Corps at a time when Canada had no air sforce (two squadrons were authorized in July 1918 but did not serve in France).

On the other hand, it is difficult to defend the diversion of skilled tradesmen to the IWT and the Army Service Corps; these men would have been invaluable to the CEF.

Whether 12,000 members of the CEF serving abroad should have been allowed to join the British army is an open question. Many were commissioned in the British army, sometimes with the aid of the CEF. Others who joined the IWT possessed badly needed skills that must have been difficult to find in wartime Britain. But the impression remains that the CEF could have been choosier about discharging men to join the British army.

MILITARY MANPOWER MANAGEMENT

Valuable as the expatriot contingents were, Canada's major contribution was the CEF in general and the Canadian Corps in particular. But, as John English has pointed out, "neither Borden nor his ministers appreciated the strain this large commitment would place upon the voluntary system of recruitment and upon the nation's economy."[92] It can also be added that neither Borden nor his ministers had a clear idea of the size or composition of the forces required or of the need for a unified system of control. These were not trivial matters. In December 1916, the Ministry of Overseas Military Forces of Canada (OMFC) had to be created in England as a government department to clean up the chaos created by Sam Hughes and to assert control over the CEF in England and France. The new ministry resolved the long-standing issue of administrative control of Canada's army overseas, but was not subordinate to the Department of Militia and Defence. This meant that Militia HQ, which was responsible for providing the manpower in the first place, had no say in the employment, number, or composition of units overseas. In effect, Canada had two armies, neither of which was beholden to the other.

Most of Canada's soldiers overseas were concentrated in five divisions, all raised under different circumstances. The 1st and 2nd Divisions were offered to Britain in 1914 as independent forces with no plan to join the two to form a corps. However, in April 1915 Hughes, apparently on his own initiative, suggested the creation of a corps to the Canadian representative at GHQ in France. The offer was gratefully accepted by the War Office, and on 13 September 1915 the Canadian Corps under the command of Lieutenant-General E.A.H. Alderson was formed in France. However, Alderson, an experienced professional officer, understood that a corps with only two divisions was unbalanced, and at his suggestion Canada offered additional units to bring the corps up to four divisions.[93]

The offer was accepted, and the 3rd and 4th Divisions were formed in England using newly arrived battalions from Canada. Lead elements of the 3rd arrived in France in December 1915, while the 4th, delayed by the need to provide reinforcements to the Canadian Corps, arrived in the summer of 1916.[94] Subsequently, in August 1916, Hughes ordered a fifth division to be organized, with a sixth to follow.[95] But manpower was becoming increasingly limited. The creation of the 5th Division was delayed until January 1917, largely because men earmarked for the division had to be sent to France to replace losses on the Somme.[96]

The 5th Division was not formed to meet any identifiable national or operational need but simply, it would appear, to save face by honouring a commitment made by Sam Hughes. Officially, the division was destined to serve in France, but OMFC staff, wrestling with the problem of finding reinforcements for the Canadian Corps, thought otherwise. As early as March 1917, the Deputy Minister OMFC warned the War Office that casualties could not be replaced if the 5th was sent to France and that it would be difficult to keep the Canadian Corps up to strength, even if the 5th were tapped for reinforcements. The warning was repeated three months later when the Minister of the OMFC, Sir George Perley, again advised the War Office that it would be necessary to use the 5th Division to keep the four divisions in France up to strength.[97] By November 1917 it was evident that maintaining the 5th was pointless, and Perley recommended that the division be broken up to provide reinforcements. Prime Minister Borden concurred, but Perley avoided taking action until February 1918, perhaps, as one historian has suggested, to avoid losing 5th Division votes in the December election.[98]

The issues surrounding the 5th Division were not straightforward, and to insist that the division simply locked up useable manpower ignores the subtleties of its history. Admittedly, the average strength was 12,843 men, many of whom were trained, fit, and eligible to be sent to the front. But this overlooks the division's unwritten role as an arm of the Canadian reserve organization in England.[99] War Office returns suggest that at least 4,800 trained soldiers from the Division were drafted to the Canadian Corps. The largest batch, 1,400 men, left in May 1917, presumably to replace losses at Vimy Ridge. As the 48th Highlanders historian wrote of the 134th Battalion in the 5th Division: "Drafts [for France] were called for regularly and then the numbers would be replaced from reserve battalions."[100] But the job of the reserve battalions was to provide reinforcements to France. Why should they continually provide men to a non-operational formation that also provided reinforcements?

All of this meant that, to some extent, the 5th was a training establishment: during its twelve-month existence, almost one third of its infantrymen at any given time were undergoing basic training.[101] Some of these trainees had little or no training. In May 1917, the 119th Battalion, a 5th Division unit, commented on a batch of 513 men from the 8th Reserve Battalion: "This draft is largely made up of men enlisted in Canada as artillerymen. Many of these men have had no shore leave; no P.T., no route marching, no BF [bayonet fighting], no armed drill and no squad drill."[102] Reserve battalions had an instructional cadre and specialized equipment to teach recruits; the 5th Division battalions did not, which calls into question how well the drafts were trained.

The Division's role as a reserve formation meant it was also a holding unit starting in February 1917, when underage soldiers at Shorncliffe, who were not employed as drummers or buglers, were posted to 5th Division units. By the end of February 1917, the division held 698 boys and, at the end of March 1917, 951 juveniles. These were the peak months, however, and when the division was broken up in February 1918 there were only fifty-nine minors on strength.[103]

Canada's willingness to step forward created other manpower problems. In March 1917, the Cabinet agreed to a British request to land drafts of the Chinese Labour Corps in British Columbia and then send them by train (under escort) to Atlantic seaports for onward passage to Europe. The decision meant that a staging area and depot had to be organized on Vancouver Island, as well as transit facilities at Camp Petawawa where drafts could wait for troop ships to become available at eastern seaports. Guards, medical orderlies, and support staff for the various camps, together with a thousand men for the Railway Service Guard, also had to be found. Although most of these men were unfit for overseas service, many could have been used elsewhere in Canada to replace fit men.[104] Guards and medical orderlies were also needed for transports, most of which sailed from Atlantic ports, although a few proceeded to Europe via the Panama Canal.

The government's failure to decide on the composition of the CEF also created problems. In March 1918, Canada agreed to raise the 1st Canadian Tank Battalion,* although there is no evidence that this would have directly benefited the Canadian Corps.[105] Subsequently, a second tank battalion was offered – and then, at the request of the War

---

* Tank battalions were not assigned to corps. In all likelihood, the Canadian unit would have been a GHQ or army resource to be used where most needed.

Office, a third. OMFC understood what Ottawa apparently did not: three tank battalions meant a Canadian Tank Brigade, with the need to find 388 men for brigade headquarters, signal company, and support services. General Turner, Chief of Staff at HQ OMFC, thought this would be difficult "[u]nless the numbers to be enlisted under the Military Service Act are likely to be increased."[106] There was also the vexing question of reinforcements, since tank crews, fitters, and signalers were specialists who required lengthy training. Fortunately, the war ended before all three battalions and the brigade components were formed.

Other changes had manning implications that were apparently not considered by HQ OMFC. In early 1918, infantry battalions in the Canadian Corps were increased by 100 men each, while engineer and machine gun companies were grouped into battalions with ninety-six guns as opposed to British machine gun battalions with only sixty-four guns.[107] Much has been made of the increase in manpower, mobility, and firepower; one historian has claimed these gave Canadian divisions the hitting power of a small British corps.[108] But this claim does stand up to scrutiny. Infantry battalions may have received an additional hundred men, but fifty were siphoned off to help form the machine gun battalions while others had to be provided to the engineer battalions; by the end of July 1918, the average Canadian battalion had only eighty-nine men more than the average British battalion with 929.[109] Nor did the new machine gun battalions provide a significant increase in firepower, since the British had corps machine-gun battalions while the Canadians did not. Furthermore, divisions did not operate independently, and additional resources were allocated by GHQ or Army HQ as needed (much like today's army). In the opening stages of the Battle of Arras on 26 August 1918, for example, the 3rd Canadian Division was supported by sixteen guns from the 1st Life Guards Machine Gun Battalion, while the divisional artillery was tripled with the addition of the 16th (British) Divisional Artillery, a field brigade from the 15th (British) Divisional artillery, and the 52nd and 126th (British) Army Field Brigades.[110]

Increasing the strength of Canadian battalions in February 1918 created some problems. HQ OMFC did not authorize a temporary increase but amended the battalion establishment, probably at Lieutenant-General Currie's suggestion.[111] Reserve units in England, therefore, were obligated to provide more men, since reinforcement demands were tied to establishments, thus creating an infantry shortfall that could not be made up until the eve of the Battle of Amiens in August.[112] Perhaps because of these difficulties, the new Canadian establishment did not last long and was quietly done away with in August 1918.[113]

Other aspects of the unique Canadian establishment created problems, and the new engineer and machine gun battalions needed 8,359 men to bring them up to strength. This generated an increase in wastage that had to be replaced. The exact cost is difficult to calculate, but it is estimated that the reorganization and increased wastage called for an additional 13,868 men. To put this figure into context, 24,132 MSA draftees were posted to the Canadian Corps in 1918.

Canada also provided troops for the rear areas in France and Belgium. Some of these, such as Medical, Service, Veterinary, and Dental Corps units, were probably Canada's share of the lines of communication needed to support the Canadian Corps. Likewise, the Canadian Cavalry Brigade and the 8th Army Field Brigade were welcome additions to the higher combat power that sustained the BEF, including the Canadian Corps. However, there were 26,632 men with railway and forestry units that did not directly support the Canadian Corps (see table 2.1). This was equivalent to twenty-seven infantry battalions – an astonishing number, given that there were forty-eight infantry battalions in the Canadian Corps. The total seems disproportionate, and it is worth noting that other Dominions did not follow suit. Australia, for example, was conscious of the need to conserve manpower and provided troops for the Lines of Communications only if they directly benefited Australian units.[114] By November 1918, railway and forestry units accounted for about 18.2 per cent of all Canadians in France and Belgium.

Contingents were also deployed to other theatres. The largest of these was the Siberian Expeditionary Force, with 3,951 officers and men. Two field artillery batteries, together with 108 instructors and 26 dog drivers with 251 dogs, served with British forces in northern Russia, as well as 41 instructors with "Dunsterforce" in the Caucasus, while a bridging company was deployed to Palestine. A total of 439 men, mainly gunners, served in St Lucia, while Bermuda was garrisoned by Canadian battalions from 1914 to 1916.[115] There seemed to be no limit to Canada's willingness to provide troops outside of France and Flanders, a willingness that included a decision in 1917 to send Russian-Canadian soldiers to Petrograd to teach Russians to drive Caterpillar tractors, which pulled siege guns provided by the British Army.[116] As J.L. Granatstein has remarked, "A small nation cannot afford to disperse its limited strength as Canada did."[117]

Table 2.1 Canadian units outside of Canadian Corps, 11 November 1918*

Element	Total
Railway troops	14,881
Forestry Corps	11,751
Cavalry Brigade	2,860
Medical Corps	2,827
Service Corps	1,732
Veterinary Corps	447
Dental Corps	156
Not specified	544
8th Army Field Artillery Brigade	900†
Total	36,098

* Miscellaneous units and detachments have not been included, i.e., the nine-man section with the Royal Engineer Messenger Dog Service and two Auxiliary Horse Transport Companies that were not part of the Canadian Corps.
† Estimated.
Source: Overseas Military Forces of Canada, *Report of the Ministry: Overseas Military Forces of Canada 1918* (London: Overseas Military Forces of Canada, 1919), 375.

SUMMARY

Apart from men diverted to industry, substantial numbers of potential recruits were lost to the CEF because they were reservists or had been recruited by other nations in Canada. The total number of potential recruits lost to British industry or other armies is uncertain but was probably in excess of 65,000 men, or substantially more than the number of MSA draftees posted overseas in 1918. Not all of these men could have been diverted to the CEF. It would have been difficult to prevent almost 21,000 British and Allied reservists in Canada from returning to their home countries. To do so would have required a rigid manpower policy from the beginning and a degree of independence in foreign affairs that Canada did not enjoy. Still, had there been a coherent government policy regarding the allocation of manpower to both industry and the military, as well as a more systematic and rational use of the forces raised, the ever-increasing difficulty in finding enough men to maintain the CEF in France and Flanders might have been ameliorated and the need for conscription delayed.

The need for coherent policies and careful management of manpower was vital, considering the need to find enough men to finish the job. After all, the national manpower pool was limited. How the CEF managed this reservoir of men forms the central theme of chapter 3.

3

Enlistment Criteria

The Canadian government may not have had specific manpower policies, but Militia HQ did. These took the form of recruiting criteria that defined precisely who was or was not acceptable to the CEF. Ironically, these criteria had the effect of reducing the number of men eligible for enlistment. Not surprisingly, standards were relaxed as the war went on and the demand for recruits increased. In effect, recruiting policies became more efficient and professional, mirroring the increasing professionalism of the CEF.

Recruiting criteria were wide-ranging, covering age, citizenship, and medical fitness (including height, dental health, eyesight, and hearing). None of these standards was absolute; they were continually changed as the war ground on, in part because of bright ideas that appealed to Sam Hughes and in part because of a growing awareness in Ottawa that carefully considered modifications to the standards would not compromise a man's ability to serve overseas either with a combatant unit or with one of the less glamorous but essential units behind the lines.

However, difficulties arose in the enforcement of standards. Men lied about their age or concealed medical problems, and some commanding officers, in keeping with the pre-war tradition of autonomy, simply flouted the rules and enlisted those who presented themselves. There were also problems with medical examinations, in part because of a lack of diagnostic tools and in part because civilian physicians, hired to offset the shortage of military doctors, applied their own standards. There were also unofficial criteria: blacks, Asians, and immigrants from Central Europe all had difficulties enlisting.

The use of recruiting criteria, whether official or unofficial, barred a considerable number of men from enlisting – which begs the question of how many were in fact fit and available for military service. This chapter therefore concludes with an estimate of the manpower available to sustain the CEF.

AGE CRITERIA

At first glance, the age standards were simple and straightforward. Men had to be between the ages of eighteen and forty-five, a standard consistent with pre-war regulations. Boys were initially excluded from the CEF, although – as discussed in chapter 1 – teens as young as thirteen could join the militia with their parents' or guardian's consent. But the peacetime notion that boys could enlist persisted, there was no clear understanding of the realities of trench warfare, and in August 1915 Militia HQ modified the CEF age standard to allow boys as young as fourteen to enlist as bandsmen, buglers, or trumpeters – a policy that was cancelled in January 1917 because juveniles were of no use as reinforcements for units in France.[1]

There was also a feeling that a man over forty-five who was capable of a hard day's work could fill a non-combatant job behind the front lines. From June 1916 onward, men could enlist in forestry units up to age forty-eight because they were "labourers only, and are not to be considered as enlisted for General Service overseas [front-line duty]."[2] In January 1917, the same age range was extended to skilled railwaymen, although medical officers were reminded that "the apparent age rather than the age given is to be taken into account and the condition of the arteries of all men 41 years of age and over is to determine acceptance or rejection."[3]

AGE CRITERIA: PROBLEMS

The Canadian age range of eighteen to forty-five created problems in England, where the CEF was governed by British regulations that restricted active service in France or Belgium to those between the ages of nineteen and forty-two.[4] The upshot was that, on arrival in England, those under nineteen or over forty-two were precluded from serving at the front.

Canadian authorities in England were initially unconcerned with the conflict in age limits. In December 1916, Sir George Perley, the minister responsible for the Overseas Military Forces of Canada (OMFC) in England, advised Prime Minister Borden that there was no maximum age limit for postings to France, although a month later his staff became concerned about the discrepancy between British and Canadian age limits. Militia HQ also picked up on the matter and expressed concerns in February 1917.[5] Subsequent queries from Ottawa to HQ OMFC were never fully answered, and it was not until January 1918 that Militia HQ set a minimum age of eighteen years and six months for drafting to England. However, this was at odds with the MSA age range of twenty (later nineteen) to thirty-five, and in March 1918 a CEF Routine Order directed a minimum age of nineteen for both enlistment and drafting to England.[6] Despite these measures, as late as 26 August 1918 there were 2,087 trained soldiers under the age of nineteen serving with reserve units in England.[7]

Dealing with those under nineteen who arrived in Britain was a challenge. Initially, there was no formal repatriation policy, but in February 1917 HQ OMFC issued regulations that returned younger boys to Canada but conserved manpower by retaining older teens with reserve units until they were of age. In brief, the policy was to repatriate boys aged sixteen and a half or younger (later seventeen) and hold the older ones with the 34th Battalion (later redesignated Young Soldiers Battalion), the Medical Corps Depot, or the 5th Division until they were old enough to be drafted to France.[8] Not all of those repatriated were discharged on arrival in Canada; District Commanders were given authority to retain suitable boys in Special Service Companies for routine garrison jobs.[9]

Despite the regulations, underage soldiers were inadvertently drafted to France and many were not returned to England. From August 1916 onward, boys were retained in France under specific conditions intended to keep them out of harm's way until they turned nineteen. Those serving within the Lines of Communication were held at a base depot, while those who had arrived in the front line could remain with their units but not in the trenches. The latter was clearly impractical. Infantry battalions had enough on their hands without worrying about young soldiers in the transport lines, and in any event the possibility of long-range shelling meant they were exposed to danger. In November 1916, therefore, GHQ directed that soldiers who were eighteen or younger would be posted to a base depot, where they would remain until they were of age.[10] The policy was further modified in May 1917, when boys between the ages of eighteen and nineteen were allowed to serve with one of the many army schools, forward of the base depots along the English Channel but still within the Lines of Communication. The policy was firm, and a proposal from the Canadian Corps in August 1918 to employ minors with a demonstration platoon at the Corps railhead was promptly scotched by HQ OMFC.[11]

Underage soldiers in France who concealed their age remained with their units, unless they confessed their age or angry parents or guardians produced birth certificates. However, there was no concerted effort to weed these minors out. In January 1918, HQ OMFC authorized Canadian Corps HQ to transfer 500 men under the age of eighteen years and six months to Britain; however, judging by unit war diaries, there was no mass exodus of juveniles.[12] Regimental histories and records support this. In 1917–18, for example, the 85th Battalion lost seventeen minors, the 102nd Battalion twenty-one, the 18th and 72nd Battalions twenty-four each, and the 21st Battalion thirty-one.

At the other end of the spectrum were the older men who could not be drafted to France. Many were identified by medical boards before embarkation to Britain and were either retained in Canada or discharged. However, some were not detected until they arrived in England; these were employed on general duties with reserve battalions. But it was illogical for older men to serve with units whose sole purpose was to feed reinforcements to Canadian units in France or Belgium, and in November 1916 over-age men were posted to the 37th Reserve Battalion.[13]

The 37th did not remain a reserve battalion for long. It was redesignated "1st Canadian Labour Battalion" and posted to France in 1917, where it was joined by three other labour battalions. These units were not composed exclusively of over-age men, but rather of those whose medical categories (including age) precluded front-line service.[14] Still, it is striking that, of the 106 Canadians from various labour units who are buried in France or Belgium, thirty-two were over the maximum age of forty-two.

Despite the regulations, over-age men in France were sometimes retained by their units. The 21st Battalion, for example, insisted on retaining both Peter Comego, a forty-seven-year-old from the Alderville First Nation, and Johnston Paudash, a fifty-two-year-old from the Hiawatha Band, because they were accomplished scouts and snipers. Eventually, however, both had to be returned to Canada with "debility."[15]

From an administrative point of view, the need to cater to the underage and over-age soldiers detracted from their usefulness. Both juveniles and seniors in England or France had to be combed out and returned to Britain or repatriated to Canada, where they were discharged. It is true that many of the young soldiers eventually reached nineteen and were deployed to France, but had they been enlisted at the proper age, a great deal of administrative effort could have been saved. In the case of the older men, particularly in England, it can be argued that their presence freed up younger men for service in France. However, these jobs could have been done by substitutes who were unfit for service at the front or by women.

HEIGHT CRITERIA

Age was not the only criterion for enlistment; men also had to meet height standards. The initial height requirement, announced on 17 August 1914, was 5' 3" for all corps –with the exception of artillery (5' 7"), engineers (5' 4"), and horse transport drivers (5' 5").[16] The infantry standard lasted less than a year, however, and in July 1915 was lowered to 5' 2". This reduction has been incorrectly attributed to a shortage of recruits.[17] In brief, Major Francis Milton, a militia officer with the 44th Battalion in Winnipeg, wrote to Sam Hughes and suggested a new battalion with men under the regulation height. Hughes was enthusiastic, but the Adjutant-General noted in June 1915 that there was no need "for herding them [undersize soldiers] in separate battalions" and it would be better to reduce the minimum height to accommodate shorter men.[18] The district commander was then consulted; he recommended a one-inch reduction in the minimum height. Hughes accepted the advice, and as of 21 July 1915 the minimum height for infantrymen was 5' 2".[19]

. Later reductions were, however, directly related to declining enlistment figures. In December 1916, the minimum height for infantrymen was reduced to 5', and a year later the standard for non-combatants was dropped to 4' 11" – four inches shorter than the minimum height established in August 1914.[20] The artillery was also affected: in June 1917, the requirement for artillery drivers was lowered to 5' 3", followed in September 1917 by a further reduction to 5' 2". Also in September 1917, the height standard for field gunners was lowered to 5' 6" (a reduction of one inch), but garrison and siege gunners who had to handle heavy equipment and ammunition for prolonged periods of time had to be at least 5' 7".[21] All of these changes to the recruiting criteria were part of a deliberate effort to enlarge the pool of potential recruits.

HEIGHT CRITERIA: PROBLEMS

Was the reduction of the infantry height standard to 5' a profitable change to the medical standard? The experience of bantam units suggests that the benefits, if any, were limited.

The idea of bantam battalions was not original, but an imitation of the British bantams, originally formed in the fall of 1914 when two battalions were raised from men standing 5' to 5' 3" (later 5' 2").[22] The concept was popular: by mid-1916, there were two bantam divisions serving in France. Neither division, however, was composed wholly of bantams; those serving with artillery, engineer, pioneer, and signals units had to meet normal height standards.[23] Bantams were not intended to supplement the British manpower pool but reflected popular enthusiasm for the war effort by providing shorter men with an opportunity to serve their country.

Not surprisingly, the CEF followed suit by raising the 143rd and 216th Bantam Battalions in 1916 as well as a bantam company for the 167th Battalion. As with the British bantams, neither of the two battalions were created because of a recruiting shortfall but resulted from lobbying by enthusiasts who were captivated by the notion of something new. Both A.B. Powley of Victoria, who commanded the 143rd Battalion, and F.L. Burton of Toronto, who commanded the 216th Battalion, had previously served in France and likely had first-hand knowledge of British bantams. In contrast, the bantam company of the 167th Battalion was authorized in November 1916 at a time when recruiting, especially for Quebec-based units, had fallen off sharply.

The concept of bantam battalions was contrary to Militia HQ's preference for homogeneous units that could be shipped overseas and absorbed by any battalion that required reinforcements. Perhaps for this reason, no one in Ottawa laid down a uniform height requirement for bantams – unlike in Britain, where standards were set by the War Office. Instead, the standard reflected the Commanding Officer's preference. The 216th recruited men who stood 5' to 5' 1½", the 143rd accepted those who were 5' 4" or shorter, and the 167th was willing to take volunteers under 5' 2".[24]

On the surface, the two battalions were successful and recruited almost a thousand men who stood less than 5' 2". However, not all of these men were a useful addition. There were 163 who could not be posted to infantry battalions in France because they stood under 5'. Three of these men were only 4' 7". There were also 141 boys between the ages of twelve and seventeen, many of whom were under the minimum height for bantams.

Some of the Bantams seem to have been stunted and not merely short; in July 1916, almost 200 men from the 143rd were weeded out by medical officers at the Sidney Mobilization Camp in British Columbia.[25] Later, in England, the battalion was examined again, and more than 155 men were consigned to the Canadian Railway Troops Depot as unfit for the infantry.[26] The 216th had problems as well, and in May 1917 doctors at Shorncliffe declared 217 men unfit for the infantry.[27] This was just the beginning. Ultimately, 300 bantams from the 216th were transferred to the Forestry Corps. In summary, the two battalions sailed with 1,666 men, of whom only 722 were fit for front-line duty.[28]

Would bantams have been useful in the front lines? In the British army the 35th (Bantam) Division found that trench parapets had to be lowered to allow men to shoot, meaning that conventional units relieving the bantams had to rebuild the parapets. Eventually, a divisional order required every man to carry two sandbags to build up the fire step. Bantams also had difficulties handling the Lee–Enfield service rifle because of its length; rifles with a special butt one inch shorter than normal were produced in 1918.[29]

As with the 143rd and 216th, many bantams in the 35th were unfit; in December 1916, medical boards inspected the 35th Division and found that 2,784 men had a "physical incapacity to perform the normal duties of a soldier in the fighting line."[30] The evidence is indirect, but the experience of the 35th suggests that allowing shorter men to enlist was of minimal benefit to the CEF.

DENTAL CRITERIA

Medical standards included dental criteria, and these were relaxed as well, starting in March 1915 when HQ MD 2 directed that men with defective or deficient teeth would be retained in Canada for treatment, "including the provision of such artificial dentures as are necessary to admit of efficient mastication."[31] The policy made sense; in May 1915, Militia HQ directed that men with partial plates or who required dental treatment could be enlisted, a regulation modified in August 1915 to allow men with full dentures to join the CEF.[32] Oddly enough, dental care was not mandatory, at least in 1915, and those who refused treatment were passed as fit "provided they are not suffering from malnutrition or digestive trouble, and are otherwise physically fit."[33]

Allowing men who required dental treatment to enlist implied an obligation to provide treatment. In April 1915 the Canadian Army Dental Corps was formed, but only for duty overseas. In Canada, districts were authorized to appoint dentists to the Medical Corps on a temporary basis. This was evidently unsatisfactory, and by July 1916 Dental Corps detachments had been established in every district. The detachments, however, were used to treat serving soldiers and not to screen recruits. The determination of dental fitness remained the purview of the medical officer conducting the examination.[34]

Did the changes to the dental standards add significantly to the number of men eligible for the CEF? In December 1916, of 20,365 Canadian soldiers examined by medical boards at Shorncliffe, Seaford, and Crowborough in England, 8,385 (41.2 per cent) were found to be dentally unfit.[35] There is no evidence that the findings reflected Canadian oral health in general, but it seems reasonable to conclude that the relaxation of standards and the provision of dental care allowed several hundred thousand men to join the CEF who might have been rejected in 1914.

VISION CRITERIA

Vision standards were also modified. Initially, recruits had to have a visual acuity of D 15/20 in the right eye and D 30/20 in the left eye.[36] In November 1915, the regulations were modified. Recruits with D 60/20 in either eye (uncorrected) were fit for general service while those with D 120/20 in the right eye could be enrolled in administrative corps.[37] The following year, recruiting slumped and the standards were relaxed even further. In August 1916, the general standard was lowered to D 80/20 for all and D 200/80 for drivers. Those with only one eye were routinely turned away until January 1917, when they could enlist in pioneer, labour, construction, forestry, and railway units, provided that the missing eye had not been lost because of an organic disease.[38]

Enrolling recruits with poor eyesight meant that eyeglasses had to be provided; from March 1915 onward, men posted from England to Flanders were issued with two pairs as required.[39] However, recruits in Canada had to provide their own – an illogical policy that was corrected in May 1916, when the Militia Council decided to provide eyeglasses to all those who needed them.[40]

The initial dental and vision standards were simple and straightforward, although the general health of Canadian males meant that many were barred from enlisting. Changes to these criteria allowed more men to join the CEF, but the need to provide dentures and eyeglasses increased the administrative overhead. Regardless of this, the changes more than benefited the CEF.

MEDICAL CRITERIA: EXCEPTIONS

Medical standards obviously varied depending on employment, but it took almost two years before Militia HQ recognized that skilled workers who did not meet infantry standards were useful in specialist corps. From June 1916 onward, Forestry recruits missing no more than one finger on each hand (other than thumb and forefinger) and one or two toes on each foot (other than the great toe) were acceptable. At the same time, the maximum age limit for skilled forestry workers such as millwrights and saw filers was extended from 45 to 48. Men with flat feet were unacceptable to the infantry, but Militia HQ made an exception for "Skilled Railway Employees" because "[a]ny men who are good enough for the railway companies are good enough for us."[41]

Not all of these changes were beneficial; they overlooked the fact that foresters for example, were expected to work "harder than infantry in the trenches, as far as the physical end is concerned."[42] Railway troops were able to cope with flat feet, but according to the Senior Medical Officer of the Railway Depot in England, most of those over forty-two or forty-three who were posted to France could not physically cope with the job, while those with only one eye had difficulties with night operations.[43]

MEDICAL CRITERIA: PROBLEMS

Many of those who joined the CEF were unfit on enrolment and were subsequently discharged. But, the designation "unfit" was relative, and it has to be kept in mind that standards were relaxed throughout the war. Arguably, a man judged to be unfit in 1914 could very well have been declared fit in 1918. Fitness was also a function of the man's corps: those discharged from infantry battalions might have been fit for the Forestry Corps or another specialist branch of the service.

The number of men released as medically unfit is not certain. In September 1916, Colonel Bruce produced a scathing report on the problem of unfit men in England, but although he gave numerous examples in his report he did not indicate the extent of the problem.[44] In a postwar speech in Montreal, General Sir Arthur Currie claimed that "100,000 men were enlisted and sent to England who were of no use to us in the field,"[45] but the source of his data is unknown. In any event, although General Currie and Colonel Bruce may have exaggerated their concerns, the problem was a serious one. Between 6 October and 5 November 1916 alone, almost one in six of all infantrymen who arrived in England were found to be medically unfit.[46] The figures shown in table 3.1 suggest this proportion was not exceptional.

A variety of factors resulted in unfit men being enlisted, according to a well-reasoned report in October 1916 by Colonel Marlow, the Director of Medical Services in MD 2: "Careless examination by medical officers or civilian practitioners, undue pressure on the part of commanding or recruiting officers anxious to increase the number in their units, attestation without further medical examination, and retention of men at small billets."[47]

There were other reasons as well, which Colonel Marlow did not comment on. The pre-war Medical Corps was small, and there were too few medical officers in the peacetime army to cope with the flood of recruits – a problem recognized on the eve of war by Lieutenant-Colonel Grant, senior medical officer of MD 6.[48] Hiring civilian physicians made up for the lack of medical officers, but this in turn helped to increase the number of unfit recruits.

Civilian physicians were paid fifty cents for each recruit examined. Not all doctors considered the tariff to be acceptable; some refused to examine recruits, while others, at least in eastern Quebec, openly said that a fifty-cent fee warranted a fifty-cent examination.[49] There was also a shortage of civilian physicians in remote areas who were willing to examine recruits. In the Gaspé, only one doctor was available. For some reason, he was willing to examine recruits but not to sign attestation forms.[50]

Even if civilian physicians were willing to examine recruits, they sometimes applied their own standards. In the Algoma District of Northern Ontario, the 119th Battalion complained of local doctors who either misunderstood or ignored medical instructions. Further south, in Victoria County, the senior doctor of MD 3 reported that civilian physicians ignored instructions, preferring to judge a man's fitness by his ability to do a day's work.[51] Trained Medical Corps doctors would have resolved these problems, but there were only a few hundred available on the outbreak of war and most were absorbed by the greatly expanded medical establishment overseas. In any event, the dispersal of the CEF in small detachments scattered across the country in the winter of 1915–16 meant that there was no choice but to rely on civilian practitioners.

For the most part, doctors conducted external examinations only. To some degree, this was not important, since most physicians could recognize obvious signs of disability such as irregular heartbeat, chronic rheumatism, or chancres. But detecting other diseases called for

Table 3.1 Unfit soldiers, 1914–18

Description	Served Canada only (actual)	Served in England (estimate)*	Total
Unfit	42,897	33,155	76,052
Found unfit by unit MO	859	21	880
Found unfit within 3 months of enrolment	4,301	15	4,316
Found unfit on reaching age 18	54	16	70
Unfit for his special duties	90	41	131
Total	48,201	33,248	81,449

* 85,673 men who served outside of Canada were discharged as medically unfit. Unfortunately, this figure includes both the wounded and those who were unfit on enrolment. However, Weekly Returns in TNA, WO 114 show the number of unfit CEF soldiers in the British Isles by unit. About 38.7 per cent were Category E not serving with the Canadian Casualty Assembly Centre, an organization intended to rehabilitate casualties. This proportion was then applied to the number of unfit men who served outside Canada.

Sources: DHH, 74/672, box 1, folder 3; TNA, WO 114/30, Weekly Returns, 28 August 1916, 25 September 1916, 30 October 1916, 27 November 1916, and 25 December 1916; TNA, WO 114/31, Weekly Returns, 29 January 1917, 26 February 1916, and 26 March 1916; TNA, WO 114/32, Weekly Returns, 30 April 1917 and 28 May 1917.

specialized tests. Tuberculosis tests were available, but cost three dollars (almost three times the daily pay of a private soldier).[52] Wasserman tests for syphilis were also available and by 1916 were common enough that the Toronto General Hospital routinely screened all admissions.[53] Whether every recruit could have been screened by these tests is uncertain, at least during the winter of 1915–16, when detachments were scattered across the country. It would have been impossible for the 119th Battalion in the remote Algoma District, for example, to send blood samples to a laboratory (probably in Toronto) for analysis. However, by the end of 1916 the centralization of units in Canada and the creation of mobilization centres meant that standing medical boards were able to make use of a wide range of diagnostic tools, including blood and sputum tests as well as x-rays.

PSYCHOLOGICAL AND PSYCHIATRIC CRITERIA

Not surprisingly, there was no psychiatric screening of recruits. Men who were mentally disabled managed to hoodwink the doctors and enlist in the CEF. In all, a total of 1,486 men were released because of mental disorders.[54] These were probably cases of mental illness ("insanity") and do not include the "mentally deficient"' or those with learning difficulties, such as the soldier with the 4th Divisional Train in British Columbia who was discharged in 1916 as unlikely to become an efficient soldier although he had been "given a great deal of individual attention and instruction but does not seem to be able to absorb anything and has shown no improvement whatever. It only seems fair to him to state that he tries hard."[55]

Soldiers such as this were a burden on units overseas; in 1916–17 there were complaints that newly arrived reinforcements were suffering from "senility," "dementia," "mental deficiency," and "delusional insanity."[56] The total is not certain, but 6,828 men were hospitalized or released with mental disorders unrelated to battle. In addition, 6,432 men were discharged as "inefficient & undesirable" without leaving Canada; some of these may have been mentally deficient.[57] Together, mental illness and impairment was found in about 2 per cent of all enlistments, a lower rate than among Canadian males in general.[58] The ratio was roughly consistent with the American Expeditionary Force, which found that about 1.5 per cent of all draftees were either mentally deficient or suffering from a mental disease.[59]

Despite the absence of formal testing, authorities in 1917 were concerned with the intelligence of trainees; medical officers were reminded that "[g]reat care is to be taken in ascertaining the mental capacity of a recruit."[60] Training officers were required to assess recruits and classify their intelligence as above average, average, or below average, while remembering that "a man may be naturally intelligent although owing to lack of educational opportunities he may appear stupid."[61] Those classified as below average were to be referred to a medical officer for observation and, if necessary, to a standing medical board for disposal.

Mental health was not assessed, and medical officers were cautioned in October 1917 that it was unwise to ask men if they had ever been admitted to a psychiatric institution. Despite this, doctors were expected to scrutinize recruits carefully for mental disorders, although the Director General of Medical Services at Militia HQ admitted in October 1917 that this would be fruitless if the individual was in remission.[62]

CITIZENSHIP CRITERIA

Initial criteria published in 1914 did not stipulate that recruits be British subjects, perhaps because they were ostensibly drawn from the militia, which accepted British subjects only.[63] Nor was citizenship a formal requirement for the 2nd Division in October 1914, perhaps because units were declared to be temporary corps of the Militia. However, this was not the case for units raised after the 2nd Division, and in August 1915 Militia HQ ruled that recruits had to be British subjects.[64]

In 1914, more than 500 men in the First Contingent were from non–English-speaking countries. Since almost half of the foreign-born in the general population had been naturalized, many were probably British subjects.[65] Thirty-eight who were from enemy states or were thought to be German sympathizers were returned to Canada for discharge in November 1914.[66] None of the others were repatriated, perhaps because the CEF in Britain was subject to the British *Army Act*, which allowed one man in every fifty to be an alien.[67]

Canadian requirements were more stringent than the British criteria. In October 1914, Militia HQ directed that "it is considered inadvisable to enlist persons of foreign birth or nationality."[68] Specific nationalities were singled out. In November 1914, it was announced that Russian subjects could not be enlisted and that those who had been were to be discharged. A few months later, in February 1915, HQ MD 10 advised the 105th Regiment in Saskatoon that CEF recruits born in the United States had to be naturalized British subjects and of British descent – an interesting exercise in genealogy.[69]

Given the decentralized nature of the Canadian Forces and the relative autonomy of military districts, regulations regarding aliens were not uniformly applied in the early years of the war. At one end of the spectrum was HQ MD 2, which in early 1915 ordered the discharge of all Italians, Danes, Greeks, and Russians serving with units in Toronto. At the same time, units recruiting in St Catharines and Brantford were forbidden to enlist foreigners, while the 51st Regiment in Sault Ste. Marie was instructed to release all CEF recruits from Belgium, the United States, France, and Russia.[70]

Not all districts were as hard-nosed as MD 2. In eastern Ontario (MD 3), the 59th Battalion enlisted more than sixty Russians, virtually all of whom sailed to England with the battalion or one of two reinforcing drafts. In MD 5, the 57th Battalion at Quebec City enlisted about a hundred Russians; sixty-four sailed to England. In total, 27.2 per cent of the men in the 57th Battalion were not British subjects by birth. The 41st Battalion, also from Quebec City, was able to reach full strength only because of a company of Russian-born recruits from western Canada.[71] A total of 221 men who were not British subjects by birth sailed in 1915 with the main body of the 41st or the reinforcing draft – about 20 per cent of the unit.

The formation of the 97th (American Legion) Battalion brought the first changes to citizenship criteria. Intended to attract Americans domiciled in Canada but not naturalized, it quickly became apparent that potential recruits were discouraged by the need to be British subjects. In November 1915, therefore, citizenship requirements were waived for the 97th, and eventually other American Legion battalions were accommodated as well.[72] With the American Legion battalions as a precedent, it was only a matter of time before other aliens were accepted as well.

The idea that aliens were acceptable in the CEF was finally recognized in April 1917, when an order in council was issued authorizing a revised enlistment oath for men who were neither Canadian citizens[*] nor British subjects.[73] Regulations were not formally suspended or amended, but the order in council was a de facto admission that non-citizens were welcome in the CEF.

A further change came in 1918 with conscription under the *Military Service Act* of 1917. In brief, draftees were required to be British subjects. Immigrants who had not been naturalized could still be drafted, but only for non-combatant service. Since the demand was for infantrymen, it can be assumed that relatively few non-British subjects were drafted.[74]

CITIZENSHIP CRITERIA: PROBLEMS

Eligibility for the CEF was clouded by the fact that foreign nations tried to control immigrants in Canada who were not British subjects. Italy allowed Italian citizens living in Canada to join the CEF, but only after obtaining a consular certificate that they were exempt from service in the Italian army. Serbs and Montenegrins were allowed to enlist, but were subject to recall by their home countries for military service.[75] Belgians were also subject to recall, and in January 1915 the 5th Field Company at Ottawa had to release seven men after representations from the Belgian consul.[76]

The enlistment of Russians was a bureaucratic nightmare, mainly because of conditions imposed by their home country. In October 1914, the Russian ambassador in Washington notified the Montreal consulate that Russians living in Canada who had fulfilled their military obligation could join the CEF. But this may have been an error; a few days later, the

---

[*] Paragraph 2(f) of *An Act Respecting Immigration*, assented to 4 May 1910, defined a Canadian citizen as someone who had been born in Canada, a British subject domiciled in Canada, or someone who had been naturalized.

consul notified External Affairs that the policy applied only to Russians living in Britain or France. Those living in Canada, therefore, could not enlist in the CEF and those who had should be discharged.[77] However, judging by a request made in December 1914 by the Russian attaché in London to allow twenty-nine Russians with the 1st Division to attend Greek Orthodox services, those serving overseas were not affected.[78]

Militia HQ promptly notified all districts, and only thirty-seven Russians are known to have enlisted in November and December 1914, mainly in the Maritimes and western Canada. In contrast, at least 119 Russians had enlisted from August to October 1914.

The Russian government insisted on maintaining a grip on all Russians, regardless of individual circumstances and Canada's status as a nation. Those who came to Canada as young children were expected to return to Russia to perform their military service. "The communications between Russia and Canada have never been interrupted," wrote the consul in March 1915, and "they are able to reach Russia, by their own means."[79] Two months later, a recruiter in Roblin, Manitoba, was told that former members of the Russian army living in Canada were not allowed to join the CEF but were expected "to join their own regiment in Russia, and have to go there by their own means."[80]

The Russian policy was clearly impractical in view of the closure of the Baltic and Black Sea ports and the difficulties of an ocean voyage from Canada to Archangel or Vladivostok. In July 1915, the Imperial Russian Consulate in Montreal notified External Affairs that the Czar had issued a decree on 18 June 1915 authorizing Russian subjects in Canada, including reservists and territorials, to enlist in the CEF. But, the edict announced, these men had to apply to the consulate for an identification certificate.[81] To obtain this certificate, men had to produce Russian identification papers (passport, military booklet, or birth certificate), provide a photograph, and pay consular fees of $1.63 – more than a day's pay for a private soldier.[82] Provided the man's credentials were in order, the consul then issued a certificate of identity in Russian, which was useless to units working in English or French. Not surprisingly, Canadian authorities were not consulted in the process of modifying enlistment procedures. Nor is there any record of the Canadian government protesting what amounted to an infringement of Canadian sovereignty.

Inevitably, there were problems with the process put in place by the Russian consul, even apart from the volume of requests (more than 7,300 Russians enlisted in the CEF).[83] In March 1916, Major-General Gwatkin, Chief of the General Staff in Ottawa, noted that a number of Russian subjects in Saskatchewan had lost or destroyed their papers and that "good men and true may be lost to the Canadian Expeditionary Force because they have the misfortune to be without papers." But the consul dismissed his concerns and insisted that local authorities at the recruit's place of birth in Russia would have to investigate the man's claims.[84] For their part, some of the Russian-born soldiers who enlisted detested the requirement for a consular certificate, were reluctant to provide their photograph to Russian authorities, and were opposed to letting the consul know they were members of the CEF.[85] The system was cumbersome, and in practice amounted to an inefficient farce despite the avowed purpose of weeding out enemy aliens trying to pass themselves off as bona fide Russians.[86]

Enemy aliens – men born in Germany, Austria-Hungary, Bulgaria and the Ottoman Empire – were automatically considered suspect by authorities, and everyone concerned understood that they could not be enlisted. But the policy was not applied uniformly, and more than 2,500 managed to join the CEF, of whom 539 served overseas.[87] Some of these men had previously served with the militia or Permanent Force, and one had fought in South Africa with the Royal Canadian Regiment.

Aliens were barred from enlistment on the basis of nationality, not ethnicity. Both Adolph Messerschmidt and Reinhold Krinke, for example, were ethnic Germans from the Baltic States and the Volhynia who had no difficulties joining because they were Russian subjects. There was, however, a tacit recognition by some recruiters that specific ethnic groups from enemy countries could be safely enlisted: those from Alsace-Lorraine, the Balkan provinces of the Austro-Hungarian Empire, Bohemia, Moravia, and Silesia, as well as Christians from the Ottoman Empire.

A number of those drafted in 1918 were enemy aliens from Germany or the Austro-Hungarian Empire. An apparent contradiction of previous regulations, this was consistent with the spirit of the *Naturalization Act 1914*, which reminded those naturalized that they were "subject to all obligations, duties and liabilities to which a natural born British subject is subject."[88] The sentiment was repeated in the *Wartime Elections Act* of 1917, which disenfranchised all those from enemy countries naturalized after 31 March 1902 but allowed those who had joined the CEF or who had been rejected as medically unfit, together with their families, to retain the vote.[89] In effect, citizenship with its attendant rights carried with it an obligation to serve the state.

Initially, immigrants from non–English-speaking countries found it difficult to join. But in the second half of 1915 the number of immigrants who enlisted was four times the number who enlisted in the first half of the year, while the total number of men who joined the CEF in the same time frame only doubled. The trend continued to the end of 1916.[90] In other words, these immigrants found it easier to enlist, which suggests that recruiters were not as zealous in enforcing citizenship requirements as they were in 1914 and the first half of 1915.

UNOFFICIAL CRITERIA

There were also unofficial criteria that reflected prevailing attitudes of the time. In theory, Chinese could enlist if they were British subjects, of age, and medically fit. However, they were not wanted, and there may have been specific rules to prevent them from joining. In April 1917, the AAG at HQ MD 2 wrote that "regulations do not permit of the enlistment of Chinamen into the Canadian Expeditionary Force."[91] The regulations invoked by HQ MD 2 have not been found, but a Military Service Branch Circular in August 1918 notified local registrars that the Militia and Defence policy was not "to enroll men with the CEF, who are obviously Chinese."[92] The Circular also noted that depot battalions had been instructed to return Chinese-Canadian draftees to the Registrar's records (i.e., to discharge them). Whether the exclusion of Chinese-Canadians was a regulation or an informal policy is not certain. Either way, it is quite clear that these men were not welcome.

Not surprisingly, very few ethnic Chinese joined the CEF. Marjorie Wong has estimated that about three hundred enlisted, but this is clearly an exaggeration: to date, only seven men have been identified, three of whom had been born in Canada. There may have been a few others. In April 1920, Hugh Guthrie, the Minister of Militia and Defence, estimated that a dozen Chinese-Canadians had served in the CEF.[93]

Japanese immigrants also had difficulties enlisting, and some may have been reluctant to step forward. Many were transient and intent on earning sufficient money to purchase a farm or house in Japan and might not have been British subjects. Language was also an issue. Militia HQ was adamant that recruits had to speak English or French but, as late as 1924–26, almost 74 per cent of Japanese immigrants in British Columbia were unable to read, write, or understand English.[94] Most of them lived in British Columbia, where the provincial government discouraged enlistment, since it could lead to enfranchisement; this sentiment was echoed by Gwatkin, the Chief of Staff at Militia HQ, who thought that "when the war is over & demobilization sets in, those of them who served in the

CEF will make themselves a nuisance. Après nous, le Déluge."[95] Elsewhere, there were no objections to recruiting Japanese-Canadians; in March 1916, when the men of the 216th Battalion in Toronto were asked if they would welcome a Japanese company, "[e]very hand in the battalion went up in the affirmative."[96]

Despite language and citizenship issues, some Japanese-Canadians were anxious to serve. In Vancouver, the Canadian Japanese Association offered to raise a battalion, while efforts were also made to form an independent company. The battalion was rejected by Militia HQ because of doubts that there would be enough recruits to form and sustain the unit. The offer was passed to Britain and Japan, but neither replied and Militia Council decided not to proceed. The independent company was also quashed because the idea of a company that could not be broken up to provide reinforcements was anathema to Militia HQ.[97]

Japanese applicants from the United States were banned from enlisting with the British Canadian Recruiting Mission, although at least ten were able to join. Ethnicity was not a bar to conscription, and at least twenty-four Japanese-Canadians or Nisei were drafted under the MSA – almost 11 per cent of all known Japanese enrolments. Surprisingly, eighteen were residents of MD 11, a district that encompassed both British Columbia and the Yukon.

Sikhs also received short shrift. Almost 99 per cent of them lived in British Columbia, where they were regarded with suspicion and contempt even though they had been born in a British colony. Some, in fact, were anxious to serve and paid their passage back to India in order to enlist.[98] In Canada, there were no objections to Sikhs enlisting provided they did so in the Indian Army and not in the CEF. In September 1914, for example, W.P. Archibald, the Dominion Parole Officer, interviewed ex-members of the Indian Army in the British Columbia Penitentiary and recommended they be allowed to join the Indian Corps in France: "These men have every appearance of strength and manhood and I am sure they are anxious to serve their country."[99] Archibald missed the point: the men in question were living in Canada, not India.

A few months later, in December 1914, a deputation of East Indians approached the premier of British Columbia, Sir Richard McBride, with an offer to raise a contingent of ex-Sepoys. McBride passed the proposal to Prime Minister Borden, but it was rejected, in part because Gwatkin, the Chief of Staff, believed that finding reinforcements would be difficult and "these men are not of the tribe or race of Sikhs who are considered the best fighters in India."[100] The proposal was then passed by Borden to the Governor General in February 1915 with a suggestion that the War Office pick up the offer of Sikh recruits from British Columbia.[101] Not surprisingly, the idea came to naught.

The number of East Indians who managed to enlist in the CEF is unknown, and one historian has gone so far as to say that none were accepted.[102] However, a search of online attestation forms has turned up fifteen East Indians who were clearly not Anglo-Indians or the sons of British expatriates. The first joined the 24th Battalion at Montreal in January 1915, while the last volunteered at Ottawa in October 1918. The sample reflects the general dislike of East Indians in British Columbia, where the overwhelming majority lived. Only three of those who enlisted were residents of British Columbia, while one, who joined the British Columbia Regiment, was a California Jew born in India who had been enlisted by the British-Canadian Recruiting Mission. In total, seven volunteers enlisted in Ontario, two in Quebec, three in Manitoba, and two in British Columbia. As with Chinese Canadians, East Indians were not supposed to be conscripted under the MSA, but at least one Sikh was: Ram Singh, from Grand Forks, British Columbia, was drafted in December 1917.

No regulations prevented blacks from enlisting, but many had difficulty in doing so. As the Adjutant-General in Ottawa noted in October 1915, "The final approval of any man, regardless of colour or other distinctions, must, of course, rest with the Officer Commanding the unit."[103] Enlistment, then, depended on the bias of the recruiter or his Commanding Officer.

There is an abundance of anecdotal evidence concerning the experiences of individual blacks who were rejected by recruiters, and these examples have been used by historians to demonstrate universal racism.[104] But this was at odds with the participation of blacks in the prewar army, and there were blacks who enlisted as volunteers from 1914 onward and served overseas: men such as Curley Christian of the 78th Battalion, who became a quadruple amputee, and Corporal James Post of the 4th Canadian Mounted Rifles, an underaged soldier who was awarded the Distinguished Conduct Medal for bravery at Passchendaele in 1917.

Also unreported by contemporary historians are efforts by authorities to ensure that blacks were able to enlist. In November 1915, for example, there were complaints that blacks had been turned away by recruiters in MD 2, and Sam Hughes demanded an explanation. The reply from the district commander was unequivocal: "Last summer [the] question arose here and I ruled they [blacks] must be accepted."[105] The district commander's reply was not a pro forma denial. A few days later, HQ MD 2 warned the Toronto Recruiting Depot that "[i]f the practice of refusing to accept colored men has been followed, it must be discontinued at once." The reply from the depot was succinct: "We make no discrimination here as to color or creed."[106]

Authorities elsewhere were also adamant that there should be no institutional discrimination. In July 1916, the Commanding Officer of No. 1 Construction Battalion wrote that the designation of a black unit as No. 2 Construction Battalion had resulted in complaints from his men, who were upset at being associated with blacks. The reply from Militia HQ was blunt and direct. Those joining No. 2 Construction Battalion were both British subjects and Canadians. Black soldiers were "recognized as comrades in arms both in France and England. It is for you, therefore, to inspire your men with correct ideas on the subject."[107]

But prejudice prevailed among some members of the CEF. In April 1918 a black street car conductor in Toronto complained to District Headquarters that when he asked a Royal Canadian Dragoons sergeant for his ticket, the NCO called him a "black son of a bitch" and said "I will punch your fucking face."[108] To their credit, HQ MD 2 insisted on an identity parade, but the miscreant was never identified.[109]

Attitudes in the CEF (and Canada for that matter) were therefore ambivalent. In November 1915, J.R.B. Whitney, publisher of the black journal *Canadian Observer*, wrote to Sam Hughes asking if the CEF would accept a black company recruited in Ontario. Hughes was taken by the suggestion but substituted a black platoon grafted on to an existing battalion. The proposal was then passed to MD 2 for review.[110]

HQ MD 2 queried thirty-seven battalions, all of which refused to accept the platoon.[111] Nineteen considered that black soldiers would deter recruiting or would be unpopular with the officers and men; the 147th Battalion in Grey County noted that "prejudice against negroes in this County is extremely bitter," and the 114th Battalion commented that the platoon would cause serious friction and discontent within the unit. Twelve battalions reported they were up to strength and did not need recruits, while the Commanding Officer of the 169th noted that his unit was up to full strength but he could offer eight blacks to help build up the platoon. Three battalions replied that they were recruiting only to fill up existing platoons, while the 133rd and 177th were willing to accept blacks, but only if they were residents of Norfolk or Simcoe County respectively.[112]

The replies reflected CEF ambivalence toward blacks. Prejudice certainly existed, but there were military considerations as well. Battalions were formed by selecting commanding officers, who then appointed a complete slate of officers, including platoon commanders, before starting recruiting.[113] The addition of a black platoon to an existing battalion, therefore, required the unit to be reorganized. Commanding officers were (and still are) very busy people. Reorganizing the battalion to accommodate a black platoon and then finding reinforcements to keep it up to strength was another burden that the Commanding Officer could do without. The platoon might have advanced the status of blacks within Canada, but it would also have been an added complication for overworked commanding officers striving to complete their battalions.[114]

The number of blacks who managed to satisfy both social and military criteria for enrolment is unknown, although the Governor General's military secretary noted in October 1915 that His Royal Highness had inspected a number of units and "come across quite a good number of coloured men."[115] However, a sample of 1,090 men who were probably black has been compiled, based on those who served in No. 2 Construction Battalion, a handful of men born in Canada, and others from the West Indies and British Guiana. The sample is incomplete, but it seems likely that more than 1,200 blacks served in the CEF. The mean enlistment date was December 1916, nine months after the CEF average. Clearly, the CEF was indifferent about black recruits. As the Adjutant-General at Militia HQ commented in April 1918, "We are not hunting for coloured recruits but merely making a place for them as they come in."[116]

Specific criteria may also have been imposed by Sam Hughes on Native recruits, at least in MD 1, from August 1914 to December 1915 after HQ MD 1 asked whether Indians could be enlisted in the First Contingent. The reply from Militia HQ, approved by Hughes (the draft is annotated "OK – SH") was succinct. Natives could not serve overseas but could enlist for home defence duties. Both the query and the reply were dated 8 August 1914. The restriction was not a reasoned, well-thought-out policy but a snap decision, typical of Hughes's approach to managing his portfolio. The same day the policy was decided upon, Hughes's military secretary, clearly oblivious to his master's decision, wrote to the Ontario M.P.P. for Huron County to assure him that Natives in his riding who wished to enlist could apply to the 32nd Huron Regiment, which was recruiting for the First Contingent.[117] The 32nd Regiment was part of MD 1.

Hughes's policy, decided on 8 August 1914, was sent to HQ MD 1, and no evidence has been found that the remaining eight districts were notified. Nor has any evidence been found of a Militia Order, General Order, or circular instruction banning Natives from enlisting in the CEF. There is some indication that the restriction was applied to MD 2 in February 1915, but this is far from certain.[118] Admittedly, the Department of Indian Affairs was notified, but not until October 1915 and only in response to a specific question.[119] In any event, the restriction was formally rescinded in December 1915, after MD 1 and MD 2 requested authority for the newly authorized 114th and 135th Battalions to recruit Natives.[120]

The effect of the supposed ban was limited. In November 1914, the 20th Battalion in MD 2 had a Native company from the 37th Regiment as well as two lieutenants, both of whom were status Indians.[121] Subsequently, Natives openly enlisted in other MD 2 units, including the 58th, 76th, 81st and 84th Battalions as well as the Canadian Mounted Rifles Depot. Aboriginal recruits were also welcomed elsewhere, and a cursory review of published embarkation rolls has turned up more than 200 Natives from every military district in Canada who enlisted before December 1915.[122]

About 3,500 to 4,000 Aboriginals served with the CEF, a creditable showing despite difficulties in recruiting.* At the Cape Mudge Reserve in British Columbia in January 1916, a group of young men warned the Indian agent that "as the Indians were not voters, and as they had not been consulted either with regard to the taking away of their original heritage, or in the formation of any of our [Canadian] laws they did not feel called upon to take up arms for the flag."[123] Also in British Columbia, there was an unofficial agreement between HQ MD 11 and Native bands that men could not enlist unless they had permission from their chief, leading one volunteer to retort "the only chief he recognized was King George V."[124] At Caughnawaga, Quebec, residents were sufficiently militant that Indian Affairs advised Militia HQ that military police hunting deserters should not enter the reserve, thus creating a safe haven for these men on Canadian soil.[125]

Many reserves were isolated, which created difficulties for recruiting parties. The 228th Battalion, for example, enlisted at least seventeen men in Moose Factory, Ontario, which was accessible only by water. In Manitoba, recruiters from the 203rd Battalion and the Forestry Corps had to use a lake steamer to enlist Natives at Norway House in June 1916

---

* At least one Inuk, August Otoon, from Alaska, enlisted in the CEF.

and Berens River in August 1917. Communities on James Bay and Hudson Bay were also difficult to reach, and in 1917 Lieutenant C.M. McCarthy hired a "gasoline boat" at an estimated cost of $1,500 to go down the Albany River and recruit forty-five men at Attawapiskat, Albany River, and Fort Albany.[126]

RECRUITING CRITERIA: LIARS

Determining fitness depended to a large extent on the candour of the recruit. Not all were honest with the doctor. In 1917, HQ MD 11 in British Columbia noted that "many men are reported to be untruthful. Such men may very easily escape the notice of the Medical Officer of the Unit for a considerable time."[127] Alcoholics, drug addicts, epileptics, and men with chronic conditions were therefore able to enlist, although in many cases the stress of military life brought their condition to the fore, as is shown in table 3.1. No doubt many of these men concealed their disability on enrolment, although the number cannot be quantified.

Another problem were those were outside of the regulation age range – men described by the Commanding Officer of the Field Ambulance Depot in Toronto as "God's beautiful liars."[128] The policies concerning age limits were clear and unequivocal but were frequently ignored, either because individuals were anxious to serve or because commanding officers were trying to fill the ranks. In all, it is estimated that more than 33,000 men who were too young or too old enlisted in the CEF. Although some made a valuable contribution to the war effort, others were a significant administrative burden.

A total of 6,548 underage soldiers were discharged from the CEF, while postwar Hollerith tabulations show that 9,355 teens under the age of eighteen enlisted.[129] But the former were only the ones who were detected, while the latter reflected only those who were candid about their age. How many concealed their true age in order to enlist?

Underage soldiers were not simply those who were a year or two shy of their eighteenth birthday. There were at least two ten-year-olds, Wesley Mickey and Reuben Rosenfield, both of whom enlisted in March 1916 and were discharged before sailing overseas.[130] The youngest who served in Flanders was probably William Hutchinson, a thirteen-year-old from Vancouver who was smuggled to England by his comrades and somehow joined the 8th Battalion, Canadian Railway Troops in Belgium.[131] The youngest who died were fifteen years old; ten shared that melancholy distinction in France and Belgium, and seven in Canada.

The number of underage soldiers who served is unknown, although an estimate can be made using Commonwealth War Graves Commission cemetery and memorial registers. About 61 per cent of the entries, compiled in the 1920s, include the age on death provided by the soldier's next of kin. The information provided by the next of kin is likely correct: Why would they lie? There are 1,412 boys listed who were under the age of nineteen when they died.[132] Assuming that this represents 61 per cent of all deaths, there must have been about 2,315 underage deaths. Given an overall death rate of 9.5 per cent, we can estimate that 24,368 youths enlisted in the CEF.

Attestation papers show that 1,025 (86.8 per cent) of those who died claimed to be eighteen or older when they enlisted, which suggests the boys were anxious to go while recruiters were willing to look the other way. In one case, an underage soldier in England claimed in 1916 that he gave his true date of birth back in Canada and "was told to run around the block, think over his age and come back again."[133] Surprisingly, more of them enlisted in 1914–15, when volunteers were plentiful, than in 1916–17, when there was a shortage of recruits. A total of 156 boys (13.2 per cent) admitted they were seventeen or younger when they enlisted. Most of these self-confessed minors (134) enlisted between August 1915 and January 1917 when boys were allowed to join with their parent's consent as bandsmen, drummers, buglers, and trumpeters.

At the other end of the spectrum were those over forty-five. A total of 1,471 of these men were released during the war, while postwar Hollerith tabulations show 1,549 overage enlistments, a figure that suggests the overwhelming majority were detected and released.[134] However, this is by no means certain. Commonwealth War Graves Commission cemetery and memorial registers compiled after the war list 533 men aged forty-seven to sixty-seven; this suggests that 9,198 older men enlisted.

Over-age soldiers were not only those who shaved a year or two off their age. In Ottawa, Alexander "Sandy" Muir, an ex-soldier of the British 11th Hussars, joined the Service Corps Detachment at Militia HQ in June 1916 at the age of eighty, thirty-five years past the maximum permissible age. He was demobilized in 1920 at the age of eighty-four.[135] The oldest soldier buried in France is probably Sapper John Kirkwood of the 4th Field Company, who died in July 1917 at the age of sixty-two.

A total of 458, or 86 per cent, of the older men commemorated by the War Graves Commission claimed to be forty-five or younger when they enlisted. In theory, these men should have been picked up during the enrolment medical, but birth certificates were not required, doctors noted the "apparent age" only, and most felt they had "no option but to accept the statement [of age]."[136] In some cases, recruiting staff simply looked the other way. In Stratford, Ontario, one man who joined the 110th Battalion at the "apparent age" of forty-three declared that his oldest son was thirty-seven. Further west, in May 1917, a man who joined the Canadian Forestry Corps at Revelstoke gave his date of birth as November 1869 and claimed to be a veteran of the 1870 Fenian raids.[137]

The enrolment of older men at a time when life expectancy was only 59 suggests a shortage of recruits, but many of these men enlisted in 1915 when there were plenty of volunteers. Their reasons can only be guessed at – patriotism, the need for a job, and – for old soldiers – a chance to return to an accustomed life with known expectations. The latter was not an inconsequential factor: 263 of those who died, or more than half, were ex-servicemen when they joined, while 67 others were current members of the militia. In round numbers, about two-thirds of the over-age men were familiar with military service when they enlisted. There was also, as there is today, an unwritten obligation to help deserving ex-soldiers, and some commanding officers went out of their way to accommodate the old sweats who wanted to soldier again.

Together, more than 33,000 men – about 5 per cent of all recruits – were outside of the normal age range when they enlisted in the CEF. This is a significant number, although not all served at the front. About 84 per cent of the underage soldiers who died were buried in France or Flanders, 5 per cent in Britain, and 11 per cent in Canada. On the other hand, 34 per cent of the over-age men who died were buried in France or Belgium, 14 per cent in Britain, and 51.9 per cent in Canada. Soldiering was a young man's game; the statistics clearly reflect this.

MEN AVAILABLE FOR MILITARY SERVICE

In 1911, there were 3,859,183 males in Canada, which suggests the nation had an ample supply of manpower.[138] However, to state the obvious, not all were eligible for military service; some were too old or too young, others were needed for essential industries, and some were medically unfit. In the case of immigrants, not all were naturalized British subjects, while those born in Germany, Austria-Hungary, Bulgaria, and the Ottoman Empire were ineligible regardless of naturalization. All of this raises the question: How many men were eligible for the CEF?

Recruits for the CEF had to be British subjects between the ages of eighteen and forty-five. Not surprisingly, these criteria reduced the number that could reasonably be expected to enlist, and of 1,720,070 men aged eighteen to forty-five, 1,526,133 were eligible for the CEF.[139]

Not all of these men were available to the CEF: essential services and industries, especially munitions plants, needed workers. However, since the Canadian government did not designate which industries were essential, the number of essential workers is therefore unknown. How many were there?

A postwar compilation of Empire recruiting statistics by the War Office commented that it was difficult to compare British and dominion recruiting rates because of staple industries in the dominions that "did not lend themselves readily to the substitution of female labour."[140] The comment is apt. Loggers, foundry workers, and miners needed not only specific skills, but also brute strength. Industries that employed relatively few women therefore can serve as a useful proxy for essential occupations in this context.

In 1911, there were 615,969 males in ten major industries[*] that employed relatively few women.[141] An estimated 443,498 of these men were of military age, and it is assumed that this was the minimum number of essential workers who could not be spared for military service. If anything, this estimate is understated: the number of wage earners in manufacturing almost doubled during the war, from 395,681 workers in 1915 to 693,116 in 1918.[142] Many of these jobs were filled by women, but heavy industry and the production of staples remained the purview of men. The pool of potential recruits should therefore be reduced to 1,082,635.

How many of these men were medically fit? In the fall of 1917, medical boards under the direction of the Military Service Branch of the Department of Justice examined all single males between the ages of twenty and thirty-five who were eligible for conscription. The results were not consistent and reflected local attitudes toward the war. Saskatchewan boards, for example, found almost 60 per cent of all men fit for combat duty overseas, whereas Quebec boards found only 36 per cent fit. Despite the results of the Quebec boards, however, the national results provide the best available snapshot of the general fitness of Canadian males in 1917 (see table 3.2).[143]

---

[*] Building trades, fishing and hunting, forestry, mining, iron and steel manufacturing, vehicle manufacturing, shipbuilding, woodworking, steam railways, and water transport. About 4.3 per cent of all woodworkers were women, although most were likely basket-makers. Agricultural workers (917,848) have been excluded, since they could have been replaced by women, men outside of the CEF age range, and those who were medically unit for active service.

Table 3.2 MSA medical board results, 1917: men aged 20–35

Medical category	Number examined (%)
Fit for combat duty overseas	128,974 (46.8)
Fit for limited duty overseas	37,192 (13.5)
Sub-total: fit for overseas duties	166,166 (60.3)
Fit for limited duty in Canada only	42,581 (15.5)
Unfit for any military service	66,733 (24.2)
Total examined	275,480

Source: Lieutenant-Colonel H.A.C. Machin, *Report of the Director of the Military Service Branch* (Ottawa: King's Printer, 1919), 78.

How accurate were the results of the MSA medical boards? In Britain, National Service medical boards examined 2,425,184 Britons in 1917–18 and found that, of every nine men, three were fit for the trenches, and two were fit for non-combatant service overseas. Of the remaining four, three were "physical wrecks" capable of little exertion and the last was "a chronic invalid with a precarious hold upon life."[144] In summary, 55.5 per cent of all men examined were fit for some form of military service overseas, a figure roughly comparable to the results of the Canadian boards.

The totals shown in table 3.3 are an estimate only and do not take into account regional attitudes toward military service and conscription. As Desmond Morton has commented, "Those who lived on farms, were married, or had jobs or deep ancestral roots in the country were least likely to enlist. By no coincidence, the Maritimes ranked only a little ahead of Quebec in recruiting rates."[145] Granatstein and Hitsman have also pointed to demographic factors: French-Canadian men were more likely to be married and to live and work in rural areas.[146] Patrice Dutil has also emphasized the Quebec sense of "isolationism."[147] His point is a good one. In September 1916, the Commander of MD 5 in eastern Quebec commented that there were no immigrants in his district and no transients. Instead, potential recruits were farmers' sons who "[thought] that the only time for them to fight would be in event of Canada itself being attacked, and their property in their immediate neighbourhood being in danger."[148] Theorists may disagree with this account of the reasons, but there is no disputing the fact that French Canadians were reluctant to enlist; this should be kept in mind in considering the figures in table 3.3.

Table 3.3 Revised manpower pool: men aged 18–45

Province	Eligible males	Fit for services overseas*	Fit for service in Canada only*	Fit for military service	Unfit for military service*
Prince Edward Island	16,792	7,859	2,267	10,126	6,666
Nova Scotia	95,850	44,858	12,940	57,798	38,052
New Brunswick	67,339	31,515	9,091	40,605	26,734
Quebec	374,297	175,171	50,530	225,701	148,596
Ontario	541,234	253,298	73,067	326,364	214,870
Manitoba	101,675	47,584	13,726	61,310	40,365
Saskatchewan	121,406	56,818	16,390	73,208	48,198
Alberta	88,810	41,563	11,989	53,552	35,258
British Columbia	118,730	55,566	16,029	71,594	47,136
Subtotal	1,526,133				
Less essential workers	443,498				
Total	1,082,635	652,829†	167,808	820,637	261,998

* MSA medical board rates have been used to calculate physical fitness or unfitness.
† Of those fit for service overseas, 506,673 were fit for service at the front and 146,156 were fit for non-combatant duties only.

SUMMARY

After factoring in age, citizenship, and medical criteria, as well as the need for essential workers, there were 820,637 men available for military service, of whom only 652,829 were fit for overseas duty. With Prime Minister Borden committed to maintaining 500,000 men in the CEF to man four divisions in the Canadian Corps, the Canadian Cavalry Brigade, a host of rear-area units in France, and a sprawling reserve organization in England, finding recruits became increasingly difficult. Developing a large professional army such as the CEF was not only a military endeavour but a national one. The failure of the Borden government to develop national manpower policies did not make the task of Militia Headquarters and the CEF any easier. Not surprisingly, the military made efforts to manage manpower more efficiently and to find alternative sources of recruits. These efforts are the theme of chapter 4.

4

Alternative Sources of Manpower

The CEF not only tinkered with recruiting standards to bring in more men, but also used alternative sources of manpower. A significant number of non-Canadian residents were enlisted, enemy aliens were drafted in 1918, and convicts were enlisted in prisons and penitentiaries. The use of manpower was also rationalized with the adoption of common medical standards that allowed fit men in non-combatant jobs to be reassigned to more demanding positions with front-line units: infantry, artillery, engineers, machine guns, and cavalry. There was also an attempt in 1918 to enlist women to free fit men in Canada for deployment overseas.

RECRUITING OUTSIDE OF CANADA

Non-Canadian residents were the first to be considered as an alternative source of recruits. Although enlistment in the CEF was restricted to British subjects, Canadian residency was not a requirement, and about 10 per cent of all those who joined the CEF were living elsewhere – particularly Bermuda, France, Belgium, and the United States.

To free a British battalion for service on the Western Front, Canada provided a garrison in Bermuda from September 1914 to September 1916. During this time, at least forty-six islanders were enrolled: thirteen by the 38th Battalion and thirty-three by the 163rd Battalion. There was no real need to enlist these men. Bermuda was not a theatre of operations, both battalions were near full strength, and reinforcements were readily available from Canada.[1] Furthermore, by recruiting Bermudians, the CEF was directly competing with efforts in the colony to raise two company-size contingents, one of which was attached to the 38th for training.

Remarkably, there were no objections by Bermuda's House of Assembly or the public at large.[2]

All thirteen Bermudians who enlisted in the 38th Battalion were expatriates. Perhaps these men, with no ties to Bermuda, preferred to take their chances with a formed unit rather than an independent Bermudian company. The 163rd Battalion also enlisted some expatriates, but twenty-two of thirty-three known recruits were blacks from Bermuda or the British West Indies who were enrolled as officers' mess waiters so that Canadians could be freed up for training with their parent companies. However, the idea of blacks serving in a white battalion upset local sensitivities, and the governor registered a stiff protest with Militia HQ in Ottawa.[3] The 163rd therefore stopped enlisting islanders, and in September 1916 left Bermuda – although without discharging the offending mess waiters.

At least thirty-one men were enlisted in France or Belgium by a variety of units: infantry, artillery, cavalry, 1st Division HQ, and Corps HQ. The majority were British subjects by birth: fourteen Canadians and thirteen Britons, one of whom claimed to be a Canadian resident. Of the remaining three, one was a Belgian ex-militiaman whose wife lived in Montreal.

Enlisting these men may have been unusual, but was not unheard of. Certainly the Canadian Section, GHQ 3rd Echelon, was willing to accept recruits and, in some cases, to frank the attestation papers of those who were enlisted in France. HQ OMFC was aware that men were enlisted on the continent and in June 1918 agreed to a proposal that Canadians with the Royal Engineers in France be allowed to join the CEF, provided, of course, the British had no objections.[4]

The CEF also recruited in Britain, starting in October 1914, when the Royal Canadian Dragoons were given permission by 1st Division HQ to recruit twenty-three men to bring the regiment up to strength.[5] A month later, in November 1914, the 17th Battalion and the Divisional Cyclist Company, both of which were under strength, placed ads in British newspapers without seeking permission.[6] Neither recruiting campaign was overly successful (the Cyclists enlisted three men and the 17th eighty-seven), but the ads drew the attention of the War Office, which ruled on 19 November 1914 that the CEF could recruit only in Canada.[7]

The War Office ruling was understandable, given the need to build up the British army, but in practice it could not be sustained. Admittedly, the CEF in England was over strength by 4,500 men on arrival in October 1914, but the haphazard mobilization at Valcartier resulted in a shortage of artificers, farriers, shoeing-smiths, and saddlers – skilled tradesmen who could not be provided from Canada because there was no coherent reinforcement system.[8] The War Office position was also illogical, since the 1st Division was tapped for more than a hundred men to serve as officers in the British army.[9] Faced with the pressing need to find skilled specialists, especially for the 1st Divisional artillery, the War Office reluctantly gave permission on 19 January 1915 for the CEF to recruit thirty skilled tradesmen in England.[10]

More than 250 Britons joined the CEF in England before the 1st Division sailed to France in February 1915. About a hundred enlisted after the War Office gave permission to recruit thirty specialists. Thirty-five – eleven of whom were skilled tradesmen – joined the artillery. Forty-two cavalrymen enlisted, but only nine had relevant civilian experience. The Canadian Army Veterinary Corps took in twenty-seven recruits, but only two had previous experience working with animals. At least twenty-five men also joined 1st Canadian Division HQ, including six grooms, two cooks, and two footmen. These men may have been specialists, but they were hardly the skilled tradesmen envisaged by the War Office.

In February 1915, the 1st Division sailed to France and recruiting in Britain virtually stopped, leaving expatriate Canadians with no alternative but to join the British army. However, in June 1915 the minister's representative, Major-General J.W. Carson of Canadian HQ in London, obtained permission from the War Office to enlist bona fide Canadians living in the United Kingdom.[11] The question of what constituted a bona fide Canadian was a thorny one, and after some deliberation Canadian HQ decided that a Canadian was a British subject who had been previously domiciled in Canada for an unspecified period of time.[12]

However, this definition was too elastic. In May 1916, Canadian HQ ruled that potential recruits had to provide documentary evidence of three years' residence in Canada.[13] In April of the following year, the rules were relaxed when the United States entered the war and "friendly or neutral" aliens in Britain became eligible to join the CEF. This policy was short-lived; from September 1917 onward, recruits had to be bona fide Canadians temporarily domiciled in Britain.[14] The definition of "Canadian" was also tightened up, and in June 1918 HQ OMFC directed that prospective recruits in Britain or France had to produce a certificate of Canadian citizenship issued by the High Commissioner.[15]

Recruiting in England was tolerated but not encouraged, and prospective recruits were expected to make their own way to a CEF unit willing to accept them.[16] There was a steady flow of recruits nevertheless, and by the end of the war 1,733 men had enlisted in the CEF in England.[17] Pay must have motivated some of the applicants: a private in the British army received a shilling a day (about 25¢), while his CEF counterpart received four times as much. But there were other reasons as well. Members of the Canadian Munition Workers Unit employed by civilian factories in Dalton-in-Furness, for example, were anxious to join the CEF when their contracts expired, but preferred to enlist in England to avoid the return trip to Canada.[18]

There were also Canadians with the British Expeditionary Force who wished to serve in the CEF. In May 1915, thirty-one Canadians with the 2/6th (Cyclist) Battalion, Royal Sussex Regiment, together with fourteen Rhodesians were transferred to the Canadian Reserve Cyclist Company. However, this was an exception; the general policy was that "[t]ransfers from the Imperial to the Canadian Forces are not permissible."[19] But, as always, the rules were modified: in June 1918, HQ OMFC notified the Canadian Section GHQ 3rd Echelon that applications to join the CEF would be accepted from those serving with the British, "but only where the men are Canadians enlisted in North America in technical units and are now being transferred compulsorily by the Imperial Authorities to the Infantry."[20] It seems unlikely that many were transferred. In April 1918, Canadians with the Royal Engineers Inland Water Transport were drafted to the Durham Light Infantry and asked HQ OMFC to intervene. Their petition was unsuccessful:

> We receive Canadian Separation Allowance from the Canadian Government and were called to sign for the land grant to Canadian Soldiers and voted in the Canadian election. We therefore ask you to claim us as Canadians. We only ask to be with our own countrymen.[21]

In terms of numbers, those enlisted in England, France, and Belgium were not a significant addition to the CEF, although the men who joined the 1st Division in 1914–15 must have been a welcome addition. Only one in five was a native Canadian, although all were required to have some connection with Canada. Whether this connection was genuine or imagined is immaterial. The care taken to enlist only Canadians (however the term was defined) meant that those who wished to serve with other Canadians were given the opportunity to do so.

THE AMERICAN CONTRIBUTION

In contrast, the United States made a very significant contribution to the manpower pool: it is estimated that more than 57,000 American residents served in the CEF from start to finish. Most had been born elsewhere.[22] They enlisted in two distinct groups: those who made their way across the border to Canada to enlist, and those who were recruited by the British Canadian Recruiting Mission in the United States.

Recruiting Americans was fraught with legal difficulties. American citizens who joined the CEF were deemed to have expatriated themselves or, in other words, to have forfeited their citizenship.[23] Foreign armies, including the CEF, were also forbidden by the United States Penal Code to recruit within the United States or to enter the United States with the intention of enticing men to leave and enlist elsewhere.[24] In Canada, CEF regulations and the *Militia Act* specified that recruits had to be British subjects.

Despite these obstacles, a steady trickle of enthusiasts travelled to Canada from 1914 onward to enlist in the CEF. At Beebe Junction in the Eastern Townships of Quebec, 123 men crossed the border in September 1914, all bound for Valcartier.[25] At Windsor, Ontario, forty-four men entered Canada from September to December 1914, declaring their intention to enlist.[26] Results were similar elsewhere, and up to May 1916, 248 men crossed at Niagara Falls to join the CEF.[27] The majority of these men had been born outside of the United States.

The steady trickle of men travelling north to join the CEF was of interest to units close to major border stations. In 1915–16 the 99th Battalion based in Windsor, Ontario, concentrated its efforts on border crossings and was able to recruit a substantial number of American residents.[28] Another Windsor-based battalion, the 241st, recruited 823 men in 1916–17, of whom 517, or 63 per cent, were American residents. Similarly, more than a quarter of those who joined the 176th Battalion at Niagara Falls in 1916–17 were American residents. In London, the 63rd Depot Battery maintained a recruiting office in Windsor, with the result that almost a third of those who joined in 1916–18 were American residents.

Some units advertised for recruits in American newspapers. In March 1916, the 99th Battalion committed a spectacular gaffe by placing ads in papers owned by Josephus Daniels, the US Secretary of the Navy. The response by Militia HQ was swift: units were prohibited from advertising in American papers.[29] But some units chose to ignore the ban, and in November 1916 Militia HQ not only repeated the prohibition but added that potential recruits could not be induced to cross the border and that district commanders would be "held personally responsible for observance of these instructions and any officer disregarding same will be subject to immediate dismissal."[30]

In some cases, measures were taken to assist potential recruits to cross the border. The 7th Field Company in London not only maintained a recruiting office in Windsor, Ontario, but hired a Detroit crimp to find likely recruits in pool halls and taverns and then escort them to Canada past immigration agents who obligingly looked the other way.[31] The co-operation extended by these agents at Windsor was not an isolated example; in November 1915, the Department of the Interior instructed immigration officials at Niagara Falls and St John's (St-Jean-sur-Richelieu), Quebec, to admit potential recruits and escort them to the nearest recruiting office. Similar instructions were given to immigration officers in Victoria, Vancouver, and Sarnia.[32] There were unofficial arrangements as well. In Winnipeg, the secretary of the Bohemian National Alliance of America (Canadian Branch), who was also the recruiting sergeant of the 223rd Battalion, wrote to the Russian Consul in 1916 that "[t]he arrangements we have made with the Emigration authorities are very satisfactory, and so far we have had no trouble getting men across the border."[33]

BRITISH-CANADIAN RECRUITING MISSION

American laws ceased to be a problem when the United States declared war on the German Empire in April 1917. The general mood of the country was distinctly pro-Allied, and after the Ambassador in Washington cleared the way Brigadier-General W.A. White, an officer with the British Mission to the United States, lost no time in soliciting congressmen for permission to enlist recruits from 700,000 British subjects in America who were neither citizens nor declarants.[34] The results were almost immediate: on 7 May 1917, the United States Congress amended the Penal Code to allow Allied nations to enlist residents who were not American citizens or declarants and had been born in the Allied nation concerned. The amendment, which allowed foreign armies to enter the United States and actively seek recruits, was a remarkable act of generosity and co-operation, even though the potential recruits were not eligible at that time to serve in the American Expeditionary Force.

White lost no time. By 6 June 1917, the British Recruiting Mission, later renamed British Canadian Recruiting Mission (BCRM), had started recruiting in New York City.[35] Developing the infrastructure and importing staff took some time, however, and in the interim US Army recruiting offices assisted the BCRM by receiving applicants, conducting medical exams, providing subsistence, and forwarding men to the nearest

CEF depot in Canada or, in the case of Britons, Jews, and Australians, to the Imperial Recruit Depot at Windsor, Nova Scotia.[36]

From a modest start in New York City, the BCRM expanded steadily. The HQ was located in New York City, and for organizational purposes the country was divided vertically into three divisions: Eastern in New York City, Western in Chicago, and Pacific in San Francisco. By November 1917, there were twenty-seven recruiting depots as well as mobile detachments that visited urban centres in the Western and Pacific Division. Canadians were part of every division, but the Western Division was staffed entirely by Canadians with a militia officer, Lieutenant-Colonel J.S. Dennis, in command.[37]

The BCRM also received civilian assistance. British consuls were instructed to assist the mission, and seventy-two recruiting committees were formed by prominent Britons and Canadians living in the United States.[38]

The BCRM recruited not only in the United States but in Canada as well to find recruits for the Jewish Legion, formed in September 1917 at the behest of the Jewish community in Britain. The original intention on the part of the War Office was to raise five battalions from British Jewry. However, it soon became evident that the pool of recruits in Britain was too small, and the War Office decided to recruit in Argentina, Canada, and the United States.[39]

Recruiting for the Jewish Legion in Canada was controlled by the BCRM – an unusual arrangement approved by Militia HQ in March 1918. To find likely recruits, the Mission organized Jewish Recruiting Committees in Montreal, Toronto, and Winnipeg.[40] The Committees were required to screen each applicant and determine "that he is not within a class called out for service under the Military Service Act of Canada, and that he is in all respects a suitable recruit for enlistment in the British Army."[41] Recruits attracted by the Committees were processed by CEF recruiting centres and then transported by the Department of Militia and Defence to the Imperial Recruit Depot at Windsor, Nova Scotia.[42]

However, there was no rush to the colours, perhaps because those Jews who were British subjects were eligible for conscription under the MSA, while many had already joined the CEF. Canadian Jewry was also divided, and Zionist support for the Legion may have inhibited recruiting, particularly in the Orthodox community. By mid-July 1918 it was apparent that the recruiting campaign was a failure, and the Jewish Recruiting Committees were disbanded.[43] The number of men enlisted in Canada is uncertain; official figures were never compiled, although Vladimir

Jabotinsky, a former officer of the Jewish Legion, estimated that about 300 Canadians were recruited, a figure confirmed by another veteran, Hyman Sokolov of Winnipeg.[44]

Apart from men joining the Jewish Legion, BCRM recruits were documented and examined in the United States and then forwarded to a Canadian depot for attestation. But men were not subject to military law until they were attested, and there were no legal means of preventing them from deserting. In March 1918, about 5 per cent of all BCRM recruits vanished before they arrived in Canada, while in August 1918 HQ MD 2 reported that more than 9 per cent had disappeared while in transit.[45] To stop this, Militia HQ directed in April 1918 that men would be attested by BCRM recruiting detachments.[46] But, since only one of the three BCRM divisions was controlled by Canadians, it is unlikely that the revised procedure had much effect.

Special efforts were made to recruit French Canadians. In June 1917, Major J.J.O.L. Daly-Gingras, who had previously served with the 22nd Battalion in France, was posted to the BCRM in the hope of enlisting French-Canadian immigrants in the New England states. The results were disappointing; in August 1917, a Catholic priest, Captain F.C.D. Doyon, who had also served with the 22nd Battalion, reported that many had already joined the American Expeditionary Force as translators and that the remainder anticipated being drafted in the near future. In summary, said Father Doyon, a concerted effort to recruit these men would be a waste of time.[47]

BCRM recruiting in the United States encountered some obstacles. Most US Army recruiting stations cooperated with the BCRM, but a few were reluctant to provide assistance or tried to entice BCRM recruits into the American Army.[48] Local draft boards were also uncooperative. In Boston, an Irish declarant who joined the Canadian Railway Troops and returned home on leave was persuaded by the local draft board to desert the CEF. In Buffalo, a BCRM recruit from the Engineer Depot at Brockville was jailed for draft evasion when he returned home on leave in uniform.[49] But others were more co-operative; in Chicago, for instance, Judge Stelk ordered non-US citizens in the Cook County Jail to be taken to the BCRM recruiting office for attestation and transport to Canada.[50]

Judging by attestation papers, BCRM medical examinations were carried out by Canadian and British Medical Corps doctors or, on occasion, by civilian physicians. The number of applicants who were medically unfit is unknown, although returns from New York City for July 1917 show that 32.8 per cent were rejected, a rate somewhat higher than the results of the MSA medical boards in Canada.[51] Those passed as fit were reassessed by medical boards on arrival in Canada. Results probably varied by district, but in MD 2, for example, 4 per cent of all arrivals were rejected by medical boards.[52] In all, it is estimated that about 63 per cent of all BCRM applicants were fit for some form of military service either in Canada or overseas.

The issue of which corps the recruits were assigned to caused some difficulties. Initially, applicants were promised they could choose any branch of the CEF and, not surprisingly, most opted to avoid the infantry. It must have come as a shock, therefore, that on arrival in Canada about 42 per cent were assigned to that corps. Not all accepted their assignment, and in MD 2 about 2 per cent of all recruits refused to be attested and were returned to the United States.[53]

By October 1918, the BCRM had provided more than 33,000 men for the CEF – about 5.5 per cent of all enlistments. But how many actually served in France, especially with the infantry, where the need for reinforcements was the greatest? A review of nominal rolls published in ten postwar regimental histories suggests that each infantry battalion received an average of 100 BCRM reinforcements. With forty-eight battalions in the Canadian Corps, it is probable that almost 5,000 BCRM infantrymen arrived in France before the Armistice. However, 58 per cent of BCRM recruits were not infantrymen, and more than 10,000 BCRM men likely served in France.

The BCRM was useful, but because it relied on voluntarism it was limited by the fact that non-declarant British subjects living in the United States who refused to volunteer for the Canadian, American, or British forces could not be compelled to serve. Conversely, American citizens living in Britain or Canada could not be drafted by British or Canadian authorities. To resolve this problem, Britain and the United States concluded a reciprocal convention that gave men a choice between returning home, where they could be conscripted, or remaining in their country of residence, where they would be subject to local draft laws. The preliminary agreement was signed on 19 February 1918; the American Senate insisted on amendments, however, and it was not until 30 July 1918 that the reciprocal convention came into effect.[54] With the introduction of conscription for those living abroad, there was no need to recruit volunteers in the United States. On 12 October 1918, the BCRM closed its doors.[55]

Whether the reciprocal convention had any practical effect on enlistments is impossible to determine, although the CEF probably had the short end of the stick. In the United States, the Provost Marshal General estimated that about 20,000 potential CEF recruits living in the United States chose to serve with the Americans rather than return home. In Canada, 18,359 Americans registered for the United States draft with consular officials and were thus exempted from conscription. No record appears to exist of the number of Americans in Canada who were drafted into the CEF, nor is there any record of the number of Canadians who trekked north under the terms of the convention.[56]

RECRUITING IN PRISONS

The CEF also accepted convicts. The first were eight prisoners from St Vincent de Paul Penitentiary in Laval who volunteered for the CEF on 14 August 1914. Their applications were reviewed by the Minister of Justice, but only one prisoner was released; in the event, he failed to enlist and was returned to prison. Others soon followed, and by December 1914 sixty-five felons had been released from penitentiaries and jails in order to join the CEF. Some were given unconditional pardons, but most were released on a "Ticket of Leave," the precursor to modern parole. About half of these ex-lags failed to enlist. Twenty-five vanished; one was deported; two, convicted of burglary after release, were returned to St Vincent de Paul; three were arrested after failing to enlist; and one enlisted but refused to go overseas and was returned to prison.[57]

For the first two years of the war, prisoners were released on the initiative of the Justice Department and not the CEF. Justice Department motives were moral: in 1915, for example, the Inspector of Penitentiaries recommended that a Kingston prisoner be allowed to enlist because "military discipline is exactly what he requires to make a man of him."[58] The Dominion Parole Officer also had faith in the uplifting nature of military service; in September 1915 he recommended the release of a chronic alcoholic from Dorchester Penitentiary: "I think if he were given a chance to go the Front he would make an excellent soldier and would redeem himself by good conduct."[59]

The CEF, however, was less concerned with morality than with manpower, and in 1916 started to take an interest in retrieving men who had been incarcerated for desertion. There were a substantial number, and a raid by military police on St Thomas, Ontario, in November 1915 netted thirty absentees. The 176th Battalion on the Niagara Peninsula had 257 deserters in less than a year, and in August 1916 there were said to be 1,500 absentees from Camp Borden, Ontario, alone.[60]

Not every deserter was caught, but there were enough to swell the prison population. Under ordinary circumstances these men would not have been welcomed back, but recruiting dropped off sharply in the latter half of 1916. An order in council was therefore issued in November 1916, allowing magistrates to suspend convictions at the request of the military provided that the offenders agreed not to desert in the future. This did nothing for those already imprisoned, however, and an amnesty was declared shortly thereafter, allowing convicted deserters to be released into the custody of the military.[61]

In 1917, the CEF took an active interest in prisoners other than deserters and began to recruit within the prisons. At Kingston, for example, a recruiting team arrived at the penitentiary on the morning of Friday, 26 May 1917, to process recruits. By noon, nine men, selected by the warden beforehand, had been interviewed, medically examined, attested, and issued with uniforms. At 1:40 p.m. that afternoon, the draft, accompanied by an escort, left for Halifax; early Monday morning, less than seventy-two hours after leaving prison, they boarded a troop ship.[62]

The passage of the *Military Service Act* in 1917 brought further changes. Nothing in the Act prevented convicts from being conscripted, although men disqualified under the *Dominion Elections Act*, a category that included prisoners, were exempt from combatant service.[63] There is no evidence that this legal nicety was followed, however, and virtually all of the convicts who are known to have been drafted served in the infantry. Although convicts may have been eligible for conscription, prisoners could be released only with a pardon or ticket of leave granted by the Justice Department.[64] Convict conscription was therefore selective, and only those deemed suitable by the Justice Department were called up.

The actual process of drafting convicts was carefully controlled. Travelling medical boards visited penitentiaries and examined those identified beforehand by prison staff. In Kingston, Warden Creighton went so far as to measure potential recruits, so that uniforms could be issued before the men left prison.[65] Convicts who were drafted were not given their freedom, but simply acquired khaki-clad turnkeys. In December 1917, prison staff from St Vincent de Paul escorted draftees directly to Peel Street Barracks in Montreal.[66] In Halifax, a recently drafted prisoner was taken under guard in May 1918 from the County Jail to the local depot, where he was to be "kept under close confinement and placed on board transport as such, with orders to the OC Troops to release him after the transport sails."[67] The methodology may have varied, depending on local circumstances, but convicts were invariably kept under close scrutiny until they were safely aboard the troop ship.

There was some concern that hardened criminals might be enlisted in the CEF. In May 1917, Militia HQ notified districts that "men who are found guilty of serious crimes are not on any account to be accepted as recruits."[68] The Department of Justice also had concerns and in October 1917 issued instructions to exclude serious cases where clemency was not justified.[69] Despite these concerns, the majority of prisoners who enlisted seem to have been good soldiers.

However, there were a small number of unsavoury recruits, such as the twenty-three convicts from Kingston Penitentiary who joined the 6th Reserve Battalion in England in July 1918. The group included one man serving a life term, two imprisoned for "white slavery," another convicted of manslaughter, one rapist, and a bank robber convicted of two counts of armed robbery and shooting with intent to wound. Two of the men confessed that they were drug addicts, and Sir Edward Kemp, the OMFC Minister, thought that the sudden increase of robberies and assaults in the vicinity of the 6th Reserve Battalion could be traced directly to these ex-prisoners.[70]

The number of men released to join the CEF is uncertain, since many of the relevant Justice Department files remain closed. Warden Creighton of Kingston Penitentiary wrote in October 1918 that he had released more than eighty prisoners for military service, including thirty-one men who were drafted under the *Military Service Act* over a three-day period in March 1918.[71] Since Kingston held about a quarter of all federal convicts, this suggests that more than three hundred men were released from federal prisons alone. On the other hand, Sessional Papers submitted to Parliament show that, from 1914 to 1918, 523 prisoners were discharged to join the CEF. These were conditional releases, however, and if pardons are included it is probable that more than 700 felons served in the CEF – a substantial number, given that there were only 4,438 men in all Canadian penal institutions at the end of 1916.[72] The estimate is consistent with the Second World War, when 598 convicts were transferred from prison to the armed forces between September 1939 and February 1943.[73]

PSYCHIATRIC HOSPITALS

Not only prisons were viewed as a source of potential recruits. In June 1918, the Military Service Branch of the Department of Justice instructed local MSA registrars to ascertain the names of potential draftees confined to "asylums, institutions for the feeble minded [and] hospitals."[74] At least one psychiatric hospital in Ontario is known to have forwarded a list of suitable inmates, but there is no evidence, in Ontario at least, that men were removed from hospital and placed in uniform.[75]

MANAGING MANPOWER

Finding alternative recruiting sources helped with manning, but for the first two years of the war there was no uniform description of a man's fitness, making it difficult to manage the pool of serving soldiers efficiently. Fitness depended on the man's corps, and without a full-blown medical examination there was no way of determining whether, for instance, a Service Corps driver was fit for the infantry. Nor was there any way to determine whether an infantryman designated as "unfit" by his battalion should be transferred to a non-combatant corps or be repatriated to Canada for discharge.

The problem was recognized by the CEF. By 1916, unfit soldiers, regardless of corps, were described as PB (permanent base), or as TB (temporary base) if the individual was expected to improve. The numbers were significant: in May 1916, of the more than 12,000 soldiers examined by CEF medical boards in England, 20.46 per cent were judged to be PB.[76] But the results were unsatisfactory, since there was no indication of the limitations on employment. Could a PB infantryman be usefully employed with the Forestry Corps, for example?

The British army had the same problem. In May 1916, Army Council Instruction (ACI) 1023 set out a universal system of medical categories that reflected individual fitness and training regardless of corps.[77] The CEF was slow to follow suit, however, probably because Canadian HQ in London was not particularly efficient and recognized neither the problem nor the remedy. However, in November 1916, Colonel A.D. McRae of Canadian HQ and Lieutenant-General Byng, the Canadian Corps commander, visited the Deputy Chief of the Imperial General Staff at the War Office and subsequently recommended the use of common standards in both France and England as well as Canada.[78] The creation of HQ OMFC shortly afterward facilitated matters, and by the end of November 1916 ACI 1023 was in use by the CEF overseas.[79] The system was then adopted in Canada when Militia HQ issued Militia Order 50 in August 1917 to identify unfit men who might otherwise be posted to England and "to utilize available material [manpower] to the best purpose."[80]

The category system established by ACI 1023 with minor modifications authorized by Militia Order 50 is summarized in table 4.1.

Table 4.1 Medical categories

Category*	General description	Remarks
A	Fit for active service	Ai – fully trained Aii – recruits Aiii – fully trained but required hardening Aiv – minors
B	Free from serious organic defects and fit for active service on the lines of communication	Bi – able to march five miles Bii – able to walk at least five miles to and from work Biii – sedentary duties only
C	Fit for home service only	Fit for service in Canada or Britain only
D	Temporarily unfit	Likely to become fit within six months
E	Unfit for categories A, B and C	Not likely to become fit within six months

* Subcategories for C and D are not included.

Once men had been categorized, the benefits of the system became obvious. In January 1917, for example, HQ OMFC directed reserve units in England to transfer all category B and C men to the Canadian Railway Troops Depot at Purfleet or to Canadian Forestry Corps companies working in England or Scotland, something that would have been impossible six months earlier without thousands of medical boards.[81]

Standard medical categories allowed fit men in non-combatant corps to be weeded out and diverted to the infantry. As early as January 1917, a draft of 399 Service Corps reinforcements from Canada "of splendid physique"[82] lost a hundred men to the infantry on arrival in England. Further transfers of category A soldiers to the infantry followed; by 9 May 1917, a total of 525 men had been transferred from the Service Corps Training Depot to reserve infantry battalions. Another 436 men were transferred to the infantry in August 1917 and a further 313 in September 1917.[83] Another 227 followed in October–November 1917.[84] In all, 1,601 Service Corps soldiers were transferred to the infantry between January and November 1917.

The results were dramatic. In January 1917, Service Corps personnel in England were virtually all category A, but by July 1918 they were virtually all category B.[85] Other corps were expected to yield category A men as well, and in the first six months of 1917, 469 pay clerks at HQ OMFC were drafted to the infantry and replaced by category B and C men.[86]

The system was not perfect. Some of the Medical Corps soldiers in the forward areas in France had to be Ai to do their job, and in May 1917 the head of medical services at HQ OMFC noted that the Medical Corps Training Depot could not afford to surrender any more category A men.[87] Similarly, the Quartermaster General reported in November 1917 that the Service Corps Training Depot had to retain a pool of category A horse transport drivers as reinforcements for divisional trains in France, because "it is feared that under the trying winter conditions, the demand for reinforcements will be exceptionally heavy if men of low category are employed."[88] Even infantry reserve battalions were affected. In January 1918, HQ OMFC urged that category A NCOs should be posted to France, although it was difficult to find competent instructors with lower categories. Still, OMFC added, the effort should be made.[89]

The process of combing out non-combatants who were fit for the front was not simply a knee-jerk reaction to the need for infantry reinforcements for France, but an effort to make the most efficient use of manpower. The general policy was set out in May 1917, when HQ OMFC directed that "all men of Category 'A' of Units and Corps other than infantry, who are surplus to the estimated requirements of reinforcements for the next 8 months, should be transferred to Infantry Reserve Battalions."[90]

Despite the success of the combing-out process, the benefit appears to have been limited – judging by the number of non-combatants posted to ten sample infantry battalions in France in 1917–18. On average, each received seventy former non-combatants. This suggests that about 3,640 men who had been combed out were posted to the fifty-two infantry and pioneer battalions in the Canadian Corps. But the total number of transfers to combatant corps must have been somewhat more, if postings to the artillery, engineers, machine gun corps, and the Canadian Cavalry Brigade are also considered.

The adoption of standard medical categories and the reassignment of men to jobs they were best suited for was not simply a bureaucratic exercise, but a realization that manpower resources were finite and had to be efficiently managed. Much has been made of the increased professionalism of the CEF in 1917–18, but there was a corresponding change in the administrative sphere, of which the categorization of manpower is but one example.

IMMIGRANTS

Although Militia HQ was able to enlarge the manpower pool by tinkering with entry requirements and making more efficient use of manpower, the reluctance of the CEF to enlist immigrants, some of whom spoke little English or French, was a missed opportunity. Only 27,351 of these men were enlisted.⁹¹ (See table 4.2 for a sample of foreign-born enlistments.) But, had they joined at the same rate as Canadians outside of Quebec, the CEF would have gained an additional 23,000 men, if not more, considering that many immigrants were males of military age. To put this number into context, the failure to fully tap the immigrant reservoir represented more than two months' wastage for the CEF in France and Flanders.

Recruiting depended not only on the criteria established by Militia HQ, but also on the willingness of units to accept volunteers and, most importantly, on the willingness of men to step forward. With this in mind, it is not surprising that the enlistment rate for immigrants from each country differed considerably. In general, the average enlistment date for immigrants was the third week in September 1916 – almost six months later than the CEF norm of March 1916. This difference can be attributed, in part, to difficulties these men had in enlisting. There is no discernable relationship between the mean enlistment date and the role of the recruit's parent country in the war, although in general those from allied nations enlisted three months before those from neutral countries. Nor is there any evidence that naturalization and enlistment rates were linked.

Attitudes to non-English speaking immigrants were mixed. Clifford Sifton, Minister of the Interior from 1896 to 1905, thought the Ukrainian immigrant, "a stalwart peasant in a sheep-skin coat," was a decided asset, but others were not as sure. J.S. Woodsworth, who was generally sympathetic to immigrants and their problems, preferred a homogeneous people who were "in accord with our democratic institutions and conducive to the general welfare."⁹² Similarly, Agnes Laut, a popular Canadian author who was not opposed to immigration per se, wrote, "These poverty-stricken Jews and Polacks and Galicians will be the wealth and power of Canada tomorrow," but added, "Will Canada remain Canada when these new races come up to power?"⁹³ Immigrants from non-English speaking countries were viewed with suspicion and were not always regarded as "one of us," regardless of their status as British subjects.

The general mistrust of immigrants prevailed in the CEF. In reply to a request to enlist naturalized Bulgarians, the Adjutant-General wrote in October 1915 that "blood being thicker than water, you should take no chances."⁹⁴ A few months later, in March 1916, a request to enlist Persians, who were bitter about Turkish persecution, was turned down because Persians "would not mix well with Anglo-Saxons."⁹⁵ Greeks could be enlisted but, as Militia HQ noted in November 1917, "No special effort,

Table 4.2 Sample of foreign-born enlistments*

Birthplace	Sample size	Mean enlistment date†	MSA enlistment, %	Naturalized, %
Belgium	1,084	April 1916	10.4	40.9
Iceland	450	April 1916	31.1	82.5
Netherlands	419	April 1916	14.3	29.6
France	1,165	May 1916	15.8	50.6
Russia	7,576	June 1916	15.6	45.5
Denmark	1,032	July 1916	8.4	44.5‡
Greece	395	September 1916	15.4	18.0
Sweden	1,779	November 1916	27.4	44.5‡
Italy	1,676	December 1916	24.7	19.9
Norway	1,581	November 1916	28.1	44.5‡
Romania	384	March 1917	32.3	46.1
Ottoman Empire	371	March 1917	15.6	39.6
Germany	243	March 1918	59.3	58.8
Austria-Hungary	1,893	May 1918	68.0	50.2
Total – All	21,400	September 1916	23.0	
Total – Allied	12,976	June 1916	16.7	
Total – Neutral	5,878	September 1916	21.8	
Total – Enemy	2,546	April 1918	58.8	
CEF total		March 1916	21.0	

* The complete sample includes men from forty-four countries.
† The mean enlistment date is the month by which half of all men in the sample had enlisted.
‡ Census data grouped all Scandinavians together.

however, should be made to recruit them."[96] However, others felt differently. In November 1914, the mayor of Fort William, Ontario, thought that "if [immigrants] could be persuaded to take up arms, there would be a profound effect on the future generation."[97] All of this must have been discouraging to the immigrants themselves, many of whom wanted "to discharge their duty to their adopted country in this war."[98]

There were concerns that men from enemy states who concealed their origins on enlistment were a security threat. Ukrainians from the Austro-Hungarian Empire, who claimed to be Russians, were suspected of maintaining ties with the old country, while some were "reported to be sending money from Canada to the United States to be forwarded from there to Austria."[99] Other groups were suspect as well. Germans were said to be passing themselves off as Scandinavians, while Austrians were suspected of claiming Serbian or Romanian citizenship.[100]

Security concerns with recruits born in enemy countries may have been exaggerated, but they had some basis in reality. In February 1917, Private George McDonald of the Royal Canadian Regiment deserted and warned VI (German) Reserve Corps of preparations for an attack at Vimy Ridge. McDonald, whose true name was Otto Ludwig Döerr, had been born in Frankfurt-am-Main, Germany, although when he enlisted at Saskatoon in 1916 he claimed to have been born in Kentucky. McDonald/Döerr evidently had an accent but accounted for this by telling his comrades he had been raised in Mexico and lived in Texas.[101]

Language was a problem because some immigrant recruits spoke little or no English or French. The number of these men who joined is unknown, although there were enough that Militia HQ found it necessary to issue repeated instructions that "no men should be enlisted who have not a satisfactory knowledge of either the French or English languages."[102] The instructions were not xenophobic: there were some very good reasons for them.

In early April 1916, Russian-born soldiers in the 39th and 41st Reserve Battalions at Shorncliffe mutinied and refused to go on parade. Unit officers questioned the men, many of whom could not speak English, but were unable to pinpoint the causes. The disturbance did not end until Lieutenant Gidony, a Russian-born CEF officer with Canadian HQ, questioned the mutineers in Russian, identified the principal causes, and suggested a remedy.[103] The whole affair was blown out of proportion simply because officers and soldiers could not communicate.

More importantly, training was hampered when men could not speak English or French. In February 1916, the Commanding Officer of the 39th Reserve Battalion in England wrote about the Russian-Canadians with his unit:

> These men are splendid soldiers and do wonderfully well under the circumstances, but they understand and speak practically no English, and have no Officers or NCOs who understand their language. It would, in consequence be impossible to depend on them to understand or set upon instructions in trench routine, fire tactics, sentry duties or reconnaissance, or to pass orders or messages, and I do not feel that I can certify them fit for overseas services. Nor can any training that we can give them would make them fit.[104]

Despite these concerns, some who spoke little English were posted to France, as Lieutenant C.A. Wells of the 1st Canadian Entrenching Battalion commented in September 1916:

My platoon is composed of kilties. Some of them are Russians. They will persist in coming on parade without their khaki aprons, so that I have to call the Russian Sergeant, and administer a scolding with him as an interpreter. What peculiar workings of military officialdom caused these Russians from Western Canada to be put into a Highland battalion, it is hard to say.[105]

Some attempts were made by reserve units in England to accommodate those who had difficulties with French or English. In April 1916, the 12th Reserve Brigade recommended that all Russians be grouped under NCOs who were fluent in both Russian and English.[106] In November 1916, the 9th Reserve Brigade commented that bilingual instructors were required for Russian-speaking reinforcements, while in June 1917 the 5th Reserve Battalion recommended that instructors who were fluent in Greek were needed for newly arrived unilingual Greeks with the 241st Battalion. A different approach was taken by the Pioneer Training Depot in 1916, and a number of Russians were promoted to lance-corporal and used to instruct their comrades. The experiment was not a success, however, because the instructors were no further advanced than their students.[107]

The use of bilingual instructors was not a satisfactory solution. Admittedly, the men would complete their training, but there was still the knotty problem of speaking English or French sufficiently well to function with units in France. The obvious solution was to conduct second-language classes. The 37th Battalion Base Company in Ontario suggested in 1915 that non-English speaking soldiers (mainly Russians) be grouped together and given an opportunity to attend language classes, but nothing came of this recommendation.[108]

The American army had the same problem, but on a much larger scale. Almost 20 per cent of their draftees were foreign-born, and many spoke English poorly or not all. The United States War Office was slow to recognize the problem, but in January 1918 the Intelligence Department in Washington created the Foreign-speaking Soldier Subsection (FSS) to facilitate the training and integration of immigrant soldiers. Under the direction of the FSS, non-English-speaking soldiers were grouped into "development battalions" with English-language instruction and military training under instructors who spoke their language.[109]

The American army was able to do this only because it was highly centralized and took in a large number of men in a relatively short period. In contrast, the CEF was decentralized and recruited fewer men over a much longer period. In short, a Canadian equivalent to the FSS was simply not possible.

RECRUITING WOMEN

Women could also have been used to replace men who were physically fit for active service, a measure that would have helped to alleviate the shortage of manpower. In England, HQ OMFC was more than willing to make use of British women from Queen Mary's Army Auxiliary Corps (QMAAC) as cooks, drivers, and mess waitresses, but there was no equivalent in Canada.

It was not as though women did not serve in the CEF: a total of 2,854 nurses served in the Medical Corps, while ten other women were commissioned as well. But there were no female soldiers, with the exception of Maude Blake, a Kingston "dental mechanic" (dental technician) who enlisted as a private in 1915 and was demobilized as a sergeant in January 1919.[110] Blake, it must be pointed out, joined as a woman and made no effort to conceal her gender.

Despite the presence of QMAAC personnel with units in England, the employment of women in the CEF was not seriously considered by Militia HQ until December 1917, when a letter signed by an anonymous "Anxious and Willin'-to-go Stenographer" in Toronto proposed a Canadian version of the QMAAC. The letter was passed to Gwatkin, the Chief of Staff at Militia HQ, who took the suggestion seriously and directed the Adjutant-General to broach the issue with the Minister's military secretary. HQ OMFC was then asked in March 1918 to investigate the use of women overseas, but the War Office rejected the idea because there were enough British women to fill the demand and there was a shortage of shipping to bring Canadian women to England.[111]

The matter did not end there. In May 1918, Colonel MacInnes at Militia HQ noted that the Royal Air Force was recruiting women for RAF Canada and observed: "Will this not, however, expose the Department to criticism, if something of the same kind is not done in connection with the Canadian Forces?"[112] MacInnes's suggestion evidently struck a chord. Militia Council considered the issue on 30 May 1918 and formed a subcommittee headed by the Quartermaster General to study the matter. The subcommittee worked slowly, however, and it was not until 18 September 1918 that Militia Council reviewed their report and approved the formation of the "Canadian Women's Army Auxiliary Corps" (CWAAC). However, Major-General S.C. Mewburn, the Minister of Militia and Defence, deferred any action until Prime Minister Bordon and the Civil Service Commission had been consulted. Nothing concrete emerged from these consultations (if, in fact, they ever took place) and the signing of the Armistice on 11 November 1918 rendered the proposal moot.[113]

Would the CWAAC have freed up a significant number of men for overseas duty? In May 1918, an estimated 90,600 soldiers were serving in Canada.[114] Many were MSA men waiting to go overseas, while others were being cared for by the Military Hospitals Commission. There were probably only a few thousand fit men employed in administrative positions who could have been replaced by members of the CWAAC. As well, had the CWAAC been formed in September 1918, only two months before the Armistice, there would have been little or no benefit to the CEF. Had the war continued into 1919, however, the CWAAC would have made a significant contribution by adding several thousand men to the reinforcement stream.

SUMMARY

By 1917-18, the CEF had come to the realization that manpower was a finite resource that had to be efficiently managed to compensate for the ever-diminishing pool of potential recruits. Alternative sources of manpower were tapped, and a substantial number of men were enlisted outside of Canada. Recruits were drawn from prisons, enemy aliens were drafted in 1918, and the use of women in uniform was seriously considered. Efforts were also made to manage serving manpower more efficiently, and the adoption of medical categories in both England and France allowed men to be employed in a manner commensurate with their medical fitness. All of this was a far cry from the chaotic early days of the war and marked the transition of the CEF from an amateur body in 1914-15 to a truly professional force.

However, efforts to add to the pool of potential recruits were not always successful, and the failure to ignore popular prejudices and encourage immigrants, blacks, and Asians to enlist probably cost the CEF thousands of recruits. These lost opportunities, together with the impact of recruits who were less than truthful on enrolment, as discussed in chapter 3, resulted in a fair amount of inefficiency and waste. To a very great extent, this was a product of the recruiting system. The evolution of this system from an ad-hoc organization in 1914 to an efficient and highly centralized structure in 1918 forms the central theme of chapter 5.

5

The Recruiting Structure 1914–18

CEF recruiting, with its monster rallies, strident newspaper stories, public demonstrations, posters, and recruiting sergeants on the streets, was a highly visible process that has been examined by a wide variety of historians. However, this picture ignores the organizational framework created by Militia HQ and the nine district headquarters across the country that made recruiting possible. Largely overlooked is the fact that recruiting was not simply a social or cultural event, but was first and foremost a military process controlled and guided by the Canadian Forces with varying degrees of success until 1918, when the Military Service Branch of the Department of Justice assumed responsibility for calling up recruits conscripted under the *Military Service Act*.

Many of the studies of recruiting for the CEF have focused on the recruiting crisis of 1915–16 and the chaos, confusion, and gross inefficiency that resulted when Sam Hughes created almost a hundred infantry battalions overnight. However, this approach gives an incomplete account of a complex process. Without denying that there was a genuine infantry recruiting crisis, it should be noted that more than one third of all recruits (36.8 per cent) were not infantrymen. These men were enlisted by a variety of agencies: corps depots, reserve squadrons, depot batteries, district recruiting offices, and – in the case of some of the forestry and railway units – the unit itself. For these agencies and units, there was no crisis.

From August 1914 to November 1916, recruiting was periodically modified as a result of snap decisions by Sam Hughes, the eccentric Minister of Militia and Defence, and it is easy to see him as the cause of all problems. In practice, however, Hughes's authority was not absolute. First, he did not concern himself with the overall policy and organization but, instead, dealt with specific issues as they arose. Second, the staff at Militia HQ, to their credit, persisted in trying to put recruiting on a rational basis. In April 1916, for example, the Militia Council took advantage of Hughes's absence from Ottawa and decided that new battalions would not be created until the existing ones had reached full strength. This action ran counter to Hughes's penchant for creating new units at the drop of a hat and, not surprisingly, A.E. Kemp, the acting president of the Council, deferred any action until Hughes returned to Ottawa.[1]

As discussed in chapter 1, district commanders expected to be consulted on matters concerning units in their district and to be kept informed of any decisions affecting their district. Not even Hughes could ignore these long-standing conventions without provoking a backlash. In August 1915, for example, Colonel W.A. Logie, the commander of MD 2, complained to the Adjutant-General in Ottawa that he had been directed to organize the 92nd Battalion in Toronto with a full slate of officers, but Hughes had already appointed Colonel J.A. Currie as the CO. Even worse, Logie learned of the appointment from Currie and not Militia HQ. His outrage was palpable. "I am at a loss to know whether I am organizing this Battalion or whether he [Currie] is organizing it," he protested, demanding to "be informed therefore, authoritatively, what status I have."[2] The reply from Ottawa was succinct: Currie would not command the 92nd, and a Commanding Officer would be appointed on the basis of Logie's recommendations.[3] The issue here was not Currie's suitability to command the new battalion, but adherence to established conventions. A few months later, in November 1915, Hughes appointed Lieutenant-Colonel R. Belcher to command the 138th Battalion in Edmonton, although Colonel Cruikshank, the District Commander, thought Belcher was unfit for command because he was sixty-six years old and "occasionally drinks to excess and then becomes unmanageable. I have been obliged to admonish him for this on two occasions."[4] In this case, there was no protest from Cruikshank because he had been consulted and had been allowed to make recommendations.

Turning to the matter of enlisting men for the newly mobilized CEF units, a variety of recruiting agencies were used: militia units, the newly mobilized CEF units themselves, and district-controlled recruiting offices. These agencies were not created sequentially, and at various times all three operated together, sometimes in the same place. In many cases, recruiting agencies had multiple functions. Militia units not only enlisted men but processed them – or, in other words, conducted medical examinations, completed documentation, and then drafted the recruits to their new units. CEF units, on the other hand, not only recruited and processed volunteers but also trained them for overseas deployment. Lastly, district-controlled recruiting offices had the same responsibilities as militia units, but starting in 1915 acted as personnel depots by holding recruits until they could be drafted to units.

MILITIA-BASED RECRUITING

Large-scale recruiting was not only a wartime phenomenon but had been considered as early as 1911, when Canada's first mobilization plan was drafted by Militia HQ. Two possibilities were considered: a *levée en masse* in the event of war with the United States, and an overseas contingent with an infantry division and a cavalry brigade drawn from the militia in the event of a European war.[5] Plans were drafted for the latter, but there is no evidence that a *levée en masse* was seriously considered.

Ideally, the overseas contingent should have been formed by select militia units to preserve regimental and regional identities. However, peacetime units were nowhere near full strength, and composite units would therefore have to be created. The issue of which militia units should be called upon was a vexing one. Too many units might result in administrative chaos. On the other hand, ignoring some of the militia units would result in howls of protest from those not selected, to say nothing of local politicians and politically well-connected honorary colonels. In the end, Militia HQ decided to form the overseas division with composite units made up of men from ninety-six militia infantry regiments, with quotas ranging from a machine gun section to five companies.[6]

Volunteers for the contingent were required to be single, physically fit, and between the ages of twenty and thirty-five – standards that excluded a significant number of serving militiamen.[7] Perhaps because of this, the mobilization plan also provided for recruiting. Both district and unit commanders retained general oversight, but the actual recruiting was to be done by the squadron, battery, and company commanders who would actually command the men enlisted. In effect, the pre-war mobilization plan relied not only on militia units for recruiting, but also on the newly mobilized units themselves, a plan that mirrored CEF recruiting early in the war. Finally, in keeping with British practice, composite units were to form regimental depots to hold both recruits and reinforcements.[8]

The pre-war scheme was not perfect. There were limited reserve stocks of clothing, equipment, and weapons, no plans existed for detailed reports or pay services, and the reliance on militia units with inexperienced staffs left much to be desired. Still, the plan was useful, because it was based on a rational consideration of national manpower resources and provided a clear starting point. Unfortunately, the scheme was abruptly cancelled by Hughes on 31 July 1914, and the orderly mobilization envisaged before the war was replaced by an improvised concentration at Valcartier, a temporary camp created by Hughes on the spur of the moment.[9] In the short term, the abrupt cancellation of the scheme had little effect on the structure of the First Contingent, which resembled the 1911 plan with an infantry division and a cavalry brigade. But, in the long term, the abandonment of pre-war plans meant that recruiting and mobilization would be an improvised business until alternative arrangements could be put in place.

The story of the First Contingent and the resultant chaos at Valcartier in August 1914 is too well known to be repeated here. Raising and dispatching the contingent in fewer than than six weeks was a considerable achievement, but the process was anything but orderly and in practice amounted to nothing more than shovelling volunteers into Valcartier, leaving a hard-pressed group of twenty-five staff officers under the direction of the camp commandant, Colonel V.A.S. Williams, the Adjutant-General, to sort things out as the troops arrived.

Calling on the militia to provide recruits for the First Contingent was not a straightforward process. Few, if any, units had full-time staff, and instructions from Ottawa had to be sent to commanding officers at their home or business and then passed to the troops by runners or newspaper advertisements. City corps could react quickly, but rural units could not. Urgent telegrams from Militia HQ took two or more days to reach the 26th Middlesex Light Infantry in southwestern Ontario, for example, because the Commanding Officer lived near Ilderton, "a considerable distance from a telegraph station."[10] Elsewhere, in Prince Edward Island, the commander of the 36th Light Horse complained that his men were scattered across the province and it was impossible to contact all of them in a reasonable period of time.[11]

Units initially had difficulties with recruiting and processing because Hughes chose to bypass district headquarters.[12] As a result, ordnance officers had no authority or basis on which to distribute uniforms and equipment from district stocks, while district paymasters had no authority (or funds) to pay recruits or call out unit staff. The 24th Kent Regiment in Chatham, for example, was forced to recruit in the evenings when officers and NCOs were free from their civilian jobs.[13] But this was only a temporary glitch, and by mid-August 1914 many units had been given authority to call out staff to handle the influx of recruits.

The number called out by each unit varied. In Stratford, the 28th Perth Regiment called out the Commanding Officer, second-in-command, medical officer, and quartermaster, together with nine clerks, medical orderlies, and storemen, to process 156 volunteers from 12–23 August 1914.[14] In Galt, the 29th Regiment used the Commanding Officer, adjutant, medical officer, quartermaster, and regimental quartermaster-sergeant to process 117 volunteers, while the 25th Regiment in St Thomas was content to rely only on the Commanding Officer and an orderly room sergeant.[15] Even small units called out regimental staff, and in Calgary Sergeant-Major Barker supervised recruiting for the 14th Service Corps Company.[16] In a few cases, support personnel were called out by rural units that chose to concentrate recruits from outlying companies at regimental headquarters, and in Parry Sound unit cooks were called out by the 23rd Northern Pioneers to feed the influx of recruits.[17]

Some militia units needed for home defence duties were unable to recruit for the First Contingent. In New Brunswick, the 73rd Regiment, a rural corps, abandoned its outlying armouries when the regiment was called out at the beginning of the war, leaving nobody behind to take in recruits. Providing guards for strategic installations was important – but so was recruiting, and on 17 August 1914 HQ MD 6 ordered one officer from each outlying company to return home and reopen the local armoury to receive recruits.[18]

One unit was unable to call on the militia for recruits: Princess Patricia's Canadian Light Infantry, a wartime creation with no ties to the peacetime militia. But regimental enthusiasts opened improvised recruiting offices in Montreal, Toronto, Winnipeg, Edmonton, and Calgary, and the battalion was quickly brought up to full strength.[19]

Almost immediately after the First Contingent sailed to England, Canada offered a Second Contingent. Unlike the First, which had been concentrated at Valcartier, the Second was dispersed across the country in improvised barracks under the command of district commanders. In the case of the fifteen infantry battalions, each district was assigned a specific quota by Militia HQ on 18 October 1914. MD 1, 3, 5, and 13 were responsible for recruiting one battalion each, MD 2, 4, 6, and 11 were tasked to recruit two battalions each, and MD 10 had to raise three battalions.[20]

As with the First Contingent, militia units were called upon to provide recruits, and district commanders kept a grip on the process. In MD 2, twenty militia regiments provided recruits to the 19th and 20th Battalions. City corps in Toronto, the Niagara Peninsula, and Sault Ste. Marie sent men to the 19th, while rural corps sent their men to the 20th Battalion.[21] Further west, in Winnipeg, HQ MD 10 assigned quotas to all infantry and cavalry units in Saskatchewan, Manitoba, and the Lakehead. The 79th, 90th, 100th, and 106th Regiments in Winnipeg, as well as the 98th Kenora Light Infantry and the 99th Manitoba Rangers in Brandon, recruited men for the 27th (City of Winnipeg) Battalion, while four Saskatchewan regiments and the 96th Lake Superior Regiment from the Lakehead recruited for the 28th (Northwest) Battalion. Lastly, each of the nine cavalry regiments in the district was called upon to provide 116 recruits for the 32nd Infantry Battalion.[22] In Quebec, both MD 4 and MD 5 sent French-speaking recruits from the 9th, 65th, and 85th Regiments to the 22nd Battalion.[23]

Not all districts were able to rely on the militia for recruits; in the Maritimes, the 25th and 26th Battalions had to recruit for themselves, probably because city militia units had been called out for home defence and rural units were not sufficiently well organized to process recruits.

In Alberta, MD 13 used a variety of methods to find recruits for the 31st Battalion. Edmonton recruits were enlisted by a battalion officer, Major Hewgill, while further south, in Calgary, Captain Morfitt of the 103rd Calgary Rifles was appointed by Hughes to recruit men for the 31st and then the 56th and 63rd Battalions.[24] Outside of Edmonton and Calgary, recruiting was delegated to militia units. In Lethbridge, Major Stewart of the 25th Independent Field Battery enlisted a hundred infantrymen for the 31st, while in Medicine Hat, Captain Oakes of the 21st Alberta Hussars and his medical officer, Captain Orr, recruited another hundred volunteers, also for the 31st Battalion.[25]

For those units that recruited for the Second Contingent, procedures were broadly similar to those followed in August 1914. In Stratford, five members of the 28th Regiment (second-in-command, medical officer, hospital sergeant, and two sergeant-clerks) were called out on 22 October 1914 to process ninety-three recruits from Perth County for the 18th Battalion at Queen's Park Barracks in London. The recruiting campaign was brief, and on 4 November 1914 the 28th staff returned to their civilian jobs.[26] Other militia regiments in MD 1 also called out staff to recruit for the 18th Battalion: the 24th in Chatham, the 29th in Galt, and the 33rd in Clinton.[27] In some cases, outlying companies were used, and the 30th Wellington Rifles opened a recruiting detachment at a company armoury in Fergus.[28]

Other districts also called out militia staff for recruiting purposes. In MD 2, members of the 23rd Regiment in Parry Sound, the 32nd in

Walkerton, and the 34th in Oshawa were called out to recruit on behalf of the 19th and 20th Battalions.[29] Non-infantry units also recruited for the Second Contingent, and in Alberta the 14th Service Corps Company employed two officers and one private from 30 November to 3 December 1914 to recruit and process thirty-two volunteers for the 2nd Divisional Train.[30]

Pre-war French-speaking militia units in eastern Quebec were weak and in 1914 were unable to recruit enough men for the 22nd Battalion. The shortfall was made up by posting men from two western Quebec battalions (the 23rd and 24th), but English-speaking recruits had to be drafted from Alberta, Ontario, British Columbia, and Manitoba units to replace the losses in the 23rd and 24th.[31]

The 2nd Divisional Artillery also drew men from militia units. In Fredericton, recruits for the 23rd and 24th Field Batteries came from all three militia field artillery brigades in Atlantic Canada.[32] In Toronto, five batteries in the local area sent their recruits directly to the 4th Field Artillery Brigade. Further west, in Winnipeg, only one of the three local militia batteries was called upon to enlist men for two batteries and the ammunition column of the 5th Field Artillery Brigade, while the third battery was raised by a militia battery in Regina.[33]

Men with technical skills not found in peacetime militia units were also needed, and various methods were used to recruit them. In Montreal, the 1st Canadian Heavy Battery turned to the Canadian Pacific Railway shops to find skilled artificers.[34] There was also a shortage of skilled electricians to operate searchlights and electrical equipment in the Halifax fortress. Fortunately, in August 1914, the Canadian General Electric Company offered to recruit and pay for twenty-five electricians. Militia HQ accepted the offer, and the men were enlisted in the Royal Canadian Engineers (PF) and sent to Halifax, where they remained until at least February 1916.[35] In Toronto, the 2nd Canadian Field Butchery did not turn to local militia units but recruited experienced butchers from December 1914 to April 1915 with the aid of Sergeant Lilley, an ex-Royal Marine butcher trained at Aldershot, England.[36] Further east, Number 5 Depot Unit of Supply in Montreal did not turn to the militia either and recruited for themselves from December 1914 to February 1915.[37]

Militia recruiting for the CEF in 1914 was not a flash in the pan; the practice continued for much of 1915, albeit on a more organized and systematic basis for longer periods of time. In Ottawa, the Governor General's Foot Guards actively recruited for the 38th and 59th Battalions from February to July 1915.[38] Further west, in Owen Sound, the

31st Regiment recruited for the 37th and 58th Battalions in February 1915 and again from April to June 1915.[39] In some cases, militia units were manning depots; they not only recruited men, but held them until drafts could be assembled and dispatched to CEF units. In MD 3, the 57th Peterborough Rangers provided men to the 39th and 80th Battalions from February to September 1915. For much of this period, drafts were forwarded weekly, but in September 1915 recruits were dispatched on a daily basis to the 80th Battalion in Belleville. As a recruiting agency, the 57th was remarkably successful, bringing in as many as 15 men a day and 198 in the month of September 1915 alone.[40]

After the initial rush in 1914, affiliations between the militia and CEF largely vanished, and those enlisted by the militia were posted on the basis of need. In August 1915 the 109th Regiment in Toronto, tasked to recruit for the 84th Battalion, could not find enough volunteers; a draft from the 108th Regiment, intended for the 83rd Battalion, was diverted to make up the shortfall in the 84th. This was not an isolated case. Men recruited by the Governor General's Body Guard for the 75th Battalion were sent instead to the under-strength 58th Battalion. The shortfall in the 75th was then made up when HQ MD 2 gave Toronto militia regiments a fresh quota of 255 men each.[41] Not all of these recruits were needed by the 75th, and in September 1915 local militia units were holding a substantial number of unallocated recruits, leading the District Commander, Colonel Logie, to request authority to raise another battalion because "[t]here are at present about 2,500 recruits in this Division of which I am handing over the authorized establishment to the 81st Battalion."[42]

Units in Atlantic Canada had little confidence in militia recruiters. In July 1915, a company commander with the 55th Battalion in New Brunswick commented that civilians were preferred because they would "do much better work than an Officer of the Militia, who, as the people would say, should be away himself. Furthermore I consider it has a dampening effect on recruiting to have in the centres Recruiting Officers who are of age and are not volunteering for overseas service and have no intention of doing so."[43] HQ MD 6 agreed, and by the end of July 1915 sacked all but four militia recruiting officers in New Brunswick because they were unable to produce a reasonable number of recruits.[44] Civilians were appointed as recruiting agents in their place, but this led to other problems.

In Woodstock, five recruiting agents were appointed: the town constable, a bank manager, the caretaker of the Woodstock armoury, a

Canadian Pacific Railway engineer, and a private from the 55th Battalion at home recovering from an appendectomy. But nobody was responsible for coordination, and all enjoyed equal status. As well, none were officers and could not attest recruits or provide them with public funds for transportation to the nearest CEF unit. In the case of the armoury caretaker, the job was considered to be part of his normal duties and there was no increase to his pay. Not surprisingly, he tried "to make money out of the recruits indirectly through his pool room."[45] Further north, in Edmunston, a local commission merchant was considered well qualified as a recruiter since he spoke both French and English, was too old for military service, and had a son with the CEF. On the other hand, "he occasionally gets on a drinking bout, which though over fairly quickly is pretty bad while it lasts."[46]

Using militia units for recruiting worked well in the short term, but in the long run part-time staff could not sustain the pace because militia officers and NCOs with jobs could not be called out for lengthy periods. The 28th Regiment in Stratford called out staff in July and August 1915 to recruit for the 34th Battalion; this was the last time the regiment responded, although one subaltern and two sergeants were called out that autumn to assist the 71st Battalion.[47]

By the fall of 1915, militia units that had been foremost in recruiting had closed, as key officers joined the CEF themselves. In Alberta, Major Stewart from Lethbridge joined the CEF in November 1914 and was followed six months later by Captains Oakes and Orr from Medicine Hat. Needless to say, there is no record of any further drafts from either the 25th Independent Field Battery or the 21st Alberta Hussars.

Other militia units were in a similar position, and by June 1916 most had lost a large proportion of their officers to the CEF. The 28th Regiment in Stratford lost nine of its eighteen officers, the 50th Regiment in Victoria lost seven of its eleven, the 8th Regiment in Quebec City lost seven out of fifteen, and the 7th Service Corps Company in Saint John, New Brunswick, lost five out of six officers.[48] With so many officers joining the CEF, many units stopped parading and were dormant by mid-1916.[49]

With the loss of key officers, units were not involved with recruiting, although individual militiamen were called out. In Toronto, HQ MD 2 was authorized by Militia HQ in June 1915 to recruit on a continuous basis. Militia units as such were not involved; instead, they provided one lieutenant and four sergeants each on a permanent basis under the command of the Toronto Recruiting Depot.[50]

UNIT-BASED RECRUITING

With the end of militia recruiting, CEF infantry battalions started to recruit for themselves. The concept was not new, but had been the custom in the peacetime militia and was part of the pre-war mobilization plan scrapped by Hughes in July 1914. Unit-based recruiting had also been extended to the CEF by Militia Order 161 of 29 March 1915, which noted that commanding officers were responsible "for the recruiting, organization, clothing, equipment and training of their units."[51]

Unit-based recruiting became the norm after the autumn of 1915, not only because the militia was declining in strength, but also because of two successive increases to the CEF. The first increase, announced by Hughes on 30 October 1915, boosted the CEF ceiling to 250,000 men, while the second, announced 1 January 1916 by Prime Minister Borden, set an establishment of 500,000.[52] In neither case was there much forethought. As one historian has remarked, Borden's announcement in particular was made "without any serious consultation with his [Cabinet] colleagues. Certainly his decision was made without the benefit of any planned study of all that this large-scale commitment of Canada's manpower would involve."[53]

The two announcements were a substantial headache for the Department of Militia and Defence. The War Purchasing Commission, for example, was caught off guard and did not discuss buying additional uniforms, let alone other equipment, until the end of January 1916. As late as 19 April 1916, contracts had not been let for the kit needed to provide for Hughes's increase announced in October 1915.[54]

With only 191,654 officers and men with the CEF at the end of December 1915, the new establishment announced by Prime Minister Borden was clearly unreasonable. After factoring in the average monthly wastage rate for 1915 (1,918 men), the CEF would have to enlist 26,613 recruits every month to reach Borden's goal by the end of 1916. Moreover, the Prime Minister did not concern himself with details such as the desired establishment for each corps. The result was, perhaps, inevitable. Recruiting depots had been created for non-infantry corps, but they were few in number, and the simplest way to meet the Prime Minister's goal was to create a large number of infantry battalions with the expectation that each would recruit its own men.

From November 1915 to July 1916, 181,438 men were enlisted in the CEF, a number that placed considerable strain on both Militia HQ and district headquarters – which had been given no warning of the increases. A recruiting officer was added to each district HQ in August 1916, but this had little effect since, in practice, the position was largely advisory.[55] In Toronto, Major-General Logie suggested in August 1916 that a system of deferred enlistment be adopted, patterned after the earlier Derby Scheme in Great Britain.[56] Militia HQ staff supported the idea, and in early September 1916 staff at Militia HQ submitted a proposal to the Adjutant-General calling for "enlistment for the CEF on a deferred basis, i.e., subject to call for training and service on notice of one, two or three months; the men remaining in their civilian occupations, but after medical examination and acceptance, receiving say twenty-five cents a day, to be paid when called and possibly receiving elementary training at night during the interim."[57]

The proposal was forwarded to districts for comment, but only four of the nine were in favour. By the end of October 1916 the idea was effectively dead. The concept might have been useful if it had been introduced to coincide with the increases announced in October 1915 and January 1916, but by the fall of 1916 there were not enough men to fill existing units. Deferring enlistment, therefore, did not make sense.

Recruiting men for the new battalions was complicated by Hughes's policy of allowing units to recruit outside of their parent district without coming under the command of the district commander concerned. The practice started in October 1915, when the Adjutant-General, probably at the behest of Hughes, announced that CEF battalions were free to recruit outside of their parent district with no reference to Militia HQ. District commanders involved were to be notified, but did not need to be consulted. The policy caused no end of confusion and animosity and was cancelled in March 1916. However, specialist units such as pioneer battalions, forestry units, and tunnelling companies were still allowed to recruit outside of their area, as were infantry units favoured by Hughes but described by the acerbic Director of Mobilization, Colonel (later Brigadier-General) Reginald Gwynn, as "marginally Gilt edged Infantry Battalions."[58]

Even though the number of units allowed to recruit outside of their parent district was limited, the policy still hampered local recruiting efforts. In December 1916, for example, HQ MD 11 in Victoria complained that seven battalions from outside of British Columbia were recruiting in Vancouver and Victoria: two from Winnipeg and the remainder from Brockville, Fredericton, Valcartier, Montreal, and Kingston.[59] Further east, Major-General Logie had the same concerns and in

December 1916 complained that six interlopers were recruiting in Toronto. Local recruiting drives were hampered, and Logie asked "that as many of these units as possible be asked to cease further recruiting in this District."[60] Despite these complaints it was not until Hughes resigned that the policy of allowing units to recruit in other areas was cancelled, and in January 1917 Militia HQ announced that units were forbidden to recruit outside of their parent district; local commanders were then able to restore some measure of control to the recruiting process.[61]

The confusion resulting from units recruiting in other districts was compounded by Hughes's willingness to accommodate local organizers. In October 1915, the 88th (New Brunswick) Battalion was renumbered as the 104th at the request of the peacetime 88th Irish Fusiliers in Victoria, who were raising a CEF battalion. The rationale for the 88th request was simply that numbering the CEF battalion to correspond with the militia regiment would boost recruiting by linking the peacetime militia with the new CEF unit.[62]

Hughes's indecisiveness also led to confusion. On 4 October 1915, he authorized the 90th Battalion to be recruited in Winnipeg, only to cancel this authorization two weeks later, on the 19th. Shortly afterward, on the 26th, he changed his mind and gave the go-ahead to raise the 90th.[63] Granted, there may have been good reason for this waffling, but it is not difficult to picture the confusion that it must have caused in Winnipeg.

Further east, in October 1915, Hughes authorized the 122nd Battalion to be raised in Simcoe County (MD 2). Lieutenant-Colonel D.M. Grant, Commanding Officer of the 35th Simcoe Foresters, moved quickly to open seven recruiting detachments; by the end of November he had recruited six hundred men. Hughes then decided that a new battalion should be raised further north, in the Muskoka District. Grant, who lived in the Muskoka District, was given command and transferred to the new unit together with the title "122nd Battalion." D.H. MacLaren, another officer from the 35th Simcoe Foresters, was then appointed Commanding Officer of the Simcoe Battalion, which was redesignated the 157th.[64] The effect of these changes on HQ MD 2 is unknown, but it must have been one of "order, counter-order, and disorder" – a state of affairs that no doubt hindered recruiting to some degree.

There were other problems as well. During the winter of 1915–16, recruits were billeted in their home town, provided that at least twenty-five or more locals enlisted.[65] The policy was probably the result of a general shortage of barrack accommodation, but there was also the hope that potential recruits would be attracted by the sight of local boys parading in uniform. The concept was well-intentioned but, inevitably, in some units, billeting areas were widely dispersed. The 151st Battalion in Alberta had men quartered in eleven communities, a state of affairs that lasted until the unit was concentrated at Sarcee in the spring of 1916.[66] The 119th Battalion in the Algoma District of northern Ontario was even worse off, with outlying detachments in fourteen communities spread out over two hundred miles. As the battalion historian later commented in May 1917,

> The administration of the B[attalio]n during the winter, while the detachments were billeted as before indicated, was very difficult. The labour entailed on the Paymaster was extreme in looking to the payment of the men and also of the battalion's monies. He was forced to travel by train and sleigh each month for 10 to 13 days in order to make the monthly pay. Has meant paying at all hours of the day and night and then moving on to the next detachment. In the extreme cold and weather [with] limited accommodation available the task was a heavy one. The same condition rendered the work of the staff in recruiting and inspecting detachments very arduous and difficult.[67]

There were some advantages to the policy of outlying detachments, however; in particular, the 135th Battalion historian thought that billeting troops in communities where there was no militia unit "undoubtedly helped recruiting to a considerable effect."[68] On the other hand, routine administration suffered. Recruiting was difficult to coordinate, training could not be closely supervised, and quartermasters had to struggle to supply the outlying detachments. Lastly, small detachments did not have medical officers or clerical staff to process recruits, and in many cases detachment officers (if there were any) were too junior to complete and approve attestation forms. The presence of uniformed troops may have attracted potential recruits, but delays created by administrative complications may have deterred some prospective recruits.

DISTRICT INVOLVEMENT

With the two increases to the CEF announced in October 1915 and January 1916 the number of enlistments increased steadily, reaching a peak of 33,960 men in March 1916. Combined with Hughes's management style, the result was chaos. New battalions were continually being created to draw in recruits, local organizers had no qualms about contacting Hughes directly with real or imagined grievances, and in many cases battalions not only competed with one another for recruits but also with units from outside of the district who had been given special dispensation by Hughes. In the end, a large number of men were enlisted in a remarkably short time, but only at the cost of bringing in thousands who were manifestly unfit and swamping reserve units in England.

District commanders tried to bring order to chaos, although each adopted a different solution. In Eastern Ontario, Brigadier-General Hemming noted in August 1916 that there were nine well-defined recruiting areas within his district, six of which had been assigned to newly formed battalions. Rather than shuffle the recruiting areas to suit existing units, Hemming requested that Militia HQ authorize three additional battalions. Not surprisingly, the request was turned down by an unsympathetic Adjutant-General, who suggested that he organize a generic depot battalion to recruit in the three unallocated areas.[69]

In Toronto, Headquarters MD 2 chose not to divide the city among the newly formed battalions, but to restrict unit recruiting campaigns to specific periods. The 123rd Battalion, for example, was allowed to recruit from December 6 to 26, 1915, and the 124th from 27 December 1915 to 18 January 1916. However, the system fell apart when the 134th and 166th were authorized and allowed to start recruiting as early as 12 January 1916. By the beginning of March 1916, five battalions in Toronto were competing for volunteers as well as three battalions in nearby Peel County, all of whom had no compunctions about recruiting in the city.[70] Under the circumstances, any attempt to allocate recruiting periods to each battalion was futile, particularly since outside units from other districts had been authorized by Hughes to recruit in Toronto. As late as December 1916, Major-General Logie complained that the 236th McLean Highlanders from Frederiction were recruiting in the city, although "my arrangement with the Commanding Officer was for him not to recruit in Toronto until after one month from the authorization of the 255th Overseas Battalion CEF."[71]

Headquarters MD 11 used several methods to control recruiting. In August 1916, for example, militia recruiters were instructed to operate only within their parent regiment's district. CEF units, on the other hand, could detail special recruiting parties to tour designated areas within the district.[72] Despite the apparent freedom given to CEF units, there was little competition for recruits. Admittedly, five battalions were recruiting simultaneously in Vancouver and Victoria, but three had specialized interests: the 143rd was a bantam battalion, the 211th was an American Legion battalion, and the 218th was composed of railway troops. The only real competition was in Vancouver, where both the 158th and the 231st Battalions were trying to build their strength.[73]

HQ MD 5 in eastern Quebec chose to divide the district into six recruiting areas, each manned by militia officers. However, the officers concerned proved to be inefficient, and in December 1915 battalions were assigned specific districts.[74] But with the departure of units for England in 1916, the recruiting structure fell apart and the district had to be reorganized with a Director of Recruiting to control district recruiting detachments.[75] Three primary district offices were established at Quebec City, Lévis and Rivière du Loup, with satellite offices at Chicoutimi and Grand-Mère. Travelling medical boards were also created, each with two Medical Corps doctors, to visit recruiting offices as necessary.[76]

In Alberta, HQ MD 13 allocated specific areas to battalions and then tried to suspend recruiting by new units until existing ones were full. In January 1916, the 113th Lethbridge Highlanders had enlisted 350 men after a three-month recruiting campaign. Despite this dismal showing, Hughes authorized two new battalions (the 191st and 192nd) to recruit in the same area as the 113th. Since there were now too many battalions chasing too few recruits, the district commander, Brigadier-General Cruikshank, recommended to Militia HQ that recruiting be deferred for the 191st and 192nd until the 113th was up to strength. But his efforts were unsuccessful, and Hughes directed that the 191st and 192nd continue recruiting.[77] Not surprisingly, none of these battalions reached full strength. The 113th sailed in September 1916 with 883 men, the 192nd in October 1916 with 424 men, and the 192nd followed in 1917 with a total of 316 men in two drafts.[78]

In some cases, battalions tried to impose controls on recruiting by individual companies. The 135th Battalion, for example, divided Middlesex County, Ontario, into company areas, with Middlesex East allocated to B Company. But Middlesex East was a rural area where only 10,666 males of all ages had been enumerated in the 1911 Census. B Company was therefore allowed to recruit in nearby London, where 21,901 males had been counted in 1911.[79] Other companies were apparently given the same privilege, and when the battalion embarked for England in August 1916, 496 men, or 54.5 per cent of the battalion, had been enlisted in London. Needless to say, recruiting for the 142nd (City of London's Own), which was restricted to London, suffered; that unit embarked for England on 31 October 1916 with only 574 men, 95 per cent of whom had been enlisted in the city.[80]

UNIT-BASED RECRUITING ENDS

Creating community-based battalions broadened the recruiting base with impressive results but, paradoxically, reduced recruiting. In brief, all of these units were organized as conventional battalions with establishments that did not provide for recruiting officers and NCOs. Recruiting, therefore, was done by officers and NCOs seconded from their platoons and sections. As long as the units remained at their home station conducting individual training, these individuals could be spared from their primary duties. But, in the spring of 1916, the new battalions were removed from their home stations and concentrated at central camps to conduct collective training from section to brigade level. Officers and NCOs employed on recruiting, therefore, had to return to their platoons and sections, which meant that recruiting was effectively halted.

The removal of battalions from their home stations in the spring of 1916 had a significant effect on recruiting. In March 1916, 33,960 men enrolled, and thereafter the numbers fell as battalions moved to central training camps: 20,200 in April, 14,572 in May, 10,059 in June, 7,961 in July, and 6,597 in August. Although there may have been other reasons for declining enrolments, a major cause was the removal of the battalions from their home bases, a point made by Brigadier-General Hemming of MD 3 in August 1916. "With reference to the 130th, 136th, 139th and 146th Battalions [from MD 3] at Valcartier," Hemming wrote to Militia HQ, "I have the honour to state that it is impossible to recruit men for these units in view of their present location."[81]

The 110th Battalion from Perth County, Ontario, enrolled 850 men between November 1915 and May 1916 while they were stationed in the County, but only 32 after the battalion was concentrated, first at London on 22 May 1916 and then at Camp Borden on 20 July 1916. Significantly, 21 of those enlisted after 22 May 1916 joined in London or Camp Borden, while only 11 were recruited in Perth County.[82] Further south, the 168th Battalion enrolled 674 men in 11 communities in Oxford County, Ontario, from January to the end of May 1916, when the unit was transferred, first to London and then to Camp Borden before embarking for England on 30 October 1916. Only 19 men were enlisted after the 168th left Oxford County, the majority (fourteen) at London or Camp Borden.

Similarly, the 107th Battalion in MD 10 recruited more than eleven hundred men during the winter of 1915–16 when it was based in Winnipeg, but only twenty-eight after the unit moved to Camp Hughes at the end of May 1916. In Saskatchewan, the diarist of the 232nd

Battalion remarked that with the unit's move to Camp Hughes on 20 July 1916, the battalion recruiting campaign had to be discontinued because "the movement [to Camp Hughes] necessitated the bringing in of all our men from outlying points."[83] The unit diarist did not exaggerate. Of the 450 men who sailed with the 232nd in April 1917, 380 had enlisted before the battalion went to Camp Hughes, while a further 17 joined before the unit moved to winter quarters at Battleford and North Battleford on 20 October 1916. Recruiting was resumed, but the momentum had been lost; only 53 additional volunteers joined the battalion before embarkation.

The policy of creating new battalions ended shortly after Hughes resigned his portfolio in mid-November 1916. His departure was not mourned at Militia HQ, particularly by Gwatkin, the Chief of Staff, who openly lamented the fact that "the lack of [a] well-regulated and firmly administered system of organization has interfered with the provision of reinforcements and impeded the upkeep of battalions overseas."[84] As early as 29 November 1916, only eighteen days after Hughes left, the Adjutant-General rejected a request for a new battalion in Selkirk, Manitoba, because if any new units "were raised, they would merely be draft-giving Depot Battalions."[85] A month later, in December 1916, the Director General of Mobilization, Brigadier-General Gwynne, recommended that a proposal to raise another battalion in New Brunswick be scotched, adding, "No new battalions have been raised [since] General Hughes left, and it would be fatal to once open the door again to do so."[86] Gwynne's recommendation was understandable, but the battalions being shipped to England as fast as troop ships could be organized constituted the infantry recruiting structure. Once they were gone, there was nothing.

REVAMPING THE SYSTEM

Both Militia HQ in Ottawa and the newly organized HQ of the Overseas Military Forces of Canada (OMFC) in London were well aware of the need for a new recruiting and reinforcing structure to replace the battalions being shipped overseas. There was an exchange of ideas between Major-General Gwatkin in Ottawa and Major-General Turner, the newly appointed General Officer Commanding Canadians in England. Both felt the infantry should be organized on a territorial basis with three linked battalions: a recruiting unit or depot in Canada, a training battalion in England, and a fighting battalion in France. The two differed only on the details: Turner recommended generic recruiting centres, while Gwatkin favoured militia units.[87]

Gwatkin's belief in the militia at this stage of the war was odd, but with the small staffs at Militia HQ and the district headquarters, creating a large-scale national recruiting organization would have taken time, whereas the militia was available immediately. Linking militia regiments to CEF battalions, Gwatkin thought, might boost recruiting. There was also the matter of the hard-won battle honours and achievements of CEF units that should be perpetuated in the post war army.[88] Others shared his faith in the militia; in January 1917, Colonel H. Osborne at Militia HQ wrote, "[O]ur greatest hope in the present situation lies in the Militia of Canada. Although dormant, with the exception of a few Regiments at the present time, it is a powerful agency, if wisely employed, not only for providing a defensive force, but also for furnishing recruits for Overseas."[89]

Gwatkin's faith in the militia seemed reasonable at the time, since a number of militia units had already succeeded in recruiting overseas contingents in 1915. Militia units had also raised drafts; in 1915, for example, the 79th Cameron Highlanders, 90th Winnipeg Rifles, and 34th Fort Garry Horse recruited six overseas drafts of about 250 men each. At the same time, the 66th Regiment in Halifax raised a draft of 250 men, while the 63rd, also from Halifax, formed 300-man drafts.

With these precedents in mind, Gwatkin circulated a proposal to Militia HQ staff on 15 January 1917 to use militia units as recruiting agencies. In brief, he noted that sixteen infantry regiments were already recruiting for the CEF and that an additional thirty-nine urban regiments should be invited to form "regimental depots with a view to raising and training reinforcements for service overseas."[90] There was no disagreement with the proposal at Militia HQ; three days later, districts were formally instructed to invite city regiments to form regimental depots to recruit and train drafts for the CEF overseas.[91]

Despite Gwatkin's optimism, expectations were not high. Regiments were expected to provide small drafts rather than company-sized drafts, which could take some time to recruit. In February 1917, the 43rd Regiment in MD 3 was allowed to form a regimental depot, but drafts were limited to one officer and fifty men.[92] Similarly, in April 1917, the 32nd Regiment in MD 1 was authorized to establish a depot in Walkerton, Ontario, to recruit reinforcements for the 160th (Bruce) Battalion, then serving with the 5th Division in England. However, as the Adjutant-General noted when he approved the new depot, "It is understood that if men are needed they will be sent over in batches of fifty under a lieutenant."[93]

The number of recruits obtained by the militia depots was disappointing. The 11th Regiment in Vancouver was able to find only fifty-one infantrymen, while in MD 1, as the District Commander reported in July 1917, six militia regiments had provided drafts but the number of recruits "is so small that it is impossible to train them separately and get satisfactory results."[94] The effort to maintain the regimental identity of the militia drafts was obviously a lost cause. In August 1917, Militia HQ directed that all recruits should be posted to the newly formed depot battalion in London and thus form part of the general reinforcement stream.[95]

Efforts were also made to use the militia to recruit men for the Canadian Defence Force (CDF), a hybrid force intended to find 50,000 men for home defence and encourage them to join the CEF. But there was little appetite in Canada for the CDF – and even less in England, where the War Office was concerned that the new force would siphon off potential recruits for the CEF.[96] It was widely expected from the start that the CDF would fail because the supply of volunteers had long since dried up. The CDF Director-General, Major-General S.C. Mewburn, for one, was "convinced that it will be impossible to raise 50,000 men for the Home Defence of Canada on the voluntary enlistment plan."[97] His sentiments were shared by the Commanding Officer of the 53rd Regiment in Sherbrooke, Quebec, who said flatly: "Compulsory training is the only way in which my Regiment can be gotten together."[98] In Winnipeg, the Commanding Officer of the 174th Battalion wrote to Militia HQ that "this latest scheme for mobilizing the Militia as the CDF is going to prove absolutely useless."[99] But the concerns were disregarded, since the CDF had a political as well as a military purpose. "It has not been made clear to me," wrote A.E. Kemp, the new Minister of Militia and Defence to the CDF Director-General in March 1917, "why we should proceed by force to enlist men for Home Defence ... without first proceeding in a voluntary way."[100]

As a recruiting venture, the CDF was a miserable failure. Forty-seven militia infantry regiments organized depots, but managed to enlist only 565 men for the CDF and 1,293 for the CEF after a three-month recruiting campaign. Some districts, such as MD 5 in eastern Quebec and MD 13 in British Columbia, found recruits for the CDF but not the CEF, while MD 6 in the Maritimes was unable to find volunteers for either component.[101] However, a few units were successful. By the end of June 1917, the 48th Highlanders in Toronto had found 133 recruits: 116 for the CEF and seventeen for home defence. Even so, the overall quality was poor. At least sixty-four volunteers had been rejected, a quarter of whom were both underage and medically unfit: boys such as Harry Brennan, an undersized, fifteen-year-old labourer with lung cancer, and seventeen-year-old Victor Callebert, who weighed only 95 pounds. Underage recruits, particularly for the home defence component, were also a problem. In June 1917, Lieutenant Haldenby of the 48th wrote: "We are to have a medical board examine the Depot on Wednesday and I think we will kiss the CDF good-by on Friday if they stick to the 18[-year-old] age limit."[102]

After three months of effort, it became apparent that few Canadians were willing to volunteer for the CDF. Recruiting was therefore suspended on 22 May 1917. However, militia depots continued to recruit for the CEF, and over the next three months the CEF recruits were transferred to the newly organized territorial depot battalions.[103]

As the CDF and the militia depots wound down, Militia HQ took stock of CEF manpower in Canada. The results were depressing. In May 1917, 6,407 men enlisted in the CEF but only 1,208 in the infantry. Figures for June 1917 were similar, with only 1,126 of 6,363 volunteers choosing the infantry. It was clear that the pool of able-bodied men in Canada willing to volunteer was virtually drained and that no recruiting organization that relied on volunteers, no matter how efficient, would be able to produce the numbers required. There was some relief when the British-Canadian Recruiting Mission was established in June 1917 and thousands of American residents joined the CEF, but this supply of manpower was dependent on the good will and co-operation of the US government. The only solution was conscription under the *Military Service Act*. However, calling men up was not the responsibility of the military but of the Military Service Branch of the Department of Justice. Thus, for the final year of the war, the Canadian Forces lost control of the principal recruiting mechanism.

CENTRALIZATION

Vital to the process of enlisting men were the conduct of medical examinations, the completion of documentation, and the issue of kit to the new recruits. Initially, this was done by militia regiments, or by CEF units, or by a combination of the two. In practice, this arrangement could not have been very efficient. It is doubtful, for example, that many militia units had adequate stocks of khaki service dress uniforms. CEF units, on the other hand, could draw from district ordnance stocks. But with the requirement to stock uniforms of various sizes, quartermasters inevitably held more uniforms than there were soldiers in the battalion. With the overall shortage of uniforms, it made no sense to allow units to maintain a surplus. Unit medical sections and orderly rooms, staffed to provide services to the unit, must also have been hard pressed at times to handle the influx of recruits. Inevitably, the CEF started in mid-1915 to centralize administrative recruiting functions.

The first recruiting depots were established in Toronto and Hamilton after the introduction of continuous recruiting in July 1915. The functions of these new depots as described at the time by the *Toronto Star* were straightforward:

> Recruiting is to go on even after the quotas for new units have been raised. According to the present plans, the [militia] regiments will continue to gather men as rapidly as possible and send them to the central and permanent recruiting stations which are to be opened. From the recruiting depot these men will be sent to Niagara in batches to be trained there until formed into battalions.[104]

Details of the actual process are sketchy, but in the case of the 48th Highlanders recruiters filled out a regimental form for each recruit with the data needed for documentation and then sent the man to the Recruiting Depot for medical examination, documentation, attestation, and issue of basic kit. In some cases, 48th staff also ensured that consent forms were completed by the next of kin of married men and minors.[105] Close ties were maintained between the depot and the militia units that provided the recruits. The Hamilton Recruiting Depot, for example, had eight companies to hold recruits: two for the infantry and the remaining six for the cavalry, artillery, engineers, Service Corps, and Medical Corps. Each company was affiliated with a specific militia unit.[106]

Other districts established recruiting centres as well. In Ottawa, the MD 3 Base Recruiting Office under Captain A.H. Thoburn opened on Sparks Street in August 1915 with a staff of one medical officer, a stenographer (Miss B. Thoburn), and four recruiting sergeants.[107] MD 1 followed in the fall of 1915 with a recruiting depot in London and the following year established a district office in Windsor as well as the 1st Hussars Recruiting Depot in Amherstburg, which despite its name processed recruits for all corps.[108]

Further west, in British Columbia, HQ MD 11 opened the Vancouver Recruiting Centre in the fall of 1915 under the command of Charles Grant Henshaw, a local commission merchant who retained his civilian status and was paid as a lieutenant-colonel.[109] His wife, Julia Willmothe Henshaw, was commissioned as a militia officer by Sam Hughes at the same time and was called out on a permanent basis as a captain with a vague mandate to promote recruiting. Captain Henshaw was later dismissed by the Militia Council in October 1917, largely because it was not apparent what she did or whom she reported to.[110] The Henshaws were, perhaps, the only officially sanctioned husband-and-wife recruiting team in either world war.

MD 10 under Brigadier-General H.N. Ruttan adopted a more systematic approach to recruiting and, in November 1915, with the approval of Militia HQ, established four "regimental areas" with headquarters in Winnipeg, Dauphin, Moose Jaw, and Prince Albert.[111] Each area was responsible for establishing outlying recruiting detachments and a central headquarters to process new recruits. For example, Recruiting Area "D" had eight detachments and a central headquarters in Prince Albert staffed by a quartermaster, medical officer, and adjutant, together with clerks and storemen. The remaining three areas were similar. Whether this would have been an efficient recruiting organization is unknown, since Hughes almost immediately authorized new battalions to recruit in the same areas. The four areas were therefore disbanded in February 1916 and the men used to provide the nucleus for the new battalions: 222nd (Area A), 226th (Area B), 188th (Area C), and 229th (Area D).[112]

By mid-1916, as discussed previously, the number of unfit men sent overseas had become a matter of serious concern, and Hughes appointed a newly commissioned Medical Corps officer, Colonel H.A. Bruce, as a "Special Inspector General" to investigate the situation in England. The matter was politically sensitive, and in August 1916, after reviewing a proposal from the Adjutant-General, Prime Minister Borden suggested to Hughes's parliamentary secretary that the Militia Council should establish mobilization centres across the country to ensure recruits were medically fit. Militia HQ reacted promptly, Hughes did not interfere (perhaps because he was in England), and three weeks later, on 12 September 1916, all districts were directed to form mobilization centres where recruits would be documented and medically examined.[113]

The new mobilization centres were intended mainly to ensure that recruits were medically fit. Medical examinations by unit medical officers and civilian physicians were regarded as preliminary, and the final decision regarding fitness was made at the mobilization centre. Each centre was to be commanded by a combatant officer with at least three medical officers, one of whom had to be an eye and ear specialist. Recruits determined to be fit would be returned to their parent unit, while those who were unfit would be compensated for their time and provided with free transportation home.[114]

In practice, districts were free to establish mobilization centres to suit local conditions as they saw fit. In October 1916, the newly formed MD 12 (Saskatchewan) created a total of eight centres across the province, while MD 11 (British Columbia) considered that centres were required only in Vancouver and Victoria. On the other hand, MD 5 (Eastern Quebec) was made up chiefly of rural parishes, and from March 1917 onward recruits were processed at the Recruiting Depot in Quebec City.[115]

In MD 2, four mobilization centres were formed to service specific regions. The Toronto Mobilization Centre handled Peel, York, Simcoe, Halton, Norfolk, Ontario, Dufferin, and Grey Counties as well as the District of Muskoka, while the Hamilton Mobilization Centre processed recruits from Wentworth, Dundas, Brant, and Haldimand Counties. Smaller offices were established in Sudbury to handle recruits from Northern Ontario, and in St Catharines to process volunteers from the Niagara Peninsula. Temporary mobilization centres were also formed as necessary, and a detachment operated in Owen Sound from April to June 1917 to process recruits for the 248th Battalion.[116]

Mobilization centres could be large organizations. In June 1917, the Toronto centre was staffed by 102 officers and men together with twenty female clerks. The Sudbury Mobilization Centre was much smaller, but in June 1918 was staffed by nine officers and men and one female clerk, as well as by two NCOs and ten men to escort recruits to a Toronto depot battalion.[117]

Each mobilization centre was, no doubt, organized differently, but in Toronto there were four sections. The administrative section provided for the needs of the individual recruit and consisted of the Main Orderly Room, with Commanding Officer, adjutant, paymaster, and clerks, as well as quartermaster stores and an attestation room with six clerks. Another section was responsible for medical examinations and consisted of thirteen "boards," each with a medical officer and an orderly. Lastly, there was a special duties section headed by the sergeant-major and a general duties section staffed with eight soldiers who looked after routine fatigues.[118]

On 1 January 1918, the first group of draftees was called up under the *Military Service Act* (MSA) to augment the 458,533 men who had volunteered previously. These men were not called up by the military but by the Military Service Branch of the Department of Justice created to administer the MSA. Recruiting was now a civil and not a military responsibility. However, the Military Service Branch handled only draftees; volunteers and men provided by the British-Canadian Recruiting Mission in the United States continued to be processed by the military.

The division of responsibility for recruiting suggests a lack of confidence in the ability of the CEF to handle draftees. However, there is no evidence that this was the case, and it entirely possible that Canada chose to follow Great Britain, where responsibility for calling out and processing conscripts had been transferred from the War Office to the Ministry of National Service in August 1917.[119] The change had been debated in the British House of Commons for some time before this, and since Canada looked to Britain as a model, there is no doubt that Canadian parliamentarians were well aware of the debate.

SUMMARY

Recruiting was not simply a matter of public rallies, strident news reports, patriotic posters, women with white feathers, and recruiting sergeants on every street corner. It was also a complex military process organized and controlled by the military. Initially, the process was simplistic and inefficient, but by 1917 an efficient, well-structured, and centralized organization was in place that served the CEF well. From an amateur beginning, the CDF developed into a highly professional structure.

In essence, recruiting was the means by which the CEF tapped the national manpower pool. Finding these men was one thing, but they also had to be trained to do their new job. This was no easy matter, since there was a chronic shortage of weapons and equipment, very little by way of an infrastructure in Canada, and no training organization in England, the CEF's overseas staging base. It took time for an efficient training structure to evolve in both Canada and England; how this occurred is the central theme of chapter 6.

6

Infantry Training

"The object to be aimed at in the training of the infantry soldier," noted *Infantry Training 1914*, the standard textbook used by thousands of Canadian officers and NCOs during the war, was "to make him, mentally and physically, a better man than his adversary on the field of battle."[1] This was far easier said than done.

Training was – and still is – a complex process shaped by a multitude of factors. First, there was the material taught, a matter overlooked by most historians. With the exception of the 1st Division's hurried training on Salisbury Plain in 1914–15, Canada was content to follow the British lead, albeit with modifications to suit local conditions. Second were the resources needed to conduct training: weapons, equipment, clothing, and facilities. These were inevitably in short supply, not only in England but even more acutely in Canada, where the CEF had to draw mainly from pre-war militia resources. Third, the challenge of producing trained soldiers who could fit into any infantry battalion implied a need for common standards, but such standards were possible only with a strong, central HQ. In Canada, Militia HQ managed for the most part to retain control of training. However, in England there was no effective Canadian military HQ until the ministry of the OMFC was created in December 1916. Not surprisingly, training suffered and the standard of infantry reinforcements posted to France ranged from poor to good. And, last, certain administrative measures hampered training. In Canada, seeding and harvesting furloughs wreaked havoc on training schedules, especially in rural units, while, in England, fatigues and garrison duties extended training well beyond the time it should have taken to complete the prescribed syllabus.

TRAINING DOCTRINE

From November 1914 onward, CEF training was based on British doctrine issued with Army Orders (AOs), War Office Instructions (WOIs), and Army Council Instructions (ACIs). Despite this, the First Contingent in 1914 devised its own training program, perhaps because it was assumed that the majority of men were trained militiamen.

First Contingent training at Valcartier in August and September 1914 was sketchy; this is not surprising, given the hasty and confused mobilization of militia units across the country. Composite units had to be organized and, in some cases, reorganized. Equipment and uniforms had to be issued, men had to be medically examined and attested, and formal parades with the inevitable rehearsals took up time that, as veteran Peter Anderson remarked, "might have been spent to better advantage."[2]

The improvised concentration at Valcartier also created organizational problems that diverted attention from training, as Lieutenant-Colonel Leckie, Commanding Officer of the 16th Battalion, commented in September 1914:

> Most of my time has been taken up here with organization. It has been quite a job to collect and organize units in this Camp. Most of the Organization should have taken place at Home Stations and this would have been done had we been furnished with the information necessary. Had we been able to bring into Camp so many Companies [at] full war strength with the proper complement of officers there would have been far less trouble.[3]

Training before departure for England was severely limited. Infantrymen were able to shoot, but only fifty rounds were available for each man. Not surprisingly, as Major Peter Anderson of the 9th Battalion commented, this yielded "poor results; it is impossible to train wholesale raw recruits to shoot."[4] There were drill classes and a number of route marches, but there was virtually no tactical training – with the exception of two short outpost exercises at night.[5] There was no comprehensive training plan, and the general consensus of those mobilized at Valcartier was that "[l]ittle useful training was conducted."[6] Artillery officer Major Leonard wrote that "[t]he Valcartier camp was an absolute waste of money and no one can have a very good idea of the vast sums squandered unless they had an opportunity of looking at things somewhat from the inside."[7]

In October 1914, the First Contingent arrived in England, and after a brief interlude to sort out baggage problems, started training in earnest on Salisbury Plain. However, the training plan was not published by Contingent HQ until 14 November 1914.[8] The plan followed a logical sequence, with three distinct phases: individual, subunit (company or squadron), and combined arms training at brigade and division level. Insofar as the infantry was concerned, they expected to devote four weeks to individual training, five weeks to company training, two weeks to battalion training, and two weeks to brigade and division training.[9]

The 1st Canadian Division had less time to prepare for battle than Territorial divisions, the British equivalent to the militia. The CEF infantry individual training plan, for example, was only four weeks, while the British AO 388 called for ten weeks. The origin of the plan is uncertain, although the official historian later wrote that the plan had been tailored to meet operational requirements after "[t]he degree of preparedness of the troops [had] been gauged."[10] However, there is no evidence that the level of training was systematically assessed. The fact that more time was devoted to collective rather than individual entry-level training suggests that Lieutenant-General Alderson, the divisional commander, felt that his men had mastered the basics and needed only a final polish before deploying to Flanders.

Training was not progressive, as set out in the official plan, which raises the question of how effective it was. A divisional exercise, for example, was staged on 27 November 1914 during the individual training phase, while another was scheduled but cancelled on 11 December because of rain. In theory, both exercises should have been held in January 1915. In the 2nd Brigade, battalion-level collective training started on 1 December and company training on 5 December, two days before the official start of the five-week company syllabus. The 1st Brigade, on the other hand, started battalion-level training on 28 December 1914 and brigade training on 4 January 1915.[11] According to the master training plan, battalion training should have started in January 1915. To be effective, training must be progressive. The soldier has to learn his basic job before mastering more complex and sophisticated training. In practice, the 1st Division plan did not do this, which calls into question whether individual soldiers were adequately trained for battle.

Apart from the lack of progressive training, bad weather and the need to provide work parties played havoc with the training program. The 16th Battalion lost two of its four days on the ranges because of snow and mist, while the 15th Battalion spent two months as common labourers.[12] Other battalions had similar problems.

First Contingent training problems did not go unnoticed by British authorities. On 16 December 1914, Lewis Harcourt, the Colonial Secretary, no doubt retailing Whitehall gossip, wrote to Lord Kitchener, the Secretary of State for War:

> I had not time yesterday to complete what I wanted to say to you about the Canadians on Salisbury Plain. I fancy that the real complaint is that they are going back in their training from that which they received at Valcartier. There they had regular shooting practice and went out for two or three days' manoeuvring under regular service conditions. On Salisbury Plain they have none of this and owing to the condition of the soil, they cannot even learn to trench. I have wondered whether it would not be possible to break up the contingent and train them in different places with the better portions of your new army. I do not believe that you will ever dare to use them as a single unit together at the front, though I should think that some of them might be fit to go there in small numbers even now.[13]

Nor was the War Office pleased with 1st Division training. In March 1915, Colonel Carson at Canadian HQ in London wrote to Colonel MacDougall of the newly created Canadian Training Division (CTD) at Shorncliffe, who had previously complained that the 23rd (British) Division had been charged with supervising his training program. "Frankly speaking, I may tell you that you are to a certain extent being punished for Salisbury Plain results," wrote Carson. "The War Office were requested not to interfere with the training of our 1st Division and did not do so, and were not satisfied with results."[14]

Was the 1st Division adequately trained when it deployed to Flanders? The evidence is uncertain, but a brief review of the British army in 1914–15 provides a basis for comparison. Broadly speaking, there were two distinct types of British battalions in 1914–15, apart from the regular army. The first were Territorials: similar to the militia, they relied on part-time soldiers and, in the event of war, required six months' training before deployment.[15] Unlike militia units, Territorial battalions were almost full strength. The Civil Service Rifles, for example, mobilized on 5 August 1914 with 849 pre-war volunteers and needed only 150 recruits to reach full strength.[16] The second type were the "New Army" battalions created after the outbreak of war; made up of raw recruits, they were led by a small number of experienced officers and NCOs.[17] Naturally, it took longer to train the latter than the former. The first Territorial division, the 46th (North Midland) Division, deployed to Flanders six months after mobilization, while the first New Army division, the 14th (Light), arrived in May 1915, eight months after mobilization.

If the 1st Division was largely made up of militiamen and others with former military service, then it received about the same amount of training as the Territorials before deploying to Belgium. On the other hand, if the division was made up largely of men with no former service, then it was on the same footing as New Army divisions and was not adequately trained by British standards.

In theory, the First Contingent consisted of experienced men, since it was drawn from militia units and ex-soldiers. One historian has concluded that about 50 per cent of the Contingent had some form of military training.[18] Another has noted: "Given the substantial number of former soldiers in its ranks 1st Division could claim to have the experience level of a Territorial division."[19] On the other hand, Colonel Duguid, the official historian and First Contingent veteran, wrote that "a large number [of the volunteers at Valcartier] were men of no training or military experience."[20] More recently, Desmond Morton has commented that "the crowds of men who jammed into the armories [in 1914] were neither militia nor even Canadian-born."[21]

The only means of determining the experience level of the 1st Division are attestation papers that required men to note whether they belonged to the militia and to declare any former service. Regulations required former soldiers to produce their discharge papers, but it appears that in many cases the attesting officers were content to accept the man's claim. The accuracy of statistical evidence of former service is therefore dependent on the honesty of the individual soldiers.

Anecdotal evidence suggests that some recruits were less than truthful. Harold Baldwin of the 5th Battalion, for example, admitted in his memoirs that he had no military experience but said he was an ex-British army regular when he reported to the Saskatoon armoury in August 1914. A month later, at Valcartier, he claimed to be a former member of the British Territorial Army.[22] Neither statement would have been accepted had he been required to produce discharge papers. Baldwin was not alone. A search of British archives for the discharge papers of forty-nine men who claimed to have been regular soldiers in the British Army turned up seventeen records – about 35 per cent.[23] Most had been civilians for more than five years, which calls into question their proficiency; one had been discharged as medically unfit; another had been discharged with ignominy; and the last had been declared "worthless and incorrigible" in 1901. The sample is not statistically conclusive, but suggests that claims of former service based solely on attestation papers should be viewed with some skepticism.

Many of those who were attested at Valcartier in September 1914 claimed to be serving militiamen. These men may have been truthful, since militia units were responsible for sending men to Valcartier, but it is likely that many joined the militia after the war broke out and were thus raw recruits. Of the 224 men provided to the 6th Battalion by the 34th Fort Garry Horse, fifty-two claimed to be members of the Regiment. However, only twenty-three were pre-war militiamen; the remainder joined after the war broke out.[24] In Ontario, only thirty-five of the hundred volunteers provided by the 24th Kent Regiment were current or former members of the regiment, while thirteen of the fifty-seven volunteers from the 22nd Oxford Rifles were pre-war militiamen.[25]

A survey of the volunteers provided by the 25th Elgin Regiment of St Thomas, Ontario, illustrates the pitfalls of relying on data from attestation papers. Of the ninety-eight men who volunteered for the CEF in August 1914, seventy-six had joined the regiment after the outbreak of war. Of the remaining twenty-two volunteers, ten had joined in the spring of 1914 and had therefore not completed any training at summer camp.[26] In a word, only 12 per cent of the volunteers from the 25th were adequately trained by militia standards. CEF attestation papers were found for forty-three of those who joined the militia after the outbreak of war. Half (twenty-two) claimed they were not serving in the militia, while twenty-one claimed they were. Moreover, some of those who joined after the war broke out were less than truthful. Private Glanville Harrison, for example, joined the 25th on 11 August 1914. But, when he was attested at Valcartier on 25 September 1914, he claimed to have been a member of the 25th since 1913. The sample is too small and specific to be conclusive, but a survey of peacetime pay lists for other militia units suggests these men were not exceptional (see table 6.1).

The evidence seems clear: the majority of men in the First Contingent were raw recruits in the same position as the British New Armies, where newly recruited infantrymen were expected to complete the ten-week syllabus specified in AO 388 of 13 September 1914 before progressing to collective training.[27] The difference between the New Armies and the First Contingent is startling. The Canadian infantryman received (in

Table 6.1 Militia volunteers, August 1914

Militia regiment	Province	Peacetime training strength*	Serving militiamen at Valcartier†	Serving militiamen who volunteered, %
72nd	B.C.	341	94	27.6
79th	Man.	470	105	22.3
5th	Que.	1,008	208	20.6
103rd	Alta.	231	45	19.5
50th	B.C.	217	36	16.6
106th	Man.	506	84	16.6
2nd	Ont.	1,184	191	16.1
104th	B.C.	437	50	11.4
25th	Ont.	219	22	10.0
105th	Sask.	506	52	10.3
9th Horse	Ont.	211	20	9.5
25th Dragoons	Ont.	263	22	8.4
71st	N.B.	473	38	8.0
7th	Ont.	294	23	7.8
43rd	Ont.	593	31	5.2
97th	Ont.	318	15	4.1
26th	Ont.	330	13	3.9
73rd	N.B.	449	13	2.9
9th	Que.	458	13	2.8
82nd	P.E.I.	420	8	1.9
Total		8,928	1,083	12.1
Percentage of the peacetime training strength with no former service				81.7

* Figures in column 3 have been taken from the last pre-war pay list.
† Column 4 lists the number who reported to Valcartier.

Sources: Colonel A. Fortescue Duguid, *Official History of the Canadian Forces in the Great War 1914–1919: Chronology, Appendices and Maps* (Ottawa: King's Printer, 1938), Appendix 85, 54–7. Peacetime data have been drawn from pay lists for annual training in LAC, RG 9, II F6, vols 216 (9th Mississauga Light Horse), 222 (25th Brant Dragoons), 22 (2nd Queen's Own Rifles), 30 (5th Regiment), 36 (7th Fusiliers), 42 (9th Voltigeurs), 76 (25th Regiment) 112 (43rd Ottawa and Carleton Rifles), 125 (50th Highlanders), 164 (71st York Regiment), 165 (72nd Seaforth Highlanders of Canada), 166 (73rd Northumberland Regiment), 176 (79th Camerons), 179 (82nd Abegweit Light Infantry), 196 (97th Algonquin Rifles), 200 (103rd Calgary Rifles), 200 (104th Westminster Fusiliers), 201 (106th Winnipeg Light Infantry and 105th Saskatoon Fusiliers), 78 (26th Middlesex Light Infantry). Most militia regiments in Nova Scotia were called out for home defence duties and are excluded from this sample. The 26th Regiment trained in 1913 but not in 1914. The 7th Fusiliers pay list for 1914 appears to exclude volunteers with the First Contingent; pay lists for the period 17 March to 24 October 1913 were used in lieu. Names on the pay lists were checked against embarkation rolls of the composite battalions that unit contingents joined on arrival at Valcartier.

theory) 162 hours of individual training, while his British counterpart received 441 hours. Granted, there were several weeks of training before the Canadian syllabus came into effect on 14 November 1914, but the length of training was still woefully short of the contemporary British standard.

Despite the abbreviated training program, the 1st Division went on to acquit itself well at the Second Battle of Ypres in April 1915. This may reflect three factors: the familiarization training conducted in February and March 1915 by British units already in the line; the fact that Ypres was a defensive battle with little manoeuvre warfare; and the skill and initiative of Canadian officers, many of whom had served in the pre-war militia.[28]

In contrast to the First Contingent, units in Canada used British training plans from November 1914 onward, when Militia HQ directed districts to use the infantry syllabus set out in AO 324 of 21 August 1914. In keeping with peacetime practices, districts were given "complete liberty of action in regard to the training."[29] AO 324 set out a gruelling schedule with ten six-day weeks of training for almost nine hours a day; this was unrealistic, as no time was allocated for routine matters such as meals and maintenance of weapons, personal equipment, and living quarters. Perhaps for this reason, AO 324 was not in use for long, and by February 1915 MD 13 was using the ten-week syllabus issued with AO 388 of 13 September 1914.[30] AO 324 and 388 set the trend, and for the rest of the war CEF units in Canada and England relied on British training programs.

That being said, given its emphasis on drill and extended order training AO 388 was out of touch with trench warfare; in June 1915, WOI 156 was issued with a revised ten-week syllabus for the infantry that was more suited to conditions at the front. The time allocated to both drill and extended order training was dramatically reduced, field work and bayonet fighting were increased, and wiring and bombing were added to the program. Conspicuous by its absence was training in gas warfare training, despite the German gas attack at Ypres almost two months earlier. Presumably, this was taught by base depots in France, which were required to issue respirators to all drafts from 29 May 1915 onward.[31]

The syllabus published in WOI 156 was used by the CEF in Canada by early 1916. In MD 10, for example, the 100th Battalion based its training in the spring of 1916 on the ten-week syllabus used in Britain.[32] Further east, in MD 6, the 112th Battalion, quartered in nine communities during the winter of 1915–16, had difficulties coordinating training; however, "[a]s nearly as possible, in the circumstances, the syllabus ordained by the War Office was adhered to."[33]

In England, the British Inspector of Infantry noted in September 1915 that reserve battalions with the CTD at Shorncliffe were using the syllabus from WOI 156. There were, however, some Canadian modifications. For example, in November 1915 the 8th Canadian Reserve Brigade adopted a syllabus similar to WOI 156, but with a twenty-six-hour reduction in drill, a thirty-six-hour reduction in physical training, and a twenty-six-hour increase in musketry. In keeping with WOI 156, there was no gas warfare training. Overall, recruits in the 8th Reserve Brigade were trained for forty-nine fewer hours than their British counterparts.[34]

The ten-week infantry syllabus was replaced by a fourteen-week training program issued in May 1916 as ACI 1103. The rationale for the new program is unknown, but evidently the War Office felt that infantry recruits required a more comprehensive course. ACI 1103 introduced a new concept: recruits were given two weeks of preliminary training before starting the syllabus in earnest. Subjects taught during preliminary training were not specified, but probably included the fitting and care of personal equipment and clothing, physical training, introductory drill, basic hygiene, and customs of the service. The remainder of the syllabus saw an increase in marching order drill, physical training, route marching, and bayonet fighting. For the first time, there was gas warfare training.[35]

ACI 1103 did not last long, however, and was replaced by a new fourteen-week syllabus issued with ACI 1968 in October 1916. More emphasis was placed on entrenching (forty-five hours), bayonet fighting (fifty-four hours), and field work (fifty-four hours). Wiring and bombing was increased to thirty-three hours, and there were also twelve hours of gas warfare training.[36]

Further refinements followed in August 1917 with ACI 1230, which reduced bombing and entrenching by twenty-three hours but added twenty-four hours of training with the Lewis machine gun or rifle grenade. ACI 1230 also included an imaginative field exercise with live ammunition, to teach recruits the use of the rifle on the battlefield –including fire and movement. The exercise was intended for men armed with rifles and bayonets, but, as the ACI noted, "[a]t a later stage, when all ranks are proficient with the rifle and bayonet, the use of Lewis guns, rifle bombs and bombs may be introduced."[37] Whether all infantrymen had the benefit of this training is unknown, although in October 1918, 4,312 trainees at Bramshott, Witley, and Seaford completed the program.[38]

By 1917, most infantry battalions in Canada were following the British fourteen-week syllabus issued with ACI 1968 in October 1916. In Eastern Ontario, HQ MD 3 reported in January 1917 that the 207th Battalion had completed the fourteen-week syllabus, with the exception of a few recruits who had just started training.[39] In March 1917, an inspector commented on training by the 236th Battalion in MD 6, where the "War Office Syllabus 1968 is being closely followed."[40] Summer training that year in both MD 10 and MD 1 was also based on ACI 1968. In August 1917, the requirement to use the fourteen-week syllabus was formalized by Militia Order 236.[41] As the CGS explained to the Minister of Militia and Defence in July 1917, "The 'fourteen weeks' as it called, was adopted for use in Canada by special request of the overseas authorities."[42]

In England, Canadian reserve battalions were quick to adopt the fourteen-week syllabus, and in June 1916 a report on the 95th Battalion at Shorncliffe noted that two companies "will be given the complete course under the new syllabus."[43] By November 1916, infantry training at Shorncliffe was based on ACI 1968, and at Bramshott a modified version of ACI 1968 was adopted in March 1917.[44]

The fourteen-week syllabus may have been the ideal, but comprehensive training was subordinate to the need to provide reinforcements. By March 1918 there was a shortage of about 282,000 infantrymen in the BEF, in part because of Prime Minister Lloyd George's decision to withhold reinforcements to stop any repetition of the costly battles of Third Ypres in 1917.[45] Most of the forty-eight British divisions in France were reduced from twelve battalions to nine; at the end of February 1918 the 55th (British) Division, for example, was able to muster only 9,115 infantrymen – as compared with Canadian divisions, which had more than 12,000 each.[46] As long as the Western Front was quiet, the manpower shortage was worrisome but did not present an immediate problem. However, on 21 March 1918 the Germans launched a series of massive attacks. The British 5th Army was driven back in disarray, and the reinforcement system in France was drained of all available infantry reinforcements. These men could be replaced only by stripping reserve battalions in England.

On 24 March 1918, the War Office issued instructions that all available trained infantrymen were to be prepared for immediate dispatch to France. Naturally, this included CEF units in England even though the Canadian Corps itself had not been caught up in the German offensive. The following day, HQ OMFC, obviously anticipating the need to provide large drafts to the Corps, issued a revised infantry syllabus that reduced training to only nine weeks.[47]

The nine-week syllabus required only 368 hours – that is, 250 fewer hours than the fourteen-week syllabus. Marching order drill, extended order drill, night work, field work, and bombing were eliminated, while drill was reduced by twenty-nine hours, entrenching by twenty-three hours, and bayonet fighting by forty-eight hours. Curiously, musketry was increased by eight hours and gas training by one hour.

The new syllabus remained in effect for the remainder of the war, although in July 1918 the General Staff at HQ OMFC reported that few reinforcements had been demanded by the Canadian Corps and that "[i]t has, therefore, been possible to extend the period of training and to train on until reinforcements are required."[48] Even so, the shortened syllabus was still used, although neither HQ OMFC nor the Canadian Corps were satisfied with the results. On 14 September 1918, Canadian Corps HQ notified the Canadian representative at GHQ 3rd Echelon that graduates of the shortened course should not be sent forward, while at the same time HQ OMFC wired the Corps that the shortened program was "considered unsound and information required as to whether necessity for this action still exists. Consider fourteen weeks be completed in England."[49]

The difficulties of reverting to the fourteen-week syllabus become apparent when strength returns are considered. Assuming a steady supply of drafts from Canada, about 29 per cent of all infantry trainees in England should have been in weeks eleven to fourteen. On 5 August 1918, however, 22.4 per cent had completed more than ten weeks of training, which suggests that many of the trainees had completed the fourteen-week syllabus. However, this proportion dropped dramatically with the need to replace the unprecedented wastage of the Hundred Days. On 21 September 1918, a week after OMFC voiced concerns with the shortened syllabus, only 3.2 per cent of all infantry trainees had completed more than ten weeks of training. The proportion continued to decline thereafter with the need to rush reinforcements to France, and on 9 November 1918 only 2.2 per cent of CEF infantry recruits in England had finished more than ten weeks of training.[50] The fourteen-week syllabus could have been restored in September 1918, but only if the flow of reinforcements was stopped for five weeks – a course of action that would have been completely unacceptable given the continuing advance of the Allied armies.

The effect of the reduction of training from fourteen weeks to nine is impossible to quantify in the absence of specific accounts. Perhaps the nine-week trainees received additional training – but where? Divisional wings at the Canadian Corps Reinforcement Camp (CCRC) routinely conducted training for reinforcements waiting to be drafted to their units, and battalions conducted training as a matter of course when they were rotated out of the front lines. It is also probable that the old hands with each battalion took the nine-week men in hand and taught them their trade on the job, so to speak. But with 8,619 infantry reinforcements arriving in August and another 10,614 arriving in September 1918, it seems likely there were some who did not receive much more than nine weeks of training.[51]

Tactics, weapons, and organizations in the various British Empire armies were not static. In 1914, the infantry was largely an unvariegated mass of riflemen manoeuvring by companies, but by 1917 the infantryman was a highly trained specialist accustomed to manoeuvring in sections and platoons equipped with grenades, rifle grenades, and Lewis guns, not only in conventional operations but also in a chemical environment. ACI 1868 and 1230 included all of these elements. Training had kept pace with technology on the Western Front, and infantrymen were now specialists in their own right.

DEVELOPMENT OF ASSESSMENT STANDARDS

By 1917 a series of comprehensive and well-thought-out training programs had been established for men with reserve units in England. But merely attending one of these programs did not mean the recruit fully understood the material that was taught or that instruction was adequate. With this in mind, a series of tests was devised by the War Office to ensure a minimum standard of training.

Initially, there were no formal training standards except for musketry. The General Musketry Course (GMC), which recruits were expected to pass, was not only a good test of basic shooting skills, but was also a comprehensive training program with clearly defined expectations. The trainee fired a total of 140 rounds at ranges varying from 100 to 600 yards in a variety of scenarios: deliberate, rapid, and snap-shooting. The GMC also offered flexibility, with parts I and II providing the basics and parts III and IV giving a final polish. Part IV of the GMC, intended for the infantry, required men to fire twenty-five rounds from a trench at an advancing target, a realistic practice that approximated actual conditions on the Western Front. The infantryman who completed parts I to IV of the GMC as well as the field firing specified in ACI 1230 of 6 August

1917, therefore, was not only well trained in basic musketry skills, but was also well schooled in shooting in combat situations.

Formal training standards for other subjects were introduced in August 1917. The standards were fairly general at first. Lewis gunners, for example, were initially required only to pass elementary handling tests, but in 1918 they had to be able to bring the gun into action within ten seconds, change the magazine in three seconds, and fill the magazine in ninety seconds. Other tests were equally specific. All infantry recruits had to pass the rapid wiring test, in which they worked as part of a team, consisting of one NCO and nine men, capable of erecting a fifty-yard length of standard French wire within fifteen minutes.[52]

Standards were also modified to reflect conditions in France. Testing in August 1917 included the cloth "PH" anti-gas helmet, but testing in 1918 did not, since by then the helmet had been phased out. Standards were also tightened up so they were more appropriate to actual conditions in the front lines. In 1917 infantry recruits had to wear the small box respirator for thirty minutes. A year later, recruits wearing fighting order and steel helmets had to don the respirator for two continuous periods of two hours of movement, one by day and one by night. These standards were not administrative requirements that reserve units were free to ignore. From August 1917 onward a certificate of qualification was pasted into the pay-book of every man drafted to France.[53]

Standards were a matter of concern for the base depots in France that handled reinforcements. In February 1915, for example, the 2nd (British) General Base Depot in France found it necessary to borrow two 18-pounders to train artillery reinforcements, some of whom had not been taught basic gun drills.[54] Infantry drafts had similar problems, and by September 1915 GHQ had posted instructors to every infantry base depot in France to ensure that reinforcements were adequately trained.[55] By February 1917, the routine at the base depots included refresher training and testing conducted by one of five base training schools, or "Bull Rings," as they were nicknamed.

Training schools were physically demanding. As John Becker, en route to the 75th Battalion in May 1917, later wrote:

> On Saturday May 5th Reveille was at 5:30 and immediately after Breakfast we marched 2 miles to the great training area known to all troops going through Le Havre, as the "Bull Ring." The day was stifling hot and we carried all equipment including helmets, gas masks and rifles. At the "Bull Ring" we went through the most strenuous

training I had yet experienced. We did everything a soldier would do under active service conditions except dodge shells and bullets.[56]

The course conducted at the base training school lasted nine days and was devoted primarily to essential skills required on the battlefield. Each of the subjects covered consisted of a review session followed by group testing under the supervision of experienced officers and NCOs seconded from divisions serving in France.* Reinforcements who failed the tests were not returned to England but were given remedial training.[57]

The training conducted by the base training schools had distinct advantages, as the British Inspector of Infantry noted in November 1917: "I do not think the system can be improved. It economizes instructors, relegates the instruction in each subject to competent hands and brings the recruit on very rapidly to the highest state of efficiency." Nevertheless, the Inspector sounded a note of caution: "The general tendency is to regard that test as final and to consider the man trained when [he] has passed it, in other words, to train for tests and not for war."[58] The Inspector did not comment, but with men being trained in batches of a thousand, monitoring individual progress must have been difficult if not impossible.

Although the base training school was a useful tool to ensure that reinforcements were sufficiently well trained, forward units complained that drafts were unduly delayed at the base depot. The Australian official historian wrote: "The delay thus imposed was often exasperating both to the drafts and to the commanders who had need of them. Moreover as a rule the sort of training really required by the drafts was inurement to war conditions which could be acquired near the front."[59] The Canadians were also concerned, and in July 1918 General Currie thought the base depot should be a staging camp: "I am not in favour of running another training establishment at the Base," Currie wrote, "as I do not see how it can be properly supervised."[60] Despite these concerns, the base depots were retained until the end of the war, when they became, as Currie had hoped, staging bases for troops returning to England.

---

* The subjects taught were weapons handling, musketry, grenade throwing, bayonet fighting, gas warfare, trench relief by day and night, drill, physical training, skirmishing, rapid wiring, judging distance, fire control orders, patrolling, entrenching, and route marching.

TRAINING RESOURCES: WEAPONS AND AMMUNITION

Comprehensive training programs that gave recruits the essential tools needed for the Western Front did not guarantee that men were well trained. Much depended on the resources available for training: weapons, ammunition, equipment, and facilities. Nor can administrative factors be overlooked.

Soldiers were expected to handle their weapons instinctively and to deliver a high volume of accurate fire in the face of an enemy assault, even at night or when cold rain or frost made fingers numb and unresponsive. "A man cannot be taught these things in a day," remarked the Chief Musketry Officer at Valcartier in 1915.[61] A man trained on one type of rifle could not readily use another type on the battlefield without some form of conversion training.

The British (and later Canadians) relied on the Short Magazine Lee-Enfield rifle (SMLE), a well-designed rifle with a ten-round magazine loaded with chargers. Only the Canadian Ross Mark III was comparable. The remaining rifles in the Canadian inventory could not be loaded with chargers and were thus obsolete and unfit for use on the battlefield. Moreover, the magazines of the Ross Marks I and II held only five rounds. Clearly, a high volume of fire was impossible with these rifles.

Ammunition was also a matter of concern. The SMLE and Ross Mark III were both designed to fire the Mark VII .303 cartridge. The Lee-Enfield Mark I and the Ross Mark I and II were intended to fire the Mark VI .303 cartridge. The difference between the two rounds was significant. The Mark VII bullet was lighter than the Mark VI and had a different shape. Muzzle velocity was 2,350 feet per second, as compared with the Mark VI, which had a muzzle velocity of 1,970 feet per second. Because of the higher muzzle velocity, the culminating point of the Mark VII at 800 yards was 9½ feet, more than 4 feet lower than the Mark VI.[62] In other words, a shooter firing the Mark VII from a rifle designed for the Mark VI would be unable to hit the target. Rifles designed for the Mark VI cartridge could not fire the Mark VII unless the rear sight was replaced and minor alterations were made to the magazine to accommodate the differently shaped bullet.

In December 1913, the Department of Militia and Defence had 110,815 rifles and carbines on hand, seemingly more than enough to arm the 1st and 2nd Divisions. However, the 5,150 carbines and the 21,465 Martini, Lee-Metford, and Lee-Enfield rifles were nineteenth-century acquisitions and useless in a modern war. The 84,200 Ross rifles, on the other hand, were relatively modern, but 19,000 were the poorly designed Mark I rifles that had been relegated to reserve stocks in 1908. Of the remaining rifles, most were obsolete because they lacked charger guides and sights for the .303 Mark VII cartridges.[63]

In August 1914, the Ross Mark III rifle with charger guides was the only up-to-date weapon held by Canada. However, there were only 16,796 rifles on hand. The Ross Rifle Company produced another 11,254 by the end of December 1914, bringing total deliveries to 28,050 rifles, but most of these were needed to arm the First Contingent.[64] By the end of December 1914, 24,575 men were undergoing training in Canada but only 11,600 Mark III rifles were in stock. Subsequent deliveries were slow, and in March 1915 HQ MD 2 reported that, with the exception of the 19th Battalion, none of the Toronto-based 2nd Division units mobilized in October 1914 had been issued with the Mark III rifle.[65] To its credit, the Ross Rifle Company was able to step up production and deliver another 118,825 rifles by 31 July 1916, but most were issued to the 2nd Division and other units sent overseas, leaving only 9,148 Mark III rifles in Canada – enough to arm 7 per cent of the 128,784 recruits undergoing training in Canada. This was the low point, however, and by the end of 1916 there were 63,937 Mark III rifles in Canada, more than enough for the 48,700 men undergoing training. By this time, the CEF in France had been re-equipped with the British SMLE and the Ross was obsolete. For much of the war, therefore, men were trained in Canada with obsolete weapons that were not used in France.

Loading by chargers was emphasized during training. In February 1915, Militia HQ reminded districts of the need for a high standard of rapid loading that could "easily be acquired by the use of dummy cartridges and chargers."[66] Musketry training was vital; in March 1915, Toronto-based units were chided for a lack of preliminary musketry training, including charger loading with dummy cartridges.[67] In 1916, the Commandant of Camp Aldershot, Nova Scotia, commented on the musketry training carried out that summer: "The results were very good except in rapid fire which was only fair. This was principally due to the fact that it was difficult to get enough Mark III Rifles and Chargers and Dummy Ammunition for practice."[68] The matter was serious. In December 1916, the CGS expressed concern in his annual report about the "serious deficiency in charger-loading rifles."[69] There was a considerable amount of musketry training in Canada, but without chargers and modern weapons the recruits could not match the sustained rapid-fire rate of the British infantryman. Inevitably, this meant that reserve units in England had to re-teach the basic musketry course.

Nevertheless, Mark III rifles were used in Canada to train recruits. In December 1915, Militia HQ decided that as Mark III rifles became available each battalion would receive forty for training purposes.[70] The policy had some merit, but the scale of issue meant that only one platoon out of sixteen in each battalion could be trained at a time, which must have made things difficult for unit musketry officers. Nor did every unit receive its allocation of forty Mark III rifles: in March 1916 the 162nd Battalion at Parry Sound reported that only one of the forty rifles promised had been issued. The battalion pressed on regardless: "We are doing what we can by taking out small squads instructing them with the one rifle available."[71] It goes without saying that this gave the individual soldier only a cursory introduction to the weapon.

At summer training camps where recruits were expected to fire their weapons, Mark III rifles were pooled in an effort to put as many men through the range practices as possible. At Valcartier in 1915, for example, 200 Mark III rifles were available, of which sixty were used to teach weapons handling and the remainder were used for shooting. At Camp Hughes that same summer, 15,000 troops fired their range practices with only 230 Mark III rifles.[72] But the rifles could not withstand heavy usage over an extended period. In June 1916, the commandant of Camp Hughes reported that 200 rifles from all units had been pooled but "they are being greatly overworked as the average number of rounds fired through each per week is in the neighborhood of 1,000 and they get no rest. It is difficult for the armourers to give them the proper attention."[73] All in all, as the General Staff at Camp Hughes pointed out in July 1916, "it is impossible under this condition to produce men proficient in Musketry Training."[74]

Because there were not enough Mark III rifles to go around, CEF units in Canada were issued with obsolete weapons, which in many cases were withdrawn or borrowed from the peacetime militia. In March 1915, the 35th Battalion in Toronto had no weapons on charge; as the Inspector General for Eastern Canada noted, "No arms of any sort issued yet – the Battalion borrows rifles daily from the Armouries but these belong to the Militia Units and cannot be retained."[75] In Eastern Ontario, the 38th Battalion in April 1915 had to borrow Ross Mark II rifles from Ottawa militia units. As late as January 1916, the 88th Battalion in Victoria had 385 Lee–Enfields on loan from their parent militia regiment. Not all militia units were cooperative. In December 1915, the 90th Battalion reported that its parent militia regiment, the 90th Winnipeg Rifles, had refused to release 106 rifles for training purposes.[76]

Equipment issued to militia units could be redistributed by district HQ, as Militia HQ reminded MD 2 in November 1915: "The distribution of Rifles is entirely in your own hands."[77] Some districts, however, did not have to be prompted; in March 1916, HQ MD 3 recalled rifles from militia units and redistributed them to CEF units.[78] But there were cases where districts, reluctant to withdraw weapons from the militia, ignored instructions from Ottawa. In August 1915, for example, the Quartermaster General noted that 5,850 rifles of all types were held by rifle associations, cadet corps, and militia units in Manitoba and sent a sharp telegram to HQ MD 10: "Please report why my instructions as to withdrawal [of] these rifles not complied with and report how many can be withdrawn at once. It is surprising to learn that Overseas Units in your District are without rifles while so many are available."[79] In February 1916, HQ MD 1 complained about a shortage of weapons but, as the Principal Ordnance Officer at Militia HQ noted, "This so-called shortage of weapons is due primarily to DOC [District Officer Commanding] not withdrawing from militia – RA's [rifle associations], CC's [cadet corps] – and too there are not enough arms in Canada to give a rifle to everyone."[80]

Unfortunately, the Principal Ordnance Officer's comment about the shortage of weapons was all too true. In January and February 1915, for example, units such as the 2nd Divisional Cyclist Company and the 35th and 50th Battalions had no weapons whatsoever.[81] The policy of billeting detachments in outlying communities in the winter of 1916 only exacerbated the problem. In St Marys, Ontario, an outlying platoon of the 110th Battalion borrowed wooden rifles from the collegiate cadet corps in February 1916. These were useful only for drill, and the platoon had to make a public appeal for sporting rifles to teach basic shooting.[82] In Sault Ste. Marie, the 119th Battalion in March 1916 was fortunate enough to have 200 rifles (type unspecified), but forty were required by the security picquet at a local steel mill and there were no rifles for seven of the outlying detachments. The 157th Battalion in Simcoe County had similar difficulties; most of its fifteen outlying detachments were not issued with rifles until they arrived at Camp Borden in the summer of 1916.[83]

In some cases, CEF units were not issued with enough rifles to arm their soldiers. In December 1915, for example, ordnance stocks in Toronto were reduced to a small stock of drill-purpose rifles; in an effort to give some to every unit, these were distributed on a scale of one to every four recruits. MD 10 had similar problems; in December 1915, the 90th Battalion had been issued with only 227 rifles, while in January 1916 the 109th held only fifty-eight rifles.[84] In considering these numbers, it must be remembered that each CEF battalion was expected to recruit about a thousand men.

For the most part, CEF units were issued with weapons withdrawn from the peacetime militia. But, as discussed in chapter 1, militia units were armed with a variety of rifles. Not surprisingly, the same trend was evident in CEF units, most of which wound up with a mixed bag that did nothing to promote efficient training. In March 1915, the 2nd Divisional Engineers in Toronto, preparing for deployment to England, had 600 Ross Mark I and 100 Ross Mark II long rifles, neither of which they would carry into action.[85] In July 1915, units at the Sarcee training camp near Calgary carried seven different types of rifles, the most modern being the obsolete Ross Mark II long rifle.[86] Later, in January 1916, the Calgary-based 82nd Battalion achieved some sort of record when it was noted as holding 565 Ross rifles: 319 single shot .22 rifles, 181 cadet rifles, 25 Mark I rifles, and 40 up-to-date Mark III rifles. In April 1916, the 101st Battalion in MD 10 was reported to hold 226 rifles of various types, while in August 1916 the 108th in Selkirk, Manitoba, was reported to hold a mixed bag of 307 rifles.[87] It goes without saying that musketry officers must have been hard pressed to conduct any sort of meaningful training program under these conditions.

Not all of the obsolete rifles issued to CEF units were serviceable. In March 1915, the 8th Canadian Mounted Rifles held only seventy-five Lee-Enfield Mark I rifles, some of which had no sights. In Toronto in November 1915, the 83rd Battalion owned 100 Ross Mark II rifles that were "[i]n fairly good condition but not safe to practice [shoot] with," while the 92nd Battalion possessed 775 Ross Mark II and Lee-Enfield Mark I rifles in "doubtful condition." In Winnipeg, the 78th Battalion were issued with a thousand Ross Mark I rifles in September 1915, but these were not safe to fire and could be used for drill purposes only.[88]

The assortment of rifles issued meant that two types of .303 ammunition had to be provided: Mark VI and Mark VII. But production by Dominion Arsenal was slow, perhaps because both types of ammunition were manufactured in the same plant. By December 1914 there were only 2,500,000 rounds of Mark VII on hand; in April 1915, HQ MD 2 commented that training was difficult for a number of reasons, including a lack of ammunition.[89] A request from HQ MD 1 in June 1915 for an allocation of 200 rounds per man was turned down by Militia HQ because "the supply of ammunition available makes it impossible to comply."[90] At Camp Hughes, Manitoba, in the summer of 1915 men were allowed to fire only forty rounds each. Even this small amount was too much; the supply of ammunition ran out and shooting had to be suspended for a month until ordnance could replenish camp stocks.[91] Matters did not improve thereafter, and in March 1916 the Master General of Ordnance noted that only a third of the Mark VII ammunition ordered had been delivered. To eke out the supply, districts were rationed to fifty rounds per man both for practice and classification (testing).[92] Recruits were therefore unable to fire 140 rounds per man as called for by the GMC, a shortfall acknowledged by Gwatkin in July 1916 when he forwarded the GMC instruction to all districts. "It will be impossible, owing to shortage of ammunition, for you to fire this course," he wrote, "but it is suggested that some of the practices might be useful in the training of the troops."[93]

With two types of ammunition in use there were inevitably problems with distribution. In an attempt to impose uniformity, the Director of Musketry recommended in March 1915 that Ontario districts (MD 1, 2 and 3) should be issued with .303 Mark VI ammunition only.[94] However, these districts had been issued with Mark III rifles, which used Mark VII ammunition, and it seems unlikely that issues were restricted to one type. Elsewhere, there were periodic shortages of ammunition; in May 1916, the 96th Battalion in Saskatchewan reported that preliminary musketry training had started, but the men could not practice loading because of a shortage of Mark VII ammunition in chargers.[95] Details are uncertain, but it is likely that other units had similar problems.

There were also problems with ammunition produced by the Dominion Arsenal in Quebec City. A pre-war investigation found that 18-pounder shells and cases were deformed by presses used in the manufacturing process. Rifle ammunition was also suspect. In 1913, Sam Hughes, Minister of Militia and Defence, condemned the ammunition on hand and ordered four years' worth of production to be destroyed. However, it appears this was not done; in 1914 Sir Charles Ross reported that some of the condemned ammunition had been fired at Valcartier and some shipped to England, where the War Office ordered it to be withdrawn.[96] Subsequently, there were a few isolated complaints about the poor quality of ammunition. In August 1915, for example, the Musketry Officer at Camp Sarcee in MD 13, confronted with deformed ammunition, reported that "since adopting the plan of gauging all bullets and eliminating the very large [i.e., oversized] ones there has not been one case of a blow-back or a stripped nickel jacket."⁹⁷ Needless to say, reports of poor-quality ammunition did little to instill confidence in the ranks.

Given a lack of weapons, a shortage of charger-loading rifles, and limited stocks of ammunition, the value of musketry training in Canada was minimal, which became evident when newly arrived units were tested by training staffs in England. The 12th Reserve Battalion, for example, reported in February 1916 that a recent draft from the 34th Battalion in MD 1 had practically no weapons training. In May 1916, the 3rd Canadian Training Brigade described the 81st Battalion from MD 2 as "not up to the mark" in rifle handling, and a month later the 1st Canadian Training Brigade judged musketry in the 90th Battalion from MD 10 and the 95th Battalion from MD 2 as "poor."⁹⁸

These were not isolated examples. From May to August 1916, Colonel Royal Burritt and his staff inspected twenty-three newly arrived infantry battalions at Shorncliffe, England, and assessed their general appearance, physique, performance on the parade square, bayonet fighting, extended order drill, and weapons proficiency.⁹⁹ Rifle handling was described as "bad" in 18 battalions, "poor" in 4 battalions, and "nil" in the 99th Battalion. It is striking that the battalions commented on came from every district in Canada. Poor musketry training was a national and not a local problem.

Much of the training had to be repeated in England, largely because of the lack of modern weapons in Canada. In May 1917, the General Staff at HQ OMFC commented on two newly arrived battalions: the 231st Battalion from MD 11, which had to repeat weeks seven to fourteen after fifteen months in Canada; and the 234th Battalion from MD 2, which had to start training from scratch after twelve months in Canada. "This, in a large measure," wrote the General Staff, "is due to the fact that all musketry training has to be reiterated in England on account of the difference in the weapons in use."¹⁰⁰

The role of the infantry is to close with and kill the enemy. The role of the Canadian infantryman in the Great War was no different. Implicit was the need for proficiency in musketry: not just the ability to shoot accurately and rapidly, but also the ability to load and operate the rifle instinctively. All of this could be acquired only through extensive training. Unfortunately, this could not be done in Canada, which meant that the men who sailed overseas had to be retrained in England, resulting in a significant loss of time and a further complication to the reinforcement system.

MACHINE GUNS

The situation was no better with respect to machine gun training. In December 1913, there were forty-three machine guns in Canada, including thirty-five outdated Maxims adopted in 1899, of which nineteen were mounted on infantry tripods and sixteen on wheeled carriages for use by the cavalry. Despite their obsolescence, the Maxims were called into use. At Valcartier in September 1914, machine gun training was based on the Maxim, with one gun issued to each of the four infantry brigades – which should have had eight.[101] In April 1915, an attempt was made by the 29th Battalion of MD 11 to train Maxim crews, but the initiative was quashed by the Director of Musketry Training at Militia HQ, who pointed out that the weapons were obsolete and that "instruction in the Maxim is wasted."[102] Despite the ruling, Maxim guns continued to be used, and in April 1917 the District Machine Gun Depot in MD 2 was reported to use the Maxim, Colt, and Lewis machine guns for training.[103] Maxim guns were also used by home defence units, and in March 1915 the 63rd (Militia) Regiment at Halifax was equipped with two guns.[104]

In view of the limited number of modern machine guns in stock, the Department of Militia and Defence had to scramble to find two machine guns for each of the seventeen battalions in the First Contingent, an allotment that was increased in February 1915 to four per battalion. The preferred weapon was the British Vickers, but factories in England were fully occupied with orders for the British army and Militia HQ decided to purchase the Colt machine gun manufactured in the United States.

American factories were not on a war footing, however, and of the 500 Colts ordered in 1915 only 402 were delivered by the end of December.[105] As with the Ross Mark III rifle, most of these guns had to be shipped overseas, leaving only seventy-five available for training in Canada. But deliveries eventually picked up, and by the end of 1917 there were 706 Colt guns available for training in Canada. However, at this point the guns were useless for training: between July and November 1916, Colts had been withdrawn from front-line units in France and replaced by the Vickers and Lewis gun.[106]

For the first two years of the war, the Colt was the principal machine gun in the CEF and there was no choice but to train with this weapon. Again, there were not enough guns to go around, and training suffered as a result. In July 1915, the 12th Canadian Mounted Rifles, 13th Canadian Mounted Rifles, 50th Battalion, and 51st Battalion at the Calgary mobilization camp were restricted to one Colt each, although the official entitlement had been increased to four. The limited scale of issue was inadequate; the Commandant of Camp Hughes noted in 1915 that "one Gun per Battalion was quite insufficient for the training of a Machine Gun section."[107]

Even with issues restricted to one Colt machine gun for each battalion, there were not enough guns for all, especially after the 86th Machine Gun Battalion was mobilized in August 1915. In November 1915, the 74th Battalion from MD 2 had to train with wooden machine guns. Nor were matters any better for the 86th Battalion: in December 1915, four months after mobilization, the unit had yet to receive any machine guns. By May 1916, however, the battalion had been equipped with four Colts as well as sixteen Lewis guns – an improvement, but still woefully short of the sixty-four Colts they should have had.[108] The need for machine guns led to the issue of whatever was on the shelf, and in March 1916 the 101st Battalion of Winnipeg reported that "[t]he Machine Gun Section continues to do good work but is somewhat handicapped on account of having only a gun without the tripod."[109] With nothing to support the gun, it seems unlikely the training was of much value.

In December 1915, the Quartermaster General reiterated that each unit was entitled to only one machine gun.[110] Even so, there were not enough guns for every battalion. In March 1916, the 118th Battalion in MD 1 complained "there is no gun and the training is consequently held back. We have indented repeatedly."[111] A few months later, in June 1916, the 153rd and 161st Battalions in London were still waiting for their gun.[112] As a substitute, Lewis light machine guns were issued to some of the infantry battalions in lieu of the Colt medium machine gun. This might have alleviated the shortage, but from a tactical point of view it made no sense, since the Lewis gun was used by rifle platoons while the Colt was used by battalion machine gun sections.

There were two aspects to machine gun training: handling the gun, and tactical drills within the machine gun section. Units that received only one Colt could train men on the former but not the latter. Likewise, units that received two or more Lewis guns as a substitute for the Colt could train men in the latter but not the former. In both cases, the gunners were inadequately trained.

Light machine guns were unheard of in 1914, but by the end of 1915 Lewis light machine guns were in use by the Canadian Corps in Belgium.[113] As with the Vickers, British factories were fully occupied filling orders for the British army; Canada therefore turned to the Savage

Arms Company in the United States, who were able to deliver 884 Lewis guns by the end of 1915. Guns had to be provided to Canadian units in England, however, and at the end of 1917 there were only 709 Lewis guns in Canadian stocks.

The purchase of Savage Lewis guns was not an unqualified success, since parts were not interchangeable with the British Lewis gun. Attempts made to modify the guns at Greenwich, England, so they were compatible were unsuccessful. In many cases, parts from one modified Savage would not fit another, leading the Quartermaster General at OMFC to comment in March 1917 that the officer responsible should be court-martialled.[114] Despite this, the guns were useful for training purposes.

As with the Colts, there were not enough Lewis guns to go around. In May 1916, for example, MD 13 possessed only two Lewis guns that were issued to various units for short periods.[115] The shortage of guns was only temporary, however, and by the spring of 1916, the 128th Battalion at Camp Hughes in MD 10 and the 134th Battalion in MD 2 had been issued with eight guns, while in September 1916 the 151st Battalion at Sarcee Camp in MD 13 was reported to have eight Lewis guns as well.[116] Infantry platoon tactics depended to a great extent on Lewis guns, but with only eight guns for sixteen platoons the training standard could not have been very high.

However, by the end of 1917, as fewer men were being trained in Canada and more guns were arriving from American factories, there were enough Lewis guns available and Militia HQ urged districts to issue "instructions so that as many men as possible of depot batteries and battalions may receive training in the use of the Lewis gun. For this purpose you are authorized to issue such numbers of these guns as can be profitably employed."[117] It seems doubtful that the reinforcements sent overseas in 1918 benefited from this largesse, since by that time men received only preliminary training before being drafted to England.

Lewis gunners were not specialists but ordinary infantrymen. In September 1916, battalions in France trained their riflemen on the Lewis gun in preparation for the Battle of the Somme, while all infantry recruits in England were trained on the gun from February 1917 onward.[118] But, in Canada, because of local shortages and the practice of treating Lewis guns as a substitute for the Colt in battalion machine gun sections, the majority of Canadian infantrymen who sailed overseas before the end of 1916 had little or no experience with the light machine gun. These men were not ready for battle until they had been trained in England. Nor were the battalion machine gunners trained with the Lewis ready; they, too, had to be trained in England. The entire situation calls into question the value of training in Canada.

Much of the training in Canada, therefore, was wasted, not only because of the lack of modern weapons but also because of a shortage even of obsolete equipment. In May 1917, the General Staff at HQ OMFC prepared a draft memorandum noting that the Canadian Corps used the Lee–Enfield rifle and Vickers machine gun, weapons that were not held in Canada, and that "training carried on in Canada, with the weapons in use there, must, to a large extent be duplicated in England."[119] The following month, Sir George Perley, Minister of the OMFC, wrote to Ottawa "that owing to the differences in armament and equipment, and to the fact that a serious degree of efficiency is lost during the ocean trip, the training period in Canada should be restricted to the minimum which will enable the recruit to appear on parade in a soldierly manner, and should not include any more advanced or technical training."[120]

FURLOUGHS

Apart from the shortage of modern equipment, training in Canada was hindered by seeding and harvesting furloughs that allowed soldiers to work on farms. Granted only to NCOs and men of good character who had an offer of employment, furloughs normally lasted thirty days, although district commanders could authorize fifteen-day extensions. Travel costs were reimbursed to a maximum of three hundred miles. Pay and allowances were withheld during the furlough but were paid to the soldier on return, provided his employer certified that the work had been done.[121] An attempt was made in September 1917 to limit furloughs to 10 per cent of unit strength, but by then most units had been sent overseas to England. Even in August 1918, when there was an urgent need for reinforcements overseas, 12,744 MSA draftees were given a thirty-day furlough, while ex-farm workers were allowed an additional fourteen days.[122]

Furloughs had a considerable effect on both training and unit cohesion. In 1915, the Commandant of Camp Hughes in MD 10 complained that "progressive training was somewhat interfered with owing to so many men being absent for some weeks on harvest furlough at a time when the weather was most favorable."[123] Similar problems were encountered in September 1916, when the 96th Battalion at Camp Hughes was reported as having made good progress in training, "although for the past month the Battalion has been disorganized by harvest leave."[124] In MD 1, the 153rd and 160th Battalions did not have enough men in camp for any meaningful training, while the 127th Battalion in MD 2 had to cancel all range practices because of the number of men on furlough. Further west, at Camp Sarcee in MD 13, 4,500 men from twelve units, including 821 from the 194th Battalion, were absent on furlough. Even the tiny Medical Corps detachment sent twelve men off to the farms.[125]

Firm evidence is lacking, but it is likely that furloughs affected rural battalions more than urban units. In the 232nd Battalion from Saskatchewan, for example, 90 per cent of the men were farmers, and therefore 90 per cent of the battalion took furlough.[126] It is doubtful that the 123rd Battalion from Toronto experienced the same problem.

The effect of furloughs was magnified because they were granted in the spring and fall, when units were concentrated at central training camps to finalize individual training and to conduct collective training at the platoon, company, and battalion level. In western Canada, where a large proportion of units were recruited in rural areas and small towns, the problem was particularly acute. In August 1916, for example, the General Staff at Camp Hughes, Manitoba, complained that training was at a standstill because most of the men were absent on harvest leave.[127] Left unsaid in the General Staff comments was that the summer concentration was the primary training season of the year. It is easy to criticize the policy of granting furloughs, but the fact remains that seasonal labour was needed on the farms. Had there been a coherent plan for the allocation of national manpower, perhaps the problem would not have arisen.

CLOTHING AND FACILITIES

Many of the newly raised units in Canada had little in the way of heated training facilities or winter clothing, which made outdoor training difficult. In January 1915, a detachment of the Division Supply Column stationed in Toronto complained of a shortage of overshoes and the absence of a heated drill room.[128] In MD 13, the shortage of accommodation and the lack of winter clothing hampered the training program of the 31st Battalion in February 1915, which was "carried out under great difficulty."[129] The 3rd Canadian Mounted Rifles also had no indoor training facilities and had to abandon training in March 1915 because of heavy snow and cold weather.[130]

Summer camps intended for peacetime militia training were useful but had no permanent facilities. On 2 October 1916, troops living in tented accommodation at Camp Hughes, Manitoba, were caught by an early winter, and the Camp Commandant urged Militia HQ to send the troops overseas immediately, since "the weather here is so bad, that great hardship is being undergone by the men in Camp. We have had very hard frost and today we are in the midst of a blinding snow storm, which prevents all drill from being carried on."[131] It was not only snow and extreme cold that hampered training. At Calgary, three days of exceptionally heavy rain and hail in June 1915 "interfered considerably with field training."[132] In the 88th Battalion at Victoria, British Columbia, training in January 1916 had to be conducted exclusively indoors because of heavy rain, snow, and muddy roads.[133] No doubt units in the Atlantic Provinces were in a similar position.

Bad weather must have been hard on morale, but units made the best of it. The historian of the 94th Battalion at Port Arthur wrote that drilling outdoors during the winter made training difficult but increased "robustness."[134] Somewhat later, the historian of the 101st Battalion at the McGregor Street Barracks in Winnipeg made light of training in sub-zero weather conditions:

> Snow or blow, or whether it was merely cold or "extremely cold," nothing interrupted the training of this go-ahead battalion. It mattered not if there was a couple of feet of snow on the parade ground, it would soon be trampled down hard and flat ... But in spite of the intense cold, the boys would soon warm to their work and ... take off their tunics and mitts in order to carry on more comfortably with their physical drill. The only command that was not appreciated to the full during the cold weather was "Stand at ease" which was usually translated by the boys into "Stand and freeze."[135]

With little or nothing in the way of heated training facilities available, training was difficult, especially during the winter of 1916 when the establishment of the CEF was dramatically increased and the Quartermaster General was hard pressed to clothe the new recruits. In January 1916, for example, the Commander of MD 1 noted the absence of winter clothing in the 91st Battalion of St Thomas, Ontario, and added: "It is to be regretted that winter caps, mittens and overshoes cannot be furnished more rapidly. The weather here is quite cold and it is impossible for the men to turn out and do efficient training unless they are warmly clad."[136] On occasion there was a limited issue of specialized equipment. In Quebec City the 33rd Battalion was given a limited issue of moccasins and snowshoes in January 1916 to allow field training to take place. A few months later, in March, the 76th Battalion Signals

Section in Simcoe County, Ontario, in the heart of the snow belt, was also equipped with snowshoes.[137] Although this equipment may have facilitated training in Canada, it did little to prepare the men for France and Flanders.

It is difficult to assess the effect of Canadian weather on training, although the challenges are easy to visualize from reports such as the one written in November 1915, which noted that the 75th Battalion in MD 2 "has not yet been issued with gloves and the men are suffering from the cold. It makes it very difficult for them to handle their rifles."[138] When the lack of winter clothing and heated training facilities is considered together with the chronic shortages of weapons, ammunition, and equipment, it comes as no surprise that training in Canada was, to a great extent, a waste of time.

SUMMARY: TRAINING IN CANADA

But how much time was actually wasted? From May 1916 onward, infantry battalions were assessed on arrival in England to determine their level of training. The length of time spent training in Canada was considered irrelevant, and placement in the fourteen-week syllabus depended entirely on unit proficiency. The results were appalling. On average, the battalions listed in table 6.2 required forty-seven weeks in Canada to attain a level of proficiency equivalent to the fourth week of the fourteen-week syllabus. This shortfall represented a colossal waste of time, energy, and resources. Much of this waste could have been avoided had there been close coordination between Militia HQ and OMFC, but this was not possible until Hughes resigned as Minister of Militia and Defence and HQ OMFC was established in England, as discussed in chapter 9.

In December 1916, the CGS wrote to HQ OMFC that Militia HQ was trying to coordinate training with England and that efforts were being made to train men as efficiently as possible despite the lack of equipment and instructors as well interruptions caused by harvest furlough.[139] The same view was reflected in the annual departmental report prepared by the CGS, who wrote that every effort "is being made to coordinate training in Canada with training in the United Kingdom. The syllabus of training in the United Kingdom is taken as a guide, and much benefit has resulted from employing on instructional duties officers recently returned from overseas."[140]

HQ OMFC accepted Gwatkin's policy of training men with the overseas syllabus as far as possible before sending them to England. However,

Table 6.2 Training levels of battalions arriving in England, 1917

Battalion	District	Weeks training in Canada	Recruiting area*	Training week on arrival in England
241st	1	40	Urban	4 (17% week 5)
149th	1	40	Rural	7
153rd	1	44	Rural	7
186th	1	52	Rural	8
248th	2	52	Rural	1
255th	2	26	Urban	1
176th	2	36	Rural	3 and 4
177th	2	40	Rural	3 (average)
182nd	2	48	Urban	3
234th	2	52	Urban	1
204th	2	52	Urban	4
208th	2	56	Urban	3 (average)
216th	2	60	Urban	5 (40% week 6, 30% week 3)
164th	2	68	Rural	4 (average)
240th	3	48	Urban	1
235th	3	52	Rural	5
253rd	3	Not stated	Urban	4
245th	4	36	Urban	3
244th	4	36	Urban	3 (35% week 5, 30% week 1)
246th	6	24	Urban	3
165th	6	60	Rural	3 (40% week 5, 40% week 1)
190th	10	52	Urban	1
229th	10	52	Rural	7 (31% week 5, 19% week 3)
181st	10	54	Rural	5
221st	10	56	Urban	5
210th	10	56	Rural	7 (18% week 8, 32% week 5)
223rd	10	60	Urban	1
141st	10	60	Rural	5
200th	10	64	Urban	5
203rd	10	Not stated	Urban	5
231st	11	52	Urban	7
Average		47		4

* The term "rural" or "urban" refers to the primary recruiting area.

Source: LAC, RG 9, III A1, vol. 53, file "Monthly Reports June 1917," Report of the General Staff for the Month of June 1917.

OMFC believed the existing system could be improved. In February 1917, the new Chief of Staff (Turner) wrote to Militia HQ noting that assessing drafts on arrival in England could be a long-drawn-out process "not conducive to economy of time, or to a satisfactory result."[141] A more efficient procedure, Turner suggested, would be for Canadian staff to assess the level of training of all drafts before they left Canada. In the absence of uniform training standards, this was easier said than done. The 204th Battalion, for example, was judged by HQ MD 2 in March 1917 to have completed the entire fourteen-week syllabus after fifty-two weeks of training. Training staff in England, however, judged that the 204th had only completed weeks 1 to 4.[142]

The case of the 204th was not unique, and in June 1917 the General Staff at HQ OMFC reported there were "[v]ariations in the stages of training and variations in the standard of training in various parts of Canada as revealed in the classification accompanying the troops."[143] The problem was not the syllabus taught in Canada but the length of time spent training with little result, which resulted in a considerable duplication of effort and waste of time. The solution was obvious: in May 1917, the General Staff Officer at OMFC recommended that "[t]he training of drafts in Canada (providing uniform training equipment cannot be provided) must be confined to a limited period and must not include anything that will require duplication on arrival in England."[144]

Sir George Perley, OMFC Minister, considered the recommendations. In June 1917, he wrote to the Minister of Militia and Defence in Ottawa to suggest that training in Canada be confined to the minimum necessary to allow the recruit to appear on parade in a soldierly manner. Nothing concrete resulted, however, and Perley wrote two hasteners in September and October 1917 urging that training in Canada be restricted to the elementary level.[145] At this point, faced with Perley's repeated requests and the impending intake of 100,000 MSA draftees, it became obvious to Militia HQ that, given the limited training resources available, advanced training in Canada was futile; from December 1917 onward, the policy was to conduct "preliminary training only as a grounding for further training in England and France."[146]

Conducting only preliminary training in Canada meant the movement of reinforcements to England was speeded up. This did not mean, however, that they went overseas shortly after enrolment, since various factors influenced the movement of reinforcements. In June 1918, for example, the 1st Depot Battalion of the New Brunswick Regiment (NBR) was unable to send drafts overseas while they were quarantined after an outbreak of cerebral meningitis.[147] As well, troop ships, which were controlled by the Allied Maritime Transport Council, had to be requested and were not always available when required, once the Americans started sending large numbers of troops overseas. As A.E. Kemp, Perley's replacement at OMFC, wrote to Prime Minister Borden in February 1918, there was "difficulty with respect to the transportation of troops from Canada, which has been aggravated by the United States using some of the ships which formerly carried Canadian troops over here to transport their own troops."[148] Kemp's observation was correct: a postwar study estimated that about 49 per cent of the two million American troops sent overseas were carried in British ships previously used by the CEF.[149] Time was also needed in Canada for basic personnel administration: documentation, medicals, kitting out, and inoculations. The upshot was that those who sailed in 1918 served an average of fourteen weeks in Canada – a lengthy period, perhaps, but a significant reduction over 1916, when the average was thirty-one weeks, and 1917, when the average was forty weeks.

How much useful training was accomplished during the fourteen weeks that the average recruit spent in Canada in 1918? In New Brunswick, the 1st Depot Battalion of the NBR, unable to send drafts overseas, endeavoured to complete the fourteen-week syllabus.[150] But the NBR was atypical: a survey of fourteen drafts with 1,809 men from Quebec and Eastern Ontario that sailed in July, August, and September 1918 shows that, on average, each draft had been trained to the midpoint of the third week of the fourteen-week syllabus only.[151]

TRAINING IN ENGLAND

Was the training in England any better? In 1915 and 1916, the quality of training in England was erratic and ranged from satisfactory to poor. Among the various reasons for this, a major one was the chaotic command and control of the CEF, which had no central HQ, competing reserve formations, and no clear chain of command. The matter has been dealt with at length elsewhere, but a brief summary is required to put the issue into context.

With the departure of the 1st Division for Belgium in February 1915, there was a need for an establishment in England to train reinforcements. The Canadian Training Depot was therefore established in Tidworth, near Salisbury Plain. Command was given to Colonel W.R.W. James, a British officer described as "a martinet and a very peppery one at that."[152] However, James was posted to France, Tidworth was too small, and in

March 1915, the depot was moved to Shorncliffe and renamed Canadian Training Division (CTD). Command of the CTD was given to Major-General J.C. MacDougall, a Canadian Permanent Force officer who had previously been appointed General Officer Commanding all Canadians in England. MacDougall did not report to Militia HQ, but rather to the British commander of Shorncliffe District.[153]

At the same time, Hughes dispatched Colonel (later Major-General) J.W. Carson to England as his personal representative. Carson's powers, as defined by an order in council, were limited; he was "to represent the Militia Department of Canada in the United Kingdom, in connection with supplies and other requirements" and to act "as the agent of Minister of Militia in maintaining the depots of articles of equipment and other supplies necessary for the upkeep and subsistence of the Canadian Expeditionary Force."[154] However, Carson interpreted this narrow mandate to give himself sweeping powers, including command of all Canadians in England.[155] To exercise this supposed authority, Carson did not establish a central military HQ but instead relied on a small secretariat housed in the Hotel Cecil in London. The secretariat, eventually styled HQ Canadians, did not have a chief of staff, which meant that Carson not only commanded the CEF in England but also had to take care of the detailed coordination. Brigadier-General R.G.E. Leckie, the former commander of the 3rd Brigade, was eventually appointed Chief of Staff in September 1916, but as an OMFC report later noted, Leckie's appointment had little effect, since his "powers were limited to inspection and suggestion."[156] The upshot was that the agency that ostensibly controlled all Canadian activities in England did not have the necessary mechanism to supervise and coordinate training.

The situation was complicated by the arrival in England of Major-General S.B. Steele, commander of the 2nd Canadian Division; considered too old for active service, he was relieved before his division deployed to France in August 1915. As a consolation prize, Steele was given a British appointment as commander of Shorncliffe District, which included the CTD under MacDougall. At this point, command and control was hopelessly confused. Both Carson and Steele claimed jurisdiction over the CTD, but Carson had no jurisdiction over Steele, who answered to HQ Southern Command. The unfortunate MacDougall in Shorncliffe now answered to two masters. All three officers freely corresponded with one another as well as with HQ Southern Command.

The command and control arrangements were reduced to a farce in October 1915 when Hughes sent another twelve battalions to England.

Only five of these battalions could be housed at Shorncliffe and the remainder were sent to Bramshott. Head of the newly formed CTD Bramshott was Brigadier-General Lord Brooke, the former commander of the 4th Canadian Infantry Brigade in France, who had been relieved as unfit for command.[157] Brooke reported to Eastern Command but in theory was also under the command of MacDougall and Carson – but not under Steele, the senior Canadian officer in England whose authority was limited to Shorncliffe District. As HQ OMFC noted in February 1917, there was "no definite head of the Canadian Organization [in England] from a military viewpoint."[158]

The roles of CTD Shorncliffe and Bramshott were never formally defined, although Steele suggested to Carson in October 1915 that reinforcements should be provided by Shorncliffe, which should then be topped up with drafts from Bramshott.[159] Steele's suggestion was evidently accepted, and in February 1916 the British Inspector of Infantry reported that Bramshott was "a Training Division – Its role being to fill up with drafts the Shorncliffe Training Division when called on. At Shorncliffe the final polish is put on."[160] The division between the two seemed clear, but in practice battalions arriving from Canada were sent to either Shorncliffe or Bramshott, depending on the availability of quarters. On occasion, Bramshott as well as Shorncliffe provided drafts directly to France.[161] As well, the Inspector of Infantry's remarks were naive, and drafts sent from Bramshott to Shorncliffe needed more than a "final polish."

In March 1916, the General Staff at Shorncliffe complained: "We have received in this Division no drafts from Bramshott which have been fully trained and fit for draft overseas."[162] As evidence of this, the General Staff pointed to thirteen drafts totalling 6,196 infantrymen recently posted from Bramshott. The most advanced was a group of 975 men from the 35th Battalion who had completed seven weeks of training, while the least advanced was a group of 52 men from the 43rd Battalion who had completed three weeks. On average, the drafts had completed four weeks of training and needed six weeks at Shorncliffe. There were other complications, and WO1 156 allowed commanders to alter the ten-week syllabus to suit local conditions. The sequence of training at Bramshott therefore may have been somewhat different, and CTD Shorncliffe was faced with a dilemma. Should the Bramshott drafts be slotted into the ten-week syllabus without regard to material taught, or should they be assessed and provided with remedial training? The system was wasteful and illogical. Unfortunately, with no central authority to organize and coordinate training, nothing could be done.

In November 1916, HQ OMFC was established to bring order to the Canadian structure in England. The changes were dramatic. MacDougall was replaced as General Officer Commanding Canadian Troops in England by Lieutenant-General Sir Richard Turner, the former commander of the 2nd Division in France. Although technically the GOC, Turner was the de facto chief of staff for the new HQ, which contained the essential directorates to coordinate and control Canadian activities: Quartermaster General, Adjutant-General, Director-General of Medical Services, paymaster, and – most important – a General Staff branch for operations and training.

From a training perspective, the General Staff branch brought about significant improvements. The new General Staff Officer 1, Lieutenant-Colonel H.F. McDonald, who had been wounded in September 1916 on the Somme while serving as the Brigade-Major of the 1st Canadian Infantry Brigade, identified two major problems: the lack of military authority and the lack of standardized training. He initiated two key reforms in February 1917. First, he "recommended that immediate application be made to the War Office for authorization for Canadian Headquarters to assume responsibility for and direction of the training of all Canadians in England."[163] This was quickly granted by the War Office, which no doubt was relieved to see a long-standing problem resolved. Second, McDonald addressed the problem of infantry training:

> The situation as regards this branch [infantry], comprising as it does the great bulk of our forces, was most serious. There appeared to be no universal syllabus of training and no continuity or coordination of training. There was no information in the General Staff office showing the stage of efficiency or the progressive results in the various areas. I at once issued orders that the Syllabus of training (covering 14 weeks) as issued by the War Office, be considered a basis for training all Canadian Infantry.[164]

Reserve units were quick to react, and on 8 March 1917 CTD Bramshott issued a general training directive to implement McDonald's instructions.[165] The Bramshott training directive laid out a detailed fourteen-week syllabus and for good measure introduced a new concept, the "squad" system. In essence, each squad of recruits was given a suite of NCOs who were responsible for taking the squad through the complete training syllabus, thus addressing the problem of continuity identified by McDonald.

The results of the reforms were evident almost immediately. Colonel J. Sutherland Brown, an officer with the Canadian Corps in France, later commented that "[t]he effect of this organization was soon felt in the field and, generally speaking it was a very great improvement over anything that preceded it."[166] This is not to say there were no problems. Reserve battalions had a fixed number of instructors, but the flow of reinforcements from Canada was uneven and the number of men undergoing training varied considerably. In June 1917, for example, the General Staff Officer 1 at HQ OMFC noted that "[i]n the early part of the month very large numbers of reinforcements from Canada were released from quarantine [in England] and placed a severe strain upon the training Staffs of the battalions concerned."[167]

Equipment problems also hampered training and were not corrected until 1917. Newly arrived troops from Canada, for example, wore the Pattern 1916 leather Oliver equipment with two ammunition pouches closed by a flap secured by two buckles next to the body. The arrangement was awkward, and in July 1916 the CTD Musketry Officer reported the results of trials of the new equipment:

> The difficulty in unbuckling the leather pouches was very marked, the men found it necessary in very many cases to lay down their rifles and use both hands [to undo the buckles]. The average time which elapsed before the first shot was fired was 18 seconds, which is about 10 seconds longer than the normal time with the [British] web equipment.[168]

The Musketry Officer also found that ninety-six men wearing the British web equipment were able to fire fifteen rounds in one minute, or a total of 1,440 rounds, whereas the same group wearing Oliver equipment could fire only 984 rounds. The British musketry standard required men to load and fire fifteen rounds in one minute. Canadians, however, could not achieve this standard wearing the Oliver equipment.

In France, Canadian infantrymen wore Pattern 1908 web, woven out of cotton, with the exception of the 4th Division, which briefly used the Oliver equipment from August 1916 until GHQ decided to issue web equipment to the division during the Battle of the Somme in October 1916.[169] The wisdom of using one type of equipment for training and another for battle is dubious. In any event, the issue was resolved by the War Office, which directed in February 1917 that web equipment would be issued to all reinforcements sent to France and half of the Canadians undergoing training in England.[170]

A much more serious problem pertained to the weapons used by Canadians in France and Flanders. Cavalry units, for example, carried the SMLE, since the Ross was too cumbersome for men in the saddle. However, reinforcements were trained with the Ross, and in May 1915 Lord Strathcona's Horse, preparing for deployment to Flanders, had to conduct conversion training for newly arrived men from the Canadian Base Depot.[171] The 1st Division had originally been armed with the Ross Mark III, but in the aftermath of the Second Battle of Ypres in April 1915 was rearmed with the British SMLE. The 2nd and 3rd Divisions, however, retained their Ross rifles until after the Battle of Mount Sorrel in June 1916. The 4th Division deployed to France in August 1916 was armed with the Ross but were able to exchange them for the SMLE in October 1916 on the eve of the Battle of the Somme.[172]

For sixteen months, therefore, from June 1915 to October 1916, there were two streams of infantry reinforcements: one trained on the Ross and the other on the SMLE. Not surprisingly, it was difficult to keep the two separate when large drafts were called for. In June 1916 the need for reinforcements during the Battle of Mount Sorrel virtually cleaned out CTD Shorncliffe, and the Canadian Base Depot in France complained that not only had reinforcements destined for 1st Division battalions (armed with the SMLE) been trained on the Ross rifle, but that had also arrived in France carrying these weapons, which then had to be exchanged for the SMLE.[173]

The answer to the problem lay in designating reserve battalions to reinforce the 1st Division and then providing them with the SMLE. But with no HQ in England to coordinate training affairs, this was not done. In January 1916, for example, the 23rd Reserve Battalion was responsible for reinforcing two battalions of the 1st Division armed with the SMLE and one battalion of the 2nd Division armed with the Ross. The 23rd had enough SMLE rifles for only one company and was therefore unable to train enough reinforcements for the 1st Division battalions.[174] An additional 300 SMLE rifles had been indented for but none were available.[175]

After the decision in October 1916 to withdraw the last of the Ross rifles from the units in France, efforts were made to issue the SMLE to all reserve infantry battalions in England. Demands were submitted to the Canadian Ordnance Depot at Ashford in November 1916 for 300 SMLE rifles for each of the fifteen reserve battalions. The ordnance depot then followed the routine procedure and indented for SMLE rifles from British stocks. However, there was no formal entitlement and the only weapons available were those surplus to British requirements. As a result, only three hundred rifles were provided to each of the six battalions at Shoreham and one hundred for each of the nine battalions at Seaford.[176] The upshot was that many of the infantry reinforcements continued to be trained with the Ross.

Needless to say, the Canadian Corps was less than pleased with this state of affairs. "Considerable criticism was found with the fact that we were using the Ross Rifles for training purposes," wrote the Deputy Minister, Colonel A.D. McRae, after a fact-finding visit to France in November 1916, "the opinion there being unanimous that it was absolutely necessary, as the Divisions in the Field were equipped with Lee-Enfield Rifles, that the training be carried out with that Rifle."[177] Shortly afterward McRae was appointed Quartermaster General at HQ OMFC. He promptly contacted the War Office, and in January 1917 the Army Council agreed to provide Canadian reserve battalions with the same weapons as British training units. The scale of issue, however, was limited: SMLE rifles for 25 per cent of the establishment; emergency or drill purpose rifles for 25 per cent of the establishment; and Pattern 1914 Enfield rifles for the remainder.[178] Ideally, there should have been enough SMLE rifles for every man undergoing training, but at least Canadian reserve battalions were now on the same footing as their British counterparts.

Not all units received their entitlement, either because of distribution problems or because of a general shortage of weapons in British stocks. In July 1917, for example, the 23rd Reserve Battalion at Shoreham had 940 Pattern 1914 Enfield rifles and thirty-five emergency rifles, but no SMLE rifles to train 1,140 men.[179] The War Office was well aware of the problem, and in October 1917 advised the 1st (British) Army that "[i]t has not yet been found possible to equip all men with their service rifles before proceeding to France but progress is being made in this direction. Every man who now lands in France equipped with a rifle will have carried out his training with that rifle."[180] However, matters improved thereafter, and by the beginning of 1918 training was no longer handicapped by a lack of weapons.

FATIGUES

Fatigues were a routine feature of life in the CEF in 1916. They interfered with the continuity of training and extended the infantry training program well beyond the intended ten weeks. The nature of these fatigues varied according to time and place, but included sentries, fire picquets, kitchen help, mess waiters, work parties to move rations and stores, and general cleanup, including garbage removal and emptying of latrines. The number of men employed on fatigues was not fixed but depended on the size of the camp and the nature of the jobs that had to be done. Someone had to do these chores, and in the absence of a dedicated work force, troops undergoing training had to be called upon. It was not a question of detailing individual soldiers; there was enough work that whole units were employed as duty battalions for a week or more.

At the risk of stating the obvious, fatigues interrupted training. In June 1915, the Reserve Artillery Brigade at Shorncliffe complained they had been employed as a duty battalion for five weeks, leaving little time for training.[181] A year later, in May 1916, the 23rd Reserve Battalion reported that "[o]wing to the heavy duties, it has, on occasion been impossible to hold a proper Battalion Parade for two or three weeks on end."[182] The length of time a unit was assigned to fatigues depended on its strength. In May 1916, the 3rd Canadian Training Brigade noted the following:

Battalions of this Brigade until two weeks ago had for some weeks been so reduced in strength that no one Battalion was able to furnish full duties, this resulted in it often being necessary to take part duties from each of the three Battalions – the one serious case was that of the 23rd Battalion which was duty battalion for two weeks running and had also to supply part duties for another two weeks, they being the only Battalion of any considerable strength.[183]

Fatigues created problems in addition to a loss of training time. As the 12th Reserve Battalion explained in May 1916, "It is a recognized fact that the detailing of a Training Battalion for a week's duty is extremely detrimental to the men, as it is found that after this Unit has been doing these duties for a Week the men are not fit to take up training where it was left off, and in most cases have to be put back a week."[184]

Reserve brigades ordinarily had four battalions. With one battalion employed on fatigues every week, men could expect at least two stints of duties during the ten-week syllabus. The infantry syllabus therefore was really twelve weeks, or fourteen if the 12th Battalion's comments on the loss of continuity are considered. The net effect of this was to increase the length of training and delay the movement of reinforcements to France.

There was no getting around the fact that fatigues had to be done. Short of a dedicated civilian work force (unlikely in wartime Britain), the job had to be done by soldiers, and efforts were made by reserve units to find a solution. In May 1916, the 70th Battalion suggested a duty company and the 30th recommended that fatigues be reduced to a minimum. The 1st Canadian Training Brigade took a broader view and suggested the establishment of a special work battalion staffed by officers and men unfit for service at the front, a solution also proposed by the Director of Recruiting and Organization.[185]

The problem was not confined to reserve battalions and brigades and required action at the training division level. In September 1916, therefore, CTD Shorncliffe established a composite duty battalion with unfit men from seven battalions that had been broken up to provide reinforcements. By October 1916, the new unit had been formally designated as a "garrison duty battalion." CTD Bramshott followed suit, and by the end of October 1916 had formed a "Garrison Depot Battalion" (later known as a garrison duty battalion), staffed initially with 176 men and later with 990, all of whom were unfit for active service.[186] Other garrison duty battalions were formed at Hastings and Shoreham. Garrison duty battalions did not last for long, however, and vanished in March 1917 when Regimental Depots of the newly organized territorial regiments were given the job of holding category B and C men to perform Command, Divisional, and Brigade fatigues to release fit men for service at the front.[187]

The problem of using recruits to do fatigues was not confined to the CEF. In January 1917, the War Office directed that all such duties in reserve units were to be reduced and that "only those men are to be retained on such work in future who are absolutely necessary to ensure that the training of drafts is not interfered with."[188] The restriction was codified by ACI 338, issued in February 1917, which stipulated that all garrison duties had to be approved by the appropriate command HQ and that only men unfit for active service could be assigned to these duties. For good measure, ACI 338 also restricted the number of men employed on unit duties. Officers' mess staff, for example, was restricted to one man for every five officers, with a maximum of ten for every hundred officers. Sergeants' mess staff was restricted to one man for every ten sergeants, with a maximum of five for every hundred sergeants. Regimental police were authorized at six per thousand men, while sanitary men were allowed at two for every company.[189] These instructions applied not only to British units, but also to the CEF.

Canadian initiatives and War Office instructions did not do away with the need for able-bodied men to carry out fatigues and other duties. Trainees were still expected to do guard duties, which were regarded as an essential part of their training.[190] But tours of guard duty were short and did not seriously affect training. Security picquets were another issue, but the numbers involved were small. In the week of 21–28 April 1918, for example, the 11th Reserve Battalion was tasked to provide twenty NCOs and seventy-eight men for various picquets in and near Folkestone. Most of the men were on duty for the weekend only, and only one NCO and six men were needed for the complete week.[191]

There was, however, the matter of unit fatigues, for which each unit had its own arrangements. Infantry reserve battalions usually drew their fatigue parties exclusively from their HQ Company, which was part of the permanent cadre not intended to be drafted to France. The Engineer and Service Corps Training Depots used low-category men, while the Shoreham area employed underage soldiers on routine chores.[192]

SUMMARY

The training structure created by the CEF during the war was complex and evolved continually. By mid-1916, training programs were clearly oriented toward the battlefield, and much of the training developed during the war would not be out of place today. Not surprisingly, given the nature of the pre-war Canadian militia, no attempt was made to develop training programs – with the exception of the First Contingent in 1914. Instead, British syllabi were used in both Canada and England, albeit with modifications to suit local needs. Given that the overseas CEF was an integral part of the British Expeditionary Force, the decision by Militia HQ was logical and professional.

The actual training doctrine endorsed by Militia HQ may have been effective, but the training system in Canada was horribly inefficient for much of the war. Those responsible for training did their best, but it was a futile effort given the shortage of modern weapons, equipment, ammunition, and training facilities. The result was that men had to be retrained on arrival in England. The duplication of effort was not only a waste of time and resources, but also slowed down the movement of reinforcements to the front. The problem was eventually rectified by the end of 1917, when Militia HQ decided that recruits would be given only preliminary training before embarking for England. The change was for the better, but came only after repeated pleas from HQ OMFC, which illustrates the difficulties of coordination between England and Canada when two separate ministries, neither subordinate to the other, were responsible for training.

Training in England was effective, but the structure was initially inefficient. The lack of uniform weapons made it difficult to train reinforcements, and the need to use trainees for fatigues lengthened the time needed to complete training. The division of responsibilities between the training divisions at Bramshott and Shorncliffe was illogical, and the two organizations at times operated at cross-purposes. Much of this resulted from the lack of a central authority to coordinate and supervise training, an authority that could not be established as long as Sam Hughes was allowed to exercise his malign influence. HQ OMFC swept much of this away when it was formed in November 1916. Command of all CEF units in England was vested in the new HQ, a proper staff was set up to control training, and arrangements were made to provide Canadian reserve units with the same equipment entitlement as their British counterparts. With the OMFC reforms, the training system in England was efficient and effective. Just as importantly, it proved to be flexible and was able to quickly modify training programs in response to the emergency in France after the German offensive of 21 March 1918. This was a well-organized, professional headquarters that proved to be instrumental in delivering a steady flow of trained reinforcements that substantially contributed to the achievements of the Canadian Corps.

Training was intended to produce trained soldiers that could be fed into the reinforcement stream. Managing this stream was not easy, and whatever system the CEF devised had to fit within British policies for providing reinforcements. However, very little has been written about these policies or about the dynamics of manpower employment and the nature of wastage at the front. These issues, which coloured the CEF's manpower policies overseas, are fully discussed in chapter 7 as a prelude to the discussion of the overseas reinforcement structure in chapters 8 and 9.

7

Reinforcements: Policy, Management, and Wastage

Reinforcements were those drafted to CEF units in France or Belgium to replace wastage – that is, the dead, wounded, missing, or sick; deserters; and those cross-posted to other units at the front or to England. The subject of reinforcements is complex, but three fundamental issues have to be considered: the doctrine that shaped the reinforcement structure in Canada, England, and France; the means by which the supply of reinforcements was managed; and wastage rates, which determined the number required.

The reinforcement system was much like a series of linked reservoirs, each flowing into the next, the first reservoir being in Canada and the final one in France or Belgium at the corps railhead behind the front-line divisions. To prevent overflow, the movement of men from one reservoir to another had to be carefully regulated. To do this, an elaborate reinforcement organization evolved that was based on British policies and procedures. Before this evolution can be understood, some explanation of these policies and procedures is needed.

The movement of reinforcements had to be carefully controlled, not only to ensure that the next reservoir did not overflow, but also to keep track of the hundreds of thousands who passed through the system. To accomplish this, a complex set of rules and procedures was instituted in France by GHQ. Although this system provided close control over the movement of men, it also created institutional delays that hindered the supply of reinforcements. In evaluating how successful the CEF reinforcement structure was, the effect of these institutional barriers must be taken into account.

Another aspect that has to be considered is the nature of wastage itself: that is, its causes, the varying rates of wastage that occurred, and the possibility of recycling some of the wastage back into the reinforcement stream. There was also the matter of those who were employed elsewhere and were therefore absent from their units. The thread that runs consistently through the administrative history of the CEF is the need for manpower, not only to replace losses but also to compensate for those absent on other duties. This thread, which in the final analysis concerns the fighting strength of units, has been overlooked by most historians. David Campbell, for example, has commented on the reduced trench strength of battalions in the 2nd Division during the Hundred Days, which resulted in some battalions reducing the number of platoons, but attributes this loss of strength to a shortage of reinforcements. Kenneth Radley, on the other hand, has noted the number of men absent from battalions in the 1st Division and the efforts made to reduce the number absent on other duties.[1]

The procedures for handling reinforcements were complex and varied considerably among the various arms and services. However, the majority of reinforcements were infantrymen; for this reason, the following discussion is focused primarily on that corps, although to put the matter into context some reference has to be made to the other arms and services.

BRITISH POLICIES AND PROCEDURES

The creation of an efficient reinforcement structure was no simple matter, because there was no precedent in Canada apart from a hundred-man draft sent to the Royal Canadian Regiment in South Africa in 1900.[2] Under the circumstances, there was no choice but to adhere to British army doctrine and procedures.

British doctrine concerning reinforcements was set out in part two of the pre-war *Field Service Regulations* (1909). The procedure was simple and straightforward. On the outbreak of war, reservists were called out not only to bring units up to full strength but also to provide "first reinforcements," amounting to 10 per cent of the unit establishment as a pool of trained soldiers immediately available as reinforcements. Once the unit left England, additional reservists were called out to provide six months' worth of reinforcements (about 40 per cent of the unit establishment in the case of infantry battalions). These men were held at regimental depots in Britain until they were needed at the front.[3] Reinforcements after the first six months would be provided by men "who were not fully trained previous to the outbreak of war, together with a proportion of men invalided and since recovered during these months, [who] will be fit to go to the front."[4]

Returning these invalids to the reinforcement stream after recovery was considered in pre-war planning. The matter was not straightforward, however, since many of those discharged from hospital were not immediately fit for active service but required a period of convalescence to rebuild their strength. If these men were retained in hospital, they became what might be termed "bed-blockers." But if they were returned to the regimental depot they became an unwelcome burden on depot staff, who were fully occupied in the training of recruits. The plan, therefore, was to form convalescent depots on the outbreak of war where recovering invalids could receive graduated exercises to rehabilitate them until they were fit and could be returned to their depots to be fed into the reinforcement stream. By 1914, a total of 4,750 beds at military bases in Lichfield, Winchester, Shorncliffe, and Warley had been earmarked for use as convalescent depots.[5]

When units arrived in a theatre of operations, they were immediately sent to the front, while the "10 per cent first reinforcements" held at base depots within the Lines of Communication (in numerical terms, amounting to 10 percent of the forward units), were under the command of the Inspector-General of Communication. As units incurred wastage, the Adjutant-General at GHQ issued instructions to the Inspector-General to forward reinforcements from the base depots, which were then filled by drafts from regimental depots in England.[6]

The pre-war structure was simple and robust, but was intended for the regular army and was too limited to provide for newly created wartime units. The regimental depot of the Northumberland Fusiliers, for example, was large enough to provide reinforcements for two regular battalions and one reserve battalion. But in 1914–15 the Fusiliers called out four Territorial battalions, created eight second- and third-line Territorial battalions, and mobilized nineteen service battalions as part of the New Armies. By mid-June 1915, thirty-three Fusilier battalions were on active service, with a combined need for reinforcements that exceeded the capacity of the pre-war regimental depot. Depot companies were established by the Territorial battalions and the wartime service battalions to train reinforcements. In practice, however, these were too small to be efficient, and in April 1915 reserve battalions were created to handle the number of men required.[7] These proved to be successful, and ultimately a total of 428 reserve battalions of all types were formed.[8]

There was a further problem in that, for some reason, the convalescent depots envisaged in peacetime were not established on the outbreak of

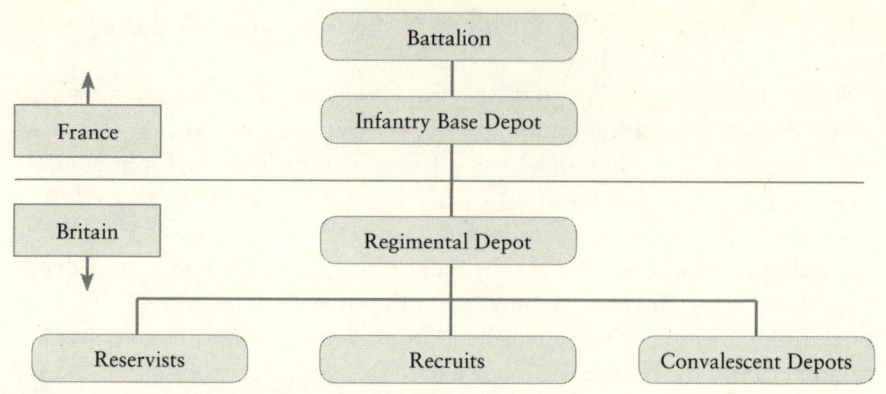

Figure 7.1 Pre-war British infantry reinforcement structure.

war. In their place, patriotic civilians provided, at their own expense, convalescent homes (later known as Class B auxiliary hospitals). These auxiliary hospitals, often quite small, were scattered across the United Kingdom, some in areas remote from major military bases; inevitably, there were problems keeping track of patients. The War Office therefore organized large military convalescent hospitals in April 1915. However, this solution was not satisfactory either, since there was a general shortage of hospital beds and many of the invalids did not require hospitalization but a regimen of graduated exercises to become fit for the front. The problem was resolved in October 1915 when a depot was formed in each of the commands in Great Britain. Known as command depots, these were not hospitals but rather convalescent centres where recovering invalids received "graduated exercises, including massage and therapeutic gymnastics, the object being to 'harden' these men to enable them to join their reserve battalions within six months fit for drafting overseas."[9] However, command depots were intended only for British troops; Dominion forces had to rely on convalescent hospitals.[10]

The pre-war model of the reinforcement organization proved to be inadequate for a modern war involving large numbers of troops. Regimental depots and depot companies in England, confronted with masses of recruits, found it difficult to complete the normal recruit training, and schools had to be added to infantry base depots in France to train men for the front. The wastage also exceeded pre-war forecasts, and more reinforcements had to be held on the continent, which resulted in overcrowding at the base depots.

To handle the additional reinforcements and relieve overcrowding, entrenching battalions were established in divisional rear areas in July 1915. These battalions had three purposes: to hold a pool of reinforcements close to the front to reduce delivery time; to conduct supplementary training for the men waiting to be called forward; and to provide a labour force to reduce the burden on the overworked infantry battalions.[11] Entrenching battalions were not overly successful. Their strength varied, depending on the number of reinforcements sent forward, while the men themselves, not unnaturally, took little or no interest in back-breaking menial labour in the rear areas. Nor did they receive much in the way of training, given the continual need to provide work parties.[12]

The difficulties did not end there. Entrenching battalions held infantrymen only, and other arms and services had to make their own arrangements. The artillery held reinforcements in brigade and divisional ammunition columns, where they could be gainfully employed hauling shells forward to battery positions until needed on the gun-line.[13] The remaining corps did not have forward establishments, and all of their reinforcements were held at base depots until called forward.

In February 1917, the British Labour Corps was created to perform labour duties in France. Because the entrenching battalions were no longer needed to provide work parties, they were replaced in September 1917 by corps schools or reinforcement camps.[14] Reinforcement camps, ideally situated near the corps railhead, were not intended to provide work parties but simply to hold "reinforcements to the extent of 100 per Battalion and 10% of other arms of the Service."[15] This is not to say the men were idle, for training was conducted under the auspices of the parent division. Not only infantrymen were held by the camps: so were reinforcements for all arms and services. The change was significant, particularly since divisions were now responsible for the training and administration of their own reinforcements.[16]

The procedure for filling reinforcement demands as set out in the *Field Service Regulations* was simple and straightforward. Divisions demanded reinforcements from the Inspector-General of Communications (IGC), who sent men forward from base depots to their divisions and then, presumably, demanded replacements from regimental depots in Britain.[17] But there was no central mechanism to control the movement of these men, which presented a very real possibility that men would become lost in the system or that units would exceed their establishment. Hence, GHQ

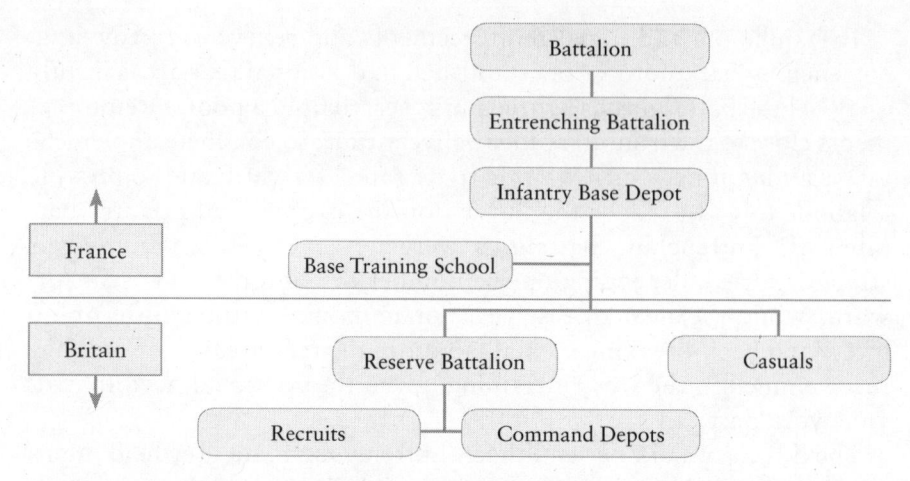

Figure 7.2 British infantry reinforcement structure, July 1915. Casuals were men returning to France from England who had been on extended leave, or had attended a course, or had been posted to France. Some were required to attend the Base Training School.

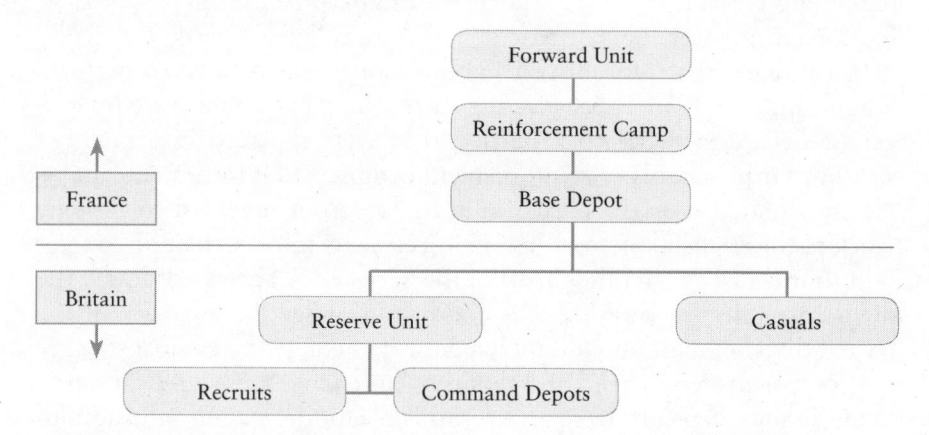

Figure 7.3 British reinforcement structure: all arms, September 1917. The reinforcement camp held reinforcements in the corps rear area for all arms and services. Base training schools at infantry base depots were suspended after the Étaples Mutiny in September 1917.

3rd Echelon was formed as the central authority for the movement of men to and from the various components of the reinforcement system. All reinforcement demands had to be submitted to the 3rd Echelon.

```
        AG GHQ 1st Echelon
    GHQ 2nd Echelon
        DAG GHQ 3rd Echelon
    Canadian Section    Dominion Sections
  OC Havre Base    Reinforcement Camp
  OC Reinforcements
  Base Depot
```

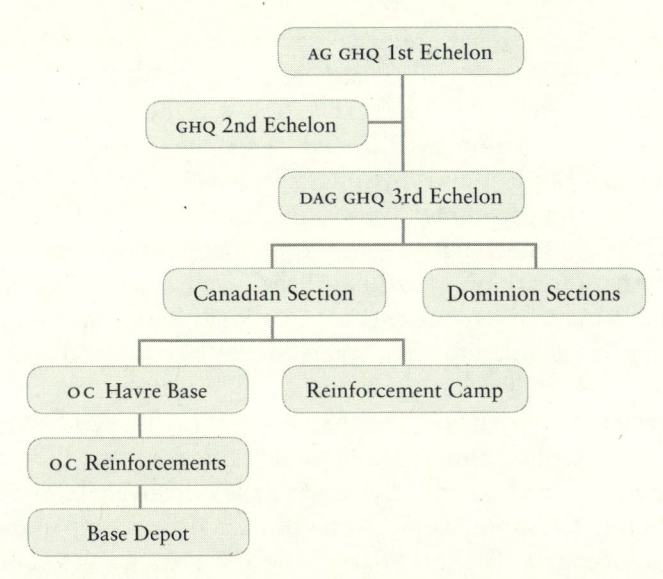

Figure 7.4 Simplified organizational control of reinforcements, September 1917. GHQ 2nd Echelon provided administrative services to the 1st Echelon, known generally as "GHQ." Both GHQ 1st and 2nd Echelons as well as the reinforcement camp were in the forward areas. The remainder were part of the Lines of Communication under command of the Inspector-General of Communications. In the case of British reinforcements, the DAG 3rd Echelon dealt directly with OC Havre (or Étaples) Base and OC Reinforcements.

CANADIAN PROCEDURES

The staff required to administer the reinforcement system was surprisingly large and grew exponentially throughout the war. The Canadian Section, GHQ 3rd Echelon at Rouen, for example, started in February 1915 with 17 officers and 73 men. By November 1918, the Section was manned by 22 officers and 486 men. Admittedly, there were four divisions on the continent, but even so the growth of what was essentially a manpower bookkeeping office is surprising.[18]

The Canadian Section dealt with all aspects of personnel management, including eligibility for working pay, promotion to acting rank, and compassionate leave to Canada. One of the more important matters the Section concerned itself with were war establishments, which listed, by rank, the number of officers, NCOs, and men to which the unit was entitled. Reinforcements could be demanded only to make up deficiencies in the establishment, and the clerks of the Canadian Section spent a good deal of their time comparing reinforcement demands against authorized establishments and strength returns to ensure that units did not accumulate surplus manpower.

Wastage generated two reports. The first was the Casualty State submitted after every action, which gave the estimated number of other ranks killed, wounded, and missing. This was not a demand for reinforcements, but "a preliminary report in order to allow the Commander to adjust his fighting strength to the requirements, and also to enable the IGC to prepare for the forwarding of the necessary reinforcements."[19] The actual demand for reinforcements, or Field Return A.F.B.213, was submitted every Sunday to GHQ 3rd Echelon by mail or dispatch rider. The return was divided into four parts, the last of which was reserved for supplementary comments. The first part was a summary showing the number of personnel, animals, and vehicles held by the unit, together with shortages, which alerted the staff to the effectiveness of each unit. The second was a summary by name of Part II Orders listing wastage together with causes. The third part of the A.F.B.213 was a summary of personnel needed by rank, trade, and technical qualifications (e.g., cook, sniper, machine gunner), together with a summary of horses and mules required by type and class to complete the establishment. This part of the return was, in effect, the reinforcement demand for both men and animals.[20]

Insofar as the CEF was concerned, field returns were submitted directly to the Canadian Section GHQ 3rd Echelon, which then compared the unit strength, losses, and reinforcements demanded against the approved establishment. Provided the numbers matched, the Section then issued instructions to the entrenching battalions or the CCRC to send reinforcements forward and notified the Canadian base depots through OC Reinforcements to refill the entrenching battalions or reinforcement camp. The Section then forwarded a request to the War Office for men to replenish the base depots. In turn, the War Office instructed CTD Shorncliffe to forward sufficient reinforcements to bring the base depots up to strength. The procedure was modified in November 1916 when reinforcement demands were submitted to HQ OMFC, but otherwise the routine remained unchanged.[21]

The system may have provided firm control over manpower, but it was cumbersome and time-consuming. Unit losses could be made up relatively quickly by the entrenching battalions or the Corps Reinforcement Camp, but the bureaucratic procedures involved delayed the movement of reinforcements from England that were needed to replenish the base depots. This could have serious consequences, depending on the amount of wastage. If a battalion suffered more than two hundred losses, for example, the stock of reinforcements in both the entrenching battalion and the base depot would have been exhausted. Obviously, this was unacceptable, and during times of heavy losses both HQ CTD and the base depot were subjected to considerable pressure to speed up the movement of reinforcements. This may have been counterproductive, however, since arguably men who had not completed their training at the base depot were prone to make more mistakes in battle and hence suffer a higher casualty rate.

Little is known about the length of time between the receipt of the casualty demand at GHQ 3rd Echelon and the dispatch of reinforcements to the base depot. In February 1916, Major-General MacDougall complained that it took an average of four weeks before demands reached CTD Shorncliffe, but matters appear to have improved somewhat thereafter.[22] A sample of seventeen drafts sent to the base depot in August, September, and October 1917 shows that demands took about three weeks to reach reserve units in England and that, on average, drafts arrived in France about thirty-two days after the initial demand was submitted to GHQ 3rd Echelon.

The time required at each stage, as shown in table 7.1, reflects the average, although individual drafts varied considerably. Draft Number 86 reached the base depot on 6 October 1917, only fourteen days after the demand was submitted to HQ OMFC, whereas Draft Number 81 took twenty-five days because of a two-week delay at the reserve unit, possibly because men had to complete their training.

WASTAGE

The number of men held at various points in the reinforcement stream was governed by the projected wastage at the front. The pre-war forecast of wastage was an annual loss of 80 per cent for infantry battalions in an active theatre of operations, but this proved to be an underestimate.[23] From August to December 1914, the wastage for British divisions in France and Belgium was 80.4 per cent or, assuming no let-up in the intensity, 193 per cent per annum.[24] The pre-war rates were therefore revised, and in April 1915 the War Office notified Canada that 6,000 infantry reinforcements had to be shipped to England every three months (or 2,000 per month) to maintain the 1st Canadian Division in the field.[25] Two months later, with the deployment of the 2nd Canadian Division to England, the War Office increased the monthly requirement to 4,000

Table 7.1 CEF average draft times

Action	Time, days	Cumulative time, days
Receipt of A.F.B. 213 at GHQ 3rd Echelon	7–9	7–9
Consolidating, checking and forwarding demands to HQ OMFC	4	11–13
HQ OMFC authority to CTD to provide drafts	6	17–19
CTD preparation of drafts	3	20–22
Issue of War Office movement order	8	28–30
Movement to base depot in France	2	30–32

Source: LAC, RG 9, III D3, vol. 5046, file 910, reel T-10938, War Diary Canadian Section GHQ 3rd Echelon, Appendix 7 to September 1917.

reinforcements.[26] The annual wastage rate of 200 per cent, therefore, clearly reflected British losses in 1914.

The revised wastage rate, however, was overstated, probably because it was based on losses during the prolonged period of intense combat that included the retreat from Mons, the Battle of the Marne, and, above all, the First Battle of Ypres, which destroyed much of the pre-war British regular army. Wastage is the product of the intensity and duration of battle; fighting after 1914 may have been intense, but it was over a shorter period. For the CEF, engaged in combat for the first time in February 1915, the annual wastage rate for the infantry was much less than the War Office forecast of June 1915.

From August 1916 to November 1918, the four divisions of the Canadian Corps, with an average strength of 64,376 all ranks, including pioneer battalions, lost on average 6,051 men every month from all causes. The annual wastage rate for the infantry was in the order of 108 per cent, a rate comparable to British Expeditionary Force infantry divisions, which had an average casualty rate of 97.2 per cent during the same period.[27] To maintain each division in the field, therefore, an average of 1,500 reinforcements were required every month from reserve battalions in England, which in turn had to be replenished by drafts from Canada. Whether Militia HQ was aware of this rate is uncertain. Still, the actual wastage rate is a useful benchmark by which to measure the effectiveness of the reinforcement stream.

Wastage did not consist only of battle casualties; men had to be replaced for a wide variety of reasons. Some died of natural causes, others were accidently killed or injured, some were posted to other units, and others fell sick and had to be evacuated to England. There was also a steady trickle of minors who were too young to serve in France, as well as men

Table 7.2 Wastage, other ranks: selected arms and services*

Corps†	Average monthly strength	Average monthly wastage, %	Battle wastage, %	Non-battle wastage, %	Men required
Machine gun	5,833	11.5	2.9	8.6	671
Service Corps	5,489	10.4	0.3	10.1	571
Infantry	64,376	9.4	5.5	4.0	6,051
Artillery	17,535	8.1	1.4	6.7	1,420
Medical Corps	4,692	7.4	0.6	6.8	347
Cavalry	2,548	5.3	2.2	3.1	135
Forestry Corps	9,738	3.2	> 1	3.2	312

* Table excludes the Canadian Engineers together with the Canadian Railway Troops, Corps HQ, and miscellaneous units.
† Infantry and Medical Corps averages are based on data from February 1916 to November 1918. The remaining averages are based on data from May 1917 to November 1918.

selected for courses in England, and a very small number who were given compassionate leave in Canada. The proportion of non-battle wastage was surprisingly high, and from February 1916 to November 1918 amounted to 60.3 per cent of all losses in France and Belgium. Interestingly, the monthly wastage rate for the Canadian Machine Gun Corps and the Service Corps was higher than for the infantry, although when it came to battle losses the infantry were clearly the worst off. But, even with a lower overall wastage rate, the infantry was the largest corps and the majority of reinforcements were therefore infantrymen.

Surprisingly, 32.4 per cent of all losses, accounting for 106,353 men, resulted from postings to other units. There were many reasons for these postings. Those with lowered medical categories were exiled to Service Corps, forestry, or labour companies; cavalrymen with poor horsemanship were posted to infantry battalions; and infantrymen were sent to other battalions. Postings could also take place when specific arms were short of reinforcements from England. In April 1918, for example, the Canadian Corps transferred 300 men to the Canadian Cavalry Brigade to bring the regiments up to strength after heavy losses at Moreuil and Rifle Woods.[28] Depending on how long a unit had been in France, the number of men posted out could vary. The 16th Battalion, for example, lost 588 men between March 1915 and November 1918, the 72nd Battalion lost 292 from August 1916 to the Armistice, and the 85th Battalion posted out 166 between February 1917 and November 1918.

Table 7.2 reflects the average monthly rate and not the product of specific actions. In April 1918, for example, after heavy fighting at Moreuil and Rifle Woods, wastage in the Canadian Cavalry Brigade shot up to 21.7 per cent, of which 18.7 per cent was related to battle. At the other end of the spectrum, in July 1918, when the Canadian Corps was largely disengaged, infantry wastage fell to 8.8 per cent, and only 0.7 per cent of all losses were battle-related. In contrast, during the bitter and intense fighting in June 1916 at Mount Sorrel, infantry battle losses were 16.3 per cent, or 19 per cent from all causes. Similarly, at Vimy Ridge in April 1917, infantry battle losses were 12.1 per cent, or 14.5 per cent overall. The reinforcement structure, therefore, had to be able to provide enough men to meet wildly varying wastage rates, not all of which could be forecast. But it was not easy to increase the number of reinforcements at the base depots and, as the Commandant of the Canadian General Base Depot pointed out in February 1917, overcrowding could lead to serious problems related to improvised tented accommodation and to washing and sanitary facilities that were intended for fewer men.[29]

Whether or not the reinforcement system maintained units at full strength, the actual number of men available was invariably less than what the establishment called for. Men who were sick and admitted to a field ambulance within the divisional area were struck off strength after seven days, which allowed reinforcements to be demanded. In contrast, those who were evacuated directly to base hospitals were struck off strength on the day of their evacuation. However, those treated for venereal disease at a rear-area hospital were not struck off strength regardless of how long they were hospitalized. Battle casualties were struck off strength the day they were known to have been killed or wounded, while the missing could not be struck off strength for twenty-one days.[30] There were also men who were "on command" or employed away from their units, often for prolonged periods, who were still on strength and could therefore not be replaced.

In some cases, those on command augmented other units. In March 1918, for example, the Canadian Light Horse had 152 men lent out to the 1st Canadian Tunnelling Company as labourers.[31] In other cases, men were placed on command to staff new units created in France, such as machine gun companies, light trench mortar batteries, tramways companies, concert parties, salvage companies, wood-cutting parties, and divisional baths. In time, some of these units were formally established. Machine gun companies had been formed from battalion machine gun sections at the end of October 1915, but the establishment of the Canadian Machine Gun Corps was not approved until April 1917. Until then, machine gunners were on strength of their parent battalions.[32] Tramway companies had been in operation since March 1916, but until they were officially established in November 1917 they had to depend on pioneer battalions for personnel.[33]

Some of those who were on command to fill rear-area administrative positions were absorbed by employment companies established in June 1917. The diarist for the 2nd Canadian Employment Company, for example, noted in June 1917 that men taken on strength were serving with a variety of agencies: Town Majors, 2nd Division schools, No. 2 Sanitary Section, divisional baths, and the Y.M.C.A.[34] Some units such as light trench mortar batteries were never given formal establishments and had to be staffed until the end of the war by men on command from their parent infantry battalions.[35]

From August 1916 until November 1918, an average of 16,833 men every month from units in France and Belgium were hospitalized for illness or wounds, or were absent, on leave, or on command. On average, about 14.3 per cent of the CEF on the continent were non-effective in the sense that they were not physically present with their units. Half of these men were on command, and although they may have been performing a useful function they were not available for their primary duties. To some degree, this situation detracted from the performance of their parent units.

Those who were sick in hospital or on command accounted for about three-quarters of all non-effectives. However, it is striking that the infantry and cavalry were the only two corps for which the number of men on command exceeded those hospitalized for illness. The infantry made up 54.9 per cent of all CEF personnel in France and Belgium, but provided 80.1 per cent of all men who were on command, perhaps because they constituted a large group with no specialized skills and were therefore a convenient manpower pool that was easy to tap.

Needless to say, commanding officers intensely disliked the effect of these detachments. In May 1916, for example, Lieutenant-Colonel Edward Hilliam of the 25th Canadian Battalion wrote to HQ 5th Canadian Infantry Brigade: "I wish very strongly to bring to your notice that although [the] nominal strength of the Battalion is 995 Other Ranks, the actual fighting strength of the Battalion very rarely exceeds, if ever, 700 men. The reason for this is wastage and sick, and men employed away from the Battalion."[36] Hilliam did not add, as he could have, that after deducting men with the unit echelon, the 25th would have had a

Table 7.3 Monthly average of non-effectives, August 1916–November 1918

Corps	Sick	On command	Non-effective*	Gross strength	Net strength	Non-effective rate, %
Infantry	2,197	6,745	11,736	64,377	52,641	18.2
Cavalry	114	166	388	2,548	2,160	15.2
Machine gun	341	191	824	5,833	5,009	14.1
Artillery	698	585	2,006	17,535	15,529	11.4
Service Corps	149	143	467	5,489	5,002	8.5
Medical Corps	148	117	441	5,320	4,879	8.3
Forestry Corps	341	49	661	9,729	9,068	6.8
All units†	4,128	8,414	16,833	117,361	100,528	14.3

* This column includes those in rear area hospitals who were expected to return, as well as those on leave or absent without leave and those listed in columns 2 and 3.

† Engineers, railway troops, tunnelling companies, and miscellaneous units are included in the total of all units together with the other corps listed.

trench strength of about 500 men. The 25th, however, was well off in comparison to the 15th Battalion, which at the end of September 1918 had 827 men but could muster only 377 for the trenches.[37]

The problem of these non-effectives was not unique to the CEF; in June 1918, GHQ estimated that every month each British infantry battalion had an average of 140 men in hospital, on leave, on command, or attending a course. Since British battalions at this time were restricted to 900 men, the non-effective rate was 15.6 per cent. But not all of the 760 men present with the battalion were available for the trenches. Sixty-one men at battalion HQ and four men with each of the four companies had administrative functions and therefore had to be left in the rear, out of harm's way. A hundred men were also left out of battle to provide a nucleus on which to rebuild the battalion should it incur heavy casualties. A fully staffed British battalion therefore had a fighting strength of 583 men, or 65 per cent of the official establishment.[38] Assuming that Canadian battalions had the same number of men employed on administrative duties and also left a hundred men out of battle, their trench strength was about 638 men – or fewer, if there was any delay in replacing wastage with reinforcements.

SUMMARY

The manpower problem, therefore, faced by Canadian commanders at all levels was how to reduce the gap between the effective strength and the established strength. Their efforts to do so not only affected units on the continent but also had a knock-on effect on the reinforcement structure in Canada and in England. The effects of this need for manpower on the reinforcement system form the underlying theme of chapters 8 and 9.

8

Reinforcements: Canada to England

Producing reinforcements in Canada was one thing, but getting them overseas was neither simple nor straightforward. Reserve units in England had to hold enough trainees to satisfy both routine and unexpected demands from units in France. However, accommodation in England was at a premium, and this meant the reinforcement stream from Canada had to be regulated to refill reserve units as they were depleted of reinforcements for France. Ideally, this should have been done by depots in Canada with the dual role of recruiting and holding men, but monthly recruit intakes varied wildly, and, for the most part, peacetime barracks were too few and accommodation had to be improvised.

Cavalry, field and siege artillery, Service Corps, Medical Corps, and Engineers were able to establish depots early that served to warehouse reinforcements until they were needed overseas. However, these corps could do this because their numbers were relatively few. In contrast, the infantry, by far the biggest corps, had to deal not only with large numbers of recruits but also with arbitrary decisions by the political leadership. The upshot was a bewildering variety of infantry reinforcement units, regional depots, reserve battalions, ad hoc drafts, militia depots, and formed infantry battalions. It was not until August 1917, when territorial depot battalions were formed, that the CEF had an efficient and rational organization by which to deliver infantry reinforcements to reserve battalions in England.

EARLY DAYS: 1914–15

As discussed in chapter 7, the pre-war British reinforcement system was based on permanent regimental depots that handled reservists recalled to the colours and trained raw recruits. However, the Canadian Forces did not have reservists, and apart from a handful of tiny Permanent Force depots, there was nothing to sustain an overseas contingent. The CEF reinforcement system therefore had to be created from scratch.

The logical basis for a reinforcement structure would have been the Militia, but inter-unit rivalry made this a difficult proposition, particularly in cities such as Toronto, where there were a number of strong, well-established militia infantry units, each of which was capable of forming a depot. Moreover, links between CEF battalions and militia regiments were tenuous, since militia units provided volunteers for composite CEF units but were not mobilized as such. Also, there were units such as the Princess Patricia's Canadian Light Infantry (PPCLI) and the Automobile Machine Gun Brigade that had no connections with the militia.

To accommodate these factors, Major-General Gwatkin, Chief of the General Staff (CGS), suggested to Sam Hughes in September 1914 that generic regional depots should be created across the country where recruits could be concentrated and where "from time to time they would be drafted to the front as reinforcements."[1] The concept was sound, but given the distances involved, sending reinforcements directly to France from Canada was unrealistic. In any event, the War Office decision in November 1914 that surplus manpower from the 1st Division should be stockpiled in England as future reinforcements meant that, for better or for worse, England would be the overseas staging base for the CEF.[2]

The regional centres envisaged by the CGS were never formed, with the exception of one depot established in Calgary on 11 October 1914 to handle reinforcements for the PPCLI and other infantry battalions if necessary.[3] However, the Calgary depot was short-lived; on 18 November 1914 it was suddenly disbanded and its personnel absorbed by the newly authorized 31st Battalion.[4] The decision to do away with the depot was probably made by Hughes, since he was the one man in the Department of Militia and Defence who could override Gwatkin. Why he would do this is unknown; perhaps, given his preference for battalions with distinct identities, he had an aversion to generic infantry institutions.

Hughes may have disliked regional reinforcement centres for the infantry, but he apparently had no objections to central depots for other arms and services and did not interfere with their establishment. In June and August 1915, for example, the artillery formed twelve depot batteries to provide reinforcements for the 1st and 2nd divisional artillery. Some of these batteries were eventually sent overseas as operational units, but others were raised in their place. By 1917, there were sixteen depot batteries in every district in Canada except MD 5 (Eastern Quebec).[5] At the same time, C Battery of the Royal Canadian Horse Artillery (RCHA) formed a depot to provide horse gunners to the RCHA Brigade overseas, while pre-war Royal Canadian Garrison Artillery depots in Kingston and Quebec City produced reinforcements for the garrison artillery, and improvised depots at Cobourg, Saint John (New Brunswick), and Halifax provided men for the siege artillery.

Medical Corps reinforcements were provided by Field Ambulance Depots formed in January 1915 in Victoria, Calgary, Winnipeg, London, Toronto, and Montreal. The following year, two others were formed at Kingston and Saint John.[6] The Service Corps also created training depots: one at Camp Sewell, Manitoba (later Winnipeg) in June 1915 for western recruits, and one in Toronto in July 1915 for eastern recruits. Service Corps depots did not mobilize units. As the Quartermaster General wrote in August 1915, "CASC Training Depots are to provide personnel only as reinforcements."[7] The depots proved their worth; in the case of No. 2 Service Corps Training Depot in Toronto, ten drafts of one to two hundred reinforcements each were sent to the Service Corps Training Depot in England between July 1915 and December 1916.

Depots were also established to provide reinforcements for new arms that had not existed in the pre-war militia or Permanent Force. For example, a total of thirteen regiments of Canadian Mounted Rifles, were raised, including one brigade from Ontario. To provide reinforcements, a depot was created in September 1915, initially in Toronto and then at Scott Barracks in Hamilton's gritty east end.[8] However, in January 1916 the amalgamation of Canadian Mounted Rifle regiments in France and their conversion to infantry altered the depot's purpose, and reinforcements were provided both to cavalry and infantry reserve units in England.

Cyclist units were another wartime creation: in August 1915, a cyclist depot was opened in Toronto to receive recruits from across Canada.[9] The arrangement was awkward, however, and by February 1917 platoon-strength cyclist depots had been established in all nine military districts to feed men to the company-sized central depot in Toronto.[10] The cyclist depots provided a steady stream of reinforcements; by July 1917, enough men were warehoused with the Canadian Reserve Cyclist Company in England to meet anticipated needs for the next twelve months. Recruiting therefore stopped, and the Cyclist Depot, together with the satellite platoons, faded away.[11] Ironically, the depot vanished because it was too successful.

Depots were also added for other corps. The Canadian Engineer Training Depot, including field engineers and signallers, had been established at Rockcliffe in Ottawa in April 1915, but when it was moved to St John's (St-Jean-sur-Richelieu), Quebec, the signals component was designated as the Signal Depot and remained at Rockcliffe until the end of the war.[12] By 1917, responsibility for forestry and railroad reinforcements had been handed to the engineers and new depots were created: a forestry depot at Brockville, a railroad construction depot at Hamilton, and a skilled railway workers' depot co-located with the Engineer Depot at St John's.[13]

Two of the three regiments in the Canadian Cavalry Brigade (Royal Canadian Dragoons and Strathcona's Horse) were Permanent Force units and were provided with reinforcements throughout the war by their pre-war depots in Toronto and Winnipeg. The last unit, the Fort Garry Horse, was a wartime creation based on the 6th Canadian Infantry Battalion, largely raised in 1914 by the 34th Fort Garry Horse from Winnipeg. In this case, reinforcements were provided by an ad hoc "service squadron" organized in March 1916 with the aim of sending a hundred-man draft overseas every three months.[14] The service squadron worked well, but there were administrative difficulties since men were not attested in the CEF until they were drafted overseas. As militiamen, the soldiers had a lower pay scale than in the CEF, and married men were not entitled to separation allowance. The problem was finally corrected in July 1917 when the squadron was recognized by Militia HQ as a bona fide CEF unit.[15]

The corps depots functioned well and, with the exception of the Cyclists, continued to operate until 1918 with no apparent difficulties. Why were the non-infantry arms and services able to form depots early on while the infantry could not? The answer may lie with the pre-war responsibilities of senior officers at Militia HQ that carried over to the wartime army. In brief, each corps had a senior officer at Militia HQ who served as the technical commander of the arm or corps in question. The Director of Artillery, for example, was also the "Officer Administering the Royal Canadian Artillery," or OA RCA. As such, he coordinated technical and organizational policies for all artillery units in Canada. Similarly, the Director General of Engineer Services was also the "Officer Administering the Royal Canadian Engineers," or OA RCE, while the Director General of Supply and Transport and the Director General of Medical Services were routinely consulted on matters concerning the organization of their corps. Other directors at Militia HQ administered the Ordnance, Pay, and Veterinary Corps.

The authority given to these officers did not supersede the normal chain of command, and the ordnance detachment in London, for example, remained under the command of HQ MD 1. However, the administrative heads at Militia HQ were routinely consulted on training and organizational matters and, as such, were able to exercise considerable influence. In contrast, the infantry had no friend in court and remained subject to local influence and to the hasty decisions of Sam Hughes.

With the abrupt cancellation of the regional infantry depots proposed by Gwatkin in 1914 there was no organization to forward infantry reinforcements to England. To resolve the problem, Militia HQ formed reserve, depot, or feeder battalions (the terminology varied) in November 1914 across the country under the command of the local district headquarters. At the same time, other battalions were raised that were intended to be fighting units. By the end of November 1914, there were fifteen battalions in Canada in various stages of recruiting, of which eight were earmarked for a second division to be formed in England, together with the four surplus battalions from the First Contingent.[16] The remaining seven battalions, together with another eight to be raised when accommodation became available after the 2nd Division sailed to England, were intended to provide reinforcements to the twenty-five battalions outside of Canada.[17]

Terminology is important: organizing *battalions* rather than *depots* created difficulties. Depots were administrative units with establishments that could readily be increased or decreased to match the reinforcement flow; battalions, on the other hand, had fixed establishments. There was no expectation for depots, as there was for battalions, that they would be sent to the front intact. The term *battalion* implied there was a place in the firing line and, not unreasonably, most reserve battalion commanding officers were convinced their battalion would be sent to the front – if only Militia HQ could be made to see reason.

By August 1915, Militia HQ had decided that each infantry battalion at the front would be linked with three reserve battalions, two in Canada and one in England. With two divisions or twenty-four battalions at the front (twenty-five, including the PPCLI) a total of seventy-five reserve battalions were required: fifty in Canada and twenty-five in England.[18] Building up the reserve establishment in England was a problem; once the reserve battalions left Canada they were no longer controlled by Militia HQ, and the War Office could transfer them from England to the front. This possibility was recognized by Gwatkin at Militia HQ, who wrote in January 1915 that the reserve battalions could "be utilized as circumstances may require, either in Canada for draft-giving purposes, or in England as training depots, or as complete units in the seat of war."[19]

Surprisingly, no formal directive was published concerning the role of reserve units, although at least forty-seven of the sixty-four battalions raised from December 1914 to September 1915 were designated in one way or another as reserve battalions. The matter was evidently considered at Militia HQ, and the Adjutant-General wrote in January 1915 that "the name might act as a deterrent [to recruiting]."[20]

The designation of reserve battalions was not kept secret, however. Militia Orders from 16 June 1915 onward routinely listed officers who had been posted to various "Depot Battalions," but these orders were administrative, not executive, and the absence of formal direction produced confusion on both sides of the Atlantic.[21] The first three reserve battalions (the 23rd, 30th, and 32nd) that arrived at Shorncliffe in February 1915 were unaware of their intended role and, as the CTD commander wrote to Militia HQ in March 1915, there were complaints because "it was not known by them until they reached here [Shorncliffe] that their Battalions were to be broken up as reinforcements for the Canadian Infantry now fighting in France."[22]

Nor were parliamentarians aware of the intended role of reserve battalions raised in their constituencies. In April 1915, Prime Minister Borden went so far as to address the House of Commons and name twenty-four reserve battalions that were intended to be used "in Canada for draft-giving purposes, or in England as training depots, or as complete units at the seat of war."[23] Even this did not clarify the matter; as late as June 1915, Major-General Carson, the minister's personal representative in England, wrote to Sam Hughes noting that he was puzzled by the designation "depot battalion" and asked whether these units should be left intact.[24]

Depot battalions were far from popular. In Manitoba, the Commander of MD 10, Colonel S.B. Steele, thought the concept broke faith with men who had enlisted in the hope of a speedy trip to the front lines with their comrades.[25] Further east, HQ MD 6 in Halifax reluctantly recommended in November 1914 that the 26th New Brunswick Battalion be used as a feeder to the 25th from Nova Scotia, but warned Militia HQ that "[t]he idea of feeding either battalion from the other would it is thought be extremely unpopular."[26] At Camp Sewell, Manitoba, in August 1915, commanding officers, struggling to keep their battalions up to strength, complained bitterly to Major-General John Hughes, the camp commandant, about the requirement to send company-sized drafts to England.

Hughes, who seems to have been aware of the role of reserve battalions, recommended to Militia HQ that the battalions be sent to England complete or remain in Canada and be formally designated as reserve units. The response was swift: the following day, the Adjutant-General notified the Commandant that units at Camp Sewell were draft-giving depot battalions. A similar message was sent to HQ MD 13 on the same day, which suggests that the same problem existed elsewhere.[27]

Reserve battalions were not free from political interference. Lieutenant-Colonel Griesbach, a prominent Alberta Conservative and member of the First Contingent, was authorized to return to Edmonton and raise the 49th Battalion. Before doing so, he received assurances from Sam Hughes that his unit would be sent to the front intact. Learning on arrival in England in June 1915 that the 49th was to be a reserve battalion providing reinforcements to the 10th and 31st Battalions in the trenches, Griesbach protested directly to Hughes.[28] Whether or not Hughes interceded on behalf of the 49th is unknown, but on 9 October 1915 the battalion embarked for France, eventually to become part of the 3rd Canadian Division – leaving Canadian HQ in London to make other arrangements to reinforce Alberta battalions at the front.

The 49th was not the only battalion to change roles. The 5th Royal Highlanders of Canada (Black Watch), a prestigious militia unit in Montreal, recruited three battalions, starting with the 13th in September 1914. A few months later, in February 1915, the Black Watch raised the 42nd Battalion. Intended by the 5th to be a depot battalion to provide reinforcements exclusively to the 13th, the 42nd was considered to be a generic reserve battalion by Militia HQ, which ruled that "should the exigencies of the service so demand, [the 42nd Battalion] might be called upon to furnish reinforcements for any unit, Highland for choice, or Lowland, or even plain Canadian."[29] In June 1915 the 42nd sailed to England, and in September the Black Watch raised the 73rd Battalion. It was then decided by Militia HQ that the 73rd would remain in Canada to reinforce the 42nd in England, which in turn would provide men to the 13th in France.

The arrangements envisaged by Militia HQ did not last long. In October 1915, the 42nd was sent from England to France to help form the 3rd Canadian Division, while the 73rd remained in Canada without providing drafts to the 13th, 42nd, or any other battalion. Subsequently, in March 1916, the 73rd Battalion sailed to England and, three months later, joined the 4th Canadian Division and embarked for France.

The 87th Battalion, raised by the Canadian Grenadier Guards, a politically well-connected Montreal militia regiment (the Honorary Colonel was Major-General J.W. Carson, Hughes's personal representative in England), was authorized on 10 September 1915. The role of the 87th was straightforward: "provide drafts [to England], consisting of 5 Lieutenants and 250 other ranks, from time to time."[30] The designation did not last long, and only three days later Militia HQ announced that the 87th would no longer be a reserve unit but would sail overseas intact as a service battalion.[31] The reason for the sudden *volte-face* is not certain; perhaps the title of "depot" or "reserve" battalion was felt by the parent militia unit to be inconsistent with the social status of a politically well-connected guards regiment, or perhaps Carson was able to lodge a protest with Hughes.

The policy of using linked reserve battalions in Canada and England to provide reinforcements to the front lasted from February until December 1915, when the last drafts sailed from Canada. The idea of using linked battalions on both sides of the Atlantic was, on paper at least, a rational solution to a knotty problem, but it was impossible to sustain because of developments in England that were beyond Ottawa's control or influence. The 1st and 2nd Divisions were raised in Canada, but the 3rd and 4th Divisions were formed overseas at the behest of the War Office. The battalions for these new formations had to come from somewhere, and ultimately the two divisions absorbed eleven reserve battalions in England. In any event, the War Office believed that one reserve battalion was capable of reinforcing two fighting battalions; as early as April 1915, it notified Sam Hughes that six more depot battalions could be forwarded, stating, "No other depot cadres are required."[32] Since there were seven reserve battalions in England at the time, plus the PPCLI Depot, this meant that only thirteen reserve units were needed to sustain twenty-five battalions at the front – about half the number envisaged by Militia HQ.

The reserve battalions in Canada were never the mainstay of the reinforcement stream: only 36.7 per cent of the 38,212 men who arrived in England in 1915 came from reserve battalions, while the remainder were provided by a handful of militia units and formed battalions. This was a harbinger of what was to come.[33]

It is easy to find fault with those responsible for creating the reinforcement structure: the CGS, Militia HQ, and district headquarters. However, creating such a large force from scratch using a peacetime army that relied on part-time soldiers was a difficult process; infrastructure, equipment, and expertise were all lacking. It might, perhaps, have been better if the 1st and 2nd Divisions had not been committed to action until an adequate reinforcement organization was put in place, but given the demand for units in France this was simply not possible. The wonder is not that the depot battalions failed, but that they were able to provide the reinforcements they did.

1916: A REINFORCEMENT TSUNAMI

The system of linked reserve battalions was overtaken when the establishment of the CEF was raised, initially to 250,000 men in October 1915 and then to 500,000 in January 1916. Recruiting took off dramatically, peaking at 33,960 men in March 1916. More than a hundred battalions were formed to accommodate the new recruits. The situation that was created can best be described as chaos. Instead of a rational, coherent reinforcement structure, new battalions were created haphazardly across the country by Hughes, often with little or no warning to the hard-pressed staff at Militia HQ. "The Minister desires that a New Overseas Battalion be located at Winnipeg," wrote Hughes's personal secretary, Ena MacAdam, to the Adjutant-General in October 1915, "to be known as the 90th; and authorized to be raised at once."[34] With so many new battalions raised between October 1915 and December 1916, Militia HQ, with a limited staff, could do little but feed, clothe, equip and house the new units. The infantry reinforcement system in Canada therefore became a matter of shipping battalions overseas as quickly as possible.

However, this was far easier said than done. Accommodation for complete battalions in England consisted not only of barracks, but also of facilities for administrative purposes: offices, messes, stables, and quartermaster stores. Regardless of the number of men on strength, each unit occupied the same amount of space. But facilities in England were limited, and as early as November 1915 the AG noted that the War Office had "notified the department that they have no accommodation for any more depot battalions at present."[35] Nor did the situation improve in the following months. In June 1916, the Adjutant-General advised Hughes that 10,000 infantrymen would be sent to England in July and recommended that, for administrative and financial reasons, drafts rather than complete units be sent. The Adjutant-General then went on to add that, although sending battalions intact might appeal to local sentiment, only fifty-two battalion lines were available in England; thus, "if complete units are sent, a corresponding number of empties must be returned to Canada."[36]

The effect of using complete battalions rather than generic depots or reserve battalions to hold reinforcements was to slow the movement of reinforcements to England. Battalions had a fixed establishment of

996 men and remained in Canada as long as possible to recruit their full complement as well as to complete both individual and collective training. It is striking that those who sailed to England with formed battalions in 1916 had served for thirty-one weeks in Canada, while those who sailed in 1917 had marked time for forty-three weeks.

Drafts, on the other hand, did not suffer from these handicaps. They were much smaller than battalions, with only 50 to 250 men. Less time was needed to recruit these numbers, and there was no need to delay departure to undergo collective training. Nor was accommodation in England a problem, since drafts were small enough to be absorbed by reserve battalions. On average, men sent to England with drafts in 1915 served only eleven weeks in Canada, whereas their counterparts in 1917 were in Canada for eighteen weeks (see tables 8.1 and 8.2).

The difference between the various groups is significant, and it is difficult not to conclude that Sam Hughes did the CEF a grave disservice by forming large numbers of infantry battalions rather than regional depots.

Keeping formed battalions in Canada for lengthy periods could also result in discipline problems and increased desertion rates. In Quebec City, orders to embark the 33rd Battalion were cancelled twice at the last minute. An anonymous officer of the 33rd wrote in November 1915 that "the men are getting so disgusted that the training and discipline of the battalion is going back instead of improving and desertions are becoming appallingly frequent. If they don't send us [to England] soon there won't be a Battalion left to send."[37] The anonymous officer was not exaggerating, and in January an anonymous "Member of the Gallant 33rd Battalion" wrote to Militia HQ complaining about being retained in Canada. He concluded, "If we are not to sail to England or be Disbanded, Please allow men to Transfer to other Regiments where there is Efficient Officers."[38]

In Valcartier, the 3rd Brigade commander noted in August 1916 that his four battalions (the 130th, 136th, 139th, and 146th) had no prospect of reaching full strength in the foreseeable future and should embark as soon as possible: "They are all sufficiently trained to proceed to England at once, and if kept in this country for any length of time, they will loose [sic] a large number of men [from desertion]."[39] The 150th and 167th Battalions at Valcartier also had a large number of deserters; in August 1916, the Director General of Mobilization reported to the Adjutant-General that the Camp Commandant "says the balance will soon disappear." Gwynne then added: "It is being arranged to send over these 2 half battalions with the reduced strength of officers, in about 2 weeks."[40] In

Table 8.1 Sample of reinforcements, service in Canada: formed battalions 1916 and drafts 1915*

Service in Canada (weeks)	Sailed with battalions 1916	(%)	Sailed with drafts 1915	(%)
0–5	362	(2.7)	551	(24.4)
6–10	370	(2.7)	856	(37.9)
11–15	537	(4.0)	378	(16.7)
16–20	761	(5.7)	74	(3.3)
21–25	1,153	(8.6)	245	(10.8)
26–30	2,908	(21.6)	79	(3.5)
31–35	3,101	(23.0)	43	(1.9)
36–40	2,105	(15.6)	29	(1.3)
41–45	1,085	(8.1)	3	(0.1)
46–50	619	(4.6)	1	(> 0.1)
< 51	456	(3.4)	1	(> 0.1)
Total	13,467		2,260	

* Based on reinforcements posted to 2 CMR, 4 CMR, 4th Battalion, 16th Battalion, 18th Battalion, 20th Battalion, 72nd Battalion, 85th Battalion and PPCLI. Relatively few men posted to these units in 1916 sailed with drafts, and those who sailed in 1915 are included for purposes of comparison only.

Table 8.2 Sample of reinforcements, service in Canada: formed battalions and drafts, 1917*

Service in Canada (weeks)	Sailed with battalions	(%)	Sailed with drafts	(%)
0–5	114	(3.5)	44	13.7
6–10	98	(3.0)	54	16.8
11–15	146	(4.4)	36	11.2
16–20	192	(5.8)	59	18.3
21–25	177	(5.4)	68	21.1
26–30	141	(4.3)	28	8.7
31–35	198	(6.0)	12	3.7
36–40	214	(6.5)	3	0.9
41–45	255	(7.7)	8	2.5
46–50	347	(10.5)	2	0.6
< 51	1,416	(42.9)	8	2.5
Total	3,298		322	

* Based on reinforcements posted to 2 CMR, 4 CMR, 4th Battalion, 16th Battalion, 18th Battalion, 20th Battalion, 72nd Battalion, 85th Battalion, and PPCLI.

the event, the 150th sailed in September with 515 men, while in November the 167th sent two small drafts overseas with eighty-one men in total after being converted to a recruiting depot.[41]

The creation of a large number of new battalions and the end of the system of reserve battalions adversely affected the infantry reinforcement stream; as Major-General Gwatkin noted in December 1916, "the lack of [a] well-regulated and firmly administered system of organization has interfered with the provision of reinforcements and impeded the upkeep of battalions overseas."[42] Gwatkin's remarks, however, applied only to the infantry. Cavalry depot squadrons as well as the Engineer, Signal, Cyclist, and Service Corps, along with the Medical Corps depots and artillery depot batteries, all continued to send a steady stream of drafts to reserve units in England.

In several cases, districts commanders made efforts to rationalize the manpower structure within their areas. In MD 10, as discussed in chapter 5, Brigadier-General Ruttan created four regimental areas based in Winnipeg, Dauphin, Moose Jaw, and Prince Albert and intended to recruit volunteers for company-sized drafts that could be sent to England.[43] Further east, Brigadier-General Shannon of MD 1 suggested in August 1916 that a depot battalion be created in London to recruit men and provide formed drafts to reserve battalions in England. It is difficult to argue with his reasoning:

> As this would be a unit for drafts entirely, it would be immaterial whether the strength were 2,000, 3,000, 4,000 or more. There would only be one Battalion organization to deal with under this scheme, and it would become expert in the matter of organization, records, training etc. The most fit of the members of this Battalion would be selected for the earliest drafts. The success that has attended the Depot Batteries in this District, and the CAMC Training Depot, leads me to believe that this would work as successfully with the Infantry. Another point in favour of a Depot Battalion would be the immense saving to the public. In place of eleven Commanding Officers and Staffs, eleven bands etc., etc., there would be only one, and when drafts were required, only Lieutenants and privates would be sent over, in place of as now a complement of senior officers who will not likely ever reach the front.[44]

The Adjutant-General at Militia HQ agreed with the concept, but Shannon evidently had second thoughts and in subsequent correspondence suggested a hold on the proposed depot battalion until all battalions in his district had filled their establishment.[45] Militia HQ did not press the point, the status quo remained, and infantry battalions continued to be shovelled overseas as troop ships and accommodation in England became available.

Sending formed battalions to England was the logical outcome of Sam Hughes's means of raising reinforcements. However, with his resignation in November 1916 the policy changed, and no consideration was given to continuing to raise new battalions. As the Adjutant-General commented two weeks after Hughes's departure, "[I]t is impossible to send them [complete battalions] overseas as such, and if they were raised, they would be merely draft giving Depot Battalions."[46] But with no new battalions being created and no depot organization in Canada for the infantry, how could reinforcements be recruited and sent overseas?

In England, the newly created HQ OMFC was also concerned about reinforcements. In December 1916, the issue was discussed at length between Gwatkin in Ottawa and Major-General Sir Richard Turner, the newly appointed Canadian commander in England. This was perhaps the first time that any serious trans-Atlantic effort was made to coordinate reinforcements for the CEF. Both agreed the infantry should be organized on a territorial basis with three linked battalions: a recruiting or depot battalion in Canada, a training battalion in England, and a fighting battalion in France. However, the two disagreed on the details. Turner favoured regional depots in major urban centres, while Gwatkin thought that militia units could form the depots required.[47]

That Gwatkin was fully aware of the difficulties in recruiting is evident from a memorandum he circulated to Militia HQ staff in January 1917:

> A solution of the problem will be difficult to find. After deducting men who have already joined the CEF, workers who cannot be spared, shirkers deaf to the call of duty, and immigrants of alien race, the balance available for military service, even for purposes of home defence, is less than might be supposed. The Militia, moreover, as an organized force has ceased to exist. To a great extent it has been absorbed into the CEF. It has not trained for three years, the period for which militiamen enlist. City corps, or some of them, have gone on recruiting; but the rural corps are empty husks.[48]

Despite this unvarnished appraisal, Gwatkin retained his faith in the militia and in the same memorandum went on to suggest that the militia should be the primary recruiting agency for the CEF. In brief, units should be reconstituted to recruit men for the CEF and train others for home defence, thus releasing members of the CEF for service overseas. City corps would be expected to raise complete units, and rural units would raise platoons or companies. City corps would also create regimental depots, which would not be independent entities but part of a regional depot group "for the purpose of providing drafts for its linked battalion in the United Kingdom."[49] All units would enlist both part-time militiamen and volunteers for the CEF; the CGS thought that some of the new militiamen would acquire a taste for soldiering and transfer to the CEF.

Initially, the idea did not seem far-fetched. A week later, on 15 January 1917, Gwatkin noted that sixteen city corps had started to recruit for the CEF. The results were promising, and Gwatkin thought that an additional thirty-nine city regiments could also be invited to form "regimental depots with a view to raising and training reinforcements for service overseas."[50] The proposal was formalized three days later, on 18 January 1917, and districts were instructed to invite city regiments to form regimental depots to raise drafts for the CEF overseas.[51]

Gwatkin's optimism was not shared by others who were closer to reality. On 13 February 1917, HQ MD 1 reported the results of a meeting with representatives of all units except for the 108th Regiment, where a resolution was "[m]oved by Lieut-Colonel H.R. Abbott, 1st Hussars, seconded by Lieut-Colonel W.T. McMullen, 22nd Regiment, that, in the opinion of this meeting the enlistment of any satisfactory number of men for the Canadian Expeditionary Force is not feasible under present recruiting conditions."[52]

Little is known about the militia regimental depots that were grouped and affiliated with reserve battalions in England. However, the "Record of History" of the 2nd Canadian Reserve Battalion at Shorncliffe noted that affiliated "draft givers were the 13th Royal Regiment, 20th Regiment (Halton Rifles), 38th Regiment (Dufferin Rifles) and the 91st Regiment (Canadian Highlanders)."[53] Three of these units (the 13th, 38th, and 91st) were city corps based in Hamilton and Brantford, while the 20th was a rural corps based in Milton with eight companies scattered across Halton County. Why the 20th was selected when Gwatkin had expressed a preference for urban units is unknown. However, Sir Donald Mann, railway magnate and one of the builders of the Canadian Northern Railway, was the Honorary Colonel of the Regiment, which may have been a factor.[54] In any event, the four regiments were unable to provide enough recruits, and the 2nd Reserve Battalion received reinforcements from virtually every militia unit in central Ontario (MD 2).

Militia units elsewhere were no more effective as draft-finding agencies than those in MD 2. In Walkerton, in MD 1, the 32nd Regiment formed a depot in April 1917 to raise drafts for the 160th Battalion, then serving with the 5th Division in England. However, the response was poor and in June the resulting handful of recruits was handed over to the Central Training Depot in London.[55] In Kitchener, also in MD 1, the 108th Regiment formed a company depot in February 1917 to raise fifty-man drafts to be sent to England. After three months of recruiting throughout Waterloo County, only forty-seven men had enlisted, thirty-four of whom elected to join either the Forestry Corps or the 256th (Railway) Battalion. In view of these results, the depot was disbanded in May 1917.[56]

To replace company depots, HQ MD 1 suggested draft-finding platoons commanded by a junior officer. This proposal was rejected in May 1917 by the Adjutant-General, who wrote that "there is no intention of authorizing officers to recruit drafts of 50 men, to proceed overseas when up to strength, as it might take 6 or 12 months for such drafts to be brought up to strength, and they might possibly never recruit to full strength."[57]

Apart from recruiting difficulties, militia depot companies were ill-suited to provide reinforcement drafts for reserve units in England. Each company was entitled to 6 officers, 10 senior NCOs, 4 buglers, and 208 rank and file.[58] However, in practice, any drafts provided would be much less than the establishment, because, after all, the depot had to maintain its corporate existence. Small drafts were inefficient. Militia HQ had to arrange troop trains, transient accommodation at or near the embarkation port, and troop ships for each draft regardless of size. HQ OMFC also had to make similar arrangements in England to receive the drafts. The administration required to fill a troop ship with small drafts was much greater than if the ship were loaded with a small number of large drafts. Lastly, from the standpoint of the senior officer on each troop ship, controlling a multitude of small drafts must have been similar to herding cats.

The depot companies were also distributed unevenly, which not only provided uneven coverage of potential recruiting areas but also made it difficult to supply routine administrative services such as pay, ordnance, and medical care. Companies in MD 1, for example, were located in Windsor, London, Woodstock, Walkerton, and St Thomas, although the administrative centre of the district was London. Providing a paymaster and medical officer for each company would have been difficult, if not impossible.

Other districts concentrated their depot companies. MD 10 had four out of six companies based in Winnipeg, while MD 2 had six of ten companies based in Toronto and Hamilton. The existence of depot companies was also dependent on the strength of local militia units. In Atlantic Canada, militia units in Atlantic Canada were weak, and it is worth noting that no depot companies were formed in either New Brunswick or Prince Edward Island.[59]

At least two district commanders took the initiative and supplemented militia efforts with central depots. Naturally, these depots were not identical in terms of organization and composition, but both were equally successful and were ultimately incorporated into territorial regiments organized in August 1917.

HQ MD 4 formed the first district depot in January 1917, when CEF units in the Montreal area were moved into the Guy Street Barracks; Lieutenant-Colonel M.A. Piché was responsible for coordinating their efforts. However, each unit was autonomous and responsible to district HQ for both training and administration. Piché, who had difficulty coordinating these units, suggested a central depot to control training, discipline, and interior economy and to eliminate superfluous staff. The proposal was promptly approved by the district commander, Major-General E.W. Wilson, and command of the new MD 4 Mobilization Depot was given to Piché.[60]

The new depot included all CEF units in the Montreal area and was divided into subunits based on corps under a senior officer of that corps. Subunits were subordinate to Depot HQ; commanders were limited to the disciplinary powers of a company commander, while Piché enjoyed the legal powers of a Commanding Officer.

The depot was a self-contained unit with a headquarters staff consisting of an adjutant, medical officer, pay officer, sergeant-major, provost sergeant, and orderly room clerks to provide normal administrative and disciplinary support. Subunit commanders were responsible for training their groups, but were under the direction of the second-in-command, Major McKergow, the District General Staff Officer.[61] Training varied among the groups, but the infantry program was "a graded course of instruction where each recruit on joining would enter a recruit class and gradually progress through the various grades. This will enable Army Order [ACI] 1968 of 1916, providing for fourteen weeks syllabus for Infantry Training to be carried out."[62]

In some respects, the MD 4 Mobilization Depot was similar to the depot battalion suggested by MD 1 and to reserve units in England, in that troops were trained, administered, and disciplined by one central authority. As a training establishment it might not have been as efficient as those in England because of limitations in equipment, training areas, and ranges, but it was ideally suited to handle large numbers of troops that spent only enough time in Canada to undergo the basic training common to all arms and corps.

Was the MD 4 experiment a success? "It has been found after four months of operation, the Mobilization Depot has fully proved its value and it is now desired to place this organization on a permanent basis," wrote the District Commander in June 1917. "In view however, of the possible adoption of selective compulsory service, at an early date, it is desired to use this organization in a new and enlarged fashion."[63] General Wilson also added that, since the majority of recruits were infantry, the depot should be organized as a reserve infantry battalion with eight companies, each holding 520 trainees or 4,160 recruits in all. Non-infantrymen could be handled by a small company with 350 men, while routine fatigues could be managed by a "Special Service" Company of low-category men to allow the other companies to focus on training. With this establishment, Wilson estimated the depot could provide a 255-man draft to England every week.[64]

Wilson's proposed establishment was well received at Militia HQ. On 16 June 1917, the Director-General of Mobilization replied, "I have talked it over with the CGS [Gwatkin] and we think some of your ideas are excellent."[65] A month later, the Adjutant-General approved Wilson's establishment – but only on a provisional basis, probably because the final form of the national reinforcement structure was under consideration at Militia HQ.[66] In the end, it was decided that all depot battalions across the country would have a uniform establishment, and on 30 August 1917 the MD 4 Mobilization Depot was absorbed by the newly created 1st Depot Battalion of the 1st Quebec Regiment.[67] The MD 4 Mobilization Depot was not eliminated because it was a failure, but because it was superseded by a national system of uniform regional depot battalions.

The commander of MD 1, Brigadier-General Shannon, had suggested forming a district depot battalion as early as August 1916. Encouraged to pursue this option by Militia HQ, Shannon elected to defer any action until all battalions in his district had filled their establishment. In April 1917, the 153rd and 241st Battalions sailed to England, leaving only the 122nd Battalion in Galt, which sailed to England the following month. This left six militia depot companies, all of which had difficulty finding recruits, as the only source within MD 1 for infantry reinforcements. Because there were so few recruits, none of these militia companies had enough men to form overseas drafts. The size of the depot companies also made training difficult; as HQ MD 1 noted in May 1917, "the number of recruits secured by the various overseas [militia] companies is so small that it is impossible to train them separately and get satisfactory results."[68]

Shannon could do nothing to overcome the general apathy toward enlisting, but he could ensure that those who joined were properly trained. His approach was to concentrate scattered detachments into a central training depot so that District instructors could conduct infantry training in bombing, machine gunning, musketry, signalling, and trench warfare, as well as basic training for other corps. The proposal was submitted to Ottawa, and on 1 June 1917 Militia HQ authorized the formation of the MD 1 Training Depot.[69]

By July 1917, the MD 1 Training Depot had absorbed 1,200 men from the 1st Hussars Depot, District Cyclist Platoon, District Forestry Depot, 1st Special Service Company, and the overseas companies of the 7th, 21st, 22nd, 25th, 32nd, and 108th Regiments. Not all units were incorporated into the depot. The 63rd and 64th Depot Batteries and the Medical Corps Depot retained their independence.

The new depot was an instant success. On 10 July 1917, Brigadier-General Shannon reported that "[t]he results of this system of organization, administration and training began to be apparent immediately after the establishment of the Depot. The discipline is good and the progress in training has been excellent – far in advance of anything I have been able to secure heretofore under the old system."[70] However, the MD 1 Training Depot was only a temporary measure. On 23 August 1917 it became part of the 1st Depot Battalion of the Western Ontario Regiment under the new system of territorial regiments.[71]

Militia HQ was well aware of the variety of training and reinforcing organizations across the country, many of which were clearly inefficient. The structure obviously needed to be reformed, particularly with the impending passage of the *Military Service Act*. This act, as Prime Minister Borden announced in June 1917, would produce 100,000 conscripts to reinforce the CEF.[72] However, the existing reinforcement structure was manifestly unsuitable for such a large number, and on 31 July 1917 Militia HQ instructed districts to form territorial regiments, each with one or more depot battalions. CEF companies and other militia depots were to be disbanded and the personnel absorbed by the depot battalions of the new regiments.[73]

A total of seventeen depot battalions were formed. The establishment changed slightly over time, but by April 1918 each depot battalion consisted of eight companies with fifty-two officers, 104 senior NCOs, ninety-six corporals, and 1,760 privates, who were intended to be drafted to England.[74] In all, the seventeen depot battalions could hold 29,920 reinforcements at any given time.

As table 8.3 indicates, depot battalions were, for the most part, co-located with their respective district headquarters, which gave them easy access to specialist instructors, key administrative services, and the district ordnance depot. There were, however, some exceptions. The 2nd Central Ontario Regiment established the 2nd Depot Battalion in Hamilton to handle recruits from the Niagara Peninsula, while the British Columbia Regiment, based in Victoria, set up a depot battalion in Vancouver. Outlying companies were also formed when justified by geography or the number of potential recruits. The 2nd Depot Battalion of the 2nd Central Ontario Regiment, for example, established detachments in Brantford and Oshawa, while the Manitoba Regiment formed H Company at the Lakehead and the Nova Scotia Regiment formed H Company in Prince Edward Island.

The new depot battalions were formed on a territorial basis so that men could serve with others from the same province or region and to provide a link with reserve battalions in England from the same region, as discussed in chapter 9. There was, however, one exception. Because the number of eligible men in Prince Edward Island was too small to justify a complete battalion, men from this province joined the Nova Scotia Regiment. The arrangement was logical, particularly since there was no infantry battalion at the front from the province and none of the reserve battalions in England were affiliated with the province.

The new depot battalions had advantages over all previous reserve establishments, apart from the large number of men who could be accommodated. The depot staff remained in situ regardless of drafts sent overseas and, over time, acquired considerable skill and expertise in training and handling recruits. Training programs could be adapted to suit local circumstances and, no doubt, equipment and training aids were stockpiled, thus avoiding the improvisation of 1916. The organization also meant that essential services provided by key staff members such as the Medical Officer, Paymaster, Musketry Sergeant, Pay Sergeant, Master Tailor, and the Sergeant Shoemaker were centralized for greater efficiency.

In theory, the new reinforcement structure should have provided an efficient means of gathering and forwarding reinforcements to England,

Table 8.3 Depot battalions in Canada, April 1918*

Regiment	Depot battalions	Headquarters	District	Remarks
Western Ontario	1st	London	1	
1st Central Ontario	1st and 2nd	Toronto	2	
2nd Central Ontario	1st	Hamilton	2	
2nd Central Ontario	2nd	Toronto	2	Oshawa and area
Eastern Ontario	1st	Kingston	3	
Eastern Ontario	2nd	Ottawa	3	
1st Quebec	1st	Montreal	4	
2nd Quebec	1st	Quebec	5	Francophones
2nd Quebec	2nd	Quebec	5	Anglophones
Nova Scotia	1st	Halifax	6	H Company in P.E.I.
New Brunswick	1st	Saint John	7	
Manitoba	1st	Winnipeg	10	H Company at the Lakehead
British Columbia	1st	Vancouver	11	
British Columbia	2nd	Victoria	11	
Saskatchewan	1st	Regina	12	
Alberta	1st	Calgary	13	

* General Order Number 57 of 15 April 1918. Locations are based on a review of attestation papers.

but it could not be fully implemented until the depot battalions were fully organized. Until then, men were sent overseas in formed battalions and drafts. A summary of infantry reinforcements sent to England in 1917 shows a chaotic total of fifty-two complete battalions (mostly under-strength), thirteen militia drafts averaging fifty men apiece, and thirty-three drafts of varying strengths from other sources, including several from the newly formed depot battalions (see table 8.4). The smallest draft was the 167th Battalion Belgian Company, which sailed in March 1917 with nine men; the largest, with 1,010 men, was provided by the 1st Depot Battalion of the 1st Central Ontario Regiment from Toronto in December 1917.

One of the principal difficulties in 1916–17 was the uneven flow of reinforcements to England, caused in part by the use of formed battalions and in part by varying monthly enlistments. The *Military Service Act*, however, provided a flow in 1918 that, although irregular at times,

Table 8.4 Infantry arrivals in England, 1917

Arrival in England	Drafts	Total strength	Formed battalions	Total strength	Total reinforcements	Reserve strength England
January 1917					Nil	25,552
February 1917	4	394	5	2,970	3,364	18,205
March 1917	1	9	1	415	424	13,691
April 1917	10 (3 Militia)	453	18	10,164	10,617	15,621
May 1917	1 (Militia)	14	16	6,997	7,011	25,095
June 1917	9 (5 Militia)	607	9	3,505	4,112	30,571
July 1917					Nil	31,165
August 1917	2 (1 Militia)	97			97	22,533
September 1917					Nil	17,688
October 1917	8 (2 Militia)	765	2	385	1,150	18,491
November 1917	2 (1 Militia)	204	1	1,029	1,233	15,400
December 1917	9	1,921			1,921	15,700
Totals	4,464		25,465	29,929		
Monthly average	372		2,122	2,494		
Units and drafts	46 (13 Militia)		52			

Source: DHH, 74/672, box 12, folder 122; DHH, 74/672, box 13; sailing lists in LAC, RG 9, II B9, vols 37, 38, 39, 40, 41, 43, 44, 45, 46, and 47; TNA, WO 114/31, Weekly Returns, 29 January 1917, 26 February 1917, and 26 March 1917; TNA, WO 114/32, Weekly Returns, 30 April 1917, 28 May 1917, 25 June 1917, and 30 July 1917; TNA, WO 114/33, Weekly Returns, 27 August 1917, 24 September 1917, 29 October 1917, 26 November 1917, and 31 December 1917.

was more consistent and provided more reinforcements to England (see table 8.5). The low point for reserve battalions in England came in March 1917, when there were only 13,691 infantry reinforcements available on the eve of the Vimy Ridge battle. By January 1918, there were 17,972 men available, and by August, during the Hundred Days

Table 8.5 Infantry arrivals in England, 1918

Arrival in England	Drafts	Total strength	Battalions	Total strength	Total reinforcements	Reserve strength England
January 1918	2	706			706	17,972
February 1918	11	4,527			4,527	20,993
March 1918	6	5,744	1	709	6,453	28,061
April 1918	21	7,849			7,849	22,257
May 1918	8	2,643			2,643	24,435
June 1918	8	3,250			3,250	24,822
July 1918	25	4,375			4,375	30,139
August 1918	35	14,230			14,230	34,531
September 1918	17	2,398			2,398	Not available
October 1918	10	854			854	Not available
Totals	143	46,558	1	709	47,285	
Monthly average	14	4,656			4,727	

Source: DHH, 74/672, box 13, folder 249; Overseas Military Forces of Canada, *Report of the Ministry: Overseas Military Forces of Canada 1918* (London: Overseas Military Forces of Canada, 1919), 66; sailing lists in LAC, RG 9, II B9, vols 47, 48, 49, 50, 52, 53, 54, 55, and 56; TNA, WO 114/34, Weekly Returns, 28 January 1918, 25 February 1918, 25 March 1918, and 29 April 1918; TNA, WO 114/35, Weekly Returns, 27 May 1918, 24 June 1918, 29 July 1918, and 26 August 1918

campaign, there were 34,531 infantry reinforcements with reserve battalions in England.

In theory, the creation of depot battalions should have resulted in an even flow of reinforcements to England. In reality, the number sent overseas was dictated by certain variables. For one thing, conscript intakes varied from 8,910 men in February 1918 to 38,336 in May 1918. There were also difficulties with both rail and sea transport. The number of troop ships was finite, and the priority went to ferrying the American Expeditionary Force to France; meanwhile, Canadian railways were periodically congested. However, the entry of the United States into the war meant that troop trains could use American lines. Strategic troop lift has received little attention from historians, but at least one troop train from the 2nd Depot Battalion of the British Columbia Regiment had to be routed through the United States in July 1918.[75]

It was difficult to coordinate the movement of troops from Western Canada with the arrival of troop ships at Halifax; this meant that transit camps had to be established near the port or in convenient facilities on major rail lines. Troop trains could also be painfully slow, adding to the coordination problem. Draft Number 105 from the 1st and 2nd Depot Battalions British Columbia Regiment, for example, left their home stations on 22 July 1918 and reached Edmonton on 25 July, Winnipeg on 27 July, and Kingston on 31 July 1918. From there, the draft was sent to transit camps at Petawawa, Ontario, and Aldershot, Nova Scotia, before embarking at Halifax on 14 August 1918.[76] This draft was fortunate in comparison with Draft Number 67, also from the British Columbia Regiment, which left Vancouver 10 June 1918, arrived at Aldershot on 20 June, and then waited until 3 August 1918 before embarking at Halifax.[77] Even with these complicating factors, however, the monthly flow was reasonably consistent and provided numbers that could be easily absorbed by reserve battalions in England.

The creation of the depot battalions allowed men to be moved promptly to England without undue delay. This, of course, had not been the case in 1916–17, when reinforcements spent an inordinate amount of time in Canada before embarking and their entry to the overseas reinforcement organization was unduly delayed. Arguably, the concern in England and France in 1917 with the shortage of reinforcements had as much to do with the length of time the men spent in Canada before transiting overseas as it did with the shortage of recruits (see table 8.6).

Although the concept of regional depots was not new, the territorial depot battalions created in mid-1917 were intended for one thing and one thing only: moving large numbers of draftees overseas in a timely manner. Although the depot battalions handled some volunteers, mainly from the British-Canadian Recruiting Mission, their raison d'etre was conscripts. Some 47,509 draftees were sent to England in 1918, of which 24,132 were taken on strength by units in France before the Armistice. Not all conscripts were sent overseas; more than 50,000 remained in Canada either on leave or with their depot battalion until they were needed overseas.

Draftees were posted to France much earlier than late summer, as is commonly supposed. On 11 April 1918, for example, a draft of eleven conscripts from British Columbia was posted to the 72nd Battalion, then serving with the 4th Division in France. Three days later, seventeen men – including four draftees – were posted to the 85th Battalion, while the 2nd Canadian Mounted Rifles did not receive their first conscripts until 11 May 1918.

Contrary to conventional wisdom, the 24,132 conscripts who arrived in France made a significant contribution. A total of 8,227 infantrymen,

Table 8.6 Comparison sample of infantry reinforcements service before embarkation, 1916–18*

Weeks in Canada before embarkation	1916 (%)		1917 (%)		1918 (%)	
0–5	362	(2.7)	166	(4.3)	425	19.3
6–10	370	(2.7)	170	(4.4)	829	37.7
11–15	537	(4.0)	203	(5.2)	432	19.6
16–20	761	(5.7)	363	(9.3)	133	6.0
21–25	1,153	(8.6)	295	(7.6)	268	12.2
26–30	2,908	(21.6)	174	(4.5)	27	1.2
31–35	3,101	(23.0	218	(5.6)	35	1.6
36–40	2,105	(15.6)	224	(5.8)	8	0.4
41–45	1,085	(8.1)	276	(7.1)	10	0.5
46–50	619	(4.6)	356	(9.1)	5	0.2
< 50	456	(3.4)	1,448	(37.2)	28	1.3
Total	13,467		3,893		2,200	
Average weeks in Canada	31		39		12	

* Based on reinforcements posted to 2 CMR, 4 CMR, PPCLI, and the 4th, 16th, 18th, 20th, 72nd, and 85th Battalions. The sample for 1918 is incomplete because printed embarkation rolls were not published. An attempt has been made to rectify this by using reserve battalion Part II Orders and sailing lists – with mixed success.

including 1,097 draftees, died in France or Belgium during the Hundred Days, 8 August to 11 November 1918. Overall, 12.5 per cent of those who died were conscripts. However, as shown in Table 8.7, the proportion of conscripts who died increased over time, which illustrates their growing importance as reinforcements.

The figures in table 8.7 are deceptive, since most draftees who died would have been with rifle companies and not battalion headquarters, transport, or quartermaster stores. Patrick Dennis has estimated that by the Battle of Cambrai, on 8 to 10 October 1918, about 25 per cent of each rifle company were draftees and that this proportion probably increased by the Armistice; again, this shows the need for conscripts to maintain the reinforcement flow.[78]

SUMMARY

Ultimately, by the fall of 1917 a comprehensive reinforcement structure was in place in Canada. Based on regional depots, the organization resembled that proposed by Gwatkin in 1914, which leads to the

Table 8.7 Infantry fatalities, Canada's Hundred Days, 8 August–11 November 1918*

Month	Volunteers	MSA conscripts	Total	MSA conscripts, %
August	3,126	173	3,299	5.2
September	2,798	487	3,285	14.8
October	1,065	303	1,368	22.4
November	206	69	275	25.1
Total	7,195	1,032	8,227	12.5

* The sample in the table excludes officers.

Source: Taken from fatalities listed by the Commonwealth War Graves Commission at www.cwgc.org/find-war-dead.aspx. Names found were checked against online attestation forms in the Soldiers of the First World War database available online from LAC.

conclusion that much of the wasted efforts and inefficiencies of the reinforcement stream in 1915–16 could have been avoided had the original plan been adopted. By 1918, the CEF had become not only a hard-hitting fighting entity that was regarded well within the British Expeditionary Force but also a highly structured and well-organized national army. The development of a complex and efficient reinforcement structure in Canada was not a unique development, but one that mirrored the transformation of the CEF into a truly professional army.

9

The Overseas *Via Dolorosa*: Reinforcements in England and France

As discussed previously, reinforcements had to be staged through reserve units in England to complete their training. Once their training was done, they were not sent directly to the front but were processed through base depots in France and holding units nearer to the forward areas. The two organizations in England and France were interrelated, but in practice did not march in tandem. For that reason, this chapter is divided into two parts, first examining reinforcements in England, and then reinforcements in France.

As in Canada, the process of creating a reinforcement establishment in England was neither easy nor straightforward. Standing up a reserve unit was easy, but with no effective control, and units scattered across southern England, there was no coordination of effort, rational structure, long-term planning, or national policies that reflected Canadian needs. The problems were legion and could not be resolved without a properly organized Canadian military headquarters – and this did not exist until the Ministry of the Overseas Military Forces of Canada (OMFC) was established in December 1916. The achievements by OMFC cannot be overstated. By mid-1917, there was a well-organized and efficient reserve structure in England, one that mirrored the transformation of the CEF into a professional army.

The situation in France was quite different, since the CEF was, to all intents and purposes, part of the British Expeditionary Force, and whatever arrangements were made with regard to the CEF had to fit within the British chain of command. This was clear enough, but the CEF did things on the cheap and used only one divisional base depot in France to handle reinforcements for all four divisions. Canadian HQ in London was well aware of the difficulties this presented, but chose to wash its hands of the matter; after all, the depot was under British command. HQ OMFC, on the other hand, took the view that Canadian interests would be best served if the depots in France were tailored to meet Canadian needs. Accordingly, this was done in the spring of 1917. Further forward, the Canadian Corps emulated British practice, initially with entrenching battalions and then, from the fall of 1917 onward, with the CCRC. At this point, all of the components of the overseas reinforcement structure had been brought together, and units in France reaped the benefits.

Part I – Reinforcements in England

PHASE ONE: THE EARLY DAYS, 1914–15

The First Contingent, which sailed to England in October 1914, did not include an organization to provide reinforcements, nor was any plan in place to create one. As a result, the reserve establishment in England was an improvised structure that continually changed over time.

The process was started in November 1914 by the War Office when orders were issued that surplus manpower in the First Contingent would be set aside as future reinforcements.[1] Depots were formed almost immediately. The Medical Corps was the first, followed shortly afterward by the artillery with three depot batteries composed of gunners made surplus after artillery brigades were reorganized from three 6-gun batteries to four 4-gun batteries.[2] Some corps, however, did not have surplus men, and both the engineer and service corps depots had to be raised in Canada and sent to England in February 1915.[3] There were no surplus cavalrymen either, but in December 1914 the War Office sanctioned the conversion of the 6th Canadian Infantry Battalion (formed by volunteers from western cavalry regiments) into a reserve cavalry regiment to provide reinforcements to the Canadian Cavalry Brigade.[4]

The infantry, with four surplus battalions, was better off. But these could not be used for reinforcements because the War Office had decided in November 1914 to use them as the basis for a second division.[5] However, on 18 January 1915 the War Office cancelled its earlier decision and directed that the 9th, 11th, 12th, and 17th Battalions would be used to reinforce the fighting battalions in the 1st Division. Together with the other depot companies and batteries, these battalions were grouped to form the Canadian Training Depot.

Accommodation was a problem. Tented bivouac sites used by the First Contingent were clearly unsuitable for long-term occupancy, and the depot was therefore allocated peacetime barracks in Tidworth, a few miles east of Salisbury Plain. Although the barracks were an improvement over the earlier tented camps, they were crowded; the 11th and 12th Battalions, for example, were housed in Kandahar Barracks, a facility built to house one peacetime unit.

The Canadian Training Depot was geographically divided. Tidworth was too small, and depot batteries were housed in improvised camps at Devizes, Market Lavington, and Beechingstoke, small towns west of Salisbury Plain.[6] Nor did the new depot hold all Canadian reserve units: specialized units were grouped with their British counterparts, perhaps to facilitate training. The Canadian Reserve Cavalry Regiment moved, in March 1915, from Tidworth to Canterbury, home of the 3rd (British) Reserve Cavalry Regiment, while from July 1915 onward Royal Canadian Horse Artillery reinforcements were trained at Woolwich, home of the British Royal Horse Artillery. However, these arrangements were only temporary, and both returned to the Canadian fold by November 1915. The Canadian Reserve Cyclist Company was another matter. Formed at Hounslow, the training centre for the British Army Cyclist Corps in May 1915, the Company was not co-located with other Canadian reserve units until October 1917.

Not all units could be provided for by the Canadian Training Depot. The 1st Automobile Machine Gun Brigade, for example, was mounted in armoured trucks and had no equivalent in the British forces apart from a handful of armoured cars in Belgium from the Royal Naval Air Service and the Motor Machine Gun Service, provided by the Royal Field Artillery and mounted on motorcycles. However, Canada did not have a naval air service, and neither the Service Corps Depot mechanical transport section nor the depot batteries were in any position to provide machine gunners, while the reserve battalions were fully taken up with basic infantry training. The unit, neither fish nor fowl, was exiled in 1915 to Kennington, about twenty kilometres from the Reserve Cavalry Regiment at Canterbury. A year later, when the Canadian Machine Gun Depot was formed, a separate branch was added to train motor machine gun reinforcements.[7]

Princess Patricia's Canadian Light Infantry (PPCLI) was nominally part of the CEF, but was deployed to Belgium with the 27th (British) Division. The Canadian Commander, Lieutenant-General Alderson, thought that providing reinforcements was none of his concern, and in December 1914 suggested that the War Office should make separate arrangements with the Canadian government or that reinforcements should be provided from British depots that supported the 27th Division.[8] Reserve units felt the same, and the Commanding Officer of the 17th Canadian Reserve Battalion objected to providing reinforcements, since the PPCLI was "not a Canadian Battalion but a private Battalion maintained by private persons."[9] The matter was finally settled in January 1915 when HQ Southern Command directed that Canadian reserve battalions would provide reinforcements.[10]

However, the PPCLI was not happy with the Canadian Training Depot, largely because of a draft of reinforcements sent by the 17th Reserve Battalion in mid-December 1915. The Commanding Officer was livid:

> The draft was to have composed of fifty men. I received no intimation as to the hour of their arrival and the first knowledge that I had was the arrival of two drunk men at the entrance to the camp. Thirteen more appeared today. I have just received a telegraphic request for an escort of four more who are under arrest at Eastleigh. The remainder appear, as far as I understand, to be scattered along the [rail] line between Salisbury and Winchester. Three NCOs accompanied the draft. They all 3 denied being in charge. Sergeant Hands appeared to me to be responsible and I placed him under arrest; he was rather the worse for liquor. One of the NCOs informed me that the draft was composed of all the worst characters in the regiment. I can, of course, express no opinion on this point, but the conduct of some of the men who have arrived here and the non-appearance of the others, can hardly inspire one with confidence.[11]

Not surprisingly the PPCLI, who did not consider themselves to be part of the First Contingent, arranged directly with Militia HQ for a five-hundred-man draft drawn from CEF units in Canada. There was no depot in England to receive the men, however, and on arrival they were posted to the 17th Reserve Battalion, which then proceeded to send a number to the 16th Canadian Scottish, some of whom were returned because they objected to wearing the kilt.[12]

The Commanding Officer of the PPCLI, Lieutenant-Colonel Farquhar, no doubt conscious that the Regiment had been privately raised with few ties to the CEF, set out to organize a regimental depot in England. Acting under his direction, Captain Agar Adamson, the senior Patricia officer in England and an officer with the Canadian Training Depot, negotiated directly with HQ Southern Command, the War Office, and Militia HQ in Ottawa.[13] His efforts were successful: in February 1915, the PPCLI Depot was added to the Training Depot at Tidworth. Strength returns suggest the new depot was an autonomous unit on the same footing as reserve battalions.[14] With no arrangements for further drafts from Canada, the new depot did not last long; by 26 April 1915, the depot held only twenty reinforcements, and in May 1915 it was done away with.[15] A joint Royal Canadian Regiment–PPCLI Depot was in existence by the end of May 1916, but since the depot reinforced two units at the front it was, in effect, a small reserve battalion.[16] This depot did not last long either, and in January 1917 was absorbed by a newly organized reserve battalion. The PPCLI Depot may have been in line with pre-war doctrine, but in the absence of a steady flow of men from Canada, the Regiment had no choice but to draw from generic Canadian reserve battalions.

Tidworth was a marked improvement over the tented camps on Salisbury Plain, but it was too small to house the additional reserve units that would be needed when the 2nd Division arrived from Canada. The War Office briefly considered moving the Canadian Training Depot to Plymouth, but in February 1915 decided to move the depot to Shorncliffe in southeastern Kent on the English Channel.[17] The new camp, occupied in March 1915, was a decided improvement, offering enough huts for 21,000 troops, summer tented camps for an additional 19,000, a nearby port (Folkestone), and ready access to the Hythe and Lyddon Spout rifle ranges, with a combined capacity of 3,000 men per week.[18]

After the move to Shorncliffe, the Canadian Training Depot was redesignated Canadian Training Division (CTD). New units arrived from Canada, and by July 1915 there were thirteen reserve battalions, all reporting directly to HQ CTD.[19] Controlling this large number of subordinate units must have made it difficult for HQ CTD to exercise effective command; perhaps because of this, the reserve battalions were grouped into three reserve brigades in September 1915. However, there was no fixed policy on the number of reserve battalions needed to reinforce the fighting battalions; as more battalions arrived from Canada, they were not broken up but were left intact and added to newly formed reserve brigades. The number of reserve brigades increased steadily, until there were twelve in December 1916.[20] Admittedly, some of these were in Bramshott, but the net effect was to recreate the command and control problems that had existed earlier.

PROBLEMS WITH THE UNFIT

Although intended to be training units, reserve battalions also held the wounded who had been evacuated from the front, some of whom could be recycled into the reinforcement stream after "hardening." The 9th

Reserve Battalion, for example, had four companies of physically fit men undergoing training, while two companies were reserved for those who were unfit.[21] Not all of these men were undergoing remedial training; because there was no administrative mechanism for disposing of those who were, for one reason or another, permanently unfit for military service, reserve battalions held these men as well.[22] Not surprisingly, the number of unfit men held by the reserve battalions increased steadily over time (see table 9.1).

Initially, the unfit were not distributed evenly among the reserve battalions. In May 1915, the 32nd Reserve Battalion held 336 convalescents, while the 23rd Reserve Battalion had none. A few months later, in September 1915, the 9th Reserve Battalion had 866 invalids, the 39th Reserve Battalion had 103, and the 48th had none. On average, the eleven reserve units had 495 unfit men each. To ease the problem, most of the unfit were concentrated in nine battalions in December 1915, leaving eight with only a few who were unfit.[23]

As shown in table 9.1, almost half of the men with reserve battalions in December 1915 were unfit for military service. From a functional point of view, there were two problems. First, more than a third of the bed spaces at Shorncliffe were taken up by invalids, leaving fewer than 14,000 spaces for fit infantry trainees. Second, the hard-pressed training staff with the reserve battalions had to devote time and energy to administering the unfit, time that should have been spent on their primary job of training reinforcements.

Obviously, something had to be done. In December 1915, Colonel F.A. Reid, the Director of Recruiting and Organization at Canadian HQ, examined the problem. His solution was to establish a Canadian casualty depot modelled on the British command depot to care for men discharged from hospital who required hardening. As Reid noted, this casualty depot would allow the reserve battalions to focus on training that "would bring them up to a far higher state of efficiency."[24] Reid's proposal was reviewed by the CTD and by the Director of Medical Services at Canadian HQ in London, both of whom added more features. As a result, Reid's proposal, approved by Canadian HQ in January 1916, went far beyond the original idea of a holding unit and instead created a comprehensive system to handle all those who were medically unfit.

Under the new system, casualties evacuated from France and Flanders to hospitals in England were posted to a new unit, the Canadian Casualty Assembly Centre (CCAC). These postings were based on casualty lists produced by GHQ 3rd Echelon, which meant that the CCAC nominal roll

Table 9.1 Reserve battalions: unfit men, April–December 1915

Month	Fit	Temporarily unfit	Permanently unfit	Convalescent	Total unfit	Ratio unfit to fit, %
April*	3,929	673	78	340	1,091	27.8
May	2,842	643	123	3,056	3,822	134.5
June	4,565	831	252	3,097	4,180	91.6
July	8,093	843	278	3,607	4,728	58.4
August	8,010	1,008	376	3,763	5,147	63.4
September	8,858	1,226	496	3,718	5,440	61.4
October†	10,029	1,730	541	3,946	6,217	62.0
November†	15,159	2,062	552	3,610	6,224	41.1
December	15,823	2,953	953	3,562	7,468	47.2

* The Infantry Base Depot and the Automobile Machine Gun Brigade have been excluded from the April return.

† Battalions earmarked for the 3rd Division have been excluded from the October and November returns.

Sources: TNA, WO 114/26, Weekly Returns, 26 April 1915; TNA, WO 114/57, Weekly Returns, 31 May 1915, 28 June 1915, 26 July 1915, and 30 August 1915; TNA, WO 114/27, Weekly Returns, 27 September 1915, 25 October 1915, 29 November 1915, and 27

was only as accurate as the information provided by the 3rd Echelon. Men who were discharged from hospital on recovery were sent to CCAC HQ at Folkestone, where they were assessed by a Standing Medical Board. Those who were fully recovered were posted to a reserve battalion and fed back into the reinforcement stream, while those who were unlikely to become fit within six months were posted to another newly created unit, the Canadian Discharge Depot, for repatriation to Canada or release in the British Isles. Men who had recovered but were fit for sedentary duties only were retained by the CCAC in a garrison duty battalion to provide workers for routine fatigues, while those who showed an aptitude for clerical work were trained by the School of Stenography in London as replacements for fit clerks who could then be posted to France.[25] Finally, those who had not fully recovered but would likely be fit within six months were posted to another unit, the Canadian Command Depot (CCD) at Monks Horton, for remedial exercises and "hardening" before rejoining the reinforcement stream.[26]

This was the basic system, but modifications were periodically made as required. In June 1916, HQ CTD ruled that men admitted to hospital from units in England would be posted to the CCAC if they were unfit for full duty. Those who were insane or suffering from epilepsy or tuberculosis would also be transferred to the CCAC for repatriation to Canada; presumably, the specialized medical care they needed was not available at the Canadian Discharge Depot.[27] Finally, it was decided in November 1916 that men with newly arrived battalions who were found to be permanently unfit by medical boards would be transferred to the CCAC for disposal.[28]

The role of the CCD was to rehabilitate casualties and return them to reserve battalions where they would be fed into the reinforcement stream. However, Reid thought reserve battalions would bungle the job; in July 1916 he wrote to the Officer in Command (OIC) Reinforcements at Canadian HQ in London that "very much better results would be secured in so far as Monks Horton [CCD] is concerned, if the men from there were drafted direct from Monks Horton to their Units in the Field. A large number of these men, after they are in shape physically, are returned to Reserve Units and are lost."[29] But, as OIC Reinforcements pointed out, it would be difficult to document, re-equip, and dispatch men to the continent directly from the CCD; as a compromise, a new unit was created to return men to their units.[30]

The new unit, known as the 1st Canadian Casualty Training Battalion, was organized at Brighton on 23 October 1916 as a reserve battalion to provide reinforcements to three fighting battalions in France.[31] By 29 January 1917, the unit held 1,168 men, although with one exception all were category Aiii (fully trained but required hardening). In effect, the new unit was not a reserve battalion but an extension of the CCD.[32] Since the battalion served no useful purpose, it was disbanded by HQ OMFC on 19 February 1917.[33]

The CCAC was intended to be "a Central Authority [in England] for the controlling of casualties."[34] To do this meant keeping accurate and up-to-date records of the whereabouts and status of all those held on strength. The CCAC, however, failed to do this and thus became an administrative nightmare instead of an efficient means of managing manpower.

The CCAC was an independent unit commanded throughout its existence by Captain E.A. Hudson (promoted to major on 18 September 1916), a remarkably junior officer to command a unit that had a peak strength in February 1917 of 41,125 men, 13,849 of whom were in hospital.[35] Each man had a personnel file, and to simplify record-keeping Hudson divided the files into five groups on the basis of the individual's corps. This was an awkward arrangement that did not acknowledge the many exceptions to the norm and led to some confusion. "Difficulty is often experienced in maintaining these categories," commented the Canadian Records Office in November 1916, "when a soldier belonging to the Infantry is attached to an Artillery unit for duty and subsequently returned."[36] The same could be said for the Service Corps driver attached to a field ambulance who was evacuated to England.

The status of the CCAC as a unit also meant that only one set of Part II Daily Orders was issued.* With more than 13,000 men posted to or from the CCAC in October 1916 alone, Part II Orders were very lengthy. Not surprisingly, given the volume of personnel transactions and the division of records, there were numerous errors. These errors were compounded when reserve units provided inaccurate or incomplete nominal rolls or, in some cases, posted men to the CCAC without notifying HQ CCAC.† Confusion reigned: in November 1916, an audit by the Canadian Records Office in London showed that a large number of men ostensibly with the CCAC were serving in France, had deserted, died, been repatriated to Canada, or simply did not exist.[37] Not surprisingly, given that the CCAC was not a particularly efficient means of managing manpower, the newly organized HQ OMFC chose to wind up operations in February 1917. However, it was the end of August 1917 before more than 6,000 missing men could be traced; until then, the CCAC records section had to remain in existence.[38]

The most successful part of this elaborate system was the CCD, designed to hold up to 4,000 men at a time in order to bring them "to the necessary fit condition in a very short time to return to duty overseas [in France or Belgium]."[39] Created in May 1916, the new unit returned a steady stream of rehabilitated casualties to reserve battalions until the end of war. The success was such that a second command depot followed in August 1916 and a third in January 1917. The three depots were then harmonized with the reserve structure in England by HQ OMFC. Number 1 CCD was affiliated with the new regimental depots in the Shorncliffe area, Number 2 with regimental depots in the Bramshott area, and Number 3 for all other regimental depots.[40]

The CCD training program was progressive and geared to the trainees' medical condition. On arrival at the CCD, men were divided into four groups: those who could do all exercises with no difficulty; those who

---

* Part II Orders listed all changes to the status of individual soldiers, including promotions and postings.
† In other words, neither the reserve battalion nor the CCAC could be sure of where the man actually was.

could not do strenuous exercises; those who could not do arm and shoulder exercises; and those who could not do much except for "gentle exercises, games and slow walks."[41] Not all convalescents were enthusiastic about being restored to full health, and in June 1916 Colonel Reid noted that "these men are not all desirous of being again fitted for the Front, and do not at all appreciate the Physical Training."[42]

The number of men returned to the reinforcement stream by the command depots is uncertain. In March 1916, Colonel Reid noted that 5,501 men had been screened by CCAC Standing Medical Boards, of whom 2,363 or 43 per cent would "be reclaimed for overseas service" after rehabilitation at the Command Depot.[43] Since 60,308 men passed through the CCAC up to December 1916, it is estimated that as many as 25,000 former casualties had been returned to duty, assuming that the majority successfully completed their training at the CCD – a very significant addition to the manpower pool.[44]

PARTLY TRAINED REINFORCEMENTS

The job of the reserve organization in England was to maintain a stream of fully trained reinforcements to meet the needs of the units in France. Insofar as the infantry was concerned, the system failed miserably. In 1916, for example, an estimated 59.2 per cent of all reinforcements provided in 1916 to nine select infantry battalions were only partly trained.[45] Other arms were in a similar position, and it goes without saying that the primary client, the Canadian Corps, was less than pleased.

In December 1915, Major-General Currie, General Officer Commanding 1st Canadian Division, complained of artillery reinforcements with little or no training on the 18-pounder:

> Now Carson, you and I know this is not only not right but d-d rotten, and the men responsible should be told so in no unmistakable terms. We have to fight these men and the least the chaps who have the soft jobs at Shorncliffe can do is to train them. They must realize that it is all high-pressure work and must be taken up with intelligence and enthusiasm. Unless they are prepared to do this, they should be kicked out of the Canadian Service.[46]

Currie's complaint was promptly investigated by HQ CTD, who determined that the Reserve Artillery Brigade had been depleted because the War Office had recently authorized three additional howitzer batteries for the 2nd Canadian Division.[47] Providing trained gunners for these new units drained the Reserve Brigade. As a result, artillery reinforcements were sent to France with as little as ten days' training; the Brigade Commanding Officer warned that "for months to come there will be no adequate reserve of trained men from which to supply two Divisions in France."[48] The crisis with the Reserve Brigade highlights a chronic weakness in the Canadian reserve structure: an inability to meet unexpected demands.

Some flexibility could have been provided by maintaining reinforcements in England over and above the number needed to replace routine wastage in France. This policy was advocated in September 1916 by the Inspector General of Canadian Forces (Alderson), who thought at least 20,000 trained infantrymen, as well as a similar number of trainees, should be available at all times to meet unexpected demands.[49] Nothing came of Alderson's recommendation, however, and in any case it is doubtful that the erratic flow of men from Canada would have permitted the stockpiling of this many reinforcements.

RESERVE UNIT ORGANIZATION 1915–16

Another problem with the reserve system in England was an inefficient organization that could not provide enough trained reinforcements to meet the demands from France. One of the primary reasons for this was the reserve system itself, which was poorly organized with two independent and uncoordinated training divisions in Shorncliffe and Bramshott. Another factor was the internal organization of reserve units and camps such as Shorncliffe.

After the creation of reserve brigades at Shorncliffe in September 1915, the training division continued to grow as troops arrived from Canada. By May 1916, ignoring administrative units, HQ CTD controlled eleven major formations as well as an independent Machine Gun School. Given the size of the organization, the continual changes, and the sprawling span of control, running the camp on a day-to-day basis took priority. Not surprisingly, the CTD commander and his administrative staff occupied the same building, while the all-important training staff was housed elsewhere. Training staff commented in June 1916 that "the Administrative Branch greatly over-shadows the General Staff Branch, and this is inimical to successful training. Matters of Training are made subordinate to Administrative questions, whereas in a *Training Division* the reverse should obtain."[50]

The emphasis on administration could have been avoided had there been enough staff to deal not simply with routine matters but with long-term issues as well. Unfortunately, the headquarters had a small staff that fluctuated monthly. In March 1916, there were fourteen officers, twenty-two NCOs, and 100 men at the Shorncliffe HQ to direct training for 20,406 infantry reinforcements.[51] By June 1916, there were 33,178 reinforcements in-house, but the HQ had dwindled to eleven officers, fourteen senior NCOs, and forty-eight men.[52] However, this was the low point: by the end of October 1916, there were sixty-three officers, thirty-five senior NCOs, and 155 men.[53] Given the continual turnover and the emphasis on administration, there was no serious effort in 1915–16 to address fundamental issues such as the organization of the reserve units themselves.

Efficient training depended on units that were specifically organized to do the job. Unfortunately, many of the reserve units at Shorncliffe in 1916 had conventional establishments that were not directed toward training, while others were ad hoc creations with no establishment. Establishments were not a meaningless exercise in military bureaucracy; they were the authority for both manpower and special training equipment such as fencing muskets and bayonet gallows. The establishment also authorized the number of training NCOs with each unit. In the case of the infantry, the British 2nd Reserve Battalion establishment not only included the same number of NCOs as a line battalion, but also provided an additional fifty-six lance-sergeants and lance-corporals and a colour-sergeant musketry instructor.[54] The instructor-student ratio in a reserve battalion, therefore, was much lower than in a line battalion.

However, the British 2nd Reserve Battalion establishment had been authorized in 1915 only for the 9th, 11th, 12th, and 17th Reserve Battalions. All other reserve battalions retained the line infantry establishment with fewer NCOs.[55] Although no doubt the conventional battalions were augmented by NCOs on command from other units, this created other problems. Those on command could not be promoted, and parent units were deprived of valuable NCOs. In September 1916, the CTD commander acknowledged that most of his reserve battalions did not have the appropriate establishment, but claimed that he could not settle on a permanent cadre until Canadian HQ in London decided how many battalions each reserve unit was to reinforce, although what this had to do with adopting the British 2nd Reserve Battalion establishment is not clear.[56]

To some extent, the question of additional instructors provided by the reserve battalion establishment was moot, since battalions arriving from

Canada in 1916 were left intact to complete their training. The efficiency of this policy was questionable, and in April 1916 the Inspector of Infantry found that reserve battalions were "depleted of men and are starving for recruits. These Draft producing units have trained Staffs of Instructors whereas the new Units when they come over are all new together, Officers, NCOs and men."[57] Three months later, Major-General Steele pointed out to Carson at Canadian HQ that "[t]he old Reserve Battalions have the Instructional Cadre composed of men thoroughly qualified to train others, and the absorption of new Battalions into the old Reserve Battalions is the only sound and practical solution to our difficulties."[58] Despite Steele's recommendation, Carson did nothing, and newly arrived battalions continued to be left intact. The policy was both wasteful and inefficient. In July 1916, for example, eleven reserve battalions had a staff of 1,947 NCOs to train 6,243 recruits – an instructor-student ratio of about 1:3. In contrast, the 69th Battalion – to name but one example – had 79 NCOs and 826 recruits – an instructor-student ratio of about 1:10.[59]

Despite the policy of leaving newly arrived battalions intact to complete their training, attempts were made to involve instructors from the established reserve battalions. However, unit pride and parochialism interfered. As the General Staff at Shorncliffe HQ noted in June 1916, "In the majority of cases the new Battalions took as few as possible of the Instructors of the old [reserve] Battalions."[60]

Some of the newly arrived battalions were able to complete their training, but others could not. The 70th Battalion, for example, arrived at Shorncliffe in May 1916, accompanied by a confidential report from HQ MD 1 that noted the battalion was weak and poorly trained but "could be made into a first class Battalion if the Senior Officers will give it that attention and supervision which they should and have not given it in the past."[61] Staff from the 1st Canadian Training Brigade tried to assist, but as Colonel Smart, the brigade commander, noted a month later, the advice had been ignored and there was no visible improvement. The fault, Colonel Smart felt, was with the senior officers, who were of little use, and with the Commanding Officer, who was "hardworking and constantly on duty but appears to have no proper sense of discipline, organization or administration generally."[62] In summary, Colonel Smart wrote, the battalion should immediately be disbanded and the men posted to the 37th Reserve Battalion to complete their training.

Despite Colonel Smart's assessment, CTD HQ left the 70th to train on its own. At the end of June 1916, when there were 504 men undergoing training, Major-General Steele reported that the battalion was proficient in drill but weak in tactical skills.[63] This was the end of the 70th Battalion training program, however, and by the end of July 1916, the unit had been reduced to cadre strength.[64]

The 69th Battalion from Montreal had similar problems and on arrival at Shorncliffe in May 1916 was described as "very slack and ill-disciplined."[65] A month later, nothing had changed. The General Staff recommended breaking up the battalion and posting the men to an established reserve battalion to complete their training, since "[t]he Officers and NCOs seem to be generally inefficient and incapable of satisfactorily training their men."[66] Despite this condemnation, the 69th continued its training under the supervision of the 6th Canadian Training Brigade. Some of the difficulties with the 69th may have been a lack of French-speaking instructors. In July 1916, the 6th Brigade commander commented that "a great number appear to speak little or no English and are very simple-minded. I find the majority of men willing to do their duty but it is difficult to make them understand."[67] In response, Shorncliffe sent an urgent request to Militia HQ in Ottawa for twenty French-speaking subalterns to help train the 69th.[68] Whether these subalterns arrived is unknown, and the 69th remained intact until 2 January 1917, when it was absorbed by the newly created 10th Reserve Battalion to provide French-speaking reinforcements to the 22nd Battalion.

Once the newly arrived battalions had completed training, they were quickly depleted of men as reinforcements were posted to France, leaving a cadre of senior officers, NCOs, and unfit men. The remnants were not disbanded but were simply put off to one side or combined to form composite battalions to perform fatigues to take some of the burden from those units that were training reinforcements.[69] At the same time, additional battalions continued to arrive from Canada. New reserve brigades were formed to handle the increase, and reserve battalions were shuffled to give each brigade a leavening of experienced units. The turmoil affected battalions trying to complete their training. "The training in England was very fragmentary," wrote the 132nd Battalion historian, and "consisted mostly in moving the Battalion from one quarters to another as the Camp was congested."[70] As Colonel Reid noted in July 1916, the continual changes led reserve brigade staffs to concentrate on the details of reorganization and the transfer of personnel and units. Together with a general lack of co-operation from the reserve units, Reid thought it no wonder that "[a]ny sudden call from the Canadian Corps for drafts has generally found the Training Division ill-prepared to meet the demand."[71]

RESERVE ESTABLISHMENTS

The issue of establishments was not unique to the infantry, as Eastern Command noted in August 1916:

> No establishment has been fixed for the Cavalry Depot or the [Reserve] Field Artillery Brigade at Shorncliffe (though the question was said to have been raised some time previously), and I expressed the opinion that an early settlement was desirable in the interests of efficient training. I again visited Shorncliffe on 23rd and 24th August [1916] and I find things remain just as they were in this respect: I can only reiterate what I said before that I regard the settlement of this question as of prime importance for the efficiency of the training.[72]

MacDougall took issue with the remarks and in September 1916 wrote that the Cavalry Depot, for example, had an establishment of thirty-nine officers but no NCOs. It is probable that he was referring only to the permanent cadre, since the overwhelming majority of military establishments included NCOs. He also noted that the Reserve Artillery Brigade had an approved establishment authorized in 1915 and intended to train enough gunners for only one division. Lastly, MacDougall noted that the Canadian Engineer Training Depot had a permanent cadre of forty officers and NCOs.[73]

MacDougall's comments make it clear that Shorncliffe had serious organizational problems. The Cavalry Depot, for example, had no permanent NCOs: Who was supposed to teach stable management, grooming, basic horsemanship, and sword drill? Regardless of MacDougall's protestation, the establishments were completely inadequate to deal with the number of trainees in the three depots: 1,178 troopers, 1,033 gunners, and 1,274 sappers. Not surprisingly, warrant officers and NCOs were placed on command to the various depots from other units. The Cavalry Depot had 200, the Reserve Artillery Brigade had 123, and the Engineer Depot had 106.[74] Although in practice these units had enough instructors, the use of borrowed NCOs meant that parent units were short-staffed.

Inadequate training establishments were bad enough, but Training Division HQ worsened the matter by forming ad hoc units. Infantry signallers, for example, were originally trained by reserve battalion signal sections. But these sections were small, and there was no guarantee each reserve unit could provide enough signallers for affiliated battalions in France. In March 1916, therefore, the 13th Reserve Brigade at Shorncliffe grouped reserve battalion signallers to form an ad hoc Signalling Base with a cadre of eight instructors (increased in May 1916 to fifteen) to handle 113 trainees. Other reserve brigades followed suit, and by July 1916 another six bases had been created with cadres varying from six in the 5th Reserve Brigade Signalling Base to twenty-three in the 3rd Reserve Brigade Signalling Base. All of these bases were improvised units whose level of manning probably depended on the availability of local talent, with the result that the instructor–student ratio varied wildly. In June 1916, the 6th Reserve Brigade Signalling Base had a cadre of eleven with no students; the 5th at Shorncliffe had a cadre of twenty-three with four students, and the 4th on St Martin's Plain had a cadre of seventeen with 229 students.[75]

No central authority was charged with signals training. As a result, there was no uniformity between the bases, and both the material taught and the standard of instruction varied widely. Nor was it easy to assemble drafts for France, since the infantry signallers were scattered among seven reserve brigades, while both the artillery and cavalry insisted on training their own. The problems were recognized by HQ OMFC, and in March 1917 the Canadian Signalling School was established to train signallers for all arms and services.[76]

Like the infantry signallers, machine gun reinforcements were originally trained by reserve battalion machine gun sections. However, in October 1915, GHQ directed that men and guns from all battalion machine gun sections in France would be pooled to form brigade machine gun companies.[77] In exchange, the battalions would be issued with Lewis light machine guns. In theory, this should not have resulted in an increased demand for gunners, since the Lewis was intended to be used by rifle platoons. But not enough Lewis guns were available, and battalions were therefore allowed to retain their Colt machine guns.[78] As a result, infantry battalions retained most of their machine gunners and Shorncliffe had to scramble to find enough trained gunners to man the new companies. The problem was a serious one. The 2nd Canadian Infantry Brigade Machine Gun Company, for example, received only 27 men from 2nd Brigade infantry battalions and needed 112 reinforcements from England to bring the unit up to the required 139 men.[79]

In response to the decision to form new machine gun companies, Shorncliffe pooled reserve battalion sections in December 1915 to form five reserve brigade machine gun companies. But the arrangement was only "a temporary measure for the purpose of placing ourselves as nearly as possible to supply demands for machine gun personnel which may be anticipated from overseas within the next few weeks."[80] The companies conducted basic training only, and trainees had to undergo two or three weeks of finishing at yet another ad hoc unit, the HQ Machine Gun School, or Machine Gun Base, as it was also known.[81]

The whole arrangement was an inefficient draft-finding organization. The five reserve brigade companies were temporary with no establishment and an uncertain future. Training capacity was also limited, since men had to be cycled through the HQ Machine Gun School to finish their training. Moreover, the standard of instruction at the school was uncertain, since the size of the cadre fluctuated from month to month. On 27 March 1916, there were thirteen officers and sixteen senior NCOs to train 145 students. In April 1916, there were seven officers and ten senior NCOs with 173 trainees, while in May 1916, there were ten officers and fifteen senior NCOs together with 220 students. In the event, the school did last long, and there is no evidence that it existed after 29 May 1916.[82]

In June 1916, the 86th Machine Gun Battalion from Hamilton arrived at Shorncliffe. Renamed Canadian Machine Gun Depot, the battalion absorbed the reserve brigade machine gun bases in Shorncliffe and quickly reached a strength of more than 2,200 men.[83] But machine gun training remained fragmented, and on 14 November 1916 there were still two reserve machine gun companies at Crowborough, almost ninety kilometres west of Shorncliffe.[84] As late as 13 September 1916, no establishment had been approved for the new depot.[85] The problem was corrected shortly afterward, but as the head of the General Staff at HQ OMFC commented in February 1917, the new establishment was for "an Infantry Reserve Battalion designed to reinforce three Active Service Battalions in the Field, an organization totally unsuitable, both from a training and draft finding point of view." However, as the General Staff Officer added, "This has now been remedied by the organization of the Canadian Machine Gun Depot on proper lines."[86]

TRAINING FACILITIES

The flow of troops from Canada increased steadily throughout 1916. By the end of December 1916 there were 130,135 Canadians in England, more than the combined capacity of both Shorncliffe and Bramshott.[87] Satellite camps at Westenhangar, Otterpool, and Upper Dibgate were added to Shorncliffe, but these were quickly filled up. Bramshott also acquired a satellite camp, Witley, later to become the home of the 5th Division.[88] Even with these additions, space was at a premium, and in

October 1916 the War Office allocated Crowborough, Shoreham, and Seaford, followed in November by Hastings and Brighton. These were not small camps, but more akin to large towns: Hastings alone held 14,000 men in December 1916.[89] In the midst of these changes, MacDougall handed over Shorncliffe to Brigadier-General E.C. Ashton in November 1916 and moved to Brighton, where he established "Brighton Command" to control the camps at Brighton, Hastings, Seaford, Shoreham, and Crowborough.[90]

The large, sprawling organization that had developed by December 1916 was not necessarily a bad thing, but the relationship between the camps was illogical, since Shorncliffe was the primary source for reinforcements to France. Admittedly, Bramshott drafted men directly to France from time to time but, as discussed in chapter 6, the camp was intended to provide initial training only for reinforcements, the "final polish" being at Shorncliffe. The same principle applied to the new camps; in October 1916, Canadian HQ muddied the waters even further by directing that "Bramshott will then supply Seaford [with reinforcements] if it be found necessary, and Seaford, after a certain amount of training, will supply Shorncliffe, who will complete the training of all Infantry troops."[91] Coordinating the training schedules of the three camps (if it was ever done) must have been difficult and time-consuming. As well, the need to shuttle troops from one camp to another must have added significantly to the time required to train men for the front. The arrangement was a complete waste of time, energy, and resources.

It is not clear who commanded the organization that had developed by December 1916. Canadian HQ in London was nominally in charge, but the actual training was controlled by the War Office, with Bramshott reporting to Eastern Command and the remainder reporting to Southern Command through various districts.[92] Major-General Carson at Canadian HQ in London had assumed command on the basis of his appointment as the Minister's representative, but his authority was ill-defined and he had not been given formal powers of command. Major-General MacDougall at Shorncliffe exercised some degree of authority, since he had been appointed General Officer Commanding Canadians in 1915, but in matters of training he was subject to the authority of Major-General Steele, who not only commanded Shorncliffe District but was also the senior Canadian officer in England. With no single agency controlling or coordinating Canadian training efforts, and reserve brigades preoccupied with administration as they were shuttled to new camps, the wonder is not that reinforcements provided to France were ill-trained and poorly prepared, but that they were provided at all.

REFORMS IN ENGLAND 1917–18

Clearly, the CEF organization in England was badly in need of reform. However, given the personalities involved in both England and Canada, merely modifying the existing structure was not enough. After several months of careful consideration, therefore, Prime Minister Borden and his cabinet approved an order in council on 27 October 1916 creating a new ministry, based in London: the Ministry of the OMFC. A few days later, on 1 November 1916, Sir George Perley, the Canadian High Commissioner, was appointed as the new minister, while Sam Hughes, in Canada, resigned his portfolio.[93]

One of Perley's first jobs was to create a military HQ to replace Carson's Canadian HQ. To do this, he brought Major-General (later Lieutenant-General) R.E.W. Turner back from France and appointed him General Officer Commanding Canadians in place of MacDougall. Steele was then sacked after providing Lord Shaughnessy with copies of confidential documents previously submitted to Sir George Perley.[94] Both MacDougall and Steele returned to Canada.

Perley wisely gave his new General Officer Commanding a free hand in selecting the principal staff officers for the new HQ. Turner chose well. Lieutenant-Colonel (later Brigadier-General) H.F. McDonald, a 1914 original with extensive staff experience in France with the 1st and 2nd Divisions, became head of the General Staff Branch responsible for training. Brigadier-General P.E. Thacker, a PF officer who had served as Director of Military Training at Militia HQ and had been seconded to the War Office in 1912, became the Adjutant-General. Lastly, Brigadier-General A.D. McRae, a talented Vancouver businessman and former Director of Supply and Transport at Canadian HQ, became the Quartermaster General. These officers took up their new positions on 5 December 1916.

On the surface, the new headquarters was similar to Militia HQ, with General Staff, Adjutant-General, and Quartermaster General branches. But there were two fundamental differences. Unlike Gwatkin in Ottawa, who was *primus inter pares* as the head of the General Staff, Turner, as General Officer Commanding Canadians, had the power to direct the subordinate branches. The second critical difference was that the principal branches controlled only those functions that were directly related to training and the support of the reinforcement structure in England. Those functions that were necessary but not directly related to the production of reinforcements were handled by the services and departments.[95] This was a mission-oriented headquarters. Not surprisingly, the faults that had developed in 1915–16 were corrected and the entire reinforcement establishment in England placed on a rational basis in a remarkably short time.

The first task of the newly appointed staff was to review the state of the reinforcement structure in England. The results were depressing. The General Staff Officer found that there was no system for the supervision or coordination of training, unit establishments were unsuitable both for training and supplying reinforcements, and there was a lack of training materiel because Canadian establishments did not correspond with British establishments. The Adjutant-General's comments were similar. Reserve units did not have formal establishments, the reserve organization was ill suited to provide reinforcements, and the control of manpower by the CCAC was unsatisfactory.[96]

The first step was to reorganize the Canadian reserve establishment in England. HQ Brighton Command, which became redundant when Major-General MacDougall was returned to Canada, was closed in January 1917. Training camps at Seaford, Shoreham, Hastings, and Crowborough, which had previously been part of Brighton Command, now reported directly to HQ OMFC, together with Shorncliffe and Bramshott.[97] The effect of these changes was that one staff officer, Lieutenant-Colonel McDonald, was in charge of the conduct and coordination of all CEF training in England.

The structure of the reinforcement organization was also rationalized. The twelve reserve brigades were disbanded and replaced by six new brigades. Two of these, together with the artillery and cavalry, were stationed at Shorncliffe, two at Bramshott, and one each at Seaford and Shoreham, an arrangement that simplified the chain of command. Crowborough was assigned to the engineers and machine gunners, while Hastings was reserved for administrative units. Finally, in February 1917, Witley was allocated entirely to the newly formed 5th Division.[98]

Unfortunately, the allocation of camps did not remain constant. In July 1917, the War Office urgently needed additional accommodation and both Crowborough and Hastings had to be vacated. A few months later, in October 1917, Shoreham was also vacated.[99] Inevitably, units had to be shuffled from one camp to another. The Machine Gun and Engineer Depots moved to Seaford, and the Reserve Cavalry Regiment and Reserve Artillery Brigade moved to a new camp at Bordon in Hampshire. Lastly, Witley became available when the 5th Division was broken up for reinforcements in February 1918 and was reoccupied by reserve infantry battalions from Shorncliffe, which then became an administrative centre.[100] In the short term, the need to move reserve units from one camp to another disrupted training, but, in the long term, the structure was more efficient and manageable with reserve units concentrated in only four camps: Seaford, Bordon, Witley, and Bramshott, as well as small camps at Sunningdale and Purfleet to accommodate forestry and railway troops.

The new structure was a vast improvement over what had previously existed. Unlike under MacDougall, the previous GOC, whose powers were uncertain, there was no ambiguity about the authority granted to Turner. His headquarters, appropriately enough, was in London near the centre of power, the Minister of the OMFC, and the War Office, instead of being isolated at Shorncliffe or Brighton. Responsibilities of the principal staff officers at the new HQ were clear, and they were unencumbered by administrative functions not directly related to the production of reinforcements. Most importantly, the new organization was specifically tailored to train recruits and provide reinforcements to France.

The reserve units themselves were also overhauled. The Engineer Training Depot at Crowborough was not only given a formal establishment, but was placed under command of Crowborough for discipline only, thus relieving the depot of any obligation to provide garrison fatigue parties. The Reserve Cavalry Brigade with three regiments was reduced to a reserve cavalry regiment with four squadrons, each intended to reinforce one of the four regiments in France. The reduction not only simplified training but also aligned the organization with the units reinforced and reduced the headquarters manning overhead. At the end of November 1916, for example, there were 406 officers, warrant officers, senior NCOs, and trumpeters with the Reserve Cavalry Brigade, as compared with 206 in the Reserve Cavalry Regiment at the end of June 1917 and 186 at the end of August 1918. The Reserve Artillery Brigade was also reorganized and given an establishment corresponding to a School of Gunnery. The Service Corps Depot at Shorncliffe was disbanded, and reinforcements were trained by Service Corps detachments supporting the various camps. Lastly, the infantry battalions were placed on British reserve establishments, a change that not only authorized the appropriate number of instructors, but, as discussed in chapter 6, entitled units to demand weapons and equipment on the same scale as their British counterparts.[101]

The infantry battalions, however, had serious problems other than their establishments. In December 1916, there were seventy battalions in

England of widely varying strengths, and the question of what constituted a reserve battalion had become hopelessly blurred. The need "for [the] provision of a stable organization for the carrying out of training was at once evident,"[102] wrote the Lieutenant-Colonel McDonald in February 1917, summarizing the state of affairs he had inherited in December 1916. HQ OMFC acted promptly in the matter; on 1 January 1917, fifty-seven battalions were absorbed by twenty-six reserve battalions affiliated with specific battalions in France, while the remaining thirteen were set aside for the 5th Division.[103] The reorganization may have been carried out in haste, but was nonetheless well thought out. Twenty-four of the new reserve battalions were intended to reinforce two fighting battalions each, while one reserve battalion provided French-speaking reinforcements to the 22nd Battalion and the last provided reinforcements to the four pioneer battalions.[104]

TERRITORIAL AFFILIATIONS

HQ OMFC also reintroduced the concept of territorial affiliation, in which battalions at the front would be reinforced with men from the same region in Canada where the fighting battalion had originally been raised. The idea, of course, was not new, and in February 1916 CTD Shorncliffe had confirmed the principle.[105] But with the erratic flow of men from Canada and the chaotic organization of the reserve structure in England, this was often not possible, and reserve battalions frequently provided drafts to six or eight battalions.[106] The result was that virtually every battalion in France contained a large proportion of men from across Canada. The 20th Battalion from Toronto, for example, received 1,218 reinforcements in 1916. But only 681 men, or 56 per cent, were from Central Ontario (although 1,186, or 97.4 per cent, were Ontarians). The remainder came from thirteen units representing every province but Prince Edward Island.

Turner's idea was to reorganize the reserve battalions in England on a territorial basis to reinforce units from the same region at the front. He also suggested that the territorial reserve battalions be refilled by drafts from affiliated territorial depots in Canada.[107] Such a system, Turner claimed, would relieve "[t]he distress and dissatisfaction caused to various parts of Canada by the system which has hitherto existed, of reinforcing Battalions at the front with men from various parts of Canada with which the Unit has no connection."[108]

The difficulty with Turner's concept was that the selection of battalions for France had not been based on demographic considerations. The result was that English-speaking Quebec in particular, was greatly overrepresented at the front. This would not have been a problem if the necessary recruits were forthcoming – but they were not, and from 1 June 1916 to 1 February 1917, English-speaking Quebec battalions were reinforced with 4,900 men from other provinces. "If the Province of Québec cannot find drafts for their Units," Turner, a peacetime resident of Quebec City, concluded, "then they are not entitled to be maintained in the Corps."[109]

The problem did not go unnoticed in Canada. On 6 December 1916, the new Minister of Militia and Defence, A.E. Kemp, telegraphed Perley: "Consider it desirable [to] remedy grievance of the general Canadian Military Districts against inadequate representation firing line in so far as compatible with military exigencies."[110] After some consideration, Turner thought the solution was to disband one of the three Black Watch battalions (13th, 42nd, and 73rd) as well as one of the other English-speaking Quebec battalions (14th, 24th, 60th, and 87th) and replace them with two battalions, one of which should be from Nova Scotia.[111]

British Columbia, with seven infantry battalions and three pioneer battalions, was also overrepresented, a serious matter with only four thousand British Columbians available as reinforcements in the reserve battalions. To resolve this, Turner recommended that two battalions be axed and replaced by two battalions from Ontario, which was under-represented.[112]

Disbanding units at the front was politically sensitive. On 20 December 1916, Sir George Perley wired the gist of Turner's recommendations to Prime Minister Borden, adding that "such action will no doubt cause considerable criticism in Montréal and British Columbia would like to know if you have any serious objections."[113] Despite Perley's observation Borden was determined to put the CEF in order and on 28 December 1916 approved the disbandment of four battalions from Quebec and British Columbia.[114] The Canadian Corps commander, Lieutenant-General Sir Julian Byng, was aware of the reorganization and wrote to Perley that "if the matter is in the interests of the Canadian Forces there will be no obstacle placed in the way by me."[115]

Predictably, there was some opposition to the proposal, not only from the commanding officers concerned but also from others such as Brigadier-General MacBrien of the 12th Canadian Infantry Brigade, who objected to losing the battle-hardened 73rd Battalion and suggested turning the 73rd into a Nova Scotia battalion by diverting the reinforcement flow. "In three to four months," MacBrien claimed, "it would be composed of 90% NOVA SCOTIANS."[116] Despite the protests, the reforms went ahead. Both the 60th and 73rd Battalions were absorbed by other units and replaced by the 116th from Ontario and the 85th from Nova Scotia. Similarly, the 3rd and 4th Pioneer Battalions from British Columbia were dissolved, while the 1st Pioneer Battalion, also from British Columbia, was transferred to the Canadian Railway Troops. In their place, the 107th Infantry Battalion from Manitoba as well as the 123rd and 124th Infantry Battalions from Toronto were converted to pioneers and posted to France in March 1917.

The reorganization was a start, but further changes were required to more closely align representation at the front with contributions from the provinces. Rather than break up experienced fighting units, however, HQ OMFC decided to divert the reinforcement flow. From August 1917 to August 1918, four battalions were given new territorial affiliations: the 54th and 102nd (British Columbia) Battalions were assigned to Central Ontario, while the 47th Battalion, also from British Columbia, was assigned to Western Ontario. Lastly, the 44th Battalion, originally from Winnipeg, was assigned to New Brunswick.

The policy of territorial affiliations for battalions in France resulted in corresponding changes to the reserve battalions in England. Originally there had been twenty-six reserve battalions, but in June 1917 the 22nd and 23rd Reserve Battalions, both of which reinforced English-speaking Quebec battalions, were amalgamated, and at the same time the 1st and 24th Reserve Battalions, which reinforced British Columbia battalions, were also amalgamated.[117] Further reductions followed when HQ OMFC decided that each reserve battalion could reinforce up to four line battalions. Six battalions were therefore disbanded in January 1918, followed by an additional five in June 1918, leaving fifteen to provide reinforcements to the forty-eight fighting battalions in France. The territorial principle was respected: the 21st Reserve Battalion, for example, provided men to the four Alberta battalions, and the 13th Reserve Battalion reinforced both New Brunswick battalions. There were, however, two exceptions. The 10th Reserve Battalion provided French-speaking reinforcements to the 22nd Battalion, while the 20th Reserve Battalion reinforced the two remaining Black Watch battalions (13th and 42nd) from Montreal.[118]

Apart from reorganizing reserve units to make the system more rational and efficient, HQ OMFC went to some lengths to ensure they were used only for their primary purpose: providing reinforcements to the front. In December 1917, for example, the War Office asked that a third siege battery be raised to complete the 3rd Canadian Garrison Artillery Brigade in France. Unlike in December 1915, when the Reserve Artillery Brigade was gutted to form new howitzer batteries, HQ OMFC made arrangements with Militia HQ for two drafts of siege gunners from Canada to man the battery.[119] Two tank battalions were also raised in 1918 at the request of the War Office. The 1st Battalion was recruited in Canada and embarked for England in April 1918. The nucleus of a second battalion was formed in England with 226 volunteers from the Reserve Cavalry Regiment, but rather than drain the cavalry reserve any further, HQ OMFC made arrangements for Militia HQ in Ottawa to provide the remainder of men needed to complete the unit.[120]

The two examples – the siege battery to be raised in December 1917, and the scond tank battalion in September 1918 – neatly illustrate the approach taken by HQ OMFC to place the reserve establishment in England on a proper footing. Clearly, the reinforcement pool had to be maintained, and if additional units were needed they had to come from Canada rather than from the hard-pressed reserve units. War Office demands were no longer filled immediately and without question. There was a new sense that Canadians should control their own destiny, as the Deputy Minister OMFC reminded the War Office in November 1917: "The Canadian Government has not delegated its powers to any British authority in England or in the Field on questions of policy or administration. In these it assumes its full responsibility."[121]

Part 2 – Reinforcements in France

BASE DEPOTS

In keeping with pre-war doctrine, base depots intended to be sent to France were created at Tidworth to hold the 10 per cent first reinforcements: the Infantry Base Depot for the 1st Division battalions and the General Base Depot for all other arms and services. The Infantry Base Depot consisted of twelve companies, one for each of the 1st Division battalions, while the General Base Depot had separate wings for the artillery, engineers, Service Corps, and Medical Corps. The plan was simple and straightforward: as the Base Depots were depleted, they would be topped up with trained soldiers from the Canadian Training Depot, which would then be refilled with drafts from Canada.[122] Both of the base depots were intended to be located in a French seaport along the English Channel.

In the event, neither of the base depots deployed to France because of a shortage of accommodation at British bases along the Channel coast. Instead, reinforcements for the 1st Division were handled by the 3rd (British) General Base Depot at Le Havre.[123] The arrangement was gratefully accepted by the CEF and continued until the newly formed Canadian General Base Depot, formerly known as the 2nd Canadian Division Infantry Base Depot, commenced operations on 27 September 1915.[124]

Logically, there was no reason to retain base depots in England to feed a base depot in France, but it appears that both were retained for record-keeping purposes although the benefits of this policy remain obscure.[125] In practice, the arrangement was inefficient and the two base depots co-located with the Canadian Training Depot were simply holding units for reinforcements waiting to be posted to the 1st Division. Posting men from a reserve unit to a base depot a few hundred yards away entailed a considerable amount of work for hard-pressed clerks and adjutants, while to the soldier who had to pack up his kit and move to a neighbouring barracks in Tidworth, the scheme must have been yet another example of the unfathomable and mysterious workings of the wartime army.

The arrangements did not last long. The Infantry Base Depot at Tidworth held enough men to replace routine wastage only, and when the unprecedented demand for reinforcements after the 2nd Battle of Ypres in April 1915 cleaned out the depot, men had to be forwarded to the 3rd (British) Base Depot in France directly from reserve battalions. Not surprisingly, the elimination of the Infantry Base Depot in England had no effect on the movement of reinforcements, and the depot was done away with shortly afterward.[126]

In September 1915, the 2nd Division deployed from England to Belgium. At the same time, the newly created 2nd Division Infantry Base Depot, intended to provide infantry reinforcements for the division, was sent to Le Havre with no warning to British authorities.[127] With the arrival of the depot at Le Havre, two agencies were responsible for Canadian reinforcements: one for 2nd Division infantrymen and the other, the 3rd (British) General Base Depot, for all others, including 1st Division infantrymen. Both depots shared Camp 19. The arrangement was clearly illogical, and after some discussion between the Havre Base Commandant and the Inspector-General of Communications, GHQ 3rd Echelon directed on 23 September 1915 that the 3rd (British) General Base Depot would vacate Camp 19 and that all Canadian reinforcements would be handled by the 2nd Division Infantry Base Depot, which would henceforth be known as the Canadian General Base Depot (CGBD).[128]

The CGBD was handicapped from the beginning, since it was intended to handle reinforcements for only one division. However, GHQ 3rd Echelon chose not to increase the establishment, despite having doubled the depot's responsibilities. As the depot war diarist noted, CGBD staff consisted of five officers and sixteen other ranks to handle reinforcements for two divisions and corps troops, while the neighbouring 47th (British) Division Infantry Base Depot had five officers and twelve other ranks to handle men for only one division.[129] The situation was clearly untenable, and three more officers were provided after an appeal to the Canadian Section GHQ 3rd Echelon in November 1915.[130]

But this was not enough. In November 1915, the CGBD Commandant, Lieutenant-Colonel Worthington, pleaded for assistance from Major-General Carson at Canadian HQ in London. However, Carson was not interested in Canadian matters in far-off France and in a note to Colonel Reid washed his hands of all responsibility: "Naturally neither you nor I nor anyone else in England have anything to do with Colonel Worthington's establishment, or the duties of his office." Carson then went on to say that Worthington should take the matter up with GHQ 3rd Echelon, "and that is about the only comfort that either you or I can give him in the premises."[131]

"Not the slightest interest has ever been taken by any of the Canadian Military Authorities in England," wrote Worthington to Lieutenant-General Turner at HQ OMFC in March 1917, "although I [have] repeatedly tried to get into communication with them as to our wants."[132] The isolation extended to correspondence that had to be forwarded through the chain of command. In the case of the CGBD, this meant that all communications with Canadian authorities in England had to pass through OC Reinforcements, the Havre Base Commander, the IGC or GHQ 3rd Echelon, War Office, and HQ Southern Command in England, HQ Shorncliffe District and, finally, HQ CTD or Canadian HQ in London. It was a slow and cumbersome process that continued until 1917 when HQ OMFC negotiated an agreement with the War Office acknowledging that "in matters of organization and administration, the Canadian Government still retained full responsibility in respect to its own Forces."[133]

The isolation of the CGBD from the rest of the CEF made it difficult to sort out problems with the training divisions at Bramshott and Shorncliffe, both of which sent ill-prepared drafts. On 29–30 January 1916, for example, 1,731 men arrived from Bramshott destined for the

3rd Division. Some were verminous, and some had contracted measles and had to be quarantined. Fortunately, these men were detected almost immediately, or, as the Commandant pointed out, the entire depot would have had to be quarantined which would have effectively shut off the flow of reinforcements to the Canadian Corps.[134] The drafts had not been instructed to bring their kit bags with spare clothing and so the CGBD Quartermaster had to make up the shortages. There were also 351 men with tunics that had been tailored and were too tight to allow cardigans or winter underwear to be worn. More than a hundred men had to exchange ill-fitting boots, 262 men had no bayonets, a handful were missing puttees, and one soldier was carrying a rifle with a metal object jammed in the bore.[135]

Worthington forwarded a complaint through the British chain of command, and at the end of February 1916 the War Office directed that HQ Southern Command take the matter up with CTD Bramshott. Almost as an afterthought, a copy of the correspondence was sent to Carson at Canadian HQ in London with the observation that "these complaints are frequent."[136] But, typically, nothing was done by Canadian HQ, Bramshott, or Shorncliffe, and until the end of December 1916 reinforcements continued to arrive at the CGBD with missing or faulty equipment, ill-fitting boots, and Canadian-pattern tunics that were too tight.[137]

Shorncliffe was no better than Bramshott. The depot war diary noted that more than a hundred reinforcements en route to the 1st Division had no training on the Lee–Enfield rifle, others had not been issued with bayonets, and some were carrying rifles with bent magazine platforms that made it virtually impossible to work the bolt.[138] Highland reinforcements were wearing kilts with no straps, or buckles that had to be fastened to shirt-tails with safety pins. Drafts also arrived at Le Havre wearing up-to-date Pattern 1908 web equipment issued shortly before they embarked for France. Not surprisingly, as a Canadian officer with the Central Training School remarked, "It is in almost every case badly fitted and the men do not appear to have received instruction as to how the equipment should be worn. Consequently on arrival in France the men are unable to march for any distance, without being caused a great deal of unnecessary fatigue."[139]

All of these problems simply generated more work for the CGBD, which was understaffed and whose quartermaster stores were not set up to make large issues of clothing and equipment. As the Commandant noted in September 1916, the quantity of material that had to be exchanged was such "that our [quartermaster] stores are not adequate to cope with the matter."[140] Correcting these deficiencies took time that could be made up only by extending work hours, curtailing training, or delaying the movement of drafts to the front. Efforts were made by the CGBD to bring these problems to the attention of Bramshott and Shorncliffe, but the tortuous chain of communication minimized the effect of these efforts and precluded a prompt resolution of the complaints. Obviously, direct liaison would have been far quicker and more efficient.

Despite their initial reluctance to assist, British authorities had a vested interest in ensuring that the CGBD had the manpower needed to do the job. As early as 28 October 1915, the Adjutant-General at GHQ increased CGBD staff to ten officers and twenty-eight other ranks, the same establishment previously used by the 3rd (British) General Base Depot. An additional six officers were added in February 1916 to compensate for the increased workload once the 3rd Canadian Division arrived in France.[141] GHQ 3rd Echelon also allowed men with "Temporary Base" or "Permanent Base" medical categories to be placed on command to the CGBD to assist with fatigues and the processing of reinforcements. As early as 30 September 1915, there were 141 additional men attached to the CGBD.[142]

Even with these increases to the establishment, the CGBD must have been hard-pressed to handle the large number of reinforcements that passed through. In December 1916 alone, 13,560 infantry reinforcements arrived at the depot. But it was not the number of men in residence that created the workload; it was the number of arrivals and departures, all of whom had to be inspected, kitted-out, and documented. On 29 November 1916, for example, the depot received 1,157 reinforcements from England and despatched 658 men to the Canadian Corps. In order to handle both drafts the staff had to work continuously from 3:30 a.m. to 11:45 p.m. But the pace did not let up. On 30 November, a draft of 4,313 men arrived from England and a draft of 913 was sent to the front. The following day a draft of 1,109 was sent forward, while on 2 December, 2,363 reinforcements arrived from England and 2,230 departed for the forward area.[143]

Comprehensive statistics of CGBD arrivals and departures have not been found, but returns from August 1916 to May 1917 illustrate the magnitude of the depot's responsibilities. Every month, on average, 6,657 reinforcements arrived from England and 2,482 men from other sources, mainly hospitals. Also, 8,169 reinforcements were dispatched to forward units every month.[144] With a monthly average of 17,266 arrivals and departures, the CGBD staff must have been very busy indeed.

The routine at the CGBD was simple and straightforward. Drafts arriving from England were met by depot staff, who collected six copies of the draft nominal roll as well as other personnel records carried by the draft conducting officer. The documents were then checked and a complete kit inspection carried out, after which the Depot Quartermaster replaced items that were unserviceable or missing. Lastly, the newcomers were medically inspected, a procedure described by a CTD medical officer during a visit to the CGBD in September 1916:

> All drafts arriving at this Base are medically examined within a few hours of their arrival. The examination is done in two of the long Dining Halls and the men are stripped and have only their overcoats on. Two Medical Officers examine in each Dining Hall, and each man is asked if his teeth and eyes are alright and if there is any specific thing which is giving him trouble. Men who are passed as [fit for] active [service] file down the centre and their paybooks are examined at the opposite door by an NCO for inoculation records etc.[145]

In cases where the medical officer was not certain whether a man was fit, he was classified as TB (Temporary Base) and held until a final judgment could be made. Those who were obviously unfit were sent forward to labour units, retained at the Depot, or returned to England. Eighteen-year-olds were retained until they turned nineteen, at which point they were fed into the reinforcement stream, while those under the age of eighteen were immediately returned to England. Men who needed fillings or extractions were treated by the Depot dental clinic, and full or partial plates were provided as required. Those with poor eyesight were classified as TB and sent to an "oculist" who provided two pairs of glasses.[146]

The CGBD routine worked well for the most part, but the size of the staff made it difficult to deal with unexpected demands. In June 1916, when the three infantry divisions with the Canadian Corps sustained heavy losses in just a few weeks during the Battle of Mount Sorrel, 9,994 reinforcements, most with little or no training in England, had to be rushed through the depot. With the need for haste, the small CGBD staff could not inspect the various drafts closely, and inevitably there were problems. Men arrived at the 28th Battalion, for example, with unsharpened bayonets and rifles still coated with ordnance grease.[147] Obviously the weapons had not been inspected, either by CTD Shorncliffe or by the CGBD. Unfit men also slipped through the CGBD; in June 1916, the

Assistant Director of Medical Services (ADMS) 3rd Canadian Division complained that more than 10 per cent of a draft of 436 reinforcements that arrived at the 42nd Battalion were medically unfit. Six men were suffering from "senility," while others had a variety of ailments including rheumatism, varicose veins, hemorrhoids, and venereal disease. Ten men required extensive dental treatment. "In some cases men had no teeth at all," wrote the ADMS, "and others only three or four in the upper jaw."[148] But these cases were the exception, and for the most part CGBD staff carried out their thankless duties quietly and efficiently.

The isolation of the CGBD ended with the creation of HQ OMFC in December 1916. Turner was concerned with the channels of communication and during a visit to France in January 1917 made a point of inspecting the CGBD, where he learned first-hand that the depot was not in touch with Canadian authorities. "This must be changed," he wrote to Perley, "in order that we should know under what conditions our men are living at this Base Camp."[149]

Like the CEF in England, the CGBD was due for an overhaul. The camp was relatively remote, and in July 1916 the Commandant requested pipers from CTD Shorncliffe, with this explanation: "Here we have had for the last two weeks about seven thousand men in camp, and as the camp is situated out in the country some 7 miles, it is a pretty lonesome place for the men."[150] The camp was also too small. Intended to hold 6,000 reinforcements, it had 10,400 men on site on 7 December 1916: "It was quite impossible to accommodate all these in tents, so that many had to sleep in Dining Rooms, Cinema Huts and other places," wrote a British medical officer, and "from a sanitary point of view, the overcrowding is very objectionable."[151] Seven acres were expropriated in December 1916, but a resentful French farmer ploughed the land twice and then top-dressed it with three or four inches of manure. Since newly arrived reinforcements had to pitch their tents in this slough of despond, there were some significant health risks. Not surprisingly, HQ OMFC complained to the War Office, noting that the base "as it existed was unsatisfactory, unhealthy and showed lack of superior supervision."[152] A few months later, in April 1917, the war diarist of the newly formed 3rd Canadian Infantry Base Depot (CIBD) noted that cramped facilities made it impossible to take over 3rd Division reinforcements from the CGBD.[153]

Action by HQ OMFC was prompt. On 13 February 1917, all Canadian training bases were notified that Canadian base depots would be transferred from Le Havre to Étaples, where better accommodation was available. As well, four infantry base depots would be formed to handle reinforcements for the four divisions in the Corps.[154] The reorganization appears to have been a Canadian initiative, and Ottawa approved an order in council on 12 March 1917 establishing the new CGBD and the four infantry base depots as units of the CEF.[155] The order in council did not change the fact that Canadian depots were under command of the local British OC Reinforcements, but meant that depots could correspond directly with HQ OMFC and the CTD in England.

The order in council also set out the establishments. The CGBD was authorized a staff of nine officers and eighteen other ranks, together with a medical officer, two paymasters, two dentists, three chaplains, and forty-five low-category fatigue men. Each of the infantry base depots was allowed three officers and six other ranks as well as a medical officer and forty-three low-category men. In all, the CGBD was staffed by eighty-seven all ranks and each infantry base depot by fifty-three all ranks.

The new CGBD no longer handled infantry reinforcements; this was the job of the infantry base depots. Instead, the CGBD cared for all non-infantry reinforcements with the exception of machine gunners, who were sent directly to the British Machine Gun Depot at Camiers, and signallers, who were sent to the British Signals Depot at Abbéville. However, this changed in January 1918 when the War Office approved a recommendation from GHQ that Canadian signallers should handled by the CGBD.[156] A few months later, in August 1918, GHQ authorized infantry machine gunners to be sent directly to the CCRC. Cavalry machine gunners were not part of the Canadian Corps, however, and continued to be processed through Camiers until the end of the war.[157]

The new depots were organized in April 1917 at Le Havre. In May 1917, the Australian base depots moved to Le Havre and the Canadians took over their facilities at Étaples.[158] The move was advantageous since the Étaples camps were near civilian facilities and the port was closer to Folkestone, where the majority of Canadian reinforcements embarked for France.

Each of the four infantry depots had an established routine, and the procedures followed by the 1st CIBD in June 1917 were probably typical. Drafts from England disembarked at Boulogne and were marched to a rest camp where they spent the night. The following day, they marched to the 1st CIBD, where they were allocated quarters and provided with showers and a hot meal. The next day rifles were issued, kit inspected and deficiencies made up, respirators fitted and tested, and medical examinations carried out. On the third day, the drafts started their nine-day course at the Central Training School. Training, however, was not continuous. One day per week was devoted to "interior economy": cleaning personal kit, tidying up the camp, mandatory bathing, and a short route march. Sundays were taken up with church parades and sports.

On completion of the training, there was another kit inspection, after which each man was required to certify in writing that his kit was complete. There was also a final medical examination followed by a pay parade. Drafts were then marched to the Étaples railway station, where they embarked for the corps railhead. On arrival at the railhead, drafts were turned over to the Railway Transportation Officer, issued with iron rations, and billeted for the night. The following day, they were marched to either the divisional entrenching battalion or the divisional school.[159]

The need for four infantry base depots was predicated on the need to hold reinforcements while they were cycled through the Central Training School. However, in September 1917 GHQ decided that reinforcements would be remain at base depots only long enough to be fitted with respirators and undergo a short course in anti-gas measures.[160] A few months later, in December 1917, this requirement was eliminated when the War Office decided that infantry reinforcements would be sent directly to corps reinforcement camps to be equipped with respirators and trained in gas warfare.[161] At this point, the base depots were nothing more than reception units for troops arriving from England.

Since infantry reinforcements were now forwarded directly to the corps reinforcement camp, the number of men held at the depots at one time was sharply reduced. At the end of December 1917, for example, there were 247 reinforcements with the 1st CIBD and only 228 at the 2nd CIBD.[162] With so few reinforcements at the infantry base depots, the GHQ 3rd Echelon Canadian Section submitted a proposal to the War Office on 22 February 1918 to reduce the number of base depots to "one General and one Infantry Base Depot, with the addition of an Overflow Depot with a small staff."[163] The recommendation was then considered by HQ OMFC and the amalgamation of the infantry base depots was approved, but not the Overflow Depot.[164]

Consolidation of the four infantry base depots was carried out 20 April 1918; the 1,636 infantry reinforcements at Étaples were absorbed by the new CIBD.[165] Thereafter, there were no changes until after the Armistice, when the CGBD and CIBD became transit camps for troops returning to England.[166] But this was only a temporary arrangement, and once the Canadian Embarkation Camp was established at Le Havre on 6 January 1919 there was no need for the CIBD, which was absorbed by the CGBD on 3 February 1919. The CGBD then continued to operate until 16 June 1919, when it was redesignated Canadian Base Details.[167]

REINFORCEMENTS NEAR THE FRONT

Unlike British Expeditionary Force base depots, the CGBD initially forwarded reinforcements directly to units, since there were no CEF entrenching battalions (see chapter 7). Other dominions were in a similar position. At a 2nd (British) Army conference in May 1916, General Sir Herbert Plumer agreed to raise the question of entrenching battalions for Dominion troops with GHQ.[168] Plumer was evidently successful, and in July 1916 GHQ approved entrenching battalions for the Canadian Corps. Four entrenching battalions, one for each division, were then mobilized by the CGBD in August 1916 and sent forward to the Corps rear area.[169]

Responsibility for the entrenching battalions was divided. Canadian Corps HQ was in command, although divisions administered their affiliated battalion and the Canadian Section GHQ 3rd Echelon controlled the movement of reinforcements from the entrenching battalions to the forward units. However, the Canadian Section GHQ 3rd Echelon found it cumbersome to issue movement orders to four entrenching battalions, and in May 1917 the Canadian Entrenching Group was formed at Corps HQ to coordinate the movement of reinforcements on behalf of the Canadian Section.[170] Training was another matter, and in August 1917 divisions became responsible for training their affiliated entrenching battalion.[171]

Entrenching battalions held the 10 per cent infantry first reinforcements, about 1,200 men for each division, as well as twenty sappers and ten drivers from the engineer pool.[172] Reinforcements for all other arms and services continued to be held by the CGBD, with the exception of machine gunners at the British Machine Gun Depot at Camiers, France, and field gunners, who served with divisional ammunition columns hauling ammunition forward until they were needed on the gun-line.[173] The constant turnover in the ammunition columns, however, made it difficult to maintain expertise and efficiency. "During the Somme fighting [in 1916] reinforcements were not available and this Unit was constantly depleted of personnel to supply batteries," wrote the war diarist of the 2nd Division Ammunition Column in hindsight in August 1918. "Officers were also being changed frequently with the result that efficiency was much lowered."[174] Not surprisingly, the practice of holding replacement gunners with ammunition columns ceased in September 1917 when the CCRC was created with a holding wing for artillery reinforcements.

PARTLY TRAINED REINFORCEMENTS

Apart from reinforcements at the CGBD or the entrenching battalions, divisions held a pool of partly trained men, who became part of the reinforcement pool after completing their training at the front. The practice originated in February 1916, when Lieutenant-General Alderson, the Canadian Corps commander, wrote to HQ Second (British) Army expressing concern about the lack of reinforcements and suggesting that partly trained infantrymen, artillerymen, and engineers could be trained by the Corps in France. "All my Divisional Commanders and Brigadiers agree with me," Alderson wrote, "that the efficiency of the Corps would be much better ensured if it were kept up to strength."[175] The War Office approved the request, but there was no accommodation at the CGBD and the idea came to naught.[176]

The concept did not die, however, but remained dormant until November 1916, when GHQ 3rd Echelon notified Canadian Corps HQ as follows:

> One hundred and fifty partially trained men will be maintained surplus to Establishment with each Canadian Battalion during the winter months. As long as these men remain untrained they are to be considered as surplus, and the actual deficiencies in the War Establishment of the Units [will be] filled by reinforcements in the ordinary way. But, as they become trained and efficient they will be absorbed into the Establishment and replaced by other untrained men by demand from England. It will therefore be necessary for this office to be informed as the 150 men of each Battalion become trained and efficient and are absorbed into the Establishment.[177]

Training these men was problematic, since the Corps did not have a training depot, but each division made its own arrangements.[178] The 4th Division, for example, formed a company of partly trained men for each battalion, each with a staff of three officers and six NCOs. The companies were grouped by brigades under a major selected by the brigade commander. Training was supervised by the Commandant of the 4th Divisional School, who determined when the men had completed their training and could be absorbed into the establishment of their parent battalion.[179] The 2nd Division, on the other hand, relied on the 2nd Division Draft Regiment.[180]

The 3rd Division formed three training battalions, one for each brigade, to conduct a four-week course for partly trained reinforcements. Not all of the new arrivals had to start in the first week; for those with extensive training in England, one week of musketry sufficed. Some of the training was directly related to trench warfare, but the remainder was at a very basic level: badges of rank, saluting, hygiene, and sanitation. Evidently, the division had little or no faith with the quality of training by reserve battalions.[181]

Not all reinforcements thought the prescribed training was useful. Private Becker of the 75th Battalion, fresh from eight months with a reserve battalion in England, commented when he arrived in the 4th Divisional School in May 1917, "we started in at squad drill again. It looked like a blind to keep some officers and NCO's in soft jobs away from the guns."[182]

The policy of maintaining untrained supernumeraries within the Corps presented no difficulties, and in January 1917 GHQ increased the number to 200 for each infantry battalion.[183] However, once HQ OMFC had reformed the training system in England, there was an adequate supply of fully trained reinforcements and therefore no need to maintain partly trained men in the forward areas. "I most respectfully submit that no partially trained men should be sent from England as long as there are any fully trained men there," wrote General Currie in April 1917, although "I have no objection to partially trained men provided no other reinforcements are available."[184] The practice was abolished by HQ 2nd (British) Army in April 1917, but the Corps managed to maintain its entitlement of 200 supernumeraries per battalion until August 1917, when GHQ 3rd Echelon placed the surplus men under control of the Deputy Adjutant-General Base Depots.[185]

The first draft of partly trained reinforcements was posted to the 1st and 2nd Divisions on 12 November 1916. From then until August 1917, there were two streams of reinforcements: trained and partly trained. The number of each is difficult to determine, but a sample of 9,085 reinforcements posted to nine battalions from November 1916 to August 1917 shows that about 26 per cent (2,718 men) had served in England for fewer than fourteen weeks and were probably partly trained. With 54,917 infantry reinforcements posted to the Corps during this period, about 14,300 men were probably partly trained.

CANADIAN CORPS REINFORCEMENT CAMP

The purpose of the base depots was to replenish entrenching battalions in the forward area near the corps railhead, which held the 10 per cent first reinforcements for the infantry battalions. However, as discussed in chapter 7, entrenching battalions were not overly successful and, in September 1917, GHQ abolished the battalions and replaced them with corps reinforcement camps that held reinforcements for all arms and services, not just the infantry.

Naturally, the Canadian Corps followed suit. On 5 September 1917, Corps HQ authorized the creation of the CCRC.[186] The new CCRC was similar to other reinforcement camps, but had distinctly Canadian features.

In the British army, divisions were rotated in and out of corps and therefore each had its own reinforcement camp, probably grouped under corps arrangements. Since British divisions had only nine battalions and one pioneer battalion by 1918, and each battalion was capped at 900, the 10 per cent first reinforcements held in the forward areas was substantially fewer than in the Canadian Corps. The British divisional camp, organized into two companies with 500 men, had an establishment of twelve officers and sixty other ranks.[187] In contrast, each Canadian divisional wing provided for twelve battalions with an establishment of eight officers and eighty other ranks. In all, the CCRC was manned by forty-six officers and 474 men.[188] A slight increase was authorized in 1918, and by the end of war the establishment called for forty-six officers and 498 other ranks.[189]

The Australians also created a reinforcement camp in November 1917; the 1st ANZAC Reinforcement Camp (known later as the Australian Corps Reinforcement Camp), similar to the CCRC. However, there were significant differences. Non-infantry reinforcements were held by a Corps Depot. Gunners and infantrymen were placed into divisional wings, but these were not co-located with the main camp and were frequently housed at the divisional railhead. Training was limited, since reinforcements spent only four or five days with the camp. In comparison with the CCRC, therefore, the Australian Corps Reinforcement Camp was considerably more decentralized.[190]

Broadly speaking, the CCRC was divided in two, with some elements quartered at the camp itself (Figure 9.1)[191] and others dispersed throughout the Corps (Figure 9.2).[192]

In some cases, reinforcements were actually with the units they were intended to reinforce. Signals reinforcements were held by the Corps

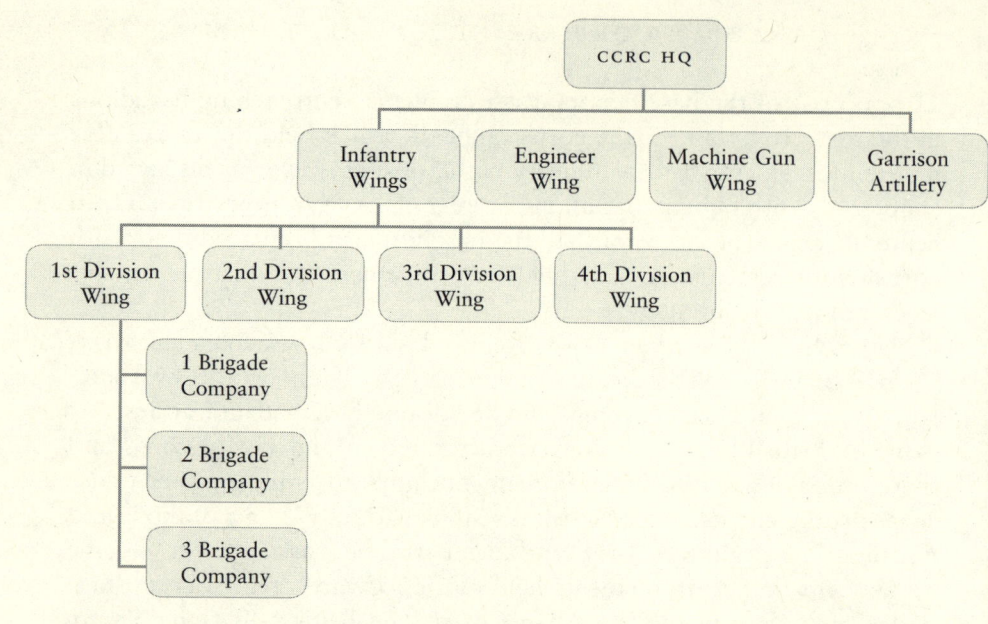

```
                        CCRC HQ
    ┌──────────────┬──────────┬──────────────┐
 Infantry      Engineer   Machine Gun    Garrison
  Wings          Wing        Wing       Artillery
    │
 ┌──────┬─────────┬─────────┬─────────┐
1st Division  2nd Division  3rd Division  4th Division
   Wing         Wing          Wing          Wing
    │
    ├── 1 Brigade Company
    ├── 2 Brigade Company
    └── 3 Brigade Company
```

Figure 9.1 Elements held in CCRC camp, 1918. Each divisional wing had an identical organization.

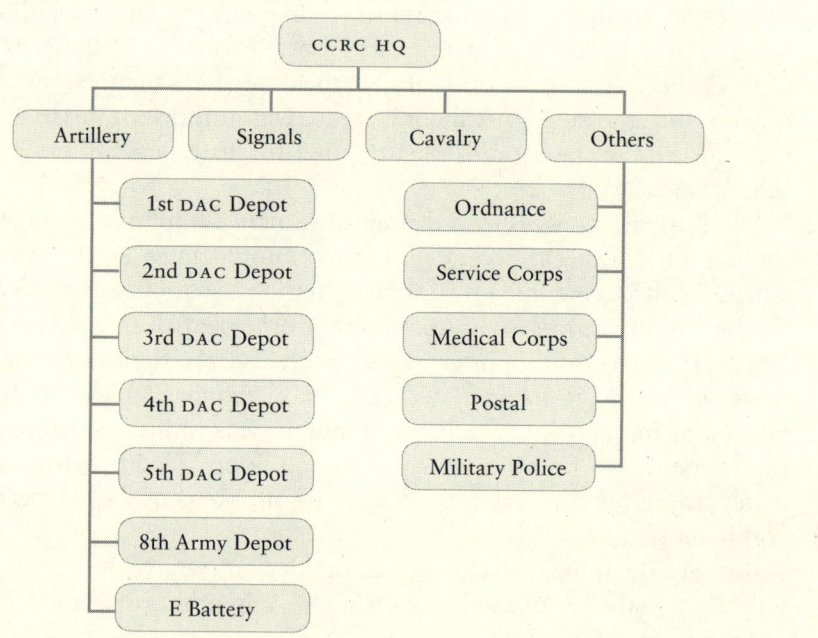

```
                 CCRC HQ
    ┌──────────┬──────────┬──────────┐
 Artillery   Signals    Cavalry    Others
    │                              │
    ├── 1st DAC Depot              ├── Ordnance
    ├── 2nd DAC Depot              ├── Service Corps
    ├── 3rd DAC Depot              ├── Medical Corps
    ├── 4th DAC Depot              ├── Postal
    ├── 5th DAC Depot              └── Military Police
    ├── 8th Army Depot
    └── E Battery
```

Figure 9.2 CCRC elements dispersed in corps area, 1918

Signals Company, anti-aircraft reinforcements were held by E Battery of the Canadian Field Artillery, and corps cavalry reinforcements were held by Canadian Light Horse Regimental HQ. Artillery reinforcements, on the other hand, were held by divisional artillery reinforcement depots attached to a Divisional Ammunition Column or, in the case of the 8th Army Brigade, by a depot attached to the Brigade Ammunition Column. Ordnance, Service Corps, Medical Corps, postal and military police reinforcements were dispersed to their respective units at Corps HQ or at the four divisions, probably because they were relatively few in number.

Infantrymen drafted from England to France were not posted to the CCRC, but to their intended unit. However, they remained with the CCRC until the Canadian Section GHQ 3rd Echelon authorized their move forward. On the other hand, artillery, engineer, machine gun, signals, medical corps, and service corps reinforcements were not posted to a unit but to a corps pool, probably because they were not subject to the same regimental and territorial constraints as the infantry.[193] Regardless of where the men were posted, they remained with the CCRC until the Canadian Section GHQ 3rd Echelon authorized them to join a forward unit.

Reinforcements held by the CCRC were normally occupied with training, although from time to time they were used for other purposes. In October 1917, for example, CCRC reinforcements in the Ypres Salient provided work parties in the rear areas, while infantry reinforcements were used as machine gun ammunition carriers on a scale of two men for each gun in a static firing position and three men for each mobile gun.[194] In August 1918, almost a thousand reinforcements were employed on various duties in the Corps rear area.[195] However, despite these diversions, the emphasis was on training the reinforcements until they were needed at the front. This was reflected in the establishment for infantry divisional wings, which called for thirty-five senior NCOs to teach drill, musketry, wiring, engineering, and bombing as well as Lewis gun and light trench mortar drills and handling.[196] Other corps trained their reinforcements as well; the Engineer Wing had ten officers and twenty-nine senior NCOs to teach drill, musketry, bombing, field engineering, tunnelling, signalling, and Lewis gun drills. Even the relatively small Garrison Artillery Depot had four senior NCOs who dealt with musketry, signalling, and gun drill.[197]

Figures 9.1 and 9.2 suggest that all reinforcements were controlled by the Commanding Officer of the CCRC. But this was not the case. Divisions were responsible for the training and administration of infantry reinforcements with their divisional wings, while field artillery reinforcements were controlled by divisional ammunition columns under the supervision of the Corps senior gunner, siege gunners were administered by the Canadian Corps Heavy Artillery, and engineer reinforcements were administered by the Corps senior Engineer.[198]

With no responsibility for training and personnel administration, the CCRC Commanding Officer was free to concentrate on other matters. His primary function was to act as a conduit for the passage of orders and instructions from both Corps HQ and the Canadian Section GHQ 3rd Echelon to the divisional wings and other components of the CCRC. Under ordinary circumstances, reinforcements could not be moved forward until the Canadian Section GHQ 3rd Echelon had issued the requisite movement orders. These were executed by the CCRC CO, who notified the component concerned, ordered transport, and ensured the men were delivered to the railhead. The Commanding Officer also responded to movement orders issued by Corps HQ concerning "battle postings" for machine gun, artillery, and signals reinforcements. These postings were approved by Corps HQ, and the Canadian Section GHQ 3rd Echelon was notified after the fact. The intention of this policy was to speed up the movement of reinforcements for critical arms when heavy fighting was in progress.[199]

The CCRC was a large, unwieldy organization that could not be moved easily at short notice. Formed at Villers au Bois, France, on 15 September 1917, the camp was moved only twice, each time to a major railhead: Calonne-Ricouart on 9 October 1917, and Aubin-Saint-Vaast in the Pas-de-Calais region on 5 May 1918.[200] During the same period, the Corps moved to a variety of areas, usually at some distance from the CCRC. On 11 November 1918, for example, the Corps was engaged in operations in and around Mons, about 180 kilometres from Aubin Saint Vaast. Reinforcements, therefore, had to be sent to whichever railhead had been allocated to the Canadian Corps. However, the railhead could be some distance from the Corps; in these cases, reinforcements faced several days of marching before they joined their new units. It must be remembered that the CCRC Commanding Officer was responsible for these men until they were safely with their units.

To speed up the movement of reinforcements, two units were deployed as necessary: the Canadian Corps Railhead Depot (CCRD) and CCRC Advanced HQ. The purpose of the CCRD was to hold reinforcements as far forward as possible until the Canadian Section GHQ 3rd Echelon issued a movement order. The number of reinforcements held at the

CCRD varied from time to time, but was decided by Canadian Corps HQ and the Canadian Section GHQ 3rd Echelon. Not all reinforcements with the CCRD were provided by the main camp at Aubin-Saint-Vaast. During periods of heavy fighting, reinforcements could be sent directly from the base depot at Étaples to the CCRD which, after all, was an arm of the CCRC.

The Advanced HQ not only controlled the CCRD, but also arranged staging camps spaced one day's march apart to provide bivouac sites and rations for reinforcements moving forward. The Advanced HQ also had an executive function. During periods of heavy casualties, the Canadian Section GHQ 3rd Echelon would speed up the movement of reinforcements by issuing movement orders directly to the Advanced HQ to avoid having CCRC HQ repeating the order to the CCRD.[201]

The CCRC was a large and complex organization with myriad rules and procedures that governed its operations. Paradoxically, the complexity of the structure and the bureaucratic maze were strengths rather than weaknesses and gave the CCRC the flexibility it needed to meet the demands of the Hundred Days and the beginning of manoeuvre warfare. Admittedly, units were short of men from time to time, but this was the product of the reinforcement flow from England and not the result of flaws in the organization.

The success of the CCRC is shown by the number of reinforcements handled from October 1917 to November 1918. In only thirteen months, 107,872 reinforcements passed through the CCRC: 60,807 for the infantry and 74,065 for the remaining arms and services. The average daily strength was 9,535 other ranks, although monthly strengths varied considerably from 9,535 men in March 1918 to 13,467 in July 1918.[202] The previous system with base depots and entrenching battalions would have had difficulties in coping with the volume and topping up depleted units in a timely manner.

SUMMARY

The reinforcement establishment in England was not a planned, well-thought-out structure but an improvisation based on surplus units in the First Contingent. As the Canadian Corps expanded to four divisions, the number of reserve battalions steadily increased. But with no properly organized Canadian Military Headquarters and a confused chain of command, there was no coordination of effort, rational structure, or long-term planning. Inevitably, training suffered and reinforcements were sent to France who were partly trained or poorly trained. Not surprisingly, the Canadian Corps had no confidence in the reserve establishment and set up divisional training schools behind the front lines to teach newly arrived reinforcements the basics of soldiering. At the same time, the CGBD in France, charged with handling soldiers from the reserve units, struggled to cope with an inadequate establishment and reinforcements from England who were poorly equipped or manifestly unfit. The problems were not insolvable, but the Depot was hampered by the fact that it was outside of the Canadian chain of command and could not communicate directly with Canadian authorities in England.

All of this changed after December 1916, when OMFC Headquarters was created in London to control all Canadian units in England. The new Headquarters, staffed by talented and efficient officers, rationalized the reserve establishment and reformed the training programs to eliminate the problems that had existed under the previous regime in 1915–16. At the same time, direct liaison was established with the General Base Depot in France, which meant the OMFC could now exercise control over all Canadian reinforcements up to the point where they were dispatched to the Canadian Corps. Not surprisingly, the Corps gained confidence in the new structure and the divisional basic training schools were done away with.

In France, the Canadian Corps had no option for handling reinforcements held in the forward area other than to adhere to British policies. Thus, entrenching battalions were formed in August 1916. However, these proved to be inefficient and in 1917 were replaced by reinforcement camps. Naturally, the Corps followed suit, but the CCRC was not simply a carbon copy of the British model; rather, its organization and policies were designed to meet Canadian needs. In practice, the new organization proved to be efficient and flexible enough to meet rapidly changing conditions at the front.

A consistent thread runs through all of these organizational changes: the CEF grew from an improvised force to a truly professional army, an army that was organized and controlled by Canadians to meet Canadian needs. No longer was the CEF part and parcel of the British army. By 1918 it was truly Canada's army.

Conclusion

This book concerns the essential aspects of manpower management in the Canadian Expeditionary Force during the First World War: finding the number of men required, training them, and then delivering them to the front. The First World War was unprecedented in Canadian history. Never before had the nation been caught up in a total war that demanded so much, particularly in the way of human resources. It was not just a matter of manpower. New organizations and policies had to be crafted to find the men, train them, and send them to the front in a timely fashion. It took time, but by mid-1917 an efficient and comprehensive system had been created to do this. At the same time, the Canadian Corps became a hard-hitting, well-organized body, an elite force within the British Expeditionary Force. Together, the operational and administrative changes that were made marked the transition of the Canadian Forces into a professional army: Canada's national army.

These changes constituted an impressive feat, considering that the peacetime army, intended only to support a part-time militia, was unprepared for general mobilization in 1914. Barracks were few and far between, and there were no manoeuvre areas in the major urban centres where most of the wartime units were raised in 1914–15. A few training camps for collective manoeuvre and artillery training existed, but for the most part the lack of infrastructure meant they could be used only in the summer. There was a general shortage of equipment, and leisurely peacetime procurement policies meant that most of the weapons held by the militia were obsolete. Thus, comprehensive training had to be conducted in England, where facilities and equipment were available.

Despite these disadvantages, the militia played a significant role in mobilization. Given the proliferation of militia detachments with their armouries and drill halls across the country, a widespread military presence was already in place that facilitated recruiting. The militia also provided an essential cadre of officers, NCOs, and trained soldiers that became the backbone of wartime units composed mainly of raw recruits. The peacetime militia was far from perfect, but in 1914–15 it provided the nucleus for Canada's first wartime army.

Manpower was not simply a military concern; men were also needed for essential industries and the production of munitions. But, from first to last, the Canadian government made no real effort to control the national manpower pool. No thought was given to allocating manpower where it was most needed, and no attempt was made to husband manpower. The size and composition of the force that could be raised and sustained was never seriously considered, and there was no acknowledgment by the government that manpower resources were finite. The result was, perhaps, inevitable: recruiting standards had to be relaxed and alternative sources of manpower explored in order to fill the ranks. Ultimately, these efforts were unsuccessful; in the end, the government was forced to adopt conscription to maintain the flow of reinforcements.

Throughout the war, Militia Headquarters and the district headquarters made concerted efforts to control recruiting – but with mixed results, owing to the decisions made by Sir Sam Hughes, the Minister of Militia and Defence, and Sir Robert Borden, the Prime Minister, both of whom ignored or failed to consult their military advisors. Both men thought of manpower in quantitative terms only and did not consider the composition and final structure of the CEF. The upshot was that most of the men enlisted were infantrymen. Even worse, they were recruited by a series of hastily organized battalions formed with no regard to the existing infrastructure. These locally based units may have assisted recruiting by appealing to local sentiment, but their proliferation threw the military into chaos. The situation was eased in late 1916, when many of the battalions were sent to England, but they were the only infantry recruiting agencies and, once gone, had to be replaced. In January 1917, Militia HQ adopted the expedient of calling on those militia units that still had a coherent command structure to organize depot companies; however, by this time, the militia was a spent force and the results were meager. The answer lay in the concept of regional depots that had originally been planned in 1914. In August 1917, faced with a very large intake of conscripts, Militia HQ created regional depot battalions across the country to recruit, train, and forward reinforcements. There is some irony in the fact that, just as a rational structure was put in place, the government enacted the *Military Service Act*, which transferred responsibility for inducting conscripts from the Department of Militia and Defence to the Military Service Branch of the Department of Justice.

Militia HQ might have had difficulties in controlling recruiting for much of the war, but it could and did control recruiting criteria. These criteria were not static, but were continually modified throughout the war mainly to expand the pool of potential recruits. Not all of the changes were productive. Reducing the minimum height for the infantry to five feet, for example, produced few soldiers who were fit for the trenches. Other changes, such as the increase to the maximum age, were not harmonized with British standards that governed the CEF overseas, with the result that men arrived in England who could not be posted to France.

Militia HQ was also ambivalent about citizenship and ethnicity, with the result that non-English speaking immigrants and visible minorities initially found it difficult to enlist. However, by 1918 immigrants, blacks, and Asians were conscripted. The initial requirement that recruits had to be British subjects remained in force throughout the war, but was relaxed in 1917; men were then able to join who would not have been eligible in 1914.

Although there were about 1,500,000 male British subjects in Canada between the ages of 18 and 45 who were eligible for military service, the manpower pool was limited. After making allowances for those who were medically unfit or those who were essential workers, there were an estimated 820,637 potential recruits, of whom 652,829, or 80 per cent, were fit for overseas service. However, these numbers are somewhat overstated, considering the opposition toward military service in some areas of Quebec. The true total of potential recruits might not have been far off the wartime establishment of 500,000 men. Not surprisingly, the CEF looked to alternative sources, including prisons and those living abroad, while efforts were made to manage serving manpower more efficiently.

Training in Canada was largely inefficient; newly mobilized units struggled to produce fully trained soldiers despite the fact that their weapons were obsolete, together with a lack of equipment, ammunition, and training facilities. The result was that men had to be retrained on arrival in England. This duplication of effort not only wasted time and resources but also slowed down the movement of reinforcements to the front. The problem was eventually rectified at the end of 1917 when Militia Headquarters decided that recruits would receive preliminary training only before embarking for England. This change was for the better, but came only after repeated pleas from Headquarters OMFC, which illustrates the difficulties of coordination between England and Canada.

Training in England was effective, but the structure by which it was delivered was inefficient. To a great extent this was due to the lack of a central authority, but such an authority could not be established as long as Sam Hughes held office. However, in November 1916, Hughes resigned after the Ministry of the OMFC was created; a properly staffed military headquarters started operations on 5 December 1916. The new headquarters was a dramatic change from the past. Command of all CEF units in England was vested in the new HQ: a proper staff was set up to control training, and arrangements were made to provide Canadian reserve units with the same equipment entitlement as their British counterparts. With these reforms, the training system in England became both efficient and effective. Just as importantly, it proved to be flexible and was able to respond quickly to new demands created by the German offensive of 21 March 1918.

The purpose of a reinforcement structure is to deliver an adequate supply of trained replacements in a timely manner to make up for unit wastage in the field. In 1915, the system, based on pre-war British policies, relied on training units in England and base depots along the Channel coast to maintain a flow of men to the 1st Division in Belgium. Although simple and straightforward, this proved to be inefficient, since reinforcements were held nowhere near the front-line units. Entrenching battalions in the forward area were created, but when the dual purposes of training reinforcements and providing work parties proved to be incompatible the entrenching battalions were replaced by a centralized Reinforcement Camp in September 1917.

Prime Minister Borden's aims evolved throughout the war. From October 1915, his goal was to shed Canada's semi-autonomous status and achieve a full voice in the affairs of the Empire.[1] To do this, he aimed at putting as many men as possible in the field. As Richard Walker has remarked, "The only currency to buy such influence was manpower."[2] The management of military manpower, therefore, was the key to Borden's war goals.

Canada's army changed dramatically during the First World War. From a hastily mobilized and poorly organized force in 1914, the CEF evolved by 1918 into a hard-hitting fighting entity: highly structured, well-organized, and a mainstay of the British army in France. The transformation did not depend solely on the efforts of the Canadian Corps but also arose from the development of an efficient and comprehensive system of recruiting, training, and reinforcing units at the front. The creation of this system during the war was difficult and at times uneven – not unlike the evolution of tactics on the Western Front. But, by 1918, the CEF had become Canada's first truly professional army, a remarkable achievement for a small country that in 1914 relied on a poorly prepared part-time militia.

Notes

INTRODUCTION

1 Keith Grieves, *The Politics of Manpower, 1914–1918* (Manchester: Manchester University Press, 1988).
2 Frederick William Perry, *The Commonwealth Armies: Manpower and Organisation in Two World Wars* (Manchester: Manchester University Press, 1988).
3 Charles Messenger, *Call to Arms: The British Army, 1914–1918* (London: Weidenfeld & Nicolson, 2005); Peter Simkins, *Kitchener's Army: the Raising of the New Armies, 1914–1916* (Manchester: Manchester University Press, 1988).
4 Ian Beckett, *The Great War* (Harlow: Pearson Education, 2007).
5 John Morton Osborne, *Voluntary Recruiting Movement in Britain, 1914–1916* (New York: Garland Publishing, 1982), 131.
6 Ian Malcolm Brown, *British Logistics on the Western Front, 1914–1919* (Westport, CT: Praeger, 1998); Michael Patrick Ryan, "Supplying the Materiel Battle: Combined Logistics in the Canadian Corps, 1915–1918" (master's thesis, Carleton University, 2005).
7 Stephen Harris, *Canadian Brass: The Making of a Professional Army 1860–1939* (Toronto: University of Toronto Press, 1988).
8 Richard J. Walker, "The Political Management of Army Leadership: The Evolution of Canadian Civil-Army Relations 1898–1945" (PhD diss., University of Western Ontario, 2003).
9 William F. Stewart, *The Embattled General: Sir Richard Turner and the First World War* (Montreal and Kingston: McGill-Queen's University Press, 2015).

10 Colonel A. Fortescue Duguid, *Official History of the Canadian Forces in the Great War 1914–1919: General Series*, vol. 1 (Ottawa: King's Printer, 1938).
11 Colonel G.W.L. Nicholson, *Official History of the Canadian Army in the First World War: Canadian Expeditionary Force 1914–1919* (Ottawa: Queen's Printer, 1962).
12 Ibid., xii.
13 Sir Andrew Macphail, *Official History of the Canadian Forces in the Great War 1914–1919: The Medical Services* (Ottawa: F.A. Acland, 1925).
14 Andrew Iarocci, *Shoestring Soldiers: The 1st Canadian Division at War, 1914–1915* (Toronto: University of Toronto Press, 2008).
15 Kenneth Radley, *We Lead, Others Follow: First Canadian Division 1914–1918* (St Catharines: Vanwell Publishing Limited, 2006).
16 David Charles Gregory Campbell, "The Divisional Experience in the C.E.F.: A Social and Operational History of the 2nd Canadian Division, 1915–1918" (PhD diss., University of Calgary, 2003).
17 Desmond Morton, *When Your Number's Up: The Canadian Soldier in the First World War* (Toronto: Random House of Canada, 1993); Desmond Morton, *A Peculiar Kind of Politics: Canada's Overseas Ministry in the First World War* (Toronto: Toronto University Press, 1982).
18 Tim Cook, *No Place to Run: The Canadian Corps and Gas Warfare in the First World War* (Vancouver: University of British Columbia Press, 1999); Bill Rawling, *Surviving Trench Warfare: Technology and the Canadian Corps 1914–1918* (Toronto: University of Toronto Press, 1992).
19 Robert Craig Brown and Donald Loveridge, "Unrequited Faith: Recruiting the CEF 1914–1918," *Revue Internationale d'Histoire Militaire*, no. 54 (1982).
20 C.A. Sharpe, "Enlistment in the Canadian Expeditionary Force: A Regional Analysis," *Revue d'Études Canadiennes / Journal of Canadian Studies* 18, no. 4 (hiver/Winter 1983–1984).
21 Jonathan F. Vance, "Research Note: Provincial Patterns of Enlistment in the Canadian Expeditionary Force," *Canadian Military History* 17, no. 2 (Spring 2008): 75–8.
22 Morton, *When Your Number's Up*, 277.
23 Robert Allen Rutherdale, *Hometown Horizons: Local Responses to Canada's Great War* (Vancouver: UBC Press, 2004).
24 Ian Hugh Maclean Miller, *Our Glory and Our Grief: Torontonians and the Great War* (Toronto: University of Toronto Press, 2002).
25 Jim Blanchard, *Winnipeg's Great War: A City Comes of Age* (Winnipeg: University of Manitoba Press, 2010).

26 James M. Pitsula, *For All We Have and Are: Regina and the Experience of the Great War* (Winnipeg: University of Manitoba Press, 2008).
27 John Herd Thompson, *The Harvests of War: The Prairie West, 1914–1918* (Toronto: McClelland and Stewart Limited, 1981).
28 Paul Maroney, "The Great Adventure: The Context and Ideology of Recruiting in Ontario, 1914–1917," in *Canadian Historical Review* 77, no. 1 (March 1996): 62–98.
29 Tim Cook, *Canadians Fighting the Great War, 1914–1916*, vol. 1, *At the Sharp End* and vol. 2, *Shock Troops* (Toronto: Viking Canada, 2007 and 2008).
30 Paddy Griffith, *Battle Tactics of the Western Front: The British Army's Art of Attack 1916–1918* (London: Yale University Press, 1994), 179–91.
31 Hampden Gordon, *The War Office* (London: Putnam, 1935), 6–7, 80, 102, 106–7; Captain Owen Wheeler, *The War Office, Past and Present* (London: Methuen & Co. Ltd., 1914), 276, 299.
32 Michael Albert Ramsay, "Tactics in Crisis: The Intellectual Origins of Modern Warfare in the British Army, 1870–1918" (PhD diss., Queen's University, 1997), 309–11.
33 LAC, RG 24, vol. 6553, file 802-6, vol. 4 contains covering letters for distribution of these publications.
34 Andrew Theobald, *The Bitter Harvest of War: New Brunswick and the Conscription Crisis of 1917* (Fredericton: Goose Lane Editions and the New Brunswick Heritage Project, 2008); Brock Millman, *Polarity, Patriotism and Dissent in Great War Canada, 1914–1919* (Toronto: University of Toronto Press, 2016).
35 Desmond Morton, *A Military History of Canada* (Edmonton: Hurtig Publishers, 1985), 154, 156.
36 Chris Sharpe, "Enlistment in the Canadian Expeditionary Force: A Re-evaluation," *Canadian Military History* 24, no. 1 (Winter/Spring 2015), 19–22.
37 A.M. Willms, "Conscription, 1917: A Brief for the Defence," *Canadian Historical Review* 37, no. 4 (December 1956).
38 J.L. Granatstein, "Conscription and My Politics," *Canadian Military History* 10, no. 4 (Autumn 2001); J.L. Granatstein, "Conscription in the Great War," in *Canada and the First World War: Essays in Honour of Robert Craig Brown*, ed. David MacKenzie (Toronto: University of Toronto Press, 2005), 63–4.
39 William Philpott, *War of Attrition: Fighting the First World War* (New York: The Overlook Press, 2014), 310–11.
40 LAC, Currie fonds, MG 30, E 100, vol. 1, Lieutenant-General Currie to J.J. Creelman, 30 November 1917.

41 Lieutenant-Colonel G. Chalmers Johnston, *The 2nd Canadian Mounted Rifles (British Columbia Horse) in France and Flanders* (Vernon, BC: Vernon News Printing & Publishing Company, c.1931); Captain S.G. Bennett, *The 4th Canadian Mounted Rifles 1914–1919* (Toronto: Murray Printing Company Limited, 1926); Captain W.L. Gibson, *Records of the Fourth Canadian Infantry Battalion in the Great War 1914–1918* (Toronto: The MacLean Publishing Company Limited, 1924); Lieutenant-Colonel H.M. Urquhart, *The History of the 16th Battalion (The Canadian Scottish) in the Great War 1914–1919* (Toronto: The Macmillan Company of Canada Limited, 1932); Major D.J. Corrigal, *The History of the Twentieth Canadian Battalion (Central Ontario Regiment), Canadian Expeditionary Force, in the Great War 1914–1918* (Toronto: Stone & Cox Limited, 1935); Bernard McEvoy and Captain A.H. Finlay, *History of the 72nd Canadian Infantry Battalion, Seaforth Highlanders of Canada* (Vancouver: Cowan & Brookhouse, 1920); Lieutenant-Colonel Joseph Hayes, *The Eighty-fifth in France and Flanders* (Halifax: Royal Print & Litho Limited, 1920); Ralph Hodder-Williams, *Princess Patricia's Canadian Light Infantry 1914–1919*, vol. 2 (London: Hodder & Stoughton Ltd., 1923); ARCC, "Records and Nominal Rolls of the 18th Battalion"; LAC, RG 150, vol. 75, part II, Orders 21st Battalion.

42 LAC, RG 9, III-B-3, vols 3764 and 3765.

CHAPTER ONE

1 Dominion of Canada, *An Act Respecting the Canadian Militia* [Militia Act], R.S.C., 1906, c. 41, ss. 2, 16, 22, 24, 26.
2 *The Quarterly Militia List of the Dominion of Canada (Corrected to 31st March 1914)* (Ottawa: Kings' Printer, 1914), 11–32.
3 Dominion of Canada, 3rd Parliament, 3rd session, *Sessional Papers* vol. 48, no. 27, 1914. Major-General W.D. Otter, Report of the Inspector-General of 30 November 1912, in *Report of the Militia Council for the Dominion of Canada, year ending March 31st, 1913*, Sessional Paper 35, p. 94, para. 50. Available: http://prod.library.utoronto.ca/maplib/dmgis/ca1_ys_s27.htm
4 General Sir Ian Hamilton, *Report on the Military Institutions of Canada* (Ottawa: Government Printing Bureau, 1913), 38.
5 James R. Steel and Captain John A. Gill, *The Battery: The History of the 10th (St Catharines) Field Battery Royal Canadian Artillery* (St. Catharines: 10th Field Battery Association, 1996), 46.
6 Jean Pariseau and Serge Bernier, *French Canadians and Bilingualism in the Canadian Armed Forces*, vol. 1, *1763–1969: The Fear of a Parallel Army*

(Ottawa: Department of National Defence, Directorate of History, 1988), 64.
7 Dominion of Canada, 3rd Parliament, 3rd session, *Sessional Papers* vol. 48, no. 27, 1914. Major-General W.D. Otter, Report of the Inspector-General of 30 November 1912, in *Report of the Militia Council for the Dominion of Canada, year ending March 31st, 1913*, Sessional Paper 35, p. 94, para. 41. Available: http://prod.library.utoronto.ca/maplib/dmgis/ca1_ys_s27.htm
8 R.C. Fetherstonhaugh, *The Royal Canadian Regiment 1883–1933* (Montreal: Gazette Printing, 1936), 185.
9 Stephen J. Harris, *Canadian Brass: The Making of a Professional Army 1860–1939* (Toronto: University of Toronto Press, 1988), 71.
10 Sir H. Jenkyns, "History of the Military Forces of the Crown," in Great Britain, War Office, *Manual of Military Law 1914* (London: HMSO, 1914; reprint 1916), 162–3.
11 Desmond Morton, *Ministers and Generals: Politics and the Canadian Militia 1868–1904* (Toronto: Toronto University Press, 1970), 186, 193; Mackey J. Hitsman, *Attempts to Integrate Canada's Armed Forces Before 1945: Report no. 15.* (Ottawa: Department of National Defence, Directorate of History, 1967), 11–13.
12 *Militia Act*, s. 7.
13 Desmond Morton, *A Military History of Canada* (Edmonton: Hurtig Publishers, 1985), 120.
14 Harris, *Canadian Brass*, 88–9.
15 Ronald Haycock, *Sam Hughes: The Public Career of a Controversial Canadian 1885–1916* (Waterloo: Wilfrid Laurier University Press, 1986), 151.
16 T.C. Willett, *A Heritage at Risk: The Canadian Militia as a Social Institution* (Boulder, CO: Westview Press, 1987), 60.
17 William Antrobus Griesbach, *I Remember* (Toronto: The Ryerson Press, 1946), 345.
18 *Quarterly Militia List (Corrected to 31st March 1914)* and *Quarterly Militia List (Corrected to 1st July 1918)*.
19 Colonel C.F. Hamilton, "Lieutenant-General Sir Willoughby Gwatkin – An Appreciation," *Canadian Defence Quarterly* 2, no. 3 (April 1925): 228, 230.
20 LAC, RG 24, series C-1, reel C-4859, HQ combined file 1295, "AG to Brigadier-General Gwynne," 30 June 1920.
21 Dominion of Canada, 3rd Parliament, 3rd session, *Sessional Papers* vol. 48, no. 27, 1914. Sam Hughes, Minister of Militia and Defence, Appendix F to *Report of the Militia Council for the Dominion of Canada, year ending*

March 31st, 1913, Sessional Paper 35, p. 85, para. 4. Available: http://prod.library.utoronto.ca/maplib/dmgis/ca1_ys_s27.htm
22 General Order no. 54, April 1913.
23 *Quarterly Militia List (Corrected to 31st March 1914)*, 26–7.
24 Pariseau and Bernier, *Fear of a Parallel Army*, 54.
25 ARCC, box X1541-43, 7th Battalion Service Roll 1899–1909.
26 Christopher J. Anstead, "Patriotism and Camaraderie in a Peacetime Militia Regiment 1907–1954." *Histoire Sociale/Social History* 26, no. 52 (November 1993), 255.
27 Desmond Morton, *The Canadian General: Sir William Otter* (Toronto: Hakkert, 1974), 152–56.
28 AO, Royal Hamilton Light Infantry Fonds, MS 843(19), reel 14, series D-2, Regimental Orders 1874–1926, Regimental Order no. 21, 1 March 1915.
29 LAC, RG 24, vol. 6427, file 257, vol. 1, "Report of the Annual Inspection of the 48th Regiment Highlanders," 10 October 1913.
30 LAC, RG 24, vol. 366, file 33-101-7, Commandant's Report Mcaulay Plains Camp 1912.
31 LAC, RG 24, vol. 1561, file HQ 683-169-5, "Misappropriation of Funds and Reorganization of 141st Battalion," September 1916.
32 Anstead, "Patriotism and Camaraderie," 255.
33 Colonel Francis B. Ware, *The Story of the Seventh Regiment Fusiliers* (London: Hunter Printing Company, 1946), 142; ARCC, box 4416, file "Correspondence 1911," OC 7th Fusiliers to DSA MD no. 1, 9 March 1911.
34 AO, Royal Hamilton Light Infantry Fonds, MS 843(19), Service Roll Book; ARCC, 7th Fusilier Service Roll.
35 LAC, RG 38, vol. 443, file "Country of Birth CEF."
36 Canada, Department of Militia and Defence, *King's Regulations and Orders for the Canadian Militia* (Ottawa: King's Printer, 1910), paras 243, 246.
37 *Hamilton Spectator*, 29 October 1912, 4.
38 *An Act Respecting Truancy and Compulsory School Attendance*, S.O. 1909, c. 92, s. 3.
39 Constance Backhouse, *Colour-Coded: A Legal History of Racism in Canada, 1900–1950* (Toronto: University of Toronto Press, 1999), 15; Sean Flynn Foyn, "The Underside of Glory: AfriCanadian Enlistment in the Canadian Expeditionary Force 1914–1917" (master's thesis, University of Ottawa, 1999), 30; see also Vic Satzewich, *Racism in Canada* (Don Mills, ON: Oxford University Press, 2011).

40 AO, Service Roll Book; LAC, RG 9, II-F-6, vol. 222, "Alberta Rangers – Annual Drill Pay List 25 June–6 July 1907"; "Annual Pay List of 23rd Alberta Rangers for the Year 1909."
41 LAC, RG 24, vol. 271, file 2-27-4, APMG Militia Headquarters to DOC MD 13, 18 November 1909.
42 Barbara M. Wilson, ed., *Ontario and the First World War 1914–1918: A Collection of Documents* (Toronto: Champlain Society, 1977), cviii; S.W. Jackman, "The Victoria Pioneer Rifle Corps, British Columbia, 1860–1866," *Journal of the Society for Army Historical Research*, 39 (1961): 41.
43 Names were taken from attestation papers on the LAC website *Soldiers of the First World War* and cross-checked with the 1911 Census to confirm racial origin. Militiamen who obviously enlisted after the outbreak of war were excluded.
44 LAC, RG 24, vol. 6297, file 39, vol. 1, "Report of the Annual Inspection 1913 of the 37th Haldimand Rifles."
45 *Quarterly Militia List (Corrected to 30th June 1914)*, 214, 222, 228, 233, 245
46 LAC, RG 9, II-F-6, vol. 89, file "32nd Regiment 1913-1914"; *Wiarton Echo*, 18 June 1913, 5.
47 *Quarterly Militia List (Corrected to 1st July 1916)*, 316; LAC, RG 24, vol. 6420, file 207, "Report of the Annual Inspection of the 18th Regiment Franc Tireurs de Saguenay," 29 June 1914.
48 LAC, RG 24, vol. 6298, file 39, vol. 1, "Report of the Annual Inspection 1912 of the 37th Regiment," 11 June 1912.
49 LAC, RG 24, vol. 6420, file 207, "Report of the Annual Inspection 1911 of the 18th Franc Tireurs du Saguenay."
50 *Quarterly Militia List (Corrected to 1st January 1915)*, 241.
51 LAC, RG 24, vol. 6298, file 39, vol. 1, "Report of the Annual Inspection 1908 of the 37th Regiment," June 1908.
52 LAC, RG 9, II-F-6, vol. 89, file "32nd Regiment 1913–1914."
53 LAC, RG 9, II-F-6, vol. 78, file "26th Regiment 1913–1914."
54 Colonel G.W.L. Nicholson, *The Gunners of Canada* (Toronto: McClelland and Stewart, 1967), 179.
55 General Sir John French, *Report* (Ottawa: King's Printer, 1910), 14.
56 R.H. Roy, *Sinews of Steel: The History of the British Columbia Dragoons* (Brampton: Charters Publishing Company, 1965), 17.
57 LAC, RG 24, vol. 363, file 33-43-32, Inspector-General to Militia Headquarters, 16 July 1912.
58 LAC, RG 24, vol. 341, file 33-7-97, Charlottetown Camp Commandant to AAG 6th Division, 11 July 1914.

59 LAC, RG 24, vol. 4267, file 14-1-17, vol.1, GOC 2nd Division to Militia HQ, 10 August 1914.
60 General Order no. 46, 15 March 1913.
61 Peterborough Centennial Museum and Archives, Frank Dobbin, *57th Regiment Peterborough Rangers: A History, written and compiled under direction of Officers of the Regiment* (unpublished ms., c. 1916), 251.
62 Steel and Gill, *The Battery*, 46–47; Lieutenant-Colonel W.S. Watson, ed., *The Brockville Rifles, Royal Canadian Infantry Corps (Allied with the King's Royal Rifle Corps): Semper Paratus, An Unofficial History* (Brockville: The Recorder Printing Company, 1966), 22.
63 LAC, RG 24, vol. 4257, file 19-1-24, "Training -1st Division – 1912" by GSO 1st Division, 30 March 1912.
64 Griesbach, *I Remember*, 352–3.
65 Militia Order no. 56, 7 February 1914.
66 LAC, RG 24, vol. 349, file 33-20-224, "Commandant's Report Petawawa Camp 1912."
67 LAC, RG 24, vol. 339, file 33-6-107, OC 3rd Division to Militia HQ, 28 July 1913.
68 LAC, RG 24, vol. 6420, file 205, "Abridged Annual Report upon 4th Regiment 'Chasseurs Canadiens' at Lévis Camp 2 July 1912"; LAC, RG 24, vol. 4537, file 3-15-6-1, "Report of the Annual Inspection of the No 2 (Montréal) Siege Company CGA at Halifax," 30 August 1913.
69 Captain A.T. Hunter, *History of the 12th Regiment, York Rangers* (Toronto: Murray Printing Company, c. 1912), 71.
70 LAC, RG 24, vol. 343, file 33-11-87, "Date and Detail of Troops Aldershot Camp 1912."
71 LAC, RG 24, vol. 358, file 33-24-79, "Officers and Men of the Active Militia trained in the year 1914 in camp & Local Hqrs in Central Camp at Calgary Alta."; LAC, RG 24, vol. 5872, file 7-54-7, "Report of the Annual Inspection of the 52nd PA Volunteers at Camp Sewell," 30 June 1913.
72 LAC, RG 24, vol. 6427, file 257, vol. 1, "Report of the Annual Inspection of the 48th Highlanders," 10 October 1913.
73 LAC, RG 24, vol. 4257, file 19-1-24, CGS Circular Letter, 4 December 1913.
74 Militia Order no. 56, 7 February 1914.
75 LAC, RG 24, vol. 346, file 33-16-101, "Commandant's Report Lévis Camp 1913," OC 5th Division to Militia HQ, 10 July 1913.
76 Lieutenant-Colonel R.J. Gwynne, *Explanations and Details for Movements in Cavalry Training* (Winnipeg: Colonial Press, 1909); LAC, RG 24, vol. 263, file 2-10-14, OC 16th Light Horse to MD 10, 13 July 1909.

77 LAC, RG 24, vol. 349, file 33-20-224, "Commandant's Report Petawawa Camp 1912."
78 LAC, RG 24, vol. 363, file 33-43-32, Inspector-General to Militia Headquarters, 16 July 1912.
79 LAC, RG 24, vol. 266, file HQ 2-23-5, CGS to DOC MD 10, 19 March 1912.
80 LAC, RG 24, vol. 6409, file 120, vol. I, "Report of the Annual Inspection 1913 of the 63rd Regiment Halifax Rifles," 22 October 1913.
81 *Toronto Globe*, 31 October 1910, 9.
82 *Toronto World*, 29 October 1912, 3; *Hamilton Spectator*, 29 October 1912, 4.
83 LAC, RG 24, vol. 363, file 33-43-45, Gramm Motor Truck Company of Canada to OC 1st Division, 20 February 1914, and OC 1st Division to CGS, 23 February 1914.
84 *Montreal Gazette*, 29 August 1914, 5; Private Betts is commemorated by the Commonwealth War Graves Commission.
85 LAC, Willoughby Garnons Gwatkin Fonds, MG30, E51, file "Correspondence A-K 1914–1916," WM Reid of Depot Harbour to Chief Commissioner of Police, 18 August 1914; GOC 2nd Division to CGS, 21 August 1914.
86 Dominion of Canada, 12th Parliament, 5th session, *Sessional Papers* vol. 50, no. 25, 1914, Sessional Paper No. 35, *Report of the Militia Council for the Dominion of Canada for the Fiscal Year Ending March 31, 1914*, p. 56. Available: http://prod.library.utoronto.ca/maplib/dmgis/ca1_ys_s27.htm; for the cost of individual uniform items, see Colonel A. Fortescue Duguid, *Official History of the Canadian Forces in the Great War 1914–1919: Chronology, Appendices and Maps* (Ottawa: King's Printer, 1938), 70.
87 Jack L. Summers and René Chartrand, *Military Uniforms in Canada* (Ottawa: Canadian War Museum, 1981), 132.
88 Brereton Greenhous, *Semper Paratus: The History of the Royal Hamilton Light Infantry (Wentworth Regiment) 1862–1977* (Hamilton: RHLI Historical Association, 1977), 122.
89 LAC, RG 24, vol. 6404, file 100, "Report of the Annual Inspection of the 86th Regiment (Three Rivers)," 8 September 1913.
90 Lieutenant-Colonel W.T. Barnard, *The Queen's Own Rifles of Canada* (Don Mills: Ont[ario] Pub[lishing] Co., 1960), 92.
91 LAC, RG 24, vol. 6409, file 123, "Abridged Annual Report upon 11th Regiment Argenteuil Rangers," 2 July 1911.

92 LAC, RG 24, vol. 5873, file 7-62-4, DOC MD 10 to Militia Headquarters, 26 May 1913, and file 7-62-5, DOC MD 10 to Militia HQ, 30 December 1913.
93 Kim Beattie, *48th Highlanders of Canada, 1891–1928* (Toronto: 48th Highlanders of Canada, 1932), 16.
94 LAC, RG 24, vol. 6420, file 205, "Abridged Annual Report Upon 4th Regiment," 29 June 1914; LAC, RG 24, vol. 341, file 33-7-97, Charlottetown Camp Commandant to AAG 6th Division, 11 July 1914.
95 LAC, RG 24, vol. 4267, file 14-1-17, vol. 1, OC 2nd Field Company to AAG Camp Niagara, 26 June 1914.
96 LAC, RG 24, vol. 4267, file 14-1-17, vol. 1, GOC 2nd Division to Militia Headquarters, 10 August 1914.
97 LAC, RG 24, vol. 6409, file 120, vol. 1, "Report of the Annual Inspection 1914 of the 63rd Regiment Halifax Rifles," 1 March 1915; LAC, RG 24, vol. 1396, file 593-6-2, vol. 5, OC Heavy Battery Depot to HQ 4th Division, 21 July 1915.
98 Canada, Department of Militia and Defence, *Canadian Militia War Establishments (Provisional), 1914* (n.p., c. 1914).
99 Carman Miller, *A Knight in Politics: A Biography of Sir Frederick Borden* (Montreal & Kingston: McGill-Queen's University Press, 2010), 205.
100 LAC, RG 24, vol. 342, file 33-8-116, Commandant Sussex camp to OC 6th Division, 21 July 1913.
101 LAC, RG 24, vol. 6427, file 261, vol. 1, "Abridged Annual Report upon No 3 Battery & Ammunition Column of PEI Heavy Brigade," 12 June 1913.
102 John S. Moir, ed., *History of the Royal Canadian Corps of Signals 1903–1961* (Ottawa: Corps Committee Royal Canadian Corps of Signals, 1962), 7.
103 *Toronto Star*, 4 November 1910, 13.
104 William F. Rannie, ed., *To the Thunderer His Arms: The Royal Canadian Ordnance Corps* (Lincoln, ON: W.F. Rannie Publisher, 1984), 35.
105 LAC, RG 24, vol. 5873, file 7-62-5, QMG to CGS, 8 November 1913.
106 LAC, RG 24, vol. 5873, file 7-62-5, CGS to QMG, 17 November 1913.
107 Upper Canada Historical Arms Society, *The Military Arms of Canada* (West Hill, ON: Museum Restoration Service, 1963), 29, 40–1.
108 Duguid, *Official History: Chronology, Appendices and Maps*, 78; Major E.G.B. Reynolds, *The Lee–Enfield Rifle* (New York: Arco Publishing Company, 1962), 188.
109 LAC, RG 24, vol. 4267, file 14-1-22, vol. 1, GOC 2nd Division to Militia Headquarters, 11 March 1913.

110 *Military Arms of Canada*, 41.
111 LAC, RG 24, vol. 5873, file 7-61-3, "Deficiencies in Arms and Equipment 59th Regt old issue," 4 January 1904; LAC, RG 24, vol. 5872, file 7-57-6, vol. 1, "Equipment Inspection Report – 55th Megantic LI, October 1905 and November 1906."
112 LAC, RG 24, vol. 6408, file 118, vol. 1, "Report of the Annual Inspection of the 56th Regiment," 25 June 1914; LAC, RG 24, vol. 6409, file 120, vol. 1, "Report of the Annual Inspection 1913 of the 63rd Regiment Halifax Rifles," 22 October 1913.
113 LAC, RG 24, vol. 6404, file 101, "Report of the Annual Inspection 1914 of the 65th Regiment CMR," 11 June 1914; LAC, RG 24, vol. 6427, file 257, vol. 1, "Abridged Annual Report upon 48th Regiment," 13 November 1914; LAC, RG 24, vol. 6427, file 258, vol. 1, "Abridged Annual Report upon 91st Regiment Canadian Highlanders," 28 October 1914.
114 LAC, RG 24, vol. 4267, file 14-1-22, CGS Circular Letter, 29 April 1914; LAC, RG 24, vol. 365, file 33-96-84, "Commandant's Report Sewell Camp 1914," vol. 1, LAC, RG 24.

CHAPTER TWO

1 Niall Ferguson, *The Pity of War: Explaining World War I* (New York: Basic Books, 1999), 267.
2 John Herd Thompson, *The Harvests of War: The Prairie West, 1914–1918* (Toronto: McClelland and Stewart, 1981), 48–9.
3 *Toronto Globe*, 26 August 1914, 4; *Toronto Star*, 25 August 1914, 3; F. Douglas Reville, *History of the County of Brant*, vol. 2 (Brantford, ON: Hurley Printing Company, 1920), 480.
4 Desmond Morton, *Canada and War: A Military and Political History* (Toronto: Butterworths, 1981), 57.
5 LAC, RG 24, vol. 1221, file 593-1-5, vol. 5, OC 1st Division to Militia HQ, 6 October 1914.
6 LAC, RG 24, vol. 1221, file 593-1-5, vol. 5, AG to OC, 1st Division, 8 October 1914.
7 LAC, RG 24, vol. 4320, file 34-318, OC 13th Brigade CFA to AAG 2nd Division, 12 November 1915.
8 LAC, RG 24, vol. 4593, file 20-10, vol. 10, MD 10 to 79th, 90th, 100th, 106th Regiments, 22 December 1914.
9 LAC, RG 24, vol. 4536, file 3-1-143, AG to OC 6th Division, 18 August 1914, Militia HQ to 6th Division, 27 August 1914; QMG to OC 6th Division, 30 August 1914.

10 DHH, 74/672, box 8, file 74/672-11-39, War Office to HQ 1st Canadian Division, 19 January 1915.
11 LAC, RG 24, vol. 4320, file 34-3-18, HQ MD 2 to Militia HQ, 6 April 1915, Militia HQ to HQ MD 2, 13 April 1915.
12 *Vancouver Sun*, 7 April 1915, 1, 2, and 9 April 1915, 2; Canada, Dominion Bureau of Statistics, *Canada Year Book 1914* (Ottawa: King's Printer, 1915), 86.
13 LAC, RG 24, vol. 4718, file 448-14-169, OC 63rd Battalion to DOC MD 13, 29 July 1915.
14 LAC, RG 24, vol. 1396, file 593-6-2, vol. 4, AG to DOC MD 13, 13 July 1915.
15 LAC, RG 24, vol. 1847, file GAQ 11-71C, "Summary 17 May 1939"; Dominion of Canada, 12th Parliament, 7th session, *Sessional Papers* vol. 52, no. 20, 1917, *Report of the Department of Labour for the Fiscal Year Ending March 31, 1916*, Sessional Paper no. 36, pp. 8–9. Available: http://prod.library.utoronto.ca/maplib/dmgis/ca1_ys_s27.htm
16 LAC, RG 9, III A1, vol. 92, file 10-12-33, Canadian High Commission to OMFC, 12 September 1917.
17 LAC, RG 9, III B1, vol. 965, file M-17-3, Canadian Corps circular letter, 16 December 1915.
18 LAC, RG 24, vol. 1847, file GAQ 11-71C, "Summary 17 May 1939."
19 DHH, 74/672, box 4, folder 15, file "Canadian Railwaymen"; *Toronto Star*, 29 September 1915, 13; 30 September 1915, 17; and 2 October 1915, 15; *Toronto Globe*, 29 September 1915, 13.
20 DHH, 74/672, box 4, folder 15, file "Canadian Railwaymen," Colonial Secretary to Governor-General, 28 September 1915.
21 LAC, RG 24, vol. 2352, file HQ C-1585-19, Chief Press Censor to *Halifax Morning Chronicle*, 3 March 1916; LAC, RG 25 B-1-b, vol. 152, file C10-20, HMS *Albemarle* to Admiralty, 4 February 1916. The ship was based in Murmansk, and the captain investigated complaints by Canadian workers.
22 *Labour Gazette*, January 1917, p. 34
23 Canada, Dominion Bureau of Statistics, *Canada Year Book, 1916–17* (Ottawa: King's Printer, 1917), 493.
24 Reville, *History of the County of Brant*, 2:480.
25 *Toronto Globe*, 16 August 1916, 7.
26 *An Act respecting the Importation and Employment of Aliens [Alien Labour Act]*, R.S.C., 1906, c. 97, s. 2; Desmond Morton, *The Canadian General: Sir William Otter* (Toronto: Hakkert, 1974), 341.
27 *Toronto Globe*, 30 January 1918, 1; *Grain Growers' Guide*, 20 March 1918, 592.

28 Adam Crerar, "Ontario and the Great War," in *Canada and the First World War: Essays in Honour of Robert Craig Brown*, ed. David MacKenzie (Toronto: University of Toronto Press, 2005), 234, 237.
29 LAC, RG 24, vol. 4740, file 448-14-262, vol. 2, GOC MD 13 to Militia HQ, 18 January 1917.
30 LAC, RG 24, vol. 4376, file 34-7-61-1, OC 129th Battalion to AAG 2nd Division, 15 December 1915.
31 LAC, RG 24, vol. 4593, file 20-10, vol. 10, HQ MD 10 Circular Letter, 21 August 1915, quoting Militia HQ Circular Letter, 19 August 1915.
32 LAC, RG 24, vol. 4427, file 26-5-64-3, vol. 1, AG Circular Letter, 16 November 1915.
33 LAC, RG 24, vol. 4376, file 34-7-61-1, 2nd Division to Chief Recruiting Officers Toronto, Hamilton, St Catharines, 29 November 1915.
34 LAC, RG 24, vol. 4376, file 34-7-61-1, Waterous Engine Works to 2nd Division 25 January 1916.
35 *Toronto Star*, 14 June 1916, 2.
36 LAC, RG 24, vol. 4427, file 26-5-64-3, vol. 1, AG Circular Letter, 16 May 1916; LAC, RG 24, vol. 4552, file 125-1-14, Chief Recruiting Officer MD 6 Circular Letters, 15 December 1915 and 5 October 1916; LAC, RG 24, vol. 6600, file 1982-1-24, OC 107th Regiment to HQ MD 11, 20 December 1916; LAC, RG 24, vol. 4509, file 17-1-49, vol. IX, AG Circular Letter, 7 February 1917.
37 LAC, RG 24, vol. 1437, file 593-6-31, vol. 1, GOC MD 11 to Militia HQ, 11 January 1918.
38 LAC, RG 24, vol. 4376, file 34-7-61-1, 2nd Division to OC 129th Battalion, 26 April 1916.
39 LAC, RG 24, vol. 4427, file 26-5-64-3, vol. 1, AD of S & T 3rd Division to AAG 3rd Division, 1 April 1916.
40 LAC, RG 24, vol. 4427, file 26-5-64-3, vol. 1, 156th Battalion to HQ MD 3, 22 March 1916.
41 LAC, RG 24, vol. 4376, file 34-7-61-1, vol. 2, AAG MD 2 to 129th Battalion, 10 May 1916.
42 Quoted in Colonel G.W.L. Nicholson, *Official History of the Canadian Army in the First World War: Canadian Expeditionary Force 1914–1919* (Ottawa: Queen's Printer, 1962), 344.
43 The MSA was reprinted in Canada, Department of Justice, *The Military Service Act 1917: Manual for the Information and Guidance of Tribunals in the Consideration and Review of Claims for Exemption* (Ottawa: King's Printer, 1918), 22.
44 Ibid., 11.

45 Canada, Dominion Bureau of Statistics, *Canada Year Book 1918* (Ottawa: King's Printer, 1919), 662.
46 *Toronto Globe*, 17 January 1918, 1.
47 Ibid., 5; *Toronto Star*, 9 January 1918, 2, and 11 January 1918, 20
48 *Labour Gazette*, February 1918, 54; *Toronto Globe*, 16 January 1918, 2; 4 February 1918, 1; and 5 February 1918, 6.
49 Grieves, *The Politics of Manpower, 1914–1918*, 149, 154, 155.
50 J. Castell Hopkins, *The Canadian Annual Review of Public Affairs: 1918* (Toronto: The Annual Review Publishing Company, 1919), 490.
51 Dominion of Canada, 13th Parliament, 4th session, *Sessional Papers* vol. 56, no. 10, 1920, *Report of the Department of Labour for the Fiscal Year Ending March 31, 1919*, Sessional Paper no. 37, pp. 21–2. Available: http://prod.library.utoronto.ca/maplib/dmgis/ca1_ys_s27.htm
52 *The Canadian Annual Review of Public Affairs: 1918*, 491; Canada, Department of Labour, *The Labour Gazette: Volume XVIII for the Year 1918*, 379.
53 Peter Simkins, *Kitchener's Army: The Raising of the New Armies, 1914–1916* (Manchester, UK: Manchester University Press, 1988), 257.
54 *Toronto Globe*, 20 October 1914, p. 2
55 Roger Sarty, "Canada and Submarine Warfare," in *The Maritime Defence of Canada*, ed. Roger Sarty (Toronto: The Canadian Institute of Strategic Affairs, 1996), 186–7.
56 Michael Bliss, *A Canadian Millionaire: The Life and Business Times of Sir Joseph Flavelle, Bart., 1858–1939* (Toronto: Macmillan Company of Canada, 1978), 257–8; Hopkins notes a speech by N.W. Rowell, President of the Privy Council at Bowmanville, Ontario, on 17 December 1918 in which he gave statistics of the IMB effort (*Canadian Annual Review of Public Affairs: 1918*, 408); Michael Bliss, "War Business as Usual: Canadian Munitions Production 1914–1918," in *Mobilization for Total War, The Canadian, American and British Experience 1914–1918, 1939–1945*, ed. N.F. Dreisziger (Waterloo, ON: Wilfrid Laurier Press, 1981), 53.
57 LAC, RG 9, III D3, vol. 5059, file 969 (reel T-11121), War Diary AG Militia HQ, 30 August 1918, and memorandum DAAG(4) to AAG, 21 October 1918.
58 Bliss, "War Business as Usual," 47.
59 TNA, WO73/97, Number of Army Reservists Who Have Permission to Reside Abroad" [July 1914], "General Monthly Return of the Regimental Strength of the British Army (including the Territorial Force): Part V; TNA, CO 42/987, Deputy Minister Department of Militia and Defence to Under Secretary of State for External Affairs, 6 January 1915; LAC, RG 9, III

AI, vol. 28, file 8-1-15, unknown correspondent to AA & QMG HQ Canadian Contingent, 7 December 1914, reported about 150 British reservists serving with the 1st Division; TNA, WO 293/2, War Office Instruction no. 13, 2 March 1915.

60 LAC, RG 9, II A2, vol. 33, *Minutes of the Militia Council*, 22 November 1916, 377.

61 LAC, RG 9, III B1, vol. 416, file E-6-1, OC A Company to OC 5th Battalion, 1 December 1914; British Ambassador to Foreign Office, 13 January 1915.

62 DHH, 74/672, box 4, folder 14, file "Recruiting," Russian Consul General to Under Secretary of State, 7 November 1914, AG Circular Letter 21 November 1914; LAC, RG 24, vol. 4331, file 43-2-18, AG Circular Letter, 2 July 1915.

63 Dominion of Canada, 13th Parliament, 4th session, *Sessional Papers* vol. 56, no. 5, 1920, *Report of the Work of the Department of Soldiers' Civil Re-establishment*, Sessional Paper no. 14, p. 75. Available: http://prod.library.utoronto.ca/maplib/dmgis/ca1_ys_s27.htm

64 DHH, 74/672, box 5, folder 20, file "Statistics," Canadians to British Service.

65 Veterans Affairs Canada, Canadian Virtual War Memorial, available: www.veterans.gc.ca/eng/remembrance/memorials/canadian-virtual-war-memorial (accessed 21–25 April 2016).

66 LAC, RG 150, acc 1992-93/166, box 4675, personnel file 490918 Alfred William Hyder; *University of Toronto Roll of Service 1914–1918* (Toronto: University of Toronto Press, 1921), xli–xlIII.

67 S.F. Wise, *Canadian Airmen in the First World War: The Official History of the Royal Canadian Air Force*, vol. 1 (Toronto: University of Toronto Press, 1981), 633–4; *In Memoriam: The Memorial Chamber, Canadian Houses of Parliament, Ottawa, Canada* (Ottawa: Photogelatine Engraving Co., Ltd., c. 1920) has illustrations of panels giving numbers.

68 Wise, *Canadian Airmen in the First World War*, 30–1, 33–4, 643.

69 Ibid., 80; P. Whitney Lackenbauer, "Pay No Attention to Sero: The Mohawks of the Bay of Quinte and Imperial Flying Training during the Great War," *Ontario History* 96, no. 2 (Autumn 2004): 146.

70 Lieutenant-Colonel L.J. Hall, *The Inland Water Transport in Mesopotamia* (London: Constable and Company, 1921), 39–40; TNA, WO 158/851, "France: History of Inland Water Transport 1914–1919."

71 Captain W.W. Murray, "Canadians in Dunsterforce," *Canadian Defence Quarterly* 8, no. 2 (January 1931): 214–15.

72 LAC, RG 24, vol. 4603, file 20-10-68, AG Circular Letter, 21 November 1916.

73 DHH, 74/672, box 5, folder 20, Summary of Canadians in British service.
74 LAC, RG 24, vol. 4603, file 20-10-68, Major W.H. Owen RE to CGS, 18 May 1917.
75 LAC, RG 24, vol. 1840, file GAC 10-20, R.W. Gornall to Historical Section, 17 March 1931.
76 LAC, RG 9, III A1, vol. 27, file 7-7-14A, A/DD S & T to D S & T, 13 October 1916; DHH, 74/672, box 5, folder 20, Canadians in British service; LAC, RG 24, vol. 4380, file 38-72-80, QMG Circular Letter, 6 November 1915.
77 LAC, RG 24, vol. 4380, file 34-7-87, vol. 1, QMG to 2nd Division, 21 November 1915.
78 LAC, RG 9, III B1, vol. 708, file 1-3-2, Canadian Records Office to HQ Canadians Shorncliffe, 17 February 1916.
79 LAC, RG 9, III A1, vol. 27, file 7-7-14, Carson to Hughes, 12 May 1916.
80 LAC, RG 9, III B1, vol. 708, file 1-8-36 vol. 1, HQ Overseas Canadians to War Office, 2 March 1916.
81 DHH, 74/672, box 4, folder 14, file "Reservists British and Allied."
82 LAC, RG 24, vol. 4517, file C/156, CGS to GOC MD 5, 16 February 1917 and 22 February 1917.
83 LAC, RG 24, vol. 425, file 54-21-1-48, vol. 1, CGS to GOC MD 6, 22 February 1917.
84 LAC, RG 24, vol. 425, file 54-21-1-48, vol. 3, Commandant Serbian Mobilization Camp to CGS, 18 January 1919.
85 Philip J. Haythornthwaite, *The World War One Source Book* (London: Arms and Armour Press, 1994), 167–8.
86 Joseph T. Hapak, "Recruiting a Polish Army in the United States, 1917–1919" (PhD diss., University of Kansas, 1972), 15–16, 22, 30–2.
87 The Polish Genealogical Society of America lists 384 recruits who were Canadian residents (see www.pgsa.org/haller.php).
88 Salaries noted in DHH, *Minutes of the Militia Council*, 18 April 1918, 321, suggest that 225 to 250 CEF soldiers were involved; Hapak claims there were 236 staff members ("Recruiting a Polish Army in the United States, 1917–1919", 108).
89 Hapak, "Recruiting a Polish Army in the United States, 1917–1919," 138; LAC, RG 24, vol. 4606, file 20-10-91, Militia HQ to GOC MD 10, 13 October 1917.
90 LAC, RG 24, vol. 4606, file 20-10-91, Polish Recruiting Centre to MD 10, 14 March 1918.
91 LAC, RG 24, vol. 6553, file HQ-808-1, Polish Recruiting Centre Montreal to GOC MD 3, 17 April 1918, GOC MD 3 to Militia HQ, 24 April 1918, and reply, 1 May 1918.

92 John English, *Borden: His Life and World* (Toronto: McGraw-Hill Ryerson Limited, 1977), 110, 112.
93 Nicholson, *Canadian Expeditionary Force 1914–1919*, 114, 133.
94 LAC, RG 9, III A1, vol. 44, file 8-5-8D, War Office to Colonial Office, 29 January 1916; Nicholson, *Canadian Expeditionary Force 1914–1919*, 138.
95 LAC, RG 9, III A1, vol. 45, 8-5-10H, Brigadier-General F.S. Meighen to Major-General J.W. Carson, 5 October 1916.
96 Desmond Morton, *A Peculiar Kind of Politics* (Toronto: University of Toronto Press, 1982), 91, 101.
97 LAC, RG 9, III A1, vol. 104, file "Fifth Division Reinforcements," Deputy Minister to War Office, 2 March 1917, Perley to War Office, 30 May 1917.
98 LAC, RG 9, III A1, vol. 104, file "Fifth Division Reinforcements," Borden to Perley, 7 November 1917, and reply, 8 November 1917; Morton *A Peculiar Kind of Politics*, 153.
99 TNA, WO 114/33, Weekly Returns, 27 August 1917, 24 September 1917, 29 October 1917, 26 November 1917, 31 December 1917; TNA, WO 114/34, Weekly Returns, 28 January 1918, 25 February 1918.
100 Beattie, *48th Highlanders of Canada: 1891–1928*, 417; TNA, WO 114/32, Weekly Returns April–July 1917.
101 TNA, WO 114/31, Weekly Returns, 26 February 1917, 26 March 1917; TNA, WO 114/32, Weekly Returns, 30 April 1917, 28 May 1917, 25 June 1917, 30 July 1917; TNA, WO 114/33, Weekly Returns, 27 August 1917, 24 September 1917, 29 October 1917, 26 November 1917, 31 December 1917; TNA, WO 114/34, Weekly Returns, 28 January 1918 and 25 February 1918.
102 LAC, RG 9, III B1, vol. 687, file E-266-2, vol. 2, 119th Battalion to HQ 15th Canadian Infantry Brigade, 28 May 1917.
103 LAC, RG 9, III A1, vol. 90, file 10-12-8, AG OMFC to Secretary OMFC, 23 February 1917; TNA, WO 114/31, Weekly Returns, 26 February 1917, 26 March 1917; TNA, WO 114/34, Weekly Returns, 25 February 1918.
104 DHH, 74/672, box 1, file "Composite Battalion Military District # 6 – Active Militia," "Short History of Work Performed by the 23rd Infantry Brigade, MD 11"; LAC, RG 24, vol. 2553, file HQCS-2103-Chinese Coolies, Inspector General Western Canada to AG 17 September 1917, Camp Commandant Petawawa to Militia HQ, 23 September 1917.
105 LAC, RG 9, III A1, vol. 54, file OMFC Progress Report, March 1918.
106 LAC, RG 9, III A1, vol. 82, file 10-9-73, CGS OMFC to Deputy Minister OMFC, 21 September 1918.

107 LAC, RG 9, III D3, vol. 4821, War Diary Canadian Corps AQ, May 1918, Appendix K.
108 Shane B. Schreiber, *Shock Army of the British Empire: The Canadian Corps in the Last 100 Days of the Great War* (Westport: Praeger, 1997), 21.
109 TNA, WO 95/26, AG GHQ War Diary, "Monthly Statement of Casualties, Reinforcements and Strengths by Divisions. Infantry and Cavalry Only: July 1918." The Australians had only 771 per battalion.
110 LAC, RG 9, III D3, Appendix 15A, "Report on Operation August 26th to 29th 1918," vol. 4986, War Diary 3rd Canadian Machine Gun Battalion, August 1918; Nicholson, *The Gunners of Canada*, 349.
111 LAC, Albert Edward Kemp fonds, MG 27 II D9, Currie to Kemp, 7 February 1918, vol. 142, file 4.
112 LAC, RG 9, III D3, VOL. 4821, reel T-7181, War Diary AA & QMG Canadian Corps, August 1918, Appendix H.
113 LAC, Albert Edward Kemp fonds, MG 27, II D9, vol. 177, file "OMFC Decisions 1-300," Meeting held 6 August 1918.
114 C.E.W. Bean, *Official History of Australia in the Great War of 1914–1918*, vol. 3, *The AIF in France 1916* (Sydney, Australia: Angus and Robertson, 1920), 55.
115 John Swettenham, *Allied Intervention in Russia 1918–1919 and the Part Played by Canada* (London: Allen & Unwin, 1967), 52; Roy MacLaren, *Canadians in Russia, 1918–1919* (Toronto: Macmillan of Canada, 1976), 9–10; AAG to 4th Garrison Battalion 24 October 1918, Acquittence Roll 19 November 1918, LAC, RG 24, vol. 4472, file 20-1-79; Lieutenant T.C. Winegard, "Dunsterforce: A Case Study of Coalition Warfare in the Middle East, 1918–1919" *Canadian Army Journal* vol. 8, no. 3 (Fall 2005); LAC, RG 24, vol. 1847, file GAC 11-58.
116 LAC, RG 9, III A1, vol. 90, file 10-12-17, Major-General Callwell at Canada House to OMFC, 17 January 1917 and 14 February 1917, CGS OMFC to Callwell, 12 February 1917.
117 J.L. Granatstein, *The Greatest Victory: Canada's One Hundred Days, 1918* (Don Mills, ON: Oxford University Press, 2014), 144.

CHAPTER THREE

1 General Orders, 13 August 1915; LAC, RG 24, vol. 4509, file 17-1-49, AG Circular Letter, 18 January 1917.
2 LAC, RG 24, vol. 4642, file 99-4-62, AG Circular Letter, 16 June 1916.
3 LAC, RG 24, vol. 4509, file 17-1-49, vol. IX, AG Circular Letter, 22 January 1917.

4 TNA, WO 293/4, ACI 1186 of 13 June 1916; TNA, WO 293/3, War Office Instruction no. 46, 6 September 1915.
5 LAC, RG 24, vol. 6600, file 1982-1-78, Perley to Borden, 21 December 1916; LAC, RG 9, III B2, vol. 3483, file 10-14-1, vol. 2, Surgeon-General to OMFC, 29 January 1917; LAC, RG 24, vol. 6600, file 1982-1-78, AG to Militia Council, 8 February 1917.
6 CEF, Routine Orders, no. 83, 22 January 1918, and no. 330, 19 March 1918.
7 TNA, WO 114/35, Weekly Returns, 26 August 1918.
8 LAC, RG 9, III A1, vol. 90, file 10-12-8, Adjutant General's Branch, AG Canadians to Secretary OMFC, 23 February 1917; LAC, RG 9, III A1, vol. 53, file "Monthly Reports: July 1917," Adjutant General.
9 Militia Order no. 146, 22 May 1917.
10 TNA, WO 123/200, BEF GRO 1754 of 24 August 1916 and GRO 1963 of 25 November 1916.
11 LAC, RG 9, III D3, vol. 5047, file 911, reel T-10939, War Diary Canadian Section GHQ 3rd Echelon, 13 August 1918.
12 LAC, RG 9, III D3, vol. 5046, file 910, reel T-10938, War Diary Canadian Section GHQ 3rd Echelon, 1 January 1918.
13 RG 9, III B1, vol. 420, file E-102-1, OMFC to HQ Brighton, 4 December 1916.
14 John Starling and Ivor Lee, *No Labour, No Battle: Military Labour During the First World War* (Stroud, Glos.: The History Press, 2009), 252.
15 LAC, RG 9, III B1, vol. 1004, file R-7-3, OC 21st Battalion to HQ 4th Canadian Infantry Brigade, 26 January 1917, Canadian Section GHQ 3rd Echelon to HQ Canadian Corps, 18 August 1917.
16 LAC, RG 24, vol. 4536, file 3-1-143, AG Circular Letter, 17 August 1914.
17 Desmond Morton, *When Your Number's Up: The Canadian Soldier in the First World War* (Toronto: Random House of Canada, 1993), 56.
18 RG 24, vol. 1396, file 593-6-2, vol. 4, AG to Private Secretary, 23 June 1915.
19 LAC, RG 24, vol. 1396, file 593-6-2, vol. 4, Major Milton to Sam Hughes, 15 June 1915, Sam Hughes to AG, 22 June 1915; LAC, RG 24, vol. 4593, file 20-10, vol. 10, AG Circular Letter, 21 Jul 1915.
20 LAC, RG 24, vol. 4509, file 17-1-49, vol. VIII, AG to GOC MD 5, 22 December 1916.
21 LAC, RG 24, vol. 4510, file 17-1-49, vol. XV, AG Circular Letter, 3 September 1917.
22 TNA, WO 162/6, "Headquarters: Directorate of Organization 1914–1918," p. 89.

23 Lieutenant-Colonel H.M. Davison, *History of the 35th Division in the Great War* (London: Sifton, Praed & Co., 1920), 3.

24 LAC, RG 9, III D 1, vol. 4701, folder 73, file 9, 143rd Battalion Historical Records; LAC, RG 24, vol. 1403, file 593-6-2, AAG(1) to GOC MD 4, 7 November 1916; LAC, RG 24, vol. 1398, file 593-6-2, vol. 11, AG to OC 2nd Division, 17 February 1916.

25 LAC, RG 24, vol. 365, file 33-95-7, MD 11 to Militia HQ, 21 December 1916.

26 LAC, RG 9, III C 1, vol. 4470 folder 6, file 6, ADRTO CRT to GOC CRT GHQ, 12 March 1917.

27 LAC, RG 9, III B 1, vol. 687, file E-266-2, "Battalions Recently Arrived From Canada in 1st Can Reserve Brigade at May 17th 1917."

28 DHH, 74/672, box 13, files 143rd Battalion and 216th Battalion.

29 Lieutenant-Colonel H.M. Davison, *History of the 35th Division*, 9; Major E.G.B. Reynolds, *The Lee–Enfield Rifle* (New York: Arco Publishing Company, 1962), 120.

30 TNA, WO 95/2472, War Diary ADMS 35th (Bantam), Division 9, December 1916; Davison, *History of the 35th Division*, 82.

31 LAC, RG 24, vol. 1144, file 54-21-51-9, vol. 1, MD 2 24/Gen No 3600 (AMD 2), 1 March 1915.

32 LAC, RG 24, vol. 4507, file 17-1-149, vol. 1, AG Circular Letter, 19 May 1915; LAC, RG 24, vol. 4507, file 17-1-149, vol. 11, AG to 5th Division 13 August 1915.

33 LAC, RG 24, vol. 1144, file 54-21-51-9, vol. 1, MD 2 24/Gen No 4113 (ADMS 2), 6 August 1915.

34 Militia Order 287 of 31 July 1916; Canada, Department of Militia and Defence, *Physical Standards and Instructions for the Medical Examination of Recruits for the Canadian Expeditionary Force and for the Active Militia of Canada* (Ottawa: King's Printer, 1917), 6.

35 LAC, RG 9, III B 1, vol. 789, file R-42-2, with reports on various units.

36 Canada, Department of Militia and Defence, *Regulations for the Canadian Medical Service 1914* (Ottawa: Government Printing Bureau, 1915), 46.

37 LAC, RG 24, vol. 4508, file 17-1-49, vol. III, AG to 5th Division, 25 November 1915.

38 LAC, RG 24, vol. 4508, file 17-1-49, vol. VI, AG Circular Letter, 24 August 1916; LAC, RG 24, vol. 4509, file 17-1-49, vol. XI, AG Circular Letter, 22 January 1917.

39 Major-General Sir W.G. Macpherson, *History of the Great War based on official documents: Medical Services General History*, vol. 1 (London: HMSO, 1921), 136.

40 DHH, *Minutes of the Militia Council 1916*, p. 82, 16 May 1916.
41 LAC, RG 4642, file 99-4-62, AG to MD 11, 16 June 1916; LAC, RG 24, vol. 1402, file 593-6-2, vol. 22, DG Mobilization to AAG(1), 2 January 1917.
42 LAC, RG 24, vol. 1437, file 593-6-31, vol. 1, OC Forestry Depot to OA RCE Militia HQ, 29 January 1918.
43 LAC, RG 9, III C1, vol. 4470, folder 7, file 8, SMO CRT Depot to Officer i/c RTS Canadians, 1 December 1917, SMO to OC CRT Depot, 8 October 1917.
44 Colonel Herbert A. Bruce, *Report on the Canadian Army Medical Service*. (London: n.p., 1916).
45 LAC, RG 24, vol. 1813, file GAC 4-12, "Gen Currie's Speeches," typed ms. of a Montreal Gazette article of 12 September 1924.
46 LAC, RG 24, vol. 1842, file GAC 10-16, DHS to C of S, 13 January 1925.
47 LAC, Albert Edward Kemp fonds, MG 27, II D9, vol. 74, file Marlow Report 1917, 20 October 1916, 4.
48 Lieutenant-Colonel J.A. Grant, "The Medical Profession and the Militia," *Canadian Medical Association Journal* 4, no. 9 (September 1914): 763.
49 Militia Order no. 87, 28 February 1916; LAC, RG 24, vol. 1144, file 54-21-51-9, vol. 1, GOC MD 5 to Militia HQ, 9 January 1917.
50 LAC, RG 24, vol. 4509, file 17-1-49, OIC Recruiting Bonaventure and Gaspé to OIC Recruiting MD 5, 24 December 1916.
51 LAC, RG 24, vol. 4380, file 34-7-91, vol. 1, 119th Battalion to AAG MD 2, 3 May 1916; LAC, RG 24, vol. 1401, file 593-6-2, vol. 18, ADMS to GOC MD 3, 21 August 1916.
52 Morton, *When Your Number's Up*, 60.
53 Jay Cassel, *The Secret Plague: Venereal Disease in Canada 1838–1939* (Toronto: University of Toronto Press, 1987), 19.
54 DHH, 74/672, box 1, folder 3, "Statistics."
55 LAC, RG 24, vol. 4642, file 99-4-55, OC 4th Company 4th Divisional Train to AAG MD 11, 3 May 1916.
56 LAC, RG 24, vol. 1836, file GAC 9-25, AG OMFC to Militia HQ, 16 January 1917; LAC, RG 9, III B1, vol. 552, file U-4-1, ADMS 3rd Canadian Division to DDMS Canadian Corps, 24 June 1916; LAC, RG 9, III C1, vol. 3483, file 10-14-1, vol. 2, OIC Moore Barracks Hospital to ADMS HQ Canadians, 8 January 1917.
57 DHH, 74/672, box 1, folder 3, "Statistics."
58 *Fifth Census of Canada, 1911*, vol. 11 (Ottawa: King's Printer, 1913), 640, table XLVI, "Number of infirm per 10,000 in each class of the population."

59 Major Albert G. Love and Major Charles B. Davenport, *Defects Found in Drafted Men: Statistical Information compiled from the Draft Records* (Washington: Government Printing Office, 1920), 124.
60 Department of Militia and Defence, *Physical Standards and Instructions*, 3.
61 LAC, RG 24, vol. 4615, file 1G 206, subfile 206-10, AG Circular Letter, 6 March 1918.
62 LAC, RG 24, vol. 4343, file 34-3-105-1, vol. 1, DGMS Circular Letter, 27 October 1917.
63 Militia Order no. 372, 17 August 1914.
64 LAC, RG 24, vol. 1311, file 593-3-7, vol. 3, General Orders, 13 August 1915.
65 Canada, Census and Statistics Office, *Special Report on the Foreign-Born Population* (Ottawa: Government Printing Bureau, 1915), 16–17.
66 LAC, RG 24, vol. 4336, file 34-3-24, CGS to GOC 2nd Division, 8 December 1914.
67 *Army Act*, s. 95(1).
68 LAC, RG 24, vol. 4336, file 34-3-24, AG to OC 2nd Division, 24 February 1915.
69 LAC, RG 24, vol. 4593, file 20-10 vol. 10, AG to DOC MD 10, 21 November 1914, DSA MD 10 to 105th Regiment, 16 February 1915.
70 LAC, RG 24, vol. 4331, file 34-2-18, 2nd Division to 38th Regiment, 11 January 1915, 2nd Division to 19th Regiment, 14 January 1915; LAC, RG 24, vol. 4336, file 34-3-24, AAG 2nd Division to 51st Soo Rifles, 17 March 1915.
71 Desmond Morton, "The Short, Unhappy Life of the 41st Battalion, CEF," *Queen's Quarterly* 81, no. 1 (Spring 1974): 75.
72 LAC, RG 24, vol. 4336, file 34-3-24, AG to OC 2nd Division, 6 November 1915; LAC, RG 24, vol. 4375, file 34-7-61, vol. 1, 2nd Division to 198th Battalion, 2 March 1916.
73 LAC, RG 9, III B1, vol. 1188, file A-42-5, vol. 1, PC 1177 of 26 April 1917.
74 LAC, RG 24, vol. 6566, file 1064-30-34, PC 111 of 17 January 1918.
75 DHH, 74/672, box 4, folder 14, file "Recruiting"; LAC, RG 24, vol. 425, file 54-21-1-48, vol. 1, AG circular letter, 4 January 1916, Colonial Secretary to Governor General 3 January 1916 and 24 January 1916.
76 LAC, RG 9, III D3, vol. 4996, reel T-10835, file 660, Part 1, War Diary 5th Field Company, 14 January 1915.
77 LAC, Likacheff–Ragosine–Mathers collection MG 30, E406, vol. 11, reel 7601, file 339, Russian Embassy in Washington to Russian Consul in Montreal, 17 October 1914; Russian Consul to External Affairs, 25 October 1914 and 10 November 1914, file 340.

78 LAC, = 9, III B1, vol. 416, file E-6-1, DMO War Office to GOC Canadian Division, 11 December 1914, repeating a request from the Russian Attaché.
79 LAC, Likacheff–Ragosine–Mathers collection, MG 30, E406, vol. 11, reel 7601, file 341, Consul to Humboldt Recruiting Officer, 4 March 1915.
80 LAC, Likacheff–Ragosine–Mathers collection, MG 30, E406, vol. 11, reel 7601, file 400, Consul to Sergeant-Major Haynes, 16 June 1915.
81 LAC, Likacheff–Ragosine–Mathers collection, vol. 11 reel 7601, file 344, Consul to External Affairs, 23 July 1915.
82 LAC, Likacheff–Ragosine–Mathers collection, MG 30 E406, vol. 11, reel 7601, file 344, Consul to CGS, [1] November 1915.
83 LAC, RG 38, vol. 443, file "Country of Birth."
84 LAC, Likacheff–Ragosine–Mathers collection, MG 30, E406, vol. 11 reel 7601, file 344, CGS to Consul, 5 March 1916 and Consul to CGS, 17 March 1916.
85 LAC, RG 24, vol. 4320, file 34-3-24, 213th Battalion to HQ MD 2, 23 November 1916.
86 LAC, Likacheff–Ragosine–Mathers collection, MG 30, E406, vol. 11, reel 7601, file 344, CGS to Russian Consul, 20 March 1916.
87 LAC, RG 38, vol. 443, file "Country of Birth CEF."
88 St Marys and District Museum, Larsson fonds, certificate of naturalization for Adolf Gottfrid Larsson granted 18 October 1916.
89 *Wartime Elections Act* [20 September 1917] article 2(g) and 2(h).
90 Richard Holt, *Filling the Ranks: Recruiting, Training and Reinforcements in the CEF* (PhD diss., University of Western Ontario, 2011), 194.
91 LAC, RG 4375, file 34-7-61, vol. 1, MD 2 to K.A. Wee of Leonia, New Jersey, 27 April 1917.
92 LAC, RG 24, vol. 4547, file 79-1-1, vol. 11, Military Service Branch Miscellaneous Circular No. 22, 22 August 1918.
93 Marjorie Wong, *The Dragon and the Maple Leaf: Chinese-Canadians in World War II* (Toronto: Pirie Publishing, 1994), 3–7; *Official Report of the Debates of the House of Commons of the Dominion of Canada*, 13th Parliament, 4th Session, vol. 142, no. 2, 29 April 1920 (Ottawa: King's Printer, 1918), 1812.
94 *Japanese Contribution to Canada: A Summary of the Role Played by the Japanese in the Development of the Canadian Commonwealth* (Vancouver: Canadian Japanese Association, 1940), 27–8, citing a 1924–26 survey done by the *Vancouver Continental Daily News*.
95 LAC, RG 24, vol. 1256, file 593-1-94, CGS to AG, 29 March 1917.
96 *Toronto Star*, 14 March 1916, 2; *Toronto World*, 15 March 1916, 4.

97 LAC, RG 9, II A2, vol. 33, "Minutes of the Militia Council 1916," 19 April 1916; LAC, RG 24, vol. 4642, file 99-4-57, CGS to OC MD 11, 22 April 1916; Ken Adachi, *The Enemy That Never Was: A History of the Japanese Canadians* (Toronto: McClelland and Stewart Limited, 1976), 102.

98 LAC, Sir Robert Bordon fonds, MG 26, II 1(c), vol. 196, p. 109546, Major (retired). R.O. Montgomery to Sir Richard McBride, 10 February 1915.

99 LAC, RG 73, C1, vol. 49 file 1-1-65, Part 1, W.P. Archibald to Minister of Justice, 11 September 1914, LAC, RG 73, C1, vol. 49 file 1-1-65, Part 1.

100 LAC, Sir Robert Bordon fonds, MG 26, II 1(c), vol. 196, p. 109533, Borden to McBride, 23 December 1914; p. 109352, McBride to Borden, 21 December 1914; p. 109545, Borden to McBride, 3 February 1915.

101 LAC, Sir Robert Bordon fonds, MG 26, II 1(c), vol. 196, p. 109544, Borden to Governor General, 22 February 1915.

102 James W. St G. Walker, "Race and Recruitment in World War I: Enlistment of Visible Minorities in the Canadian Expeditionary Force," *Canadian Historical Review* 70, no. 1 (March 1989), 4.

103 LAC, RG 24, vol. 1206, file 297-1-21, AG to T.J. Stewart of Hamilton, 16 October 1915.

104 Walker, "Race and Recruitment in World War I"; Calvin W. Ruck, *The Black Battalion: 1916–1920: Canada's Best Kept Military Secret* (Halifax: Nimbus Publishing, 1987).; Sean Flynn Foyn, "The Underside of Glory: AfriCanadian Enlistment in the Canadian Expeditionary Force, 1914–1917" (master's thesis, University of Ottawa, 1999).

105 LAC, RG 24, vol. 4375, file 34-7-61, vol. 1, Minister of Militia and Defence to OC 2nd Division, 18 November 1915, and reply, 18 November 1915, LAC, RG 24.

106 LAC, RG 24, vol. 4375, file 34-7-61, vol. 1, AAG 2nd Division to Toronto Recruiting Depot, 19 November 1915, and reply, 22 November 1915.

107 LAC, RG 24, vol. 1400, file 593-6-2, vol. 16, AG to OC No. 1 Construction Battalion, 10 July 1916.

108 LAC, RG 24, vol. 4375, file 34-7-55, vol. 3, Charles Richardson to HQ MD 2, 29 April 1918.

109 LAC, RG 24, vol. 4375, file 34-7-55, vol. 3, HQ MD 2 to Royal Canadian Dragoons Depot Squadron, 7 May 1918.

110 DHH, 74/672, box 8, file 74/672-11-36, "Enlistment of Colored Men in the CEF," J.R.B. Whitney to Minister of Militia and Defence, 24 November 1915; LAC, RG 24, vol. 1206, file 297-1-21, AG to OC 2nd Division, 3 February 1916, LAC, RG 24, vol. 1206, file 297-1-21.

111 LAC, RG 24, vol. 4387, file 34-7-141, vol. 1, MD 2 circular letter, 3 April 1916.
112 LAC, RG 24, vol. 4387, file 34-7-141, vol. 1, Unit replies to MD 2 circular letter, 3 April 1916.
113 Canada, Department of Militia and Defence, *Canadian Expeditionary Force Units: Instructions Governing Organization and Administration* (Ottawa: Government Printing Bureau, 1916), 4.
114 See *Canadian Observer* 3, no. 5 (8 January 1916), 4, concerning the benefits of a formed platoon to the black community.
115 LAC, RG 24, vol. 1206, file 297-1-21, Military Secretary to John T. Richards of Saint John, 11 October 1915.
116 LAC, RG 24, vol. 1833, file GAC 9-34A, AG to GOC MD 1, 30 April 1918, "Labour Units."
117 LAC, RG 24, vol. 122, file 593-1-7, part 1, OC 1st Divisional Area to Militia HQ, AG to OC 1st Division 8 August 1914; AO, Alexander Emerson Belcher fonds, F18 reel MS 93, MU 5813-5814, Military Secretary to A.E. Belcher, 8 August 1914.
118 LAC, RG 24, vol. 1221 file 593-1-7, vol. 1, OC 2nd Division to Militia HQ, 23 November 1915.
119 LAC, RG 10, vol. 6767, file 452-13, Deputy Minister Militia and Defence to Indian Affairs, 22 October 1915.
120 LAC, RG 24, vol. 1221 file 593-1-7, vol. 1, OC 2nd Division to Militia HQ, 23 November, 27 November, and 3 December 1915; OA 1st Division to Militia HQ, 2 December 1915; AG circular letter, 10 December 1915.
121 LAC, RG 9, II B5, vol. 5, file "CEF: 18th, 19th–22nd, 24th–27th Battalions," Examination – Board of Officers. Canadian Expeditionary Forces. Report on 20th Batt. 29 January 1915; *Toronto World*, 14 November 1914, 2.
122 Richard Holt, "Research Note – First Nations Soldiers in the Great War," *Native Studies Review* 22, no. 1 (July 2013).
123 LAC, RG 10, vol. 6766, file 452-13, Kwawkewlth Agent to Indian Affairs, 7 January 1916.
124 LAC, RG 10 vol. 6766, file 452-13, BC Inspector of Indian Agencies to Indian Affairs, 8 January 1917.
125 LAC, RG 10 vol. 6767 file 451-16 part 1, Indian Affairs to Militia HQ, 29 May 1917.
126 LAC, RG 10 vol. 6766 file 452-13, C.M. McCarthy to Reverend R.J. Renison, 14 April 1917.
127 LAC, RG 24, vol. 1144, file 54-21-51-9, vol. 2, OC MD 11 to Militia HQ, 19 April 1917.

128 Walter McRaye, *Town Hall Tonight* (Toronto: The Ryerson Press, c. 1929), 69.
129 DHS, 74/672, box 1, folder 3, "Disposition on Discharge"; LAC, RG 38, vol. 443, "Age on Appointment of Enlistment in the CEF."
130 LAC, RG 150, acc 1992-93/166, box 6153, 267541 Wesley Mickey of the 214th Battalion; LAC, RG 150, acc 1992-93/166, box 8464, 701232 Reuben Rosenfield of the 101st Battalion.
131 LAC, RG 150, acc 1992-93/166, box 4663, 258572 William Henry Hugh Hutchinson of the 211th Battalion,
132 I am indebted to Ms Johanne Neville of the Commonwealth War Graves Commission, Canadian Agency, for providing the initial list of over-age and underage soldiers based on Commission records. A review of 3,190 surnames beginning with "Mc" indicated that 61.1 per cent of all entries included age.
133 LAC, RG 9, III A1, vol. 37, file 8-2-10, Medical Board Folkestone to Director of Recruiting and Organization, 22 August 1916.
134 DHS, 74/672, box 1, folder 3, "Disposition on Discharge"; LAC, RG 38, vol. 443, file "Age on Appointment or Enlistment CEF."
135 LAC, RG 150, acc 1992-93/166, box 6459, 1282269 Alexander Muir.
136 LAC, RG 24, vol. 1144, file 54-21-51-9, vol. 1, ADMS MD 10 to AAG MD 10, 11 January 1917.
137 LAC, RG 150 acc 1992-93/166, box 1734, 727193 Frank Clark; LAC, RG 150, acc 1992-93/166, box 4076, 2368456 Charles Frederick Harrigan.
138 *Fifth Census of Canada, 1911*, vol. II (Ottawa, King's Printer, 1913), 440, Table XVII, "Birthplace of the people by provinces."
139 Canada, Dominion Bureau of Statistics, *The Canada Year Book 1918* (Ottawa: King's Printer, 1919), 99.
140 Great Britain, War Office, *Statistics of the Military Effort of the British Empire during the Great War* (London: HMSO, 1922), 379.
141 *Fifth Census of Canada, 1911*, vol. VI, "Occupations of the People," 2–7.
142 Canada, Dominion Bureau of Statistics, *Canada Year Book 1922–23* (Ottawa: King's Printer, 1924), 433.
143 Lieutenant-Colonel H.A.C Machin, *Report of the Director of the Military Service Branch* (Ottawa: King's Printer, 1919), 78; Morton *When Your Number's Up*, 66–7, concerning different standards of local tribunals. No doubt the same applied to medical boards.
144 Great Britain, Ministry of National Service, *Report*, vol. 1. *Upon the physical examination of men of military age by National Service medical*

boards from November 1st, 1917 – October 31st, 1918 (London: HMSO, 1920), 3–4.
145 Desmond Morton, *A Military History of Canada* (Edmonton: Hurtig Publishers, 1985), 152–3.
146 J.L. Granatstein and J.M. Hitsman, *Broken Promises: A History of Conscription in Canada* (Toronto: Toronto University Press, 1977), 29.
147 Patrice A. Dutil, "Against Isolationism: Napoléon Belcourt, French Canada and La grande guerre," in *Canada and the First World War: Essays in Honour of Robert Craig Brown*, ed. David Mackenzie (Toronto: University of Toronto Press, 2005), 99.
148 DHH, 74/672, box 10, file 74/672, 11 – 69, "French-Canadian Battalion" GOC MD 5 to Militia HQ, 25 September 1916.

CHAPTER FOUR

1 Jean-Pierre Gagnon, "Canadian Soldiers in Bermuda During World War One," *Histoire Sociale–Social History* 23, no. 45 (May 1990): 17–18.
2 Jennifer Ingham, *Defence Not Defiance* (Bermuda: privately published, n.d.), 50; No reference to Canadian recruiting was found in the Bermuda *Royal Gazette* 1914–1916, *House of Assembly Debates* 1914–1915, *House of Assembly Debates* 1915–1916, or in the Bermuda Archives, CS 6/1/28, "Governor's Despatches 1913–1916."
3 DHH, 74/672, box 8, file 74/672-11-36, Governor of Bermuda to Militia HQ, 18 August 1916.
4 LAC, RG 9, III D3, vol. 5047, file 911, reel T-10938, War Diary Canadian Section GHQ 3rd Echelon, June 1918, Appendix 6.
5 Colonel A. Fortescue Duguid, *Official History of the Canadian Forces in the Great War 1914–1919: Chronology, Appendices and Maps* (Ottawa: King's Printer, 1938), 140.
6 LAC, RG 9, III B1, vol. 419, file E-90-1, Chief Paymaster CEF to HQ Canadian Contingent, c. 15 November 1914; Duguid, *Official History: Chronology, Appendices and Maps*, 116; W.D. Ellis, ed., *Saga of the Cyclists in the Great War 1914–1918* (n.p.: Canadian Corps Cyclist Battalion Association, 1965), 4–5.
7 DHH, 74/672, box 8, file 74/672-11-39, War Office to OC 1st Canadian Contingent, 19 November 1914; LAC, RG 150, file "17th Reserve Battalion," Daily Orders, 5 November 1914 to 20 January 1915; LAC, RG 9, III D3, vol. 4956, reel T-10773, War Diary 1st Canadian Divisional Cyclist Company, November–December 1914.

8 LAC, RG 24, vol. 1811, file GAC 3-9, "Memorandum on the Canadian Expeditionary Force" by Colonel W.G. Gwatkin, CGS, 3 October 1914.
9 LAC, RG 9, III B1, vol. 419, file E-90-1, GOC Canadian Contingent to Southern Command, 8 December 1914.
10 DHH, 74/672, box 8, file 74/672-11-39, War Office to 1st Canadian Division, 19 January 1915.
11 LAC, RG 9, III A1, vol. 28, file 8-1-11, Carson to War Office, 25 May 1915; Carson to Canadian Training Division Shorncliffe, 14 June 1915.
12 LAC, RG 9, III B1, vol. 439, file E-479-1, vol. 1, HQ Canadians to all units, 30 June 1915.
13 LAC, RG 9, III A1, vol. 28, file 8-1-11, Director of Recruiting and Organization to HQ Canadians London, 9 May 1916.
14 LAC, RG 9, III A1, vol. 92, file 10-12-33, High Commissioner to HQ OMFC, 12 September 1917.
15 LAC, RG 9, III B1, vol. 1260, file E-55-5, Canadian Section GHQ 3rd Echelon to AAG(C) GHQ 3rd Echelon, 4 June 1918.
16 LAC, RG 9, III A1, vol. 28, file 8-1-11, Officer i/c Enlistments to Director of Recruiting and Organization, 8 January 1916.
17 Overseas Military Forces of Canada, *Report of the Ministry: Overseas Military Forces of Canada 1918*, (London: Overseas Military Forces of Canada, 1919), 44.
18 LAC, RG 9, III A1, vol. 28, file 8-1-11, W.G. Hunter, British Army Recruiting Officer to Major-General Carson, 4 October 1915; Carson to Hunter, 7 October 1915.
19 LAC, RG 9, III B1, vol. 1260, file E-55-5, Canadian Section GHQ 3rd Echelon to AAG(C) GHQ 3rd Echelon, 4 June 1918.
20 LAC, RG 9, III D1, vol. 5047, file 911 reel T-10938, War Diary Canadian Section GHQ 3rd Echelon, June 1918, Appendix 6; HQ OMFC to Canadian Section GHQ 3rd Echelon, 10 June 1918.
21 LAC, RG 9, III B1, vol. 1260, file E-55-5, petition submitted to OC Canadian General Base Depot in April 1918. One of the men was a Native soldier from British Columbia.
22 From November 1915 to 31 May 1917, 5.5 per cent of 9,161 men enlisted by one of six major depots were United States residents. These depots recruited from a broad area, thus eliminating local factors: LAC, MD 10/11 CAMC (Western Canada), MD 2 CASC, C Battery RCHA and CMR (Ontario and Quebec) and the Engineer Depot St John's (Eastern Canada). Of the 406,147 enlistments made by 31 May 1917 it is estimated that at least 22,338 were American residents. To this should be added 33,335 enlisted by the BCRM.

23 United States, *Statutes at Large of the United States of America*, vol. 34, part 1 (Washington: Government Printing Office, 1909), 1228. An Act in reference to the expatriation of citizens and their protection abroad, s. 2.
24 United States, *Statutes at Large of the United States of America*, vol. 35, part 1, 1088. An Act to codify, revise and amend the penal laws of the United States [Penal Code], s. 10.
25 LAC, RH 76 reel T-5462, file Beebe Junction Border Entries April 1914–December 1918, Border Entries for the period 14–18 September 1914.
26 LAC, RG 75, reel T-5506, "Windsor Border Entries October 1913–June 1917," Border entries for September, October, November and December 1914.
27 LAC, RG 76, reel 5489, "Border Entries Niagara Falls August 1914 to September 1915," Border Entries Niagara Falls October 1915 to May 1916.
28 LAC, RG 9, III D1, vol. 4699 folder 68, file 1, 99th Battalion historical report, March 1918.
29 *Charlotte Daily Observer*, 26 February 1916, p. 1, commented at length on the ad and quoted the *Washington Times*; LAC, RG 24, vol. 4427, file 26-6-64-3, vol. 1, AG circular letter, 17 March 1916.
30 LAC, RG 24, vol. 782, file 1982-1-56, AG circular telegram, 16 November 1916.
31 Roy A. McLellan, *Day to Day Experiences during World War I and World War II* (privately printed, c. 1958), 19.
32 DHH, 74/672, box 5, folder 18, file "United States Citizens – Enlistment of in Canadian Forces," Department of the Interior to Minister of Militia and Defence, 3 November 1915; LAC, RG 24, vol. 289, file 13-123-5, Superintendent of Immigration to Militia HQ, 14 June 1917.
33 LAC, Likacheff–Ragosine–Mathers collection, MG 30, E406, vol. 11, reel 7603, file 400, August Fibiger to Consul, 3 May 1916 and 11 November 1916.
34 Colonel W.G. Lyddon, *British War Missions to the United States* (London: Oxford University Press, 1938), 197–8; United States, Bureau of the Census, *Historical Statistics of the United States, Colonial Times to 1970*, Part I (Washington: US Government Printing Office, 1975), 116.
35 Lyddon, *British War Missions to the United States*, 198; *New York Times*, 4 June 1917, 6.
36 LAC, RG 24, vol. 289, file 13-123-5, U.S. Army General Recruiting Service Circular Letters 1917 Number 69 of 31 May 1917; Lyddon, *British War Missions to the United States*, 198; *New York Times*, 31 May 1917, 5; *Boston Daily Globe*, 4 June 1917, 1.

37 LAC, Albert Edwin Kemp fonds, MG 27, II D9, vol. 76, file 127, Appendix 1; LAC, RG 24, vol. 4615, file 1G 1, vol. 3, Undated memorandum c. September 1917, *European War: Memorandum No. 4 respecting Work of the Department of Militia and Defence from January 1, 1917 to December 31, 1917* dated 6 February 1918.

38 LAC, RG 24, vol. 289, file 13-123-5, HQ British Recruiting Mission to Militia HQ 29 June 1917, Memorandum to Minister 20 June 1917; LAC, Edward Albert Kemp fonds, MG 27, II D9, vol. 76, file 127, undated summary of BCRM c. September 1917.

39 Martin Watts, *The Jewish Legion and the First World War* (Basingstoke, Hampshire: Palgrave Macmillan, 2004), 148; Elias Gilner, *War and Hope: A History of the Jewish Legion* (New York: Herzl Press, 1969), 184–55; Michael Keren and Shlomit Keren, *We Are Coming, Unafraid: The Jewish Legions and the Promised Land in the First World War* (Plymouth: Rowman & Littlefield Publishers, 2010), 5–6.

40 LAC, RG 24, vol. 4490, file 48-21-3, DAG Organization to MD 4, 5 March 1918 and 1 May 1918.

41 LAC, RG 24, vol. 4490, file 48-21-3, Militia HQ to MD 4, 1 May 1918.

42 LAC, RG 24, vol. 4490, file 48-21-3, AG to MD 4, 23 April 1918.

43 LAC, RG 24, vol. 4490, file 48-21-3, BCRM to AG, 16 July 1918.

44 Vladimir Jabotinsky, *The Story of the Jewish Legion* (New York: Bernard Ackerman, 1945), 164; Gilner, *War and Hope*, 186; Hyman Sokolov, "The Jewish Legion for Palestine," in *Jewish Life and Times: A Collection of Essays* (Winnipeg: Jewish Historical Society of Western Canada, 1983), 56.

45 DHH, 74/672, box 1, folder 2, file British-Canadian Recruiting Mission, Synopsis of Recruits, 12 March 1918; LAC, RG 24, vol. 4313, file 341-59-R vol. 4, OC Toronto Mobilization Centre to District Record Officer, 5 September 1918.

46 LAC, RG 9, II B3, vol. 77, CEF Routine Order Number 475 of 23 April 1918.

47 *New York Times*, 19 June 1917, 2; LAC, Albert Edward Kemp fonds, MG 27, II D9, vol. 76, file 127, OC Boston Depot to GOC BCRM, 29 August 1917.

48 LAC, RG 24, vol. 289, file 13-123-5, A/AG to Minister of Militia and Defence, 23 July 1917.

49 TNA, FO 115/2440, HQ BCRM to British Ambassador Washington, 31 May 1918, Memo Eastern Division BCRM 28 May 1918, BCRM Buffalo to Eastern Division BCRM 29 May 1918.

50 Michael Willrich, *City of Courts: Socializing Justice in Progressive Era Chicago* (Cambridge: Cambridge University Press, 2003), 165.

51 LAC, Albert Edward Kemp fonds, MG 27, II D9, vol. 76, file 127, Statements of Recruits in New York City for week ending 14 July 1917, 21 July 1917, and 28 July 1917.
52 LAC, RG 24, vol. 4313, file 341-1-59R, vols 1 and 2, Weekly statements of BCRM recruits in MD 2, 1 July 1917 to 7 September 1918.
53 LAC, RG 24, vol. 4312, file 34-1-59R, vol. 1, OC Toronto Mobilization Centre to AAG & QMG MD 2 27 August 1917; LAC, RG 24, vol. 4313, file 341-1-59R, vols 1 and 2, Weekly statements of BCRM recruits in MD 2, 1 July 1917 to 7 September 1918.
54 Christian L. Wiktor, ed., *Unperfected Treaties of the United States of America: 1776–1976*, vol. 4 (Dobbs Ferry, NY: Oceana Publications, 1979), 379 and 383; United States, *Treaties, Conventions, International Acts, Protocols and Agreements between the United States and Other Powers, 1910–1923*, vol. 3 (Washington: Government Printing Office, 1923), 2650–4 and 2654–7.
55 *New York Times*, 20 September 1918, 12.
56 Major-General E.H. Crowder, *Second Report of the Provost Marshal General to the Secretary of War on the Operations of the Selective Service System to December 20, 1918*. (Washington: Government Printing Office, 1919), 36–7; Lieutentant-Colonel H.A.C Machin, *Report of the Director of the Military Service Branch* (Ottawa: King's Printer, 1919), 113.
57 LAC, RG 73, C1, vol. 49, file 1-1-65 Part I, Warden St Vincent de Paul Penitentiary to Inspector of Penitentiaries 14 August 1914 and reply 17 August 1914; LAC, RG 73, vol. 196, file "Ticket of Leave 1912–14," Inspector D. Hogan to Chief of Remissions Branch, 25 October 1915.
58 LAC, RG 73, C1, vol. 49, file 1-1-65 Part I, Inspector Stewart to Minister of Justice 27 May 1915, Dominion Parole Officer to Department of Justice, 10 September 1915.
59 LAC, RG 73, vol. 196, file Correspondence Ticket of Leave Act 1915–1916, Dominion Parole Officer to Department of Justice, 10 September 1915.
60 *London Advertiser*, 5 November 1915, 2; LAC, RG 9, II B5, vol. 6, Abridged Report Upon 176th Overseas Battalion, 29 March 1917; *Toronto Globe*, 10 August 1916, 5.
61 LAC, RG 73, vol. 196, file "Ticket of Leave 1915-1916," PC 2741 of 4 November 1916, Department of Justice to Provincial Attorneys-General, 29 November 1916.
62 LAC, RG 73, vol. 186, file "Remission Branch: Tickets of Leave: Correspondence 1916–1924," MD 3 Recruiting Officer to Minister of Justice, 31 May 1917.

63 *Military Service Act*, s. 12; *Dominion Elections Act*, R.S.C. 1906, vol. I, s. 67.
64 LAC, RG 24, vol. 4615, file 206-8, "Circular Memorandum to Wardens of Penitentiaries and Gaols re Military Service Act 1917," 19 November 1917.
65 LAC, microfilm reel T-2001 (Kingston Warden's Letter Book, 11 January 1918–16 October 1918), Warden Creighton to Major A.T. Kidd of HQ MD 3, 4 July 1918.
66 LAC, RG 73 C1, vol. 49, file 1-1-65, Warden G.S. Malepart to Dominion Parole Officer, 20 December 1917.
67 LAC, RG 24, vol. 4552, file 125-1-79, DAA & QMG MD 6 to OC 1st Depot Battalion Nova Scotia Regiment, 10 May 1918.
68 DHH, 74/672, box 1, file 3, AG circular letter, 10 May 1917.
69 LAC, RG 73, C1, vol. 49, file 1-1-65, Deputy Minister Department of Justice to Inspector of Penitentiaries, 16 October 1917.
70 LAC, Albert Edward Kemp fonds, MG 27, II D9, vol. 135, file "Convicts 1918," Sir Edward Kemp to Major-General S.C. Mewburn, 27 July 1918.
71 LAC, reel T-2001 (Kingston Warden's Letter Book 11 January 1918–16 October 1918), Creighton to Inspector WS Hughes, 19 October 1918.
72 M.C. Urquhart and K.A.H. Buckley, eds, *Historical Statistics of Canada* (Toronto: The Macmillan Company of Canada, 1965), 42.
73 LAC, RG 73, vol. 186, file "Ticket of Leave, vol. 8, January 1934–1944," LAC, RG 24, vol. 4547, file 79-1-1, "Table prepared by Remissions Branch, Department of Justice, 4 March 1943."
74 LAC, RG 24, vol. 4547, file 79-1-1, Department of Justice, Military Service Branch Circular Memorandum #2, 24 June 1918.
75 AO, RG 8-5, box 78, file "Military Service Act," Superintendent Hamilton Hospital for the Insane to Provincial Secretary, July 1918. Patient ledgers for the Queen Street Mental Hospital, Brockville Asylum and Penetanguishene do not list any patients who were discharged to join the CEF.
76 LAC, RG 9, III B1, vol. 439, file E-105-1, Medical Board Department to Director of Recruiting and Organization at Canadian HQ, 20 May 1916.
77 TNA, WO 293/4, ACI 1023 of 19 May 1916.
78 LAC, RG 9, III A1, vol. 74, file 10-8-22, vol. 1, Deputy Minister to Sub-Militia Council in England, 2 November 1916.
79 LAC, RG 9, III B1, vol. 789, file R-42-2, vol. 3, AA & QMG CTD Shorncliffe to all units, 26 November 1916.
80 Militia Order 50 of 6 August 1917.
81 LAC, RG 9, III C1, vol. 4470, folder 7, file 6, Director of Organization to all commands, 24 January 1917.

82 LAC, RG 9, III B1, vol. 774, file R-9-2, vol. 6, CTD Shorncliffe to HQ OMFC 4 January 1917.
83 LAC, RG 9, III B1, vol. 789, file R-43-2, vol. 4, CASC Training Depot to HQ Canadian Troops Shorncliffe, 9 May 1917; LAC, RG 9, III A1, vol. 53, file Monthly Reports, Quartermaster General, Monthly Reports, August and September 1917.
84 LAC, RG 150, vol. 237, Canadian Army Service Corps Base Depot, Daily Orders Part II for 9 October, 20 October,s and 16 November 1917.
85 LAC, Richard Ernest William Turner fonds, MG 30, E46, vol. 10, file 63, QMG to AG HQ OMFC, c. July 1918.
86 LAC, RG 9, III A1, vol. 85, file 10-12-1, Chief Paymaster to Deputy Minister OMFC, 10 July 1917.
87 LAC, RG 9, III B1, vol. 789, file R-43-2, vol. 4, ADMS HQ OMFC to HQ Canadian Training Division, 8 May 1917.
88 LAC, RG 9, III A1, vol. 53, file "Monthly Reports November 1917," Quartermaster General.
89 LAC, RG 9, III C13, vol. 4605, folder 22, HQ OMFC to HQ Canadians Bramshott, 11 January 1918.
90 LAC, TH 9, III B1, vol. 789, file R-32-2, vol. 4, HQ omfc to HQ Canadian Troops Shorncliffe, 4 May 1917.
91 LAC, RG 38, vol. 443, file "Place of Birth CEF"; LAC, RG 9, III B1, vol. 789, file R-32-2, vol. 4.
92 J.S. Woodworth, *Strangers within Our Gates or Coming Canadians* (Toronto: Missionary Society of the Methodist Church, 1909), 277.
93 Agnes Laut, *The Canadian Commonwealth* (Chautuaqua, New York: Chautuaqua Press, 1915), 119.
94 LAC, RG 24, vol. 4320, file 34-1-90, AG to OC 2nd Division, 19 October 1915.
95 LAC, RG 24, vol. 858, file 54-21-12-30, MD 10 to Militia HQ, 16 March 1916 with minute by CGS, AG to HQ MD 10, 23 March 1916.
96 LAC, RG 24, vol. 436, file 54-21-1-91, AG to GOC MD 6, 3 November 1917.
97 LAC, RG 24, vol. 4593, file 20-10, vol. 10, Mayor of Fort William to Minister of Militia and Defence, 27 November 1914.
98 LAC, Albert Edward Kemp fonds, MG 27, II D9, vol. 71, file 31, Prime Minister Borden to A.E. Kemp 14 December 1916 regarding a delegation of Ruthenians [Ukrainians].
99 LAC, RG 24, vol. 4509, file 17-1-49, vol. VIII, AG circular letter, 7 November 1916.

100 LAC, RG 24, vol. 1402, file 593-6-2, vol. 21, AG to DOC MD 12, 22 November 1916; LAC, RG 24, vol 1206, file 297-1-29, AG circular letter, 12 July 1916.
101 LAC, RG 150, acc 1992-93, acc 166, box 6720, Personnel file 261286 George McDonald, "Proceedings of a Court of Enquiry 16 June 1917."
102 LAC, RG 24, vol. 1397, file 593-6-2, vol. 8, AG circular letter, 9 September 1915; LAC, RG 24, vol. 4427, file 26-5-64-3, vol. 1, AG circular letter, 14 January 1916.
103 LAC, RG 9, III B1, vol. 486, file R-34-1, vol. 1, Precis for the Information of the General Officer Commanding, 14 April 1916.
104 LAC, RG 9, III B1, vol. 488, file R-34-1, 39th Reserve Battalion to HQ 12th Canadian Reserve Brigade, 25 February 1916.
105 O.C.S. Wallace, ed., *From Montreal to Vimy Ridge and Beyond: The Correspondence of Lieut. Clifford Almon Wells, B.A., of the 8th Battalion, Canadians, B.E.F. November 1915–April 1917* (Toronto: McClelland, Goodchild & Stewart, 1917), 188.
106 LAC, RG 9, III A1, vol. 30, file 8-1-65, 12th Reserve Brigade to HQ Canadian Training Division, 8 April 1916.
107 LAC, RG 9, III A1, vol. 52 file 8-7-3, 9th Reserve Brigade to HQ Canadian Training Division, 26 November 1916; LAC, RG 9, III B1, vol. 790 file R-46-2, vol. 4, 5th Reserve Battalion to HQ 1st Canadian Reserve Brigade, 21 June 1917; LAC, RG 9, III B1, vol. 560 file A-84-2, vol. 1, Canadian Pioneer Training Depot to 5th Canadian Training Brigade, 16 June 1916.
108 LAC, RG 24, vol. 4331, file 34-2-18, OC Base Company 37th Battalion to HQ MD 2, 1 September 1915.
109 Nancy Gentile Ford, *Americans All! Foreign-Born Soldiers in World War I* (Texas A&M University Press, 2001) 66, 68, 76–7.
110 LAC, RG 150, acc 1992-93/166, box 803, Personnel file 95 Maude Blake.
111 LAC, RG 24, vol. 493, file 54-21-4-147, "Anxious and Willin'-to-go Stenographer" to Department of Militia and Defence, 28 December 1917, AG to Military Secretary 31 December 1917, Militia HQ to OMFC 17 March 1918, War Office to HQ OMFC, 22 March 1918.
112 LAC, RG 9, III B2, vol. 3745, file "Adami Papers (1). Miscellaneous," DAG Organization to AG Militia HQ, 10 May 1918.
113 DHH, KE6848 A329 C309, *Minutes of the Militia Council 1918*, vol. II, 30 May 1918, 453–4; DHH, KE6848 A329 C309, *Minutes of the Militia Council 1918*, vol. III, 18 September 1918, p. 872; LAC, RG 24, vol. 1744, file DHS 4-62, Deputy Minister to War Committee, 11 October 1918.

114 LAC, RG 9, III B3, vol. 3765: 153,061 men were in France or Flanders at the end of May 1918; TNA, WO 114/35, Weekly Returns, 27 May 1918 show 101,087 men were in Britain; 344,757 men were in the CEF at the end of May 1918: Colonel G.W.L. Nicholson, *Official History of the Canadian Army in the First World War: Canadian Expeditionary Force 1914–1919* (Ottawa: Queen's Printer, 1962), 547.

CHAPTER FIVE

1 LAC, RG 9, II A2, vol. 33, *Minutes of the Militia Council 1916*, p. 45, 6 April 1916.
2 LAC, RG 24, vol. 1396, file 593-6-2, vol. 6, OC 2nd Division to Militia HQ, 2 August 1915.
3 LAC, RG 24, vol. 1396, file 593-6-2, vol. 6, AG to OC 2nd Division, 5 August 1915.
4 LAC, RG 24, vol. 1398, file 593-6-2, vol. 9, DOC MD 13 to AG, 8 November 1915.
5 Colonel A. Fortescue Duguid, *Official History of the Canadian Forces in the Great War 1914–1919: Chronology, Appendices and Maps* (Ottawa: King's Printer, 1938), 11.
6 LAC, RG 24, vol. 1810, file GAC 1-4, "Notes re Pre War Mobilization Scheme for raising of a Canadian Division."
7 Duguid, *Official History: Chronology, Appendices and Maps*, 12.
8 Canada, Department of Militia and Defence, *Mobilization Regulations 1913* (Ottawa: Government Printing Bureau, 1912), 9, 18, 22.
9 AG Circular Letter, 31 July 1914, quoted in Duguid, *Official History: Chronology, Appendices and Maps*, 10–11; Ronald Haycock, *Sam Hughes: The Public Career of a Controversial Canadian 1885–1916* (Waterloo: Wilfrid Laurier University Press, 1986), 182; Stephen Harris, *Canadian Brass: The Making of a Professional Army 1860–1939* (Toronto: University of Toronto Press, 1988), 95.
10 LAC, RG 24, vol. 1221, file 593-1-5, OC 1st Division to Militia HQ, 8 August 1914.
11 LAC, RG 4536, file 3-1-143, OC 36th Light Horse to 6th Division, 11 August 1914.
12 Colonel J. Sutherland Brown, "Military Policy of Canada, 1905–1924 and Suggestions for the Future," *Canadian Defence Quarterly* 1, no. 4 (July 1924): 27.
13 LAC, RG 24, vol. 1221, file 593-1-5, AG to Lieutenant-Colonel A.R. Lavergne of Quebec, 7 August 1914; *Chatham Daily Planet*, 7 August 1914, 1.

14 LAC, RG 9, II F9, vol. 30, file 28th Regiment, Pay sheets, 12–23 August 1914.
15 LAC, RG 9, II F9, vol. 30, file 29th Regiment Headquarters August 1914 to December 1914, Pay sheets, 6–22 August 1914; LAC, RG 9, II F9, vol. 29, file "25th Regiment Details October 1914 to August 1915." Despite the title, the file contains pay sheets for 7–22 August 1914.
16 LAC, RG 9, II F9, vol. 1535, file CASC No 14 Company, Pay sheet 12–21 August 1914.
17 LAC, RG 9, II F9, vol. 224, file 23rd Regiment Aug 1914–July 1915, Pay sheets 12–20 August 1914.
18 LAC, RG 24, vol. 4536, file 3-10143, AAG 6th Division to 73rd Regiment, 17 August 1914.
19 Stephen K. Newman, *With the Patricia's in Flanders 1914–1918: Then & Now* (Saanichton, British Columbia: Bellewaerde House Publishing, 2000), 2–5.
20 Colonel A. Fortescue Duguid, *Official History of the Canadian Forces in the Great War 1914–1919: General Series,* vol. 1 (Ottawa: King's Printer, 1938), 161, 425.
21 LAC, RG 9, III D3, vol. 4926, reel T-10722, War Diary 19th Battalion, 6 November 1914; LAC, RG 9, II B5, vol. 5, file "CEF: 18th, 19th-22nd, 24th-27th Bns," Examination – Board of Officers' Report on 20th Batt, 29 January 1915.
22 Bruce Tascona, *From the Forks to Flanders Fields: The Story of the 27th City of Winnipeg Battalion, 1914–1919* (Winnipeg: Bunker to Bunker Books, 1995), 10; Major D.G. Scott Calder, *The History of the 28th (Northwest) Battalion CEF (October 1914 – June 1919).* (Regina: n.p., 1961), 16–17; LAC, RG 9, III A1, vol. 52, file 8-7-1A, OC 32nd Battalion to GOC Canadians, 23 March 1915.
23 Serge Bernier, *The Royal 22e Regiment 1914–1999* (Montreal: Art Global, 2000), 31.
24 LAC, RG 24, vol. 1398, file 593-6-2, vol. 9, Hughes to AG 14 November 1915; *Edmonton Daily Bulletin,* 3 November 1914, 1; 4 November 1914, 4, 8, 10.
25 *Lethbridge Daily Herald,* 11 November 1914, 1; *Medicine Hat News,* 19 November 1914.
26 LAC, RG 9, II F6, vol. 68, file 28th Regiment, Pay sheets recruiting 22 October–4 November 1914.
27 LAC, RG 9, II F9, vol. 29, file "24th Regt Details August 1914 to October 1914," Paysheets 22 October–4 November 1914; LAC, RG 9, II F9, vol. 30, file 29th Regiment Headquarters August 1914 to December 1914,

Paysheets for 21 October–4 November 1914; LAC, RG 9, II F9, vol. 31, file 33rd Regiment August 1914 to October 1916, Paysheets for October–4 November 1914.

28 LAC, RG 9, II F9, vol. 30, file 30th Regiment August 1914 to December 1914, Paysheets 24 October–3 November 1914 for Fergus and Guelph.

29 LAC, RG 9, II F9, vol. 224, files 23rd Regiment, Aug 1914–July 1915, and 34th Regiment, Aug 1914–April 1915, Paysheets – 23rd Regiment, 27 October–4 November 1914 and 34th Regiment, 26 October–9 November 1914; LAC, RG 9, II F9, vol. 31, file 32nd Regiment September 1914 to June 1917, Paysheets 32nd Regiment, 26 October–3 November 1914.

30 LAC, RG 9, II F9, vol. 1535, file CASC No 14 Company April 1914–July 1915, Paysheets 30 November–3 December 1914.

31 Duguid, *Official History: Chronology, Appendices and Maps*, 344–5.

32 Captain M.S. Hunt, *Nova Scotia's Part in the Great War* (Halifax: The Nova Scotia Veteran Publishing Co. 1920), 41.

33 Colonel G.W.L. Nicholson, *The Gunners of Canada*, vol. 1 (Toronto: McClelland and Stewart, 1967), 236–8.

34 Lieutenant-Colonel N.O. Carr, "The Man Behind the Gun," *Canadian Defence Quarterly* 8, no. 3 (April 1931), 374.

35 *Toronto Globe*, 8 August 1914, 7; OA RCE Ottawa to CRCE 2nd Division, 7 September 1914, GOC 2nd Division to Militia HQ, 16 September 1914. LAC, RG 24, vol. 4331, file 34-1-14; the file contains correspondence up to February 1916 regarding GE workers.

36 LAC, RG 24, vol. 1166, file 64-82-1, vol. 3, Report of the Annual Inspection 1915 – Field Butchery – Toronto, 1 March 1915.

37 LAC, RG 9, III D3, vol. 5021, file 784, reel T-10906, War Diary Number 6 Depot Unit of Supply, 3 December 1914 and 20 January 1915.

38 LAC, RG 9, II F9, vol. 551, files Governor General's Foot Guards Nov 1914–Jan 1916 and Governor General's Foot Guards June 1915–July 1915, Regimental Order 15, 11 June 1915.

39 LAC, RG 9, II F9, vol. 224, file 31st Regiment Overseas Contingent pay list and File 31st Regiment Apr 1915–June 1915, Pay sheets 31st Regiment quota for 37th Provisional Battalion and pay sheets for recruits for the 37th and 58th Battalions.

40 LAC, RG 9, II F9, vol. 563, file, "57th Regiment Overseas Detachment MD 3 Daily Orders Aug 1914–Aug 1915" and "57th Regiment Overseas Detachment MD 3 Daily Orders Sept 1915–April 1917."

41 *Toronto Star*, 5 August 1915, 2.

42 LAC, RG 24, vol. 1397, file 593-6-2, vol. 8, OC 2nd Division to Militia HQ, 27 September 1915.

43 LAC, RG 24, vol. 4552, file 125-1-13, OC Depot Company 55th Battalion to HQ 6th Division, 31 July 1915.
44 LAC, RG 24, vol. 4552, file 125-1-23, GOC 6th Division to Militia HQ, 20 July 1915 and reply 28 July 1915.
45 LAC, RG 24, vol. 4552, file 125-1-13, Lieutenant-Colonel Armstrong to HQ 6th Division, 12 August 1915.
46 LAC, RG 24, vol. 4552, file 125-1-13, Lieutenant-Colonel Armstrong to AAG 6th Division, 14 August 1915.
47 LAC, RG 9, II F9, vol. 30, Pay sheets "Recruiting for CEF July 2, 1915–July 27, 1915" and "Recruiting for CEF August 6, 1915–August 30, 1915"; RG 9, II F9, vol. 30, Pay sheets "Recruiting Men for 71st Battalion" 23 September–9 November 1915 and 2–21 September 1915.
48 *The Quarterly Militia List of the Dominion of Canada (Corrected to 1st July 1916)*, (Ottawa: King's Printer, 1916), 262, 288, 317, 409.
49 DHH, KE 6848 A329 C309, *Minutes of the Militia Council 1916*, p. 196, 10 August 1916.
50 LAC, RG 24, vol. 1396, file 593-6-2, vol. 4, AG to Minister of Militia and Defence, 28 June 1915; *Toronto Star*, 21 August 1915, 5.
51 Militia Order 161 of 29 March 1915.
52 *Official Report of the Debates of the House of Commons of the Dominion of Canada, 12th Parliament, 6th Session*, vol. 122 (Ottawa: King's Printer, 1916), 25, with Borden's address, 17 January 1916; Henry Borden, ed., *Robert Laird Borden: His Memoirs* (Toronto: Macmillan of Canada, 1938), 527–8; Robert Craig Brown, *Robert Laird Borden: a Biography*, vol. 2, *1914–1937* (Toronto: Macmillan of Canada, 1980), 34; LAC, RG 2, vol. 1131, file PC 36 1433 E, vol. 879, PC 36/1916 of 12 January 1916.
53 Colonel G.W.L. Nicholson, *Official History of the Canadian Army in the First World War: Canadian Expeditionary Force 1914–1919* (Ottawa: Queen's Printer, 1962), 216.
54 Canada, War Purchasing Commission, *Report of the War Purchasing Commission*, vol. 2 (Ottawa: King's Printer, 1916), 603–5.
55 LAC, RG 24, vol. 4508, file 17-1-49, vol. vi, AG to GOC MD 5, 31 August 1916; TNA, CO 42/994, PC 2688 of 23 September 1916.
56 LAC, RG 24, vol. 858, file 54-21-12-33, GOC MD 2 to Militia HQ, 26 September 1916.
57 LAC, RG 24, vol. 858, file 54-21-12-33, AAG(1) to AG, 8 September 1916.
58 LAC, RG 24, vol. 4552, file 125-1-23, AG Circular Letter, 1 October 1915; LAC, RG 24, vol. 6600, file 1982-1-24, vol. 1, Director of Mobilization to AG, 27 December 1916.

59 LAC, RG 24, vol. 6600, file 1982-1-24, vol. 1, DOC MD 11 to Militia HQ, 6 December 1916.
60 LAC, RG 24, vol. 6600, file 1982-1-24, vol. 1, GOC MD 2 to Militia HQ, 5 December 1916.
61 LAC, RG 24, vol. 6600, file 1982-1-24, vol. 1, AG Circular Telegram, 2 January 1917.
62 LAC, RG 24, vol. 1397, file 593-6-2, vol. 7, AG to Director of Mobilization, 20 October 1915, AG to OC 6th Division, 20 October 1915.
63 LAC, RG 24, vol. 1397, file 593-6-2, vol. 8, Private Secretary to AG, 4 October 1915; AG to DOC MD 10, 5 October 1915; AG to DOC MD 10, 20 October 1915, AG to DOC MD 10, 26 October 1915.
64 LAC, RG 9, III D 1, vol. 4700, folder 71, file 6, 122nd Battalion historical summary.
65 University of Western Ontario Area Research and Collections Centre, box 5100, Divisional Orders, 27 November 1915, quoting instructions from Militia HQ.
66 LAC, RG 24, vol. 1583, file 683-239-5, Report of the Annual Inspection 1916 of the 151st Overseas Battalion CEF, Sarcee Camp, 23 September 1916.
67 LAC, RG 9, III D 1, vol. 4700, folder 70, file 20, 119th Battalion Historical summary.
68 LAC, RG 9, III D 1, vol. 4700, folder 72, file 14, 135th Battalion Historical summary.
69 LAC, RG 24, vol. 1401, file 593-6-2, vol. 19, GOC MD 3 to Militia HQ, 22 August 1916 and reply 30 September 1916.
70 LAC, RG 9, III D 1, vol. 4700 folder 71, files 8 and 11, Historical Summaries 123rd Battalion and 124th Battalion; *Toronto Globe*, 1 March 1916, 8; Desmond Morton, *When Your Number's Up: The Canadian Soldier in the First World War* (Toronto: Random House of Canada, 1993), 59.
71 LAC, RG 24, vol. 6600, file 1982-1-24, vol. 1, GOC MD 2 to Militia HQ, 5 December 1916.
72 LAC, RG 24, vol. 4670, file 99-4-7, vol. 3, AAG i/c Administration to Militia HQ, 30 August 1916.
73 DHH, 74/672, box 13, folders 143, 158, 172, 211, 218 and 231.
74 LAC, RG 24, vol. 4508, file 17-1-49, vol. III, 5th Division to Militia HQ, 11 November 1915.
75 LAC, RG 24, vol. 4509, file 17-1-49, vol. XV, MD 5 to Militia HQ, 18 January 1917.

76 LAC, RG 24, vol. 4509, file 17-1-49, vol. VIII, MD 5 to Militia HQ, 22 September 1916, and MD 5 to Militia HQ, 11 November 1916.
77 LAC, RG 24, vol. 1398, file 593-6-2, vol. 11, MD 13 to Militia HQ, 26 January 1916, AG to Minister, 28 January 1916, AG to DOC MD 13, 3 February 1916.
78 DHH, 74/672, box 12 folder 113, box 13, folders 191 and 192.
79 LAC, RG 9, III D 1, vol. 4700 folder 72, file 14, Historical summary 135th Battalion.
80 DHH, 74/672, box 13, folder 142.
81 LAC, RG 24, vol. 1402, file 593-6-2, vol. 21, MD 3 to Militia HQ, 26 August 1916.
82 LAC, RG 9, II B 10, vol. 22, file 110th Battalion, weekly returns of recruits, 26 November 1915 to 29 October 1916.
83 LAC, RG 24, vol. 4680, file 18-29-2, Historical Record of the 232nd Overseas Battalion CEF.
84 LAC, RG 24, vol. 413, file 54-21-1-20 vol. 1, Draft "Statement by Department of Militia and Defence from 1st February to 31st December 1916," dated 1 December 1916.
85 LAC, RG 24, vol. 1402, file 593-6-2, vol. 21, AG to DOC MD 10, 29 November 1916.
86 LAC, RG 24, vol. 1402, file 593-6-2, vol. 22, DG Mobilization to CGS, 30 December 1916.
87 LAC, Albert Edward Kemp fonds, MG 27 II D9, vol. 73, file 68, Summary of memorandums from Gwatkin and Turner compiled by the Parliamentary Secretary, 15 January 1917.
88 LAC, RG 24, vol. 413, file 54-21-1-20, vol. 1, Draft Statement by Department of Militia and Defence from 1st February to 31st December 1916, dated 1 December 1916.
89 LAC, Albert Edward Kemp fonds, MG 27, II D9, vol. 73, Colonel H. Osborne to A. Claude Macdonnell M.P., 18 January 1917.
90 DHH, 74/672, box 4, folder 13, file CDF, CGS to AG, 15 January 1917.
91 DHH, 74/672, box 4, folder 13, file CDF, AG Circular Letter, 18 January 1917.
92 LAC, RG 24, vol. 1403, file 593-6-2, vol. 21, AG to GOC MD 3, 5 February 1917.
93 LAC, RG 24, vol. 4257, file 6-14-10, AAG MD 1 to OC 32nd Regiment, 28 February 1917, AG to OC MD 1, 4 April 1917.
94 LAC, RG 24, vol. 336, file 33-2-117, OC MD 1 to Militia HQ, 10 July 1917.
95 LAC, RG 24, vol. 336, file 33-2-117, AG to DOC MD 1, 23 August 1917.

96 TNA, CO 42/1004, War Office to Under Secretary of State for the Colonies, 9 May 1917.
97 LAC, Albert Edward Kemp fonds, MG 27, II D9, vol. 73, Colonel S.C. Mewburn to Kemp, 6 March 1917.
98 LAC, RG 24, vol. 5872, file 7-55-23, OC 53rd Regiment to GOC MD 4, 30 March 1917.
99 LAC, RG 24, vol. 1403, file 593-6-2, vol. 25, OC 174th Battalion to DG Mobilization, n.d. but late March 1917.
100 AO, Sydney Chilton Mewburn fonds, ms 798, reel 1, Series 1, Kemp to Mewburn, 8 March 1917.
101 DHH, 74/672, box 4 folder 13, file CDF.
102 48th Highlanders of Canada Regimental Museum, box CDF, R.E. Haldenby to Mr. White, 17 June 1917.
103 LAC, RG 24, vol. 4547, file 78-1-1, AG circular letter, 22 May 1917.
104 *Toronto Star*, 20 July 1915, 2.
105 48th Highlanders Regimental Museum, box CDF, Regimental recruiting forms for 203 men rejected between May 1915 and June 1917.
106 *Hamilton Spectator*, 6 August 1915, 1, 14.
107 LAC, RG 24, vol. 4425, file 26-5-64-2, vol. 1, MD 3 to Militia HQ 1 June 1917; taken from scattered correspondence in vols 1–3.
108 LAC, RG 9, II F9, vol. 39, file "Recruiting March 1916 to November 1916," Pay lists London Recruiting Depot, Windsor Recruiting Officer and Windsor Mobilization Centre; *London Advertiser*, 29 December 1916, 11.
109 LAC, RG 9, II F9, vol. 1383, file MD 11, Recruiting Staff Nov 1915– March 1917.
110 DHH, *Minutes of the Militia Council 1917*, p. 1172, 18 October 1917.
111 LAC, RG 24, vol. 4593, file 20-10, vol. 10, AG to MD 10, 4 November 1915.
112 LAC, RG 9, II F9, vol. 1296, files "MD 10 Recruiting Area B February 1916," "MD 10 Recruiting Area C December 1915–January 1916," and 'MD 10 Recruiting Area D November 1915–February 1916'; LAC, RG 9, II F9, vol. 1297, "MD 10 Recruiting Area D February 1916"; LAC, RG 24, vol. 4593, file 20-10 vol. 10, HQ MD 10 to 188th Battalion, 10 February 1916.
113 LAC, RG 24, vol. 1311, file 593-3-7, Prime Minister to F.B. McCurdy, 18 August 1916; AG to Militia Council, 23 August 1916; AG Circular Letter, 12 September 1916.
114 LAC, RG 24, vol. 4311, file 34-1-59-M, AG Circular Letter, 12 September 1916.

115 LAC, RG 24, vol. 1311, file 593-3-7, DOC MD 12 to AG, 25 October 1916; LAC, RG 24, vol. 4509, file 17-1-49, vol. XII, MD 11 to Militia HQ, 28 September 1916; MD 5 to Militia HQ, 29 March 1917.
116 *Toronto Star*, 1 February 1917, 14. Details of mobilization centres c. spring 1918 were found in LAC, RG 24, vol. 4311, file 34-1-59-L; LAC, RG 4311, file 24-1-59-M, vol. 1, 248th Battalion to Chief Recruiting Officer MD 2, 23 April 1917.
117 LAC, RG 24, vol. 4311, MD 2 to Militia HQ, 18 July 1918, RG 42, vol. 4311, file 34-1-59-L, Toronto Mobilization Centre to HQ MD 2, 28 November 1917.
118 LAC, RG 24, vol. 4310, file 34-1-59, vol. 2, Toronto Mobilization Centre to HQ MD 2, 20 August 1917.
119 Great Britain, House of Commons, The War Cabinet. *Report for the Year 1917* (London: HMSO, 1918), 85.

CHAPTER SIX

1 War Office, Great Britain, *Infantry Training 1914* (London: HMSO, 1914), 1.
2 Peter Anderson, *I That's Me: Escape from a German Prisoner-of-War Camp* (Edmonton: Bradburn, c. 1920), 23.
3 LAC, Leckie fonds, MG 30, E84, OC 16th Battalion to A/OC 72nd Regiment [Vancouver], 20 September 1914.
4 Anderson, *I That's Me*, 23.
5 R.C. Fetherstonhaugh, *The Thirteenth Battalion, Royal Highlanders of Canada, 1914–1919* (Montreal: The Thirteenth Battalion, Royal Highlanders of Canada, 1925), 9; Kenneth Radley, *We Lead, Others Follow: First Canadian Division 1914–1918* (St Catharines: Vanwell Publishing Limited, 2006), 59.
6 Daniel Dancocks, *Gallant Canadians: The Story of the Tenth Canadian Infantry Battalion, 1914–1919* (Calgary: The Calgary Highlanders Regimental Funds Foundation, 1994), 8; Lieutenant-Colonel H.M. Urquhart, *The History of the 16th Battalion (The Canadian Scottish) in the Great War 1914–1919* (Toronto: The Macmillan Company of Canada Limited, 1932), 17.
7 Lauren Abrams et al., eds. *The Hour of Trial & Sorrow: The Great War Letters of the Leonard Family* (London, ON: University of Western Ontario, 2015), 74.
8 LAC, RG 9, III D3, vol. 4823, file 35-36, Part 2, reel T-7182, War Diary 1st Canadian Division General Staff, 14 November 1914, Appendix 8.

9 LAC, RG 9, III C3 folder 51, file 5, GOC Canadian Contingent to HQ Southern Command, 6 November 1914.
10 Colonel A. Fortescue Duguid, *Official History of the Canadian Forces in the Great War 1914–1919: General Series,* vol. 1 (Ottawa: King's Printer, 1938), 130.
11 LAC, RG 9, III D3, vol. 4866, file 187, reel T-10665, 1st Brigade War Diary, 27 November and 11 December 1914; LAC, RG 9, III D3, vol. 4870, file 200, reel T-10668, 2nd Brigade War Diary 27 November 1914.
12 Kenneth Radley, *We Lead, Others Follow: First Canadian Division 1914–1918* (St Catharines: Vanwell Publishing Limited, 2006) 67–9.
13 TNA, Kitchener papers, PRO 30/57/56, Lewis Harcourt to Lord Kitchener, 16 December 1914.
14 LAC, RG 9, III A1, vol. 44, file 8-5-10, War Office to HQ Eastern Command and 23rd Division, 19 March 1915; MacDougall to Carson, 24 March 1915; Carson to MacDougall, 25 March 1915.
15 Gordan Corrigan, *Mud, Blood and Poppycock* (London: Cassell, 2003), 45.
16 Jill Knight, *The Civil Service Rifles in the Great War: "All Bloody Gentlemen"* (Barnsley, South Yorkshire: Pen & Sword Military, 2005), 31.
17 Captain Basil Williams, *Raising and Training the New Armies* (London: Constable and Company, 1918), 10.
18 Andrew Iarocci, *Shoestring Soldiers: The 1st Canadian Division at War, 1914–1915* (Toronto: University of Toronto Press, 2008), 270.
19 Radley, *We Lead, Others Follow,* 47.
20 Duguid, *Official History: General Series,* vol. 1, 53.
21 Desmond Morton, *When Your Number's Up: The Canadian Soldier in the First World War* (Toronto: Random House of Canada, 1993), 9.
22 Harold Baldwin, *Holding the Line* (Chicago: A.C. McClurg & Co., 1918), 3.
23 Taken from discharge papers in WO 97. It is acknowledged that the sample is too small to be statistically reliable. Nor is there any evidence that the discharge papers in WO 97 are complete.
24 Fort Garry Horse Regimental Museum (Winnipeg), The Fort Garry Horse – Nominal Roll – Pre World War I (unpublished mss, n.d.).
25 *Chatham Daily Planet,* 20 August 1914, 8; Oxford Museum, box Oxford Rifles Number 3 22nd Regiment, Record of Service 1907–1923.
26 Elgin Military Museum, 25th Regiment Service Roll.
27 TNA, WO 123/56, Army Order 388 of 13 September 1914.
28 George H. Cassar, *Hell in Flanders Fields: Canadians at the Second Battle of Ypres* (Toronto: Dundurn Press, 2010), 64.

29 TNA, WO 123/56 Army Order 324 of 21 August 1914; LAC, RG 24, vol. 1335, file 593-3-21, vol. 1, CGS to OC 6th Division, 12 December 1914.
30 LAC, RG 24, vol. 782, file 54-21-8-12, Condensed Report by Inspector General of Western Canada: Units Mobilized in MD 13, Calgary, 26 February 1915.
31 TNA, WO 293/2, War Office Instruction 156 of 16 June 1915, Appendix VI; TNA, WO 123/199, BEF Routine Order 163 of 29 May 1915.
32 LAC, RG 9, III D1, vol. 4699 folder 68, file 3, 100th Battalion Historical Records compiled 14 December 1916; HQ MD 10 "Syllabus for Ten Weeks Training." Issued spring 1916. The syllabus is almost identical to WO1 156, in DHH, 74/672, box 10, file "Training in Canada."
33 LAC, RG 9, III D1, vol. 4699 folder 69, file 15, Historical Record 112th Battalion.
34 LAC, Joseph Phillipe Landry fonds, MG 30, E17, vol. 22, file 22-13, Syllabus for a Ten Week's Training, 17 November 1915.
35 TNA, WO 293/4, ACI 1103 of 31 May 1916.
36 TNA, WO 293/5, ACI 1968 of 15 October 1916.
37 TNA, WO 293/7, ACI 1230 of 6 August 1917.
38 LAC, RG 9, III A1, vol. 54, file Progress Reports October 1918, General Staff Report.
39 LAC, RG 9, II B5, vol. 7, Abridged Annual Report Upon the 207th Overseas Battalion CEF, 16 January 1917.
40 LAC, RG 24, vol. 1403, file 593-6-2, vol. 24, Lieutenant-Colonel C.J. Mersereau to GOC New Brunswick Troops, 16 March 1917.
41 LAC, RG 24, vol. 347, file 33-18-45, Commandant's Report 1917 [St Charles, Manitoba, 9 July–7 October 1917]; LAC, RG 24, vol. 336, file 33-2-117; Militia Order 236 of 27 August 1917, MD1 to Militia HQ, 10 July 1917.
42 LAC, Albert Edward Kemp fonds, MG 27, D9, vol. 75, file 100 "Reinforcements 1917," CGS to Minister, 16 July 1917.
43 LAC, RG 9, III B1, vol. 773, file R-9-2, 1st Canadian Training Brigade to HQ CTD, 10 June 1916.
44 LAC, RG 9, III B1, vol. 510, file T-81-1, HQ Crowborough to HQ CTD Brighton, 13 November 1916; LAC, RG 9, III D3, vol. 4865, file 184, reel T-10655, War Diary Canadian HQ Bramshott, February 1917 Appendix 3, dated 8 March 1917.
45 TNA, WO 32/9557, "Number of Men Necessary to Maintain the Forces in the Field," 29 March 1918; Charles Messenger, *Call to Arms: The British Army, 1914–1918* (London: Weidenfeld & Nicolson, 2005), 274–5.
46 TNA, WO 95/26, War Diary AG GHQ, Monthly Statement of Casualties, Reinforcements and Strength by Divisions: Infantry and Cavalry only, February 1918.

47 LAC, RG 9, III D3, vol. 4865, file 185, reel T-10665, War Diary Canadian Troops Witley, 24 March 1918, Annex D.
48 LAC, RG 9, III A1, vol. 54, file Progress Reports July 1918, General Staff Report.
49 LAC, RG 9, III A2, vol. 354, file 39, HQ OMFC to HQ Canadian Corps, 15 September 1918.
50 LAC, RG 9, III A4, vol. 354, file 30, Strength returns of men in training by week.
51 TNA, WO 95/26, WD AG GHQ, Monthly Statement of Casualties, Reinforcements and Strength by Divisions: Infantry and Cavalry only, August and September 1918.
52 TNA, WO 293/7, ACI 1230 of 6 August 1917 and ACI 1807 of 12 December 1917; TNA, WO 293/9, ACI 876 of 7 August 1918 and ACI 1253 of 9 November 1918.
53 TNA, WO 293/7, ACI 1230 of 6 August 1917.
54 TNA, WO 95/4185, War Diary 2nd General Base Depot, 15 February 1915.
55 LAC, RG 9, III A2, vol. 355, file 5, OC No. 3 (British). Base Depot to DA AG Canadian Section GHQ 3rd Echelon, 10 September 1915.
56 John Harold Becker, *Silhouettes of the Great War: The Memoir of John Harold Becker 1915–1919* (Ottawa: CEF Books, 2001), 57–8.
57 LAC, RG 9, III C1, vol. 3870, folder 112, file 13, *System of Testing & Training Reinforcements carried out by Base Training Schools*, BEF issued by Lieutenant-General J.J. Asser, C.B., GOC L. of C. Area (Army Printing and Stationary Services, n.d. c. February 1917).
58 LAC, RG 9, III C13, vol. 4605 folder 21, 5th Canadian Reserve Brigade Circular Letter, 23 November 1917, with a copy of the Inspector of Infantry's report on the Bull Ring.
59 C.E.W. Bean, *Official History of Australia in the Great War of 1914–1918*, vol. 3, *The AIF in France 1916* (Sydney, Australia: Angus and Robertson, 1920), 177.
60 LAC, RG 9, III B1, vol. 974, file O-136-3, GOC to DAA & QMG Canadian Corps, 7 July 1918.
61 LAC, RG 24, vol. 366, file 33-127-11, Chief Musketry Officer to GSO Camp Valcartier, 28 October 1915.
62 Major E.G.B. Reynolds, *The Lee–Enfield Rifle* (New York: Arco Publishing Company, 1962), 114.
63 Unless otherwise noted all data concerning weapons and ammunition holdings has been taken from LAC, RG 24, Series C-1-b reel C-5050, Parts 8, 9, 10, 11, and 12, "Naval, Military and Air Resources – Annual Returns."

64 Roger F. Phillips, Francis Dupuis, and John Chadwick, *A Technical Appraisal of the Ross Rifle* (Antigonish: Casket Printing and Publishing Co., 1984), 459.

65 LAC, RG 24, vol. 4335, file 34-3-15, OC 2nd Division to Militia HQ, 12 March 1915.

66 LAC, RG 24, vol. 4335, file 34-3-15, Director of Musketry circular letter, 4 February 1915.

67 LAC, RG 24, vol. 4335, file 34-3-15, GSO 2nd Division to 4 CMR, 19th and 20th Battalions, 7 March 1915.

68 LAC, RG 24, vol. 344, file 33-11-142, Report on Aldershot Camp Nova Scotia 1916, 14 December 1916.

69 LAC, RG 24, vol. 413, file 54-21-1-20 vol. 1, Draft "Memorandum (No 3), Respecting the Work of the Department of Militia and Defence from 1st February to 31st December 1916," signed by CGS, 1 December 1916.

70 LAC, RG 24, vol. 1337, file 393-2-21, vol. 7, MGO to MD 1 30 December 1915.

71 LAC, RG 24, vol. 1337, file 593-3-21, vol. 8, 162nd Battalion Training Report for Week Ending March 25th 1916.

72 LAC, RG 24, vol. 336, file 33-127-11, Chief Musketry Officer to GSO Valcartier, 28 October 1915; LAC, RG 24, vol. 365, file 33-96-104, Report on the Training Camp Held at Camp Hughes, Man., from May 22nd until 3rd November 1915.

73 DHH, 74/672, box 10, folder Training XVI-6, Commandant Camp Hughes to Militia HQ, 17 June 1916.

74 LAC, RG 24, vol. 1339, vol. 13, file "Training 2nd and Subsequent Contingents, European War," GSO Camp Hughes to DMT Militia HQ, 9 July 1916.

75 LAC, RG 24, vol. 1167, file 64-82-1, vol. 3, Abridged Annual Report upon 35th Battalion, 26 March 1915.

76 LAC, RG 24, vol. 1167, file 64-82-1, vol. 3, Report of the Annual Inspection 1915 of the 38th Battalion, 15 April 1915; LAC, RG 9, III B5, vol. 6, file "80th–89th Battalions CEF," Abridged Annual Report upon 88th Overseas Battalion CEF, 20 January 1916; LAC, RG 24, vol. 1337, file 593-3-21, vol. 7, Weekly Training Report of the 90th Canadian Overseas Battalion (Winnipeg Rifles), for week ending December 18th 1915.

77 LAC, RG 24, vol. 1337, file 593-2-21, vol. 6, QMG to OC 2nd Division, 5 November 1915.

78 LAC, RG 24, vol. 1337, file 593-2-21, vol. 8, OC 3rd Division to Militia HQ, 14 March 1916.

79 LAC, RG 24, vol. 1337, file 593-2-21, vol. 6, QMG to DOC MD 10, 6 August 1915.
80 LAC, RG 24, vol. 1337, file 593-2-21, vol. 8, Principal Ordnance Officer to Director of Military Training, 15 February 1916.
81 LAC, RG 24, vol. 1335, file 593-3-1, vol. 2, 2nd Divisional Cyclist Company to GSO 2nd Division, 25 January 1916; Inspector General's Report on 50th Battalion, 26 February 1915; Inspector General's Report on 35th Battalion, February 1915.
82 *St. Marys Argus*, 3 February 1916, 4.
83 LAC, RG 9, III D 1, vol. 4701, folder 74, file 17, 119th Battalion to HQ MD 2, 25 March 1916, DHH, 74/672, box 10, folder Training XVI-6; 157th Battalion Historical Records, 6 December 1916.
84 LAC, RG 24, vol. 1337, file 593-3-21, vol. 7, GOC 2nd Division to Militia HQ, 5 January 1916; LAC, RG 24, vol. 1337, file 593-3-21, vol. 7, Weekly Training Report, 18 December 1915; DHH, 74/672, box 10, file Training XVI-6, Abridged Annual Report upon 109th Battalion, 9 January 1916.
85 LAC, RG 24, vol. 1166, file 64-82-1, vol. 1, Abridged Annual Report upon 2nd Divisional Engineers, 18 March 1915.
86 LAC, RG 24, vol. 1337, file 593-3-21, vol. 6, Sarcee Camp Commandant to Militia HQ, 12 July 1915.
87 LAC, RG 9, II B 5, vol. 6, file 80th–89th Battalions CEF, Report of the Annual Inspection 1916 of the Eighty-Second Battalion CEF, 11 January 1916; LAC, RG 9, II B 5, vol. 6, file 100th–109th Battalions CEF, Abridged Annual Report upon 101st Overseas Battalion CEF 10 April 1916 and Abridged Annual Report upon 108th Overseas Battalion CEF, 9 August 1916.
88 LAC, RG 24, vol. 1166, file 64-82, vol. 1, Abridged Annual Report upon 8th Regt Canadian Mounted Rifles, 19 March 1915, 1; LAC, RG 9, II B 5, vol. 6, file 80th–89th Battalions CEF, Abridged Inspection Report upon the 83rd Overseas Battalion, 18 November 1915; LAC, RG 9, II B 5, vol. 6, file 90th–99th Battalions CEF, Abridged Annual Report upon 92nd Battalion, 23 November 1915; LAC, RG 9, II B 5, vol. 6, file 70th–79th Battalions CEF, Abridged Annual Report upon 78th Battalion, 23 September 1915.
89 LAC, RG 24, vol. 4335, file 34-3-15, OC 2nd Division to Militia HQ, 28 April 1915.
90 LAC, RG 24, vol. 1336, file 593-3-21, vol. 5, OA 1st Divisional Area to Militia HQ, 30 June 1915 and reply 3 July 1915.
91 LAC, RG 24, vol. 365, file 33-96-104, Report on the Training Camp for Units of the Canadian Expeditionary Force Held at Camp Hughes, Man., from May 22nd until 3rd November 1915.

92 LAC, RG 24, vol. 413, file 54-21-1-20, vol. 1, MGO to Deputy Minister, 9 March 1916; LAC, RG 24, vol. 1336, file 593-3-21, vol. 3, Director of Musketry to Director of Clothing and Equipment, 31 March 1915.
93 LAC, RG 24, vol. 6553, file 802-8, vol. 4, CGS circular letter, 15 July 1916.
94 LAC, RG 24, vol. 1336, file 593-3-21, vol. 3, Director of Musketry to Director of Clothing and Equipment, 18 March 1915.
95 LAC, RG 24, vol. 1339, file 593-3-21, vol. 13, 96th Battalion to GSO MD 10, 27 May 1916.
96 Colonel G.W.L. Nicholson, *The Gunners of Canada*, vol. 1 (Toronto: McClelland and Stewart, 1967), 178; Roger F. Phillips, Francis Dupuis, and John Chadwick, *The Ross Rifle Story* (Sydney, Nova Scotia: J.A. Chadwick, 1984), 79–81, 83.
97 LAC, RG 24, vol. 1337, file 593-3-21, vol. 6, Camp Musketry Officer to Commandant Camp Sarcee, 7 August 1915.
98 LAC, RG 9, III B1, vol. 773, file R-9-2, vol. 1, 12th Reserve Battalion to 10th Reserve Brigade, 7 February 1916, 3rd Canadian Training Brigade to Canadian Training Division, 17 May 1916; LAC, RG 9, III B1, vol. 773, file R-9-2, vol. 2, 1st Canadian Training Brigade to Canadian Training Division, 10 June 1916.
99 LAC, RG 9, III B1, vol. 773, file R-4-2, vol. 1, 2, 3, and 4 with inspection reports for various units.
100 LAC, RG 9, III A1, vol. 53, file Monthly Reports June 1917, General Staff Report.
101 LAC, RG 24, vol. 1833, file GAC 8-19, p. 4, Colt and Lewis Machine Guns.
102 LAC, RG 24, vol. 1336, file 593-3-21, vol. 3, Director of Musketry to MD 11, 6 April 1915.
103 LAC, RG 24, vol. 4387, file 34-7-139, Chief Instructor Canadian School of Musketry to HQ MD 2, 18 April 1917.
104 LAC, RG 24, vol. 6409, file 120, vol. 1, Report of the Annual Inspection of the 63rd Regiment Halifax Rifles, 1 March 1915.
105 LAC, RG 24, vol. 413, file 54-21-1-20, vol. 1, MGO to Deputy Minister, 9 March 1916.
106 Lieutenant-Colonel C.S. Grafton, *The Canadian Emma Gees: A History of the Canadian Machine Gun Corps* (London, ON: Hunter Printing Company, c. 1938), 37; LAC, RG 9, III B1, vol. 511, file T-83-1, HQ Eastern Command to HQ Canadians Brighton, 24 November 1916.
107 LAC, RG 24, vol. 365, file 33-96-104, Report on the Training Camp Held at Camp Hughes, Man., from May 22nd until 3rd November 1915.

108 LAC, RG 9, II B5, vol. 6, file 70th–79th Battalions CEF, Abridged Annual Report Upon the 74th Overseas Battalion, 30 November 1915; LAC, RG 24, vol. 1831, file GAC 7-46, HQ MD 2 to Militia HQ, 3 May 1916.
109 DHH, 74/672, box 10, folder Training XVI-6, 101st Battalion to HQ MD 10, 18 March 1916.
110 LAC, RG 24, vol. 1337, file 593-3-21, vol. 7, QMG to OC 1st Division, 30 December 1915.
111 DHH, 74/672, box 10 folder Training XVI-6, 118th Battalion training report, 4 March 1916.
112 DHH, 74/672, box 10 folder Training XVI-6, 153rd Battalion to HQ MD 1, 29 June 1916, 161st Battalion to HQ MD 1, 30 June 1916.
113 Bill Rawling, *Surviving Trench Warfare: Technology and the Canadian Corps, 1914–1918* (Toronto: University of Toronto Press, 1992), 58.
114 LAC, RG 9, III A1, vol. 53, file "Monthly Reports 1917," QMG OMFC to War Purchasing Committee, 1 March 1917
115 DHH, 74/672, box 10, folder Training XVI-6, HQ MD 13 to Militia HQ, 5 May 1916.
116 LAC, RG 24, vol. 1583, file 683-239-5, "Report of the Annual Inspection 1916 of the 151st Overseas Battalion CEF," 23 September 1916; LAC, RG 9, III D1, vol. 4700 folder 71, file 20; LAC, RG 9, III D1, vol. 4700 folder 72, file 12, 128th Battalion Historical Record, 31 March 1917, 134th Battalion Historical Records, 8 January 1917. LAC, RG 24, vol. 4259, file 34-26-1, Militia HQ circular letter, 24 December 1917.
117 LAC, RG 24, vol. 4259, file 34-26-1, Militia HQ circular letter 24 December 1917.
118 LAC, RG 9, III D3, vol. 4865, reel T-10655, War Diary Canadian HQ Bramshott February 1917, Appendix 2; Rawling, *Surviving Trench Warfare*, 75.
119 LAC, Richard Ernest William Turner fonds, MG 30, E46, vol. 10, file 72, Memorandum on Training of Reinforcements in Canada and England forwarded by General Staff to GOC OMFC, 25 May 1917.
120 LAC, Richard Ernest William Turner fonds, MG 30, E46, vol. 10, file 72, Sir George Perley to Sir Edward Kemp, 13 June 1917.
121 LAC, RG 24, vol. 4372, file 34-7-45, AG to OC 2nd Division 1– July 1915; LAC, RG 9, II A2, vol. 33, file Minutes of the Militia Council 1916, Militia Order 72 of 1916; Minutes p. 79, 8 May 1916.
122 DHH, CEF General Instruction Number 73 of 24 September 1917; DHH, CEF Routine Order Number 882 of 7 August 1918.

123 LAC, RG 24, vol. 365, file 33-96-104, Report on the Training Camp Held at Camp Hughes, Man., from May 22nd Until 3rd November 1915.
124 LAC, RG 9, II B 5, vol. 6, file 90th–99th Battalions CEF, Report of the Annual Inspection 1916 of the 96th Overseas Battalion CEF, 19 September 1916.
125 DHH, 74/672, box 10, folder Training XVI-6, DOC MD 1 to Militia HQ, 28 July 1916, DOC MD 2 to Militia HQ, 28 July 1916, Commandant Camp Sarcee to Militia HQ, 11 September 1916.
126 LAC, RG 24, vol. 4680, file 18-29-2, Historical Record of the 232nd Overseas Battalion CEF.
127 DHH, 74/672, box 10, folder Training XVI-6, GSO Camp Hughes to Militia HQ, 20 August 1916.
128 LAC, RG 24, vol. 1335, file 593-3-21, vol. 2, OC Divisional Supply Column to GSO 2nd Division, 25 January 1915.
129 LAC, RG 24, vol. 1335, file 593-3-21, vol. 2, MD 13 to Militia HQ, 4 February 1915.
130 LAC, RG 9, II B 5, vol. 5, file Miscellaneous CEF Units, Condensed Report by Inspector General of Western Canada, 3rd Regiment CMR, 6 March 1915.
131 LAC, RG 24, vol. 1401, file 593-6-2, vol. 19, Commandant Camp Hughes to Militia HQ, 2 October 1916.
132 LAC, RG 24, vol. 358, file 33-24-102, Commandant Mobilization Camp, Calgary to Militia HQ, 28 June 1915.
133 LAC, RG 9, II B 5, vol. 6, file 80th–89th Battalions CEF, Abridged Annual Report upon the 88th Battalion CEF, 20 January 1916.
134 LAC, RG 9, III D 1, vol. 4698, folder 67, file 10, 94th Battalion Historical Records.
135 LAC, RG 9, III D 1, vol. 4699, folder 68, file 5, 101st Battalion Historical Records.
136 LAC, RG 24, vol. 1337, file 593-3-21, vol. 8, OA 1st Divisional Area to Militia HQ, 19 January 1916.
137 LAC, RG 24, vol. 1337, file 593-3-21, vol. 7, QMG to 5th Division, 15 January 1916; Simcoe County Archives, *Barrack Bugle* 1, no. 15 (20 March 1916), 2.
138 LAC, RG 9, II B 5, vol. 6, file 70th–79th Battalions CEF, Abridged Annual Report upon the 75th Overseas Battalion CEF, 16 November 1915.
139 LAC, Albert Edward Kemp fonds, MG 27, II D9, vol. 73, file 68, Gwatkin to "My Dear General" (Turner), 31 December 1916.

140 DHH, 74/672, box 10, file "Training in Canada," Extract from Memorandum No. 3: Work of Dept Mil & Def from February 1, 1916 to December 31, 1916.
141 LAC, Richard Ernest William Turner fonds, MG 30, E46, vol. 10, file 72, Turner to Militia HQ, 19 February 1917.
142 LAC, RG 9, III A1, vol. 53, file Monthly Reports, June 1917, General Staff Report.
143 LAC, RG 9, III A1, vol. 53, file Monthly Reports, June 1917, General Staff Report.
144 LAC, Richard Ernest William Turner fonds, MG 30, E46, vol. 10, file 72, GSO HQ OMFC to GOC OMFC, 25 May 1917.
145 LAC, Richard Ernest William Turner fonds, MG 30, E46, vol. 10, file 72, Perley to Kemp, 13 June 1917; LAC, RG 9, III A1, vol. 74, file 10-08-21, part 1, Perley to Kemp, 12 October 1917,
146 LAC, RG 24, vol. 4615, file 1G 1, vol. 3, European War. Memorandum No. 4 Respecting Work of the Department of Militia and Defence from January 1, 1917 to December 31, 1917.
147 LAC, RG 9, III D3, vol. 5062, file 981, reel T-11126, War Diary 1st Depot Battalion, New Brunswick Regiment, HQ MD 7 to Militia HQ, 26 June 1918.
148 LAC, Albert Edward Kemp fonds, MG 27, II D9, vol. 142, file 4, Kemp to Borden, 8 February 1918.
149 J.A. Salter, *Allied Shipping Control: An Experiment in International Administration* (Oxford: Clarendon Press, 1921), 153–4, 185.
150 LAC, RG 9, III D3, vol. 5062, file 981, reel T-11126, War Diary 1st Depot Battalion New Brunswick Regiment, Training Orders, c. 2 July 1918.
151 LAC, RG 24, vol. 1437, file 593-6-26, vol. 4, Abridged Reports on Drafts 69, 79, 80, 88, 89, 91,120, 127, 129, 130, 131, 132.
152 LAC, RG 9, III A1, vol. 44, file 8-5-10, Carson to Minister of Militia and Defence, 18 February 1915.
153 DHH, Historical Report No. 98, n.d., declassified 3 December 1986, *The Command of the Overseas Military Forces of Canada in the United Kingdom, 1914–1918*, pp. 13–15; Desmond Morton, *A Peculiar Kind of Politics* (Toronto: University of Toronto Press, 1982), 37.
154 P.C. 107 of 15 January 1915, reproduced in Colonel A. Fortescue Duguid, *Official History of the Canadian Forces in the Great War 1914–1919: Chronology, Appendices and Maps*, 136–7.
155 Morton, *A Peculiar Kind of Politics*, 37.

156 LAC, RG 9, III A1, vol. 53, file Monthly Reports February 1917, Adjutant General and General Staff Reports.
157 DHH, Historical Report no. 98, n.d., declassified 3 December 1986, *The Command of the Overseas Military Forces of Canada in the United Kingdom, 1914–1918*, 27–8; Morton, *A Peculiar Kind of Politics*, 48–9.
158 LAC, RG 9, III A1, vol. 53, file Monthly Reports February 1917, General Staff Report.
159 LAC, RG 24, vol. 1841, file GAC 10-39D, Steele to Carson, 12 October 1915.
160 LAC, RG 9, III B1, vol. 719, file 1-118-2, Inspector of Infantry to HQ Home Forces, 12 February 1916.
161 Fred Bagley and Harvey Daniel Duncan, *A Legacy of Courage: Calgary's Own 137th Overseas Battalion, CEF* (Calgary: Plug Street Books, 1993), 98–9; James L. McWilliams and R. James Steel, *The Suicide Battalion* (Edmonton: Hurtig Publishers, 1978), 25–6.
162 LAC, RG 9, III A1, vol. 52, file 8-7-1A, GSO to GOC CTD Shorncliffe, 31 March 1916.
163 LAC, RG 9, III A1, vol. 53, file Monthly Reports February 1917, General Staff Report.
164 LAC, RG 9, III A1, vol. 53, file Monthly Reports February 1917 General Staff Report.
165 LAC, RG 9, III D3, vol. 4865, file 184, reel T-10665, War Diary CTD Bramshott February 1917, GS/C-301, 8 March 1917.
166 LAC, RG 24, vol. 1813, file GAC 4-15L, The Expansion of the Canadian Militia for the War 1914–1918, 30 March 1925.
167 LAC, RG 9, III A1, vol. 53, file Monthly Reports June 1917, General Staff Report.
168 LAC, RG 9, III B1, vol. 418, file E-60-1, General Staff (Musketry) to GOC CTD, 17 July 1916.
169 LAC, RG 9, III A1, vol. 53, file Monthly Reports February 1917, GHQ to War Office 6 October 1916.
170 LAC, Albert Edward Kemp fonds, MG 27, II D9, vol. 71, file 28, Minister of Militia and Defence Private Secretary to QMG 26 February 1916, quoting OMFC telegram of 23 February 1917.
171 LAC, RG 9, III D3, vol. 4955, file 494, reel T-10772, War Diary Lord Strathcona's Horse, 1 May 1915.
172 Rawling, *Surviving Trench Warfare*, 63–5.
173 LAC, RG 9, III B1, vol. 552, file U-4-1, CGBD to CTD, 19 June 1916.
174 LAC, RG 9, III vol. 52, file 8-71, CTD Routine Order 1459 of 19 July 1915, the 23rd to provide reinforcements to the 14th and 24th

Battalions; LAC, RG 9, III B1, vol. 494, file R-147-1, CTD Routine Order 2969 of 13 October 1915, the 23rd to reinforce the 3rd Battalion.
175 LAC, RG 9, III B1, vol. 678, file E-137-2, 23rd Reserve Battalion to HQ 12th Canadian Reserve Infantry Brigade, 8 January 1916.
176 LAC, RG 9, III B1, vol. 511, file T-86-1, HQ Brighton to Chief Ordnance Office Ashford, 23 November 1916, referring to indents, and HQ CTD to Musketry Officer HQ Brighton, 25 November 1916.
177 LAC, RG 9, III A1, vol. 74, file 10-8-22, vol. 1, Deputy Minister to Chairman Sub-Militia Council, 2 November 1916.
178 LAC, RG 9, III A1, vol. 53, file Monthly Reports February 1917, War Office to QMG, 27 January 1917.
179 LAC, RG 9, C13, vol. 4605, folder 1, HQ Shoreham to 23rd Reserve Battalion, 16 July 1917; TNA, WO 114/32, Weekly Returns 30 July 1917.
180 LAC, RG 9, III C1, vol. 3870, folder 112, file 13, First (British) Army to Canadian Corps, 8 October 1917, quoting a War Office letter of 7 October 1917.
181 LAC, RG 9, III B1, vol. 687, file 25-2-172, OC Reserve Brigade CFA to HQ Canadians, 2 June 1915.
182 LAC, RG 9, III B1, vol. 707, file 1-2-2, vol. 3, 23rd Reserve Battalion to HQ 3rd Canadian Training Brigade, 23 May 1916.
183 LAC, RG 9, III B1, vol. 707, file 1-2-2, vol. 3, 3rd Canadian Training Brigade to HQ CTD, 22 May 1916.
184 LAC, RG 9, III B1, vol. 707, file 1-2-2, vol. 3, 12th Reserve Battalion to HQ 1st Canadian Training Brigade, 22 May 1916.
185 LAC, RG 9, III B1, vol. 707, file 1-2-2, vol. 3, 1st Canadian Training Brigade to HQ CTD, 25 May 1916; RG 9, III A1, vol. 45, file 8-5-10F, Director of Recruiting and Organization to Major-General Carson, 24 July 1916.
186 TNA, WO 114/30, Weekly Returns, 30 October 1916 and 27 November 1916.
187 LAC, RG 24, vol. 1844, file GAC 11-11C, Instructions for Dealing with Casualties and Non-Effectives Generally of the Canadian Overseas Military Forces issued by AG HQ OMFC, 26 February 1917.
188 LAC, Joseph Phillipe Landry fonds, MG 30, E17, vol. 22, file 22-23, War Office circular letter, 26 January 1917.
189 LAC, Joseph Phillipe Landry fonds, MG 30, E17, vol. 22, file 22-23, Army Council Instruction 338 of 24 February 1917.
190 LAC, RG 9, III B1, vol. 752, file O-64-2, CTD Instruction, 13 January 1917.
191 LAC, RG 150, vol. 115, Daily Orders 11th Reserve Battalion, 18 April 1918.

192 LAC, RG 9, III B1, vol. 752, file O-64-2, CTD Instruction, 13 January 1917; LAC, RG 9, III B1, vol. 418, file E-62-1, Engineer Training Depot to OC CTD, 10 October 1916; LAC, RG 9, III B1, vol. 789, file R-43-2, CASC Training Depot to AD of Supply and Transport Shorncliffe Area, 9 January 1917; LAC, RG 9, III C13, vol. 4605, folder 21, HQ Shoreham to 23rd Reserve Battalion, 26 August 1917.

CHAPTER SEVEN

1 David Charles Gregory Campbell, "The Divisional Experience in the C.E.F.: A Social and Operational History of the 2nd Canadian Division, 1915–1918" (PhD diss., University of Calgary, 2003), 538; Kenneth Radley, *We Lead, Others Follow: First Canadian Division 1914–1918* (St Catharines: Vanwell Publishing Limited, 2006), 101–3.
2 R.C. Fetherstonhaugh, *The Royal Canadian Regiment: 1883–1933* (Montreal: Gazette Printing, 1936), 133.
3 War Office, Great Britain, *Field Service Regulations,* part 2, *Organization and Administration,* 1909 (London: HMSO, 1909), 53–6.
4 *Field Service Regulations: Part II,* 54.
5 Major-General Sir W.G. Macpherson, *History of the Great War based on official documents: Medical Services General History,* vol. 1 (London: HMSO, 1921), 18–19.
6 *Field Service Regulations: Part II,* 53–6.
7 Brigadier E.A. James, *British Regiments 1914–1918* (London: Samson Books, 1978), 46–7.
8 Charles Messenger, *Call to Arms: The British Army, 1914–1918* (London: Weidenfeld & Nicolson, 2005, 109; James, *British Regiments 1914–1918,* Table C.
9 MacPherson, *History of the Great War: Medical Services General History,* vol. 1, 91.
10 LAC, RG 9, III A1, vol. 48, file 8-5-58, War Office circular letter, 2 November 1915.
11 John Starling and Ivor Lee, *No Labour, No Battle: Military Labour During the First World War* (Stroud, Glos.: The History Press, 2009), 84–5.
12 Messenger, *Call to Arms,* 222; LAC, RG 9, III D3, vol. 5046, file 910 reel T-10938, War Diary Canadian Section GHQ 3rd Echelon, 5 August 1917.
13 LAC, RG 9, III C4, vol. 4257, folder 37, file 9, Canadian Section GHQ 3rd Echelon to OC CCRC, 14 October 1917.
14 Messenger, *Call to Arms,* 221–2, 273; Australian War Memorial 33/8/2, War Diary 4th Australian Division Base Depot, 30 September 1917.

15 LAC, RG 9, III D3, vol. 5046, file 910, reel T-10938, War Diary Canadian Section GHQ 3rd Echelon, 4 September 1917.
16 DHH, 74/672, box 4, folder 14, file Reinforcements England-France, Historical Summary of the Canadian Corps Reinforcement Camp, Canadian Corps circular letter of 5 September 1917; LAC, RG 9, III D3, vol. 5047, file 913 reel T-10939, War Diary Canadian Corps Reinforcement Camp, 15 September 1917 and 17 October 1917.
17 *Field Service Regulations: Part II*, 56.
18 LAC, RG 9, III D3, vol. 5046, file 910, reel T-10938, War Diary Canadian Section GHQ 3rd Echelon, 13 March 1917 and 30 November 1918.
19 Major G.R.N. Collins, *Military Organization and Administration* (London: Hugh Rees, 1918), 321.
20 Ibid., 321–4.
21 LAC, RG 9, III B1, vol. 489, file R-38-1, vol. 1, HQ Canadians to HQ Brighton, 14 November 1916; LAC, RG 24, vol. 1810, file GAC 1-6, "Canadian Corps Reinforcement Camp."
22 DHH, 74/672, box 33 folder 48, file 2, GOC Canadian Corps to HQ Second (British) Army, 8 February 1916.
23 *Field Service Regulations 1909: Part II*.
24 Brigadier-General J.E. Edmonds, *History of the Great War Based on Official Documents: Military Operations, France and Belgium 1914* (London: Macmillan and Co. 1925), 467.
25 Colonel G.W.L. Nicholson, *Official History of the Canadian Army in the First World War: Canadian Expeditionary Force 1914–1919* (Ottawa: Queen's Printer, 1962), 223.
26 Colonel A. Fortescue Duguid, *Official History of the Canadian Forces in the Great War 1914–1919: General Series*, vol. 1 (Ottawa: King's Printer, 1938), 547.
27 Lieutenant-Colonel T.B. Nicholls, *Organization, Strategy and Tactics of the Army Medical Services in War* (London: Bailliere, Tindall and Cox, 1937), 51.
28 LAC, RG 9, II D3, vol. 5046, file 910, reel T-10938, War Diary Canadian Section GHQ 3rd Echelon, 9 April 1918.
29 LAC, Richard Ernest William Turner fonds, MG 30, E46, vol. 10, file 69, OC CGBD to OC Reinforcements Havre, 20 February 1917.
30 LAC, RG 9, III D3, vol. 5047, file 911, reel T-10938, War Diary Canadian Section GHQ 3rd Echelon, August 1918 Appendix 8; Canadian Section GHQ 3rd Echelon to HQ 1st Canadian Division, 18 August 1918 Appendix 11; Canadian Section GHQ 3rd Echelon to HQ OMFC, 30 August 1918.

31 LAC, RG 9, III D3, vol. 4955, file 490, reel T-10771, War Diary Canadian Light Horse March 1918, Appendix B.
32 Lieutenant-Colonel C.S. Grafton, *The Canadian Emma Gees: A History of the Canadian Machine Gun Corps*, 73.
33 LAC, Albert Edward Kemp fonds, MG 27, II D9, Secret Memorandum on Engineer Services, 7 February 1918, vol. 142, file 4, part 3; Colonel A.J. Kerry and Major W.A. McDill, *The History of the Corps of Royal Canadian Engineers*, vol. 1, 1749–1939 (Ottawa: The Military Engineers Association of Canada, 1962), 129.
34 LAC, RG 9, III D3, vol. 5008, file 711, reel T-10857, War Diary 2nd Canadian Employment Company 18, 25, and 27 June 1917.
35 Overseas Military Forces of Canada, *Report of the Ministry: Overseas Military Forces of Canada 1918* (London: Overseas Military Forces of Canada, 1919), 238.
36 LAC, RG 9, III C3, vol. 4119, folder 4, file 10, OC 25th Battalion to GOC 5th Canadian Infantry Brigade, 16 May 1916.
37 LAC, RG 9, III D3, vol. 4924, file 394, reel T-10719, War Diary 15th Canadian Battalion September 1918, Appendices 209 and 226.
38 TNA, WO 106/411, GHQ to First, Second, Third, Fourth and Fifth Armies, IX Corps, XXII Corps, 14 June 1918.

CHAPTER EIGHT

1 LAC, Willoughby Garnons Gwatkin fonds, MG 30, E51, file Correspondence A–K 1914–1916, Gwatkin to Hughes, 21 September 1914.
2 LAC, RG 24, vol. 1810, file GAC 1-6, Organization of Base Depots and System of Providing Reinforcements.
3 DHH, 74/672, box 10, file 74/672-11-56, CGS to Acting Minister of Militia, 11 October 1914; DHH, 74/672, box 33, folder 48, file 1, AG to MD 13, 15 October 1914.
4 DHH, 74/672, box 33, folder 48, file 1, AG to MD 13, 18 November 1914.
5 DHH, 74/672, box 33, folder 48, file 3, Canadian Army Medical Corps.
6 LAC, RG 24, vol. 1395, file 593-6-2, vol. 1, AG Mobilization to DGMS, 19 January 1915; DHH, 74/672, box 33, folder 48, file 3, Canadian Army Medical Corps.
7 LAC, RG 24, vol. 1397, file 593-6-2, vol. 7, QMG to OC 2nd Division, 11 August 1915.
8 LAC, RG 24, vol. 1397, file 593-6-2, vol. 7, QMG to OC 2nd Division 11 August 1915, AG to Minister of Militia and Defence, 9 September 1915.

9 LAC, RG 24, vol. 1396, file 593-6-2, vol. 6, AG to OC 2nd Division, 11 August 1915.

10 LAC, RG 24, vol. 1403, file 593-6-2, vol. 24, AG to GOC MD 2, 2 February 1917.

11 LAC, Albert Edward Kemp fonds, MG 27, II D9, vol. 75, file 100, Kemp to CGS and AG, 4 July 1917; LAC, RG 24, vol. 1404, file 593-6-2, vol. 2, Militia HQ to HQ OMFC, 5 September 1917.

12 DHH, 74/672, box 33, folder 48, file 3, "Reinforcements by Arms."

13 LAC, RG 24, vol. 4311, file 34-1-59-M, vol. 1, MD 2 to Militia HQ, 26 December 1917.

14 LAC, RG 24, vol. 4606, file 20-10-94, vol. 1, AG to MD 10, 14 March 1916.

15 LAC, RG 24, vol. 4606, file 20-10-94, vol. 1, A&PMG Militia HQ to MD 10, 19 December 1916, AG to MD 10, 24 July 1917.

16 LAC, RG 24, vol. 4593, file 20-10, vol. 10, AG to MD 10, 21 November 1914; DHH, 74/672, box 10, folder 56.

17 DHH, 74/672, box 4, folder 14, file Reinforcements Canada–England, AG circular telegram, 2 November 1914, and Deputy Minister to Governor General, 18 November 1914.

18 LAC, RG 24, vol. 1396, file 593-6-2, vol. 6, AG to Minister of Militia and Defence, 4 August 1915.

19 LAC, RG 9, III A1, vol. 98, file 10-14-19, vol. 3, *Memoranda Respecting Work of the Department of Militia and Defence: European War 1914–1915* (Ottawa: Government Printing Bureau, n.d.), 8.

20 LAC, RG 24, vol. 4593, file 20-10 vol. 10, AG to DOC MD 10, 28 January 1915.

21 Militia Order Number 301 of 16 June 1915 to Militia Order Number 495 of 9 November 1915.

22 LAC, RG 9, III A1, vol. 52, file 8-7-1A, GOC Canadians to Militia HQ, 26 March 1915.

23 *Official Report of the Debates of the House of Commons of the Dominion of Canada*, 12 Parliament, 5th Session, vol. 121, p. 2368 [within Prime Minister Borden's speech of 10 April 1915] (Ottawa: King's Printer, 1915).

24 LAC, RG 9, III vol. 52, file 8-71, Carson to Hughes, 14 June 1915.

25 LAC, RG 24, vol. 4593, file 20-10, vol. 10, DOC MD 10 to CGS, 14 November 1914.

26 LAC, RG 24, vol. 4536, file 31-1-143, vol. 2, 6th Division to Militia HQ, 4 November 1914.

27 LAC, RG 24, vol. 1396, file 593-6-2, vol. 6, Commandant Camp Sewell to Militia HQ, 4 August 1915 and reply 5 August 1915; AG to MD 13, 5 August 1915.

28 LAC, RG 9, III A1, vol. 52, file 8-7-1A, CTD Routine Order 1459 of 19 July 1915; LAC, William Antrobus Griesbach fonds, MG 30, E15, vol. 1, file Griesbach to Hughes, 21 July 1915.
29 LAC, RG 24, vol. 1395, file 593-6-2, vol. 1, AG to 4th Division, 16 February 1915.
30 LAC, RG 24, vol. 1397, file 593-6-2, vol. 7, AG to 4th Division, 10 September 1915.
31 LAC, RG 24, vol. 1397, file 593-6-2, vol. 7, AG to 4th Division 13 September 1915.
32 DHH, 74/672, box 33, folder 50, file 1, War Office to Minister of Militia, 29 April 1915.
33 Colonel A. Fortescue Duguid, *Official History of the Canadian Forces in the Great War 1914–1919: Chronology, Appendices and Maps*, 368–72.
34 LAC, RG 24, vol. 1397, file 593-6-2, vol. 8, Private Secretary to AG, 4 October 1915.
35 LAC, RG 24, vol. 1399, file 593-6-2, vol. 12, AG to Minister, 29 November 1915.
36 LAC, RG 24, vol. 1400, file 593-6-2, vol. 15, AG to Minister in Council, 8 June 1916.
37 LAC, RG 24, vol. 1399, file 593-6-2, vol. 12, H.D. Symes to Secretary to Governor General, 19 November 1915, quoting a letter from an unnamed officer of the 33rd Battalion, 17 November 1915.
38 LAC, RG 24, vol. 1298, file 593-6-2, vol. 10, Anonymous soldier to Militia HQ, January 1916.
39 LAC, RG 24, vol. 1401, file 593-6-2, vol. 18, 3rd Infantry Brigade to GOC Camp Valcartier, 29 August 1916.
40 LAC, RG 24, vol. 1401, file 593-6-2, vol. 18, DG Mobilization to AG, 13 September 1916.
41 DHH, 74/672, box 13, folder 150 (150th Battalion) and folder 167 (167th Battalion).
42 LAC, RG 24, vol. 413, file 54-21-1-20, vol. 1, Draft "Statement by Department of Militia and Defence From 1st February to 31st December 1916," signed by CGS, 1 December 1916.
43 LAC, RG 24, vol. 4593, file 20-10, vol. 10, AG to MD 10, 4 November 1915.
44 LAC, RG 24, vol. 1402, file 593-6-2, vol. 22, MD 1 to Militia HQ, 31 August 1916.
45 LAC, RG 24, vol. 1402, file 593-6-2, vol. 22, AG to DG Mobilization, 7 November 1916, OA MD 1 to Militia HQ, 25 November 1916.
46 LAC, RG 24, vol. 1402, file 593-6-2, vol. 21, AG to MD 10, 29 November 1916.

47 LAC, Albert Edward Kemp fonds, MG 27, II D9, vol. 73, file 68, Summary of memorandums from Gwatkin and Turner compiled by the Parliamentary Secretary, 15 January 1917.
48 DHH, 74/672, box 4 folder 13, file CDF, Memorandum by CGS, 7 January 1917.
49 DHH, 74/672, box 4 folder 13, file CDF, Memorandum by CGS, 7 January 1917.
50 DHH, 74/672, box 4, folder 13, file CDF, CGS to AG, 15 January 1917.
51 DHH, 74/672, box 4, folder 13, file CDF AG, Circular Letter, 18 January 1917.
52 LAC, Albert Edward Kemp fonds, MG 27, II D9, vol. 73, file 68, HQ MD 1 to Militia HQ, 13 February 1917.
53 LAC, RG 9, III D1, vol. 4707, folder 89, file 3, Record of the history of the 2nd Canadian Reserve Battalion, 15 February 1918.
54 *The Quarterly Militia List of the Dominion of Canada (Corrected to 1st July 1916)*, (Ottawa: King's Printer, 1916), 279.
55 LAC, RG 24, vol. 4257, file 6-14-10, AG to MD 1, 14 April 1917.
56 LAC, RG 24, vol. 4257, file 6-19-5, AG to MD 1, 17 February 1917, AG to MD 1, 10 May 1917, MD 1 to Militia HQ, 15 May 1917.
57 LAC, RG 24, vol. 4257, file 6-19-5, MD 1 to AG, 7 May 1917 and AG to MD 1, 10 May 1917.
58 DHH, 74/672, box 4, folder 13, file CDF, Director-General CDF to MD 6, 19 March 1917.
59 DHH, 74/672, box 4 folder 13, file CDF, Summary prepared by Edwin Pye, 25 April 1943.
60 LAC, RG 24, vol. 4488, file 48-1-5, Lieutenant-Colonel M.A. Piché to AAG MD 4, 26 January 1917, and District Order No. 60 of 27 January 1917.
61 LAC, RG 24, vol. 4488, file 48-1-5, District Order No. 60 of 27 January 1917.
62 LAC, RG 24, vol. 4488, file 48-1-5, Lieutenant-Colonel M.A. Piché to AAG MD 4, 26 January 1917.
63 LAC, RG 24, vol. 4488, file 48-3-1, MD 4 to Militia HQ, 11 June 1917.
64 LAC, RG 24, vol. 4488, file 48-3-1, MD 4 to Militia HQ, 11 June 1917.
65 LAC, RG 24, vol. 4488, file 48-3-1, DG Mobilization to MD 4, 16 June 1917.
66 LAC, RG 24, vol. 4488, file 48-3-1, AG to MD 4, 3 July 1917.
67 LAC, RG 24, vol. 4488, file 48-3-1, AG to MD 4, 23 August 1917.
68 LAC, RG 24, vol. 336, file 33-2-117, MD 1 to Militia HQ, 15 May 1917.
69 LAC, RG 24, vol. 336, file 33-2-117, MD 1 to Militia HQ, 15 May 1917, and AG to MD 1, 1 June 1917.

70 LAC, RG 24, vol. 336, file 33-2-117, MD 1 to Militia HQ, 10 July 1917.
71 LAC, RG 24, vol. 336, file 33-2-117, AG to MD 1, 23 August 1917.
72 Colonel G.W.L. Nicholson, *Official History of the Canadian Army in the First World War: Canadian Expeditionary Force 1914–1919* (Ottawa: Queen's Printer, 1962), 344.
73 DHH, 74/672, box 4, folder 13, file CDF, Summary prepared by Edwin Pye, 25 April 1943.
74 General Order Number 58 of 15 April 1918.
75 LAC, RG 9, II B9, vol. 48, file 1089A, Part II, Order 7 of 28 July 1918.
76 LAC, RG 9, II B9, vol. 55, file 1393, Part II Orders Draft 105, British Columbia Regiment.
77 LAC, RG 9, II B9, vol. 54, file 1371, Part II Orders Draft 67, British Columbia Regiment.
78 Patrick Dennis, "A Canadian Conscript Goes to War – August 1918: Old Myths Re-examined," *Canadian Military History* 18, no. 1 (2009): 14.

CHAPTER NINE

1 DHH, 74/672, box 33 folder 50, file 1, War Office to GOC Canadian Division, 23 November 1914.
2 LAC, RG 24, vol. 1810, file GAC 1-6, Organization of Base Depots and System of Providing Reinforcements; Colonel A. Fortescue Duguid, *Official History of the Canadian Forces in the Great War 1914–1919: General Series,* vol. 1 (Ottawa: King's Printer, 1938), 157.
3 Colonel A.J. Kerry and Major W.A. McDill, *The History of the Corps of Royal Canadian Engineers,* vol. 1, 1749–1939 (Ottawa: The Military Engineers Association of Canada, 1962), 75; Duguid, *Official History: General Series,* vol. 1, 53.
4 DHH, 74/672, box 33 folder 48, file 3, Reinforcements by Arms-Cavalry, War Office to HQ Canadian Division, 8 December 1914.
5 DHH, 74/672, box 33, folder 50, file 1, War Office to GOC Canadian Division, 23 November 1914.
6 Colonel A. Fortescue Duguid, *Official History of the Canadian Forces in the Great War 1914–1919: Chronology, Appendices and Maps,* 164.
7 Cameron Pulsifer, *The Armoured Autocar in Canadian Service* (Ottawa: Service Publications, 2007), 10, 14; LAC, RG 9, III D3, vol. 4986, file 625 Part 1, reel T-10818, War Diary 1st Canadian Motor Machine Brigade, 13–16 June 1915.
8 LAC, RG 9, III B1, vol. 485, file R-14-1, GOC, 1st Canadian Division to HQ Southern Command, 8 December 1914.

9 LAC, RG 9, III B1, vol. 485, file R-14-1, OC 17th Nova Scotia Highlanders to GOC 1st Canadian Division, 15 December 1914.
10 DHH, 74/672, box 33, folder 50, file 1, First Contingent Order 924 of 18 January 1915.
11 LAC, RG 9, III B1, vol. 485, file R-14-1, CO PPCLI to HQ 80th (British) Infantry Brigade, 17 December 1914.
12 LAC, RG 9, III B1, vol. 485, file R-14-1, 1st Canadian Division to Southern Command, 3 February 1915.
13 LAC, Adamson fonds, MG30, E149, vol. 2, Agar Adamson to Mabel Adamson, 6 February 1915 and 9 February 1915.
14 TNA, WO 114/26, Weekly Returns, 8 March 1915, 15 March 1915, 22 March 1915, 29 March 1915, 5 April 1915, 12 April 1915, and 19 April 1915.
15 TNA, WO 114/26, Weekly Returns, 26 April 1915.
16 TNA, WO 114/29, Weekly Returns, 29 May 1916.
17 LAC, RG 9, III A1, vol. 44, file 8-5-10, War Office to Carson, 18 February 1915.
18 LAC, RG 9, III B1, vol. 719, file 1-118-2, Inspector of Infantry to GOC Canadians, Shorncliffe, 4 April 1916; LAC, RG 24, vol. 1841, file GAC 10-39D, Minutes of a Conference held at the War Office, 28 April 1916.
19 LAC, RG 9, III A1, vol. 52, file 8-7-1A, CTD Routine Order of 19 July 1915.
20 LAC, RG 9, III A1, vol. 53, file Monthly Reports 1917, Adjutant General's Report.
21 LAC, RG 9, III D3, vol. 4950, file 476, reel T-10761, Medical Officer's War Diary, 28 July 1915.
22 TNA, WO 293/2, War Office Instruction 148 of 18 May 1915.
23 TNA, WO 114/57, Weekly Returns, 31 May 1915; TNA, WO 114/27, Weekly Returns, 27 September 1915, 25 October 1915 and 27 December 1915.
24 LAC, RG 24, vol. 1844, file GAC 11-11C, Director of Recruiting and Organization to OIC Records, Westminster, 9 December 1915.
25 LAC, RG 9, III A1, vol. 74, file 10-8-22, vol. 1, AG HQ Canadians to Perley, 7 November 1916; [Colonel F.A. Reid], *System of Handling and Disposition of Casualties in the Canadian Expeditionary Force* (London: n.p., 31 October 1916).
26 LAC, RG 24, vol. 1844, file GAC 11-11C, Chart shewing progressive steps in disposal of a casualty dated 11 January 1916.
27 LAC, RG 24, vol. 1844, file GAC 11-11C, HQ CTD circular letter, 1 June 1916.

28 LAC, RG III B1, vol. 490, file R-50-1, HQS Brighton to GOC Canadian Troops Seaford, OC Canadian Troops Crowborough and OC Canadian Troops Seaford, 20 November 1916.
29 LAC, RG 9, III A1, vol. 48, file 8-5-58, Director of Recruiting and Organization to OIC Reinforcements, 21 July 1916.
30 LAC, RG 9, III A1, vol. 48, file 8-5-58, OIC Reinforcements to Director of Recruiting and Organization 22 July 1916; *System of Handling and Disposition of Casualties*, 87.
31 LAC, RG 9, III B1, vol. 420, file E-103-1, Draft CTD Orders, 24 October 1916.
32 TNA, WO 114/31, Weekly Returns, 29 January 1917.
33 LAC, RG 24, vol. 1844, file GAC 11-11C, HQ OMFC Routine Order 762 of 10 March 1917.
34 LAC, RG 24, vol. 1844, file GAC 11-11C, Director of Recruiting and Organization to Canadian Records Office, 9 December 1915.
35 LAC, RG 24, vol. 184, file GAC 11-11C, Canadian Casualty Assembly Centre.
36 LAC, RG 24, vol. 1844, file GAC 11-11C, Memorandum Relating to Organizing the CCAC in Relation to Its Effect on Record Office, 24 November 1916.
37 LAC, RG 24, vol. 1844, file GAC 11-11C, Memorandum Relating to Organizing the CCAC in Relation to Its Effect on Record Office, 24 November 1916, and HQ CTD Shorncliffe circular letter, 1 June 1916.
38 LAC, RG 24, vol. 184, file GAC 11-11C, Canadian Casualty Assembly Centre.
39 LAC, RG 9, III A1, vol. 48, file 8-5-58, CTD i/c BF & PT to Director of Recruiting and Organization, 19 July 1916.
40 LAC, RG 24, vol. 1844, file GAC 11-11C, HQ Canadians Routine Order 1307 of 22 August 1916, and HQ OMFC AG circular letter, 7 January 1917.
41 *System of Handling and Disposition of Casualties*, 80.
42 LAC, RG 9, III A1, vol. 48, file 6-5-58, Director of Recruiting and Organization to Major-General Carson, 27 June 1916.
43 LAC, RG 24, vol. 1844, file 11-11C, Director of Recruiting and Organization to GOC Shorncliffe, 28 March 1916.
44 LAC, RG 24, vol. 1844, file 11-11C, Canadian Casualty Assembly Centre.
45 Based on a sample of 9,138 reinforcements received by 2 CMR, 4 CMR, PPCLI, and the 4th, 16th, 18th, 20th, 72nd, and 85th Battalions.
46 LAC, RG 9, III A1, vol. 52, file 8-7-1, Major-General Currie to Major-General Carson, 9 December 1915.

47 LAC, RG 9, III A1, vol. 52, file 8-7-1, GSO CTD to Carson, 15 December 1915.
48 LAC, RG 9, III A1, vol. 46, file 8-5-20, Comments by OC CFA Reserve Brigade, c. January 1916.
49 LAC, RG 9, III A1, vol. 45, file 8-5-10F, Lieutenant-General Alderson to HQ Home Forces, 8 September 1916.
50 LAC, RG 9, III A1, vol. 45, file 8-5-10E, Notes on Canadian Training Division Shorncliffe, 6 June 1916.
51 TNA, WO 114/28, Weekly Returns, 27 March 1916.
52 TNA, WO 114/29, Weekly Returns, 26 June 1916.
53 TNA, WO 114/30, Weekly Returns, 30 October 1916.
54 War Office, Great Britain, *War Establishments: 1915, Revised Establishments for certain reserve units and depots,* part 5, p. 42, "A 2nd Reserve Battalion, Infantry of the Line."
55 LAC, RG 24, vol. 1841, file GAC 10-39D, Summary of CTD.
56 LAC, RG 9, III A1, vol. 45, file 8-5-10F, MacDougall to Carson, 13 September 1916.
57 LAC, RG 9, III B1, vol. 719, file 1-119-2, Inspector of Infantry to GOC Shorncliffe, 4 April 1916.
58 LAC, RG 9, III A1, vol. 45, file 8-5-10E, Steele to Carson, 25 July 1916.
59 TNA, WO 114/29, Weekly Returns, 31 July 1916.
60 LAC, RG 9, III A1, vol. 45, file 8-5-10E, Notes on Canadian Training Division, Shorncliffe, 6 June 1916.
61 LAC, RG 9, III B1, vol. 771, file R-4-2, vol. II, Confidential Report on 70th Overseas Battalion, CEF c. April 1916.
62 LAC, RG 9, III B1, vol. 771, file R-4-2, vol. 2, Commander 1st Canadian Training Brigade to HQ CTD, 7 June 1916.
63 LAC, RG 9, III A1, vol. 45, file 8-5-10E, Steele to Carson, 27 June 1916; TNA, WO 114/29, Weekly Returns, 26 June 1916.
64 TNA, WO 114/29, Weekly Returns, 31 July 1916.
65 LAC, RG 9, III B1, vol. 771, file R-4-2, vol. II, GSO CTD to GOC CTD, 8 May 1916.
66 LAC, RG 9, III B1, vol. 771, file R-4-2, vol. II, GSO CTD to GOC CTD, 3 June 1916.
67 LAC, RG 9, III B1, vol. 771, file R-4-2, vol. II, OC 6th Canadian Training Brigade to HQ CTD, 6 July 1916.
68 LAC, RG 9, III B1, vol. 771, file R-4-2, vol. II, HQ CTD to Militia HQ, 8 August 1916.
69 LAC, RG 9, III A1, vol. 45, file 8-5-10F, Undated CTD instruction, c. late August 1916 or early September 1916.

70 LAC, RG 9, III D1, vol. 4700, folder 72, file 8, 132nd Battalion Historical Records, n.d. but probably 1917.
71 LAC, RG 9, III A1, vol. 45, file 8-5-10F Colonel Reid to Major-General Carson, 24 July 1916.
72 LAC, RG 9, III A1, vol. 45, file 8-5-10F, GOC Eastern Command to GHQ Home Forces, 28 August 1916.
73 LAC, RG 9, III A1, vol. 45, file 8-5-10F, MacDougall to Carson, 13 September 1916.
74 TNA, WO 114/30, Weekly Returns, 25 September 1916,
75 TNA, WO 114/28, Weekly Returns, 27 March 1916; TNA, WO 114/29, Weekly Returns, 29 May 1916, 26 June 1916, and 31 July 1916.
76 LAC, RG 9, III D1, vol. 4718, folder 113, file 15, compiled 1 December 1918.
77 LAC, RG 9, III C3, vol. 4009, folder 10, file 17, Notes of a discussion between Colonel Hutchison GHQ and MGGS 2nd (British) Army, 16 October 1915.
78 LAC, RG 9, III C3, vol. 4009, folder 10, file 17, GOC 1st Canadian Division to GOC Canadian Corps, 22 May 1916; LAC, RG 9, III B1, vol. 489, file R-38-1, vol. 1, HQ Home Forces to HQ Eastern Command 16 September 1916; LAC, RG 9, III B1, vol. 419, file E-88-1, HQ Eastern Command to HQ CTD Shorncliffe, 20 September 1916.
79 LAC, RG 9, III D3, vol. 4982, file 602, reel T-10812, War Diary 2nd Canadian Machine Gun Company, 1 February, 16 February, and 23 February 1916.
80 LAC, RG 9, III B1, vol. 752, file O-64-2, HQ CTD to all Canadian reserve brigades, 15 December 1915.
81 LAC, RG 24, vol. 1840, file GAC 10-39, Major-General Lessard to Sam Hughes, May 1916.
82 TNA, WO 114/28, Weekly Returns, 27 March 1916 and 24 April 1916; WO 114/29, Weekly Returns, 29 May 1916.
83 LAC, RG 9, III D1, vol. 4698, folder 66, file 1, 86th Battalion Historical Records, 3 March 1917.
84 LAC, RG 9, III B1, vol. 426, file E-250-1, OC Canadian Troops Crowborough to Commandant Canadian Machine Gun Depot, 14 November 1916.
85 LAC, RG 9, III A1, vol. 45, file 9-5-10F, MacDougall to Carson, 13 September 1916.
86 LAC, RG 9, III A1, vol. 53, file Monthly Reports February 1917, General Staff Report.
87 TNA, WO 114/30, Weekly Returns, 25 December 1916.

88 TNA, WO 114/28, Weekly Returns, 28 February 1916; TNA, WO 114/29, Weekly Returns, 29 May 1916 and 26 June 1916; TNA, WO 114/30, Weekly Returns, 25 September 1916.
89 TNA, WO 114/30, Weekly Returns, 30 October 1916 and 27 November 1916; LAC, RG 9, III D3, vol. 4865, file 183, reel T-10665, War Diary Canadian HQ Hastings, April 1917, p. 2.
90 LAC, RG 9, III A1, vol. 53, file Monthly Reports, February 1917, General Staff, Adjutant General.
91 LAC, RG 9, III A1, vol. 45, file 8-5-10H, Memorandum Allotment of Canadian Troops in England, n.d., c. late October 1916.
92 LAC, RG 9, III A1, vol. 53, file Monthly Reports, February 1917, General Staff, Adjutant General.
93 Desmond Morton, *A Peculiar Kind of Politics* (Toronto: University of Toronto Press, 1982), 88–9.
94 Ibid., 98; LAC, RG 9, III A1, vol. 74, file 19-8-22, vol. 1, Major-General Steele to Sir George Perley, 18 November 1916, Major-General Steele to Lord Shaughnessy, 19 November 1916, Sir George Perley to Major-General Steele, 24 November 1916.
95 TNA, WO 33/814, Composition of Headquarters of Overseas Dominion Forces in the British Isles, 20 March 1917.
96 LAC, RG 9, III A1, vol. 53, file Monthly Reports, February 1917, General Staff and Adjutant General.
97 LAC, RG 9, III A1, vol. 53, file Monthly Reports, February 1917, Adjutant General Report.
98 LAC, RG 9, III A1, vol. 53, file Monthly Reports February 1917, Adjutant General Report; TNA, WO 33/814, Composition of Headquarters of Overseas Dominion Forces in the British Isles, 20 March 1917.
99 LAC, RG 9, III A1, vol. 53, file Monthly Reports, July 1917, Adjutant General Report; LAC, RG 9, III A1, vol. 53, file Monthly Reports, October 1917, General Staff Report.
100 Overseas Military Forces of Canada, *Report of the Ministry: Overseas Military Forces of Canada 1918* (London: Overseas Military Forces of Canada, 1919), 59–61.
101 LAC, RG 9, III A1, vol. 53, file Monthly Reports, February 1917, Adjutant General, General Staff; LAC, RG 9, III B1, vol. 717, file 1-89-2, HQ Shorncliffe to HQ OMFC, 2 March 1917; LAC, RG 9, III A1, vol. 70, file 10-8-4, QMG HQ OMFC to AG HQ OMFC, 30 January 1917; LAC, RG 9, III A1, vol. 53, file Monthly Reports, August 1917, Quartermaster General; TNA, WO 114/30, Weekly Returns, 27 November 1916; TNA, WO 114/32, Weekly Returns, 25 June 1917; TNA, WO 114/35, Weekly Returns, 31 August 1918.

102 LAC, RG 9, III A1, vol. 53, file Monthly Reports, February 1917, General Staff Report.
103 LAC, RG 9, III A1, vol. 53, file Monthly Reports, February 1917, Adjutant General Report.
104 LAC, RG 9, III B1, vol. 489, file R-38-1, vol. 1, DAA & QMG HQ Canadians Brighton to Brigadier-General Landry, 21 December 1916.
105 LAC, RG 9, III B1, vol. 1357, file R-17-5, War Office to GHQ 3rd Echelon, 16 February 1916.
106 LAC, RG 9, III B1, vol. 489, file R-38-1, vol. 1, HQ Brighton to Brigadier-General Landry, 21 December 1916.
107 LAC, Albert Edward Kemp fonds, MG 27, II D9, vol. 73, file 68, Memorandum for the Honourable the Minister – Suggested Reorganization of the Canadian Expeditionary Force and Association with the Militia of Canada, 15 January 1917.
108 LAC, Albert Edward Kemp fond, MG 27, II D9, vol. 76, file 121, Turner to Perley, 16 December 1916.
109 LAC, Richard Ernest William Turner fonds, MG 30, E46, vol. 10, file 71, Turner to GOC 4th Canadian Division, 22 March 1917.
110 LAC, RG 9, III A1, vol. 73, file 10-8-17, Kemp to Perley, 6 December 1917.
111 LAC, RG 9, III A1, vol. 73, file 10-8-17, Turner to Perley, 11 December 1916.
112 LAC, Richard Ernest William Turner fonds, MG 30, E46, vol. 10, file 71, Turner to Perley, 16 December 1916.
113 LAC, Richard Ernest William Turner fonds, MG 30, E46, vol. 10, file 71, Perley to Prime Minister Borden, 20 December 1916.
114 LAC, Richard Ernest William Turner fonds, MG 30, E46, vol. 10, file 71, Borden to Perley, 28 December 1916.
115 LAC, Richard Ernest William Turner fonds, MG 30, E46, vol. 10, file 71, Lieutenant-General Byng to Perley, 18 December 1916.
116 LAC, Richard Ernest William Turner fonds, MG 30 E46, vol. 10, file 71, GOC 12th Canadian Infantry Brigade to GOC 4th Canadian Division, 29 January 1917.
117 LAC, RG 9, III A1, vol. 53, file Monthly Reports, June 1917, Adjutant General.
118 LAC, RG 9, III A1, vol. 53, file Monthly Reports, October 1917, Adjutant General; *Report of the Ministry: Overseas Military Forces of Canada 1918* (London: Overseas Military Forces of Canada, 1919), 56, 59–61.
119 Adjutant General, LAC, RG 9, III A1, vol. 54, file Monthly Reports, December 1917

120 LAC, RG 9, III A1, vol. 82, file 10-9-73, CGS HQ OMFC to Deputy Minister, 21 September 1918.
121 TNA, WO 32/5139, Deputy Minister OMFC to War Office, 23 November 1917.
122 LAC, RG 24, vol. 1810, file GAC 1-6, "Organization of Base depots and System of Providing Reinforcements."
123 Colonel G.W.L. Nicholson, *Official History of the Canadian Army in the First World War: Canadian Expeditionary Force 1914–1919* (Ottawa: Queen's Printer, 1962), 222; LAC, RG 9, III B1, vol. 485, file R-13-1, Inspector-General of Communications to War Office, 4 February 1915.
124 LAC, RG 9, III D3, vol. 5048, file 917, reel T-10940, War Diary Canadian General Base Depot, 27 September 1915.
125 LAC, RG 9, III B1, vol. 485, file R-13-1, CEF Pay and Record Office London to Canadian Training Depot, 22 February 1915.
126 DHH, 74/672, box 33, folder 48, file 3, Reinforcements by Arms, p. 65; LAC, RG 9, III A1, vol. 52, file 8-7-1A, Major-General Carson to Lieutenant-General Alderson, 11 May 1915.
127 LAC, RG 9, III D3, vol. 5048, file 5048, reel T-10940, War Diary Canadian General Base Depot, 14 September 1915.
128 LAC, RG 9, III B1, vol. 425, file E-203-1, HQ IGC to GHQ 3rd Echelon, 23 September 1915.
129 LAC, RG 9, III D3, vol. 5048, file 917, reel T-10940, War Diary Canadian General Base Depot, 15 September 1915.
130 LAC, RG 9, III D3, vol. 5048, file 917, reel T-10940, War Diary Canadian General Base Depot November 1915, OC Canadian Base Depot to OC Reinforcements Havre, 8 November 1915.
131 LAC, RG 9, III B1, vol. 425, file E-203-1, Carson to Director of Recruiting and Organization, 17 November 1915.
132 LAC, Richard Ernest William Turner fonds, MG 30, E46, vol. 10, file 69, Commandant CGBD to Lieutenant-General Turner, 3 March 1917.
133 *Report of the Ministry, Overseas Military Forces of Canada, 1918*, 1.
134 LAC, RG 9, III B1, vol. 622, file C-197-2, vol. 1, Commandant CGBD to OC Reinforcements Havre, 8 February 1916.
135 LAC, RG 9, III B1, vol. 622, file C-197-2, vol. 1, CGBD Quartermaster to Commandant, 1 February 1916.
136 LAC, RG 9, III B1, vol. 622, file C-197-2, vol. 1, War Office to Carson, 25 February 1916, War Office to HQ Southern Command, 25 February 1916.

137 LAC, RG 9, III B1, vol. 489, file R-38-1, vol. 1, CGBD Commandant to OC Reinforcements Havre, 28 September 1916; LAC, RG 9, III D3, vol. 5048, file 917, reel T-10940, War Diary CGBD, 17 December 1916.
138 LAC, RG 9, III D3, vol. 5048, file 917, reel T-10940, War Diary CGBD, 4 December 1915, 30 January 1916, and 7 June 1916.
139 LAC, RG 9, III B1, vol. 489, file R-38-1, vol. 1, Major H.C. Gibbins, 43rd Battalion instructor with Central Training School to OC Central Training School, 23 September 1916.
140 LAC, RG 9, III B1, vol. 489, file R-38-1, vol. 1, CGBD Commandant to OC Reinforcements Havre, 28 September 1916.
141 LAC, RG 9, III D3, vol. 5048, file 917, reel T-10940, War Diary Canadian General Base Depot, November 1915, Staff of Canadian Base Depot: Establishment, 25 February 1916, AG GHQ 3rd Echelon to IGC, 28 October 1915.
142 LAC, RG 9, III D3, vol. 5048, file 917, reel T-10940, War Diary Canadian General Base Depot, 30 September 1915.
143 LAC, RG 9, III D3, vol. 5048, file 917, reel T-10940, War Diary Canadian General Base Depot, 29–30 November 1916, 1–2 December 1916.
144 LAC, RG 9, III D3, vol. 5048, file 917, reel T-10940, War Diary Canadian General Base Depot, April 1917, Appendix B and daily entries for May 1917.
145 LAC, RG 9, III B1, vol. 552, file U-4-1, DADMS CTD to ADMS CTD, 4 September 1916.
146 LAC, RG 9, III B1, vol. 552, file U-4-1, DADMS CTD to ADMS CTD, 4 September 1916; LAC, RG 9, III D3, vol. 5048, file 917, reel T-10940, War Diary Canadian General Base Depot, 23 May 1916.
147 LAC, RG 9, III A1, vol. 52, file 8-7-1A, 2nd Division Armourer Officer to 2nd Division DADOS, 12 June 1916.
148 LAC, RG 9, III B1, vol. 552, file U-4-1, ADMS 3rd Canadian Division to DDMS HQ Canadian Corps, 24 June 1916.
149 LAC, RG 9, III A1, vol. 80, file 10-9-26, Turner to Perley, 10 January 1917.
150 LAC, RG 9, III B1, vol. 440, file F-11-1, Commandant CGBD to HQ CTD Shorncliffe, 13 July 1916.
151 LAC, Richard Ernest William Turner fonds, MG 30, E46, vol. 10, file 69, Commandant CGBD to OC Reinforcements Havre, 20 February 1917, Annex D.
152 LAC, RG 9, III A1, vol. 80, file 10-9-26, HQ OMFC to War Office, January 1917.

153 LAC, RG 9, III D3, VOL. 5048, file 921, reel T-10940, War Diary 3rd Canadian Infantry Base Depot, 21 April 1917.
154 LAC, RG 9, III B1, vol. 685, file E-254-2, HQ OMFC to Shorncliffe, Seaford, Shoreham and Bramshott, 13 February 1917.
155 LAC, RG 24, vol. 1437, files 593-6-28 and 593-6-29, PC 659 dated 12 March 1917.
156 LAC, RG 9, III D3, VOL. 5046, file 910, reel T-10938, War Diary GHQ 3rd Echelon Canadian Section, 18 January 1918.
157 LAC, RG 9, III B1, vol. 1004, file R-19-3, AG GHQ to GHQ 3rd Echelon and Canadian Corps, 29 August 1918.,
158 TNA, WO 95/4027, War Diary Étaples Camp Commandant, Appendix to May 1917.
159 LAC, RG 9, III C1, vol. 3870, folder 112, file 13, OC 1st Canadian Infantry Base Depot to HQ 1st Canadian Division, 16 June 1917.
160 LAC, RG 9, III C1, vol. 3870, folder 112, file 13, GHQ to all armies, 21 September 1917.
161 LAC, RG 9, III B1, vol. 967, file O-12-3 1st (British) Army to I, XIII, XV, and Canadian Corps, 15 December 1917.
162 LAC, RG 9, III D3, vol. 5048, file 919, reel T-10940, War Diary 1st Canadian Infantry Base Depot, 31 December 1917; LAC, RG 9, III D3, vol. 5048, file 920, reel T-10940, War Diary 2nd Canadian Infantry Base Depot, 31 December 1917.
163 LAC, RG 9, III D3, vol. 5046, file 910, reel T-10938, War Diary GHQ 3rd Echelon Canadian Section, 22 February 1918.
164 LAC, RG 9, III A1, vol. 54, Adjutant General, file Progress Reports, February 1918; LAC, RG 9, III D3, vol. 5046, file 910, reel T-10938, War Diary GHQ 3rd Echelon Canadian Section, 19 March 1918.
165 LAC, RG 9, III D3, vol. 5048, file 918, reel T-10940, War Diary Canadian Infantry Base Depot, 20–21 April 1918.
166 LAC, RG 9, III D3, vol. 5048, file 918, reel T-10940, War Diary Canadian Infantry Base Depot, 24 December 1918.
167 LAC, RG 9, III D3, vol. 5048, file 917, reel T-10940, War Diary Canadian General Base Depot, 16 June 1919; LAC, RG 9, D3, vol. 5048, file 918, reel T-10940, War Diary Canadian Infantry Base Depot, 3 February 1919; LAC, RG 9, III D3, vol. 5047, file 914, reel T-10939, War Diary Canadian Embarkation Camp, 6 January 1919.
168 LAC, RG 9, III C1, vol. 3827, folder 6, file 16, Minutes of 2nd Army Corps Commanders' Conference, 24 May 1916.
169 LAC, RG 9, III D3, vol. 5009, file 716, reel T-10857, War Diary 1st Canadian Entrenching Battalion 1 August 1917; LAC, RG 9, III D3,

vol. 5009, file 717, reel T-10858, War Diary 2nd Canadian Entrenching Battalion, August 1917, with a summary of the first year of activities.

170 LAC, RG 9, III D3, vol. 5047, file 912, reel T-10939, War Diary Camp Commandant Canadian Corps, 19 May 1917.

171 LAC, RG 9, III C1, vol. 3864, folder 99, file 9, BGGS, Canadian Corps to 1st, 2nd, 3rd, and 4th Canadian Divisions, 21 August 1917.

172 LAC, RG 9, III C1, vol. 3864, folder 99, file 7, DAG GHQ 3rd Echelon to AG GHQ, 25 January 1917; LAC, RG 9, III B1, vol. 1332, file R-1-5, vol. 2, Canadian Section GHQ 3rd Echelon to CRE Canadian Corps, 12 June 1917.

173 LAC, RG 9, III B1, vol. 1004, file R-19-3, AAG GHQ to Canadian Section GHQ 3rd Echelon and Canadian Corps, 8 August 1918, and AG GHQ to Canadian Section GHQ 3rd Echelon, 29 August 1918.

174 LAC, RG 9, III D3, vol. 4978, file 585, reel T-10807, War Diary 2nd Division Ammunition Column, 31 August 1918.

175 LAC, RG 9, III B1, vol. 1332, file R-1-5, vol. 6, Canadian Corps Commander to HQ Second Army, 8 February 1916.

176 LAC, RG 9, III C1, vol. 3887, folder 39, file 13, War Office to GHQ 1st Echelon, 3 March 1916, and AG GHQ to HQ Second (British) Army, 6 March 1916.

177 LAC, RG 9, III C1, vol. 3866, folder 103, file 13, DAG GHQ 3rd Echelon to HQ Canadian Corps, 28 November 1916.

178 LAC, RG 9, III C1, vol. 3866, folder 103, file 13, HQ Canadian Corps to DAG 3rd Echelon GHQ, 30 November 1916.

179 LAC, RG 9, III C1, vol. 3866, folder 103, file 13, HQ 4th Division to HQ Canadian Corps, 10 December 1916.

180 David Charles Gregory Campbell, "The Divisional Experience in the C.E.F.: A Social and Operational History of the 2nd Canadian Division, 1915–1918" (PhD diss., University of Calgary, 2003), 292.

181 LAC, RG 9, III C1, vol. 3866, folder 103, file 16, HQ 3rd Division to 7th, 8th, and 9th Canadian Infantry Brigades, 18 December 1916.

182 John Harold Becker, *Silhouettes of the Great War: The Memoirs of John Harold Becker* (Ottawa: CEF Books, 2001), 62.

183 LAC, RG 9, III B1, vol. 1009, file R-43-3, vol. 2, AAG GHQ to BGGS GHQ, 27 January 1917, and BGGS GHQ to AG GHQ, 30 January 1917.

184 LAC, RG 9, III C1, vol. 3866, folder 103, file 13, GOC 1st Canadian Division to HQ Canadian Corps, 30 April 1917.

185 LAC, RG 9, III C1, vol. 3870, folder 112, file 13, HQ First Army to I, II, XI, XIII, Canadian Corps, 23 April 1917; LAC, Arthur William Currie fonds, MG 30 E100, vol. 35, file 16, DAG GHQ 3rd Echelon to Canadian

Corps HQ, 3 August 1917, and AG HQ OMFC to Canadian Section GHQ 3rd Echelon, 14 August 1917.
186 LAC, RG 9, III C1, vol. 3864 folder 99, file 9, HQ Canadian Corps circular letter, 5 September 1917.
187 TNA, WO 33/901, Great Britain, War Office, *War Establishments*, part 7A, (London: HMSO, 1918), 199–200.
188 LAC, RG 9, III D3, vol. 4839, file 90, reel T-1922, War Diary 1st Canadian Division Administrative Branches of the Staff Appendix H to December 1917.
189 TNA, WO 33/938, Great Britain, War Office, *War Establishments*, part 16, *Canadian Forces (France), 1919* (London: HMSO, 1919), 289.
190 Australian War Memorial, Australian Corps Reinforcement Camp November 1917–May 1918, 4 Item 33/2/2.
191 LAC, RG 24, vol. 1810, file GAC 1-6, Summary of the Canadian Corps Reinforcement Camp; LAC, RG 9, III D3, vol. 4839, file 90, reel T-1922, War Diary 1st Canadian Division Administrative Branches of the Staff, Appendix H.
192 LAC, RG 24, vol. 1810, file GAC 1-6, Summary of the Canadian Corps Reinforcement Camp; LAC, RG 9, III D3, vol. 4839, file 90, reel T-1922, War Diary 1st Canadian Division Administrative Branches of the Staff, Appendix H.
193 LAC, RG 9, III C3, vol. 4021, folder 48, file 6, HQ Canadian Corps circular letter, 28 April 1918; LAC, RG 9, III C4, vol. 4257, folder 37, file 9, GHQ 3rd Echelon Canadian Section to OC CCRC, 14 October 1917.
194 LAC, RG 9, III C1, vol. 3866, folder 103, file 10, HQ Canadian Corps circular letter October 1917; LAC, RG 9, III C1, vol. 3885, folder 32, file 5, 1st Canadian Division Administrative Instruction No. 13 of 27 October 1917.
195 LAC, RG 24, vol. 1810, file GAC 1-6, Summary of the Canadian Corps Reinforcement Camp.
196 TNA, WO 33/938, Great Britain, War Office, *War Establishments*, part 16, *Canadian Forces (France), 1919* (London: HMSO, 1919), 291.
197 LAC, RG 9, III B1, vol. 937, file E-19-3, HQ Canadian Corps circular letter, 26 October 1918, and HQ Canadian Corps circular letter, 17 December 1918.
198 LAC, RG 9, III C1, vol. 3864, folder 99, file 9, HQ Canadian Corps circular letter, 5 September 1917; LAC, RG 9, III B1, vol. 967, file O-12-3, HQ Canadian Corps to HQ 1st (British) Army, 2 December 1917; LAC, RG 24, vol. 1833, file GAC 8-34, Notes on the Canadian Corps Reinforcement Camp.

199 LAC, RG 24, vol. 1810, file GAC 1-6, Summary of the Canadian Corps Reinforcement Camp.
200 LAC, RG 24, vol. 1833, file GAC 8-36, Notes on the Canadian Corps Reinforcement Camp.
201 LAC, RG 24, vol. 1810, file GAC 1-6, Summary of the Canadian Corps Reinforcement Camp; LAC, RG 24, vol. 1833, file GAC 8-36, Notes on the Canadian Corps Reinforcement Camp; RG 9, III B1, vol. 1003, file R-5-3, vol. 16, Memoranda on Canadian Corps Railhead Depot operations during the Battle of Amiens, 18 August 1918; LAC, RG 9, III D3, vol. 4821, file 29 reel T-7180, War Diary Canadian Corps HQ Administrative Branches of the Staff, April 1918, Appendix F; LAC, RG 9, III B1, vol. 972, file O-70-3, HQ Canadian Corps to Canadian Section GHQ 3rd Echelon, c. August or September 1918.
202 LAC, RG 24, vol. 1833, file GAC 8-36, Notes on the Canadian Corps Reinforcement Camp.

CONCLUSION

1 Robert Craig Brown, *Robert Laird Borden: 1914–1937* (Toronto: Macmillan of Canada, 1980), 33.
2 Richard J. Walker, "The Political Management of Army Leadership: The Evolution of Canadian Civil-Army Relations 1898–1945" (PhD diss., University of Western Ontario, 2003), 175.

Bibliography

ARCHIVAL SOURCES

Library and Archives Canada (LAC)
- RG 2   Privy Council Office
- RG 9   Department of Militia and Defence
- RG 10   Indian Affairs
- RG 13   Department of Justice
- RG 24   Department of National Defence
- RG 25   Department of External Affairs
- RG 38   Department of Veterans Affairs
- RG 73   Department of Justice
- RG 76   Immigration
- RG 150   Ministry of the Overseas Military Forces of Canada
- MG 27   Personal papers
- MG 30   Personal papers

Department of National Defence, Directorate of History and Heritage (DHH)
- 74/672 (Edwin Pye Fonds)
- CEF   General Instructions and Routine Orders
-          Minutes of the Militia Council

The National Archives of Great Britain (TNA)
- CO   Colonial Office
- FO   Foreign Office
- WO   War Office

Archives of Ontario (AO)
Bermuda Archives
Elgin Military Museum
48th Highlanders of Canada Regimental Museum

Peterborough Centennial Museum and Archives
Simcoe County Archives
The Royal Canadian Regiment Museum
Western University: Archives and Research Collection Centre
Woodstock City Museum

PUBLISHED SOURCES

Adachi, Ken. *The Enemy That Never Was: A History of the Japanese Canadians*. Toronto: McClelland and Stewart Limited, 1976.
Allinson, Sidney. *The Bantams: The Untold Story of World War I*. Oakville, Ontario: Mosaic Press, 1983.
Anderson, Peter. *I That's Me: Escape from a German Prisoner-of-War Camp*. Edmonton: Bradburn, c. 1920.
Backhouse, Constance. *Colour-Coded: A Legal History of Racism in Canada, 1900–1950*. Toronto: University of Toronto Press, 1999.
Bagley, Fred, and Harvey Daniel Duncan. *A Legacy of Courage: Calgary's Own 137th Overseas Battalion, CEF*. Calgary: Plug Street Books, 1993.
Baldwin, Harold. *Holding the Line*. Chicago: A.C. McClurg & Co., 1918.
Barnard, Lieutenant-Colonel W.T. *The Queen's Own Rifles of Canada*. Don Mills: Ont[ario] Pub[lishing] Co., 1960.
Bean, C.E.W. *Official History of Australia in the Great War of 1914–1918*, vol. 3. *The AIF in France 1916*. Sydney, Australia: Angus and Robertson, 1920.
Beattie, Kim. *48th Highlanders of Canada, 1891–1928*. Toronto: 48th Highlanders of Canada, 1932.
Beckett, Ian. *The Great War*. Harlow: Pearson Education Limited, 2007.
Bennett, Captain S.G. *The 4th Canadian Mounted Rifles 1914–1919*. Toronto: Murray Printing Company Limited, 1926.
Bernier, Serge. *The Royal 22e Regiment 1914–1999*. Montreal: Art Global, 2000.
Blanchard, Jim. *Winnipeg's Great War: A City Comes of Age*. Winnipeg: University of Manitoba Press, 2010.
Borden, Henry, ed. *Robert Laird Borden: His Memoirs*. Toronto: Macmillan of Canada, 1938.
Brown, Atholl Sutherland. *Buster: A Canadian Patriot and Imperialist, The Life and Times of Brigadier James Sutherland Brown*. Waterloo, ON: Laurier Centre for Military Strategic and Disarmament Studies, 2004.
Brown, Ian Malcolm. *British Logistics on the Western Front, 1914–1919*. Westport, CT: Praeger, 1998.

Brown, Robert Craig. *Robert Laird Borden: A Biography*, vol. 2. 1914–1937. Toronto: Macmillan of Canada, 1980.
Bruce, Colonel Herbert A. *Report on the Canadian Army Medical Service.* London: n.p., 1916.
Canada, Census and Statistics Office. *Special Report on the Foreign-Born Population.* Ottawa: Government Printing Bureau, 1915.
Canada, Department of Justice. *The Military Service Act 1917: Manual for the Information and Guidance of Tribunals in the Consideration and Review of Claims for Exemption.* Ottawa: King's Printer, 1918.
Canada, Department of Militia and Defence. *Canadian Expeditionary Force Units: Instructions Governing Organization and Administration.* Ottawa: Government Printing Bureau, 1916.
– *Canadian Militia War Establishments (Provisional) 1914.* n.p.: c. 1914.
– *Mobilization Regulations 1913.* Ottawa: Government Printing Bureau, 1912.
– *Quarterly Militia List of the Dominion of Canada (Corrected to 31st March 1914).* Ottawa: King's Printer, 1914.
– *Quarterly Militia List of the Dominion of Canada (Corrected to 1st July 1916).* Ottawa: King's Printer, 1916.
– *Quarterly Militia List of the Dominion of Canada (Corrected to 1st July 1918).* Ottawa: King's Printer, 1918.
– *King's Regulations and Orders for the Canadian Militia.* Ottawa: King's Printer, 1910.
– *Physical Standards and Instructions for the Medical Examination of Recruits for the Canadian Expeditionary Force and for the Active Militia of Canada.* Ottawa: King's Printer, 1917.
– *Regulations for the Canadian Medical Service 1914.* Ottawa: Government Printing Bureau, 1915.
– *Rifle and Musketry Exercises for the Ross Rifle.* Ottawa: Government Printing Bureau, 1915.
Canada, Dominion Bureau of Statistics. *Canada Year Book 1914.* Ottawa: King's Printer, 1915.
– *Canada Year Book, 1915.* Ottawa: King's Printer, 1916.
– *Canada Year Book, 1916–17.* Ottawa: King's Printer, 1917.
– *Canada Year Book 1918.* Ottawa: King's Printer, 1919.
– *Canada Year Book 1922–23.* Ottawa: King's Printer, 1924.
Canada, Dominion of. *An Act Respecting the Canadian Militia* R.S.C., 1906. Ottawa: King's Printer, 1907.
– *Fifth Census of Canada 1911.* Ottawa: King's Printer, 1912.
– 12th Parliament, 5th session. *Sessional Papers* vol. 50, no. 25, 1914, Sessional Paper No. 35, *Report of the Militia Council for the Dominion of Canada for the Fiscal Year Ending March 31, 1914.*

- 12th Parliament, 7th session. *Sessional Papers* vol. 52, no. 20, 1917, *Report of the Department of Labour for the Fiscal Year Ending March 31, 1916*, Sessional Paper no. 36.
- 13th Parliament, 4th session. *Sessional Papers* vol. 56, no. 5, 1920, *Report of the Work of the Department of Soldiers' Civil Re-establishment*, Sessional Paper no. 14.
- 13th Parliament, 4th session. *Sessional Papers* vol. 56, no. 10, 1920, *Report of the Department of Labour for the Fiscal Year Ending March 31, 1919*, Sessional Paper no. 37.

Canada, Overseas Military Forces of Canada. *Report of the Ministry: Overseas Military Forces of Canada* London: Overseas Military Forces of Canada, 1919.

Canada, Parliament, House of Commons. 12th Parliament, 6th Session. *Official Report of the Debates of the House of Commons.* Vol. 122. Ottawa: King's Printer, 1916.

- 12th Parliament, 7th Session. *Official Report of the Debates of the House of Commons*. Vols 126 and 128. Ottawa: King's Printer, 1918.

Canada, War Purchasing Commission. *Report of the War Purchasing Commissioni, vol. 2. Minutes from Minute No. 1, May 4 1915 to Minute No 6616, April 28, 1916*. Ottawa: King's Printer, 1916.

Canadian Japanese Association. *Japanese Contribution to Canada: A Summary of the Role Played by the Japanese in the Development of the Canadian Commonwealth*. Vancouver: Canadian Japanese Association, 1940.

Cassar, George H. *Hell in Flanders Fields: Canadians at the Second Battle of Ypres*. Toronto: Dundurn Press, 2010.

Cassel, Jay. *The Secret Plague: Venereal Disease in Canada 1838–1939*. Toronto: University of Toronto Press, 1987.

Collins, Major G.R.N. *Military Organization and Administration*. London: Hugh Rees, 1918.

Cook, Tim. *At the Sharp End: Canadians Fighting the Great War, 1914–1916*. Vol 1. Toronto: Viking Canada, 2007.

- *No Place to Run: The Canadian Corps and Gas Warfare in the First World War*. Vancouver: University of British Columbia Press, 1999.
- *Shock Troops: Canadians Fighting the Great War, 1917–1918*. Vol 2. Toronto: Viking Canada, 2008.

Corrigal, Major D.J. *The History of the Twentieth Canadian Battalion (Central Ontario Regiment), Canadian Expeditionary Force, in the Great War 1914–1918*. Toronto: Stone & Cox Limited, 1935.

Corrigan, Gordon. *Mud, Blood and Poppycock*. London: Cassell, 2003.

Crowder, Major-General E.H. *Second Report of the Provost Marshal General to the Secretary of War on the Operations of the Selective Service System to December 20, 1918*. Washington: Government Printing Office, 1919.

Dancocks, Daniel. *Gallant Canadians: The Story of the Tenth Canadian Infantry Battalion, 1914–1919.* Calgary: The Calgary Highlanders Regimental Funds Foundation, 1994.

Davison, Lieutenant-Colonel H.M. *History of the 35th Division in the Great War.* London: Sifton, Praed & Co., 1920.

Duguid, Colonel A. Fortescue. *Official History of the Canadian Forces in the Great War 1914–1919: Chronology, Appendices and Maps.* Ottawa: King's Printer, 1938.

– *Official History of the Canadian Forces in the Great War 1914–1919: General Series,* vol. 1. Ottawa: King's Printer, 1938.

Dupuis, Francis, and John Chadwick. *A Technical Appraisal of the Ross Rifle.* Antigonish: Casket Printing and Publishing Co., 1984.

Edmonds, Brigadier-General J.E. *History of the Great War Based on Official Documents: Military Operations, France and Belgium 1914.* London: MacMillan and Co. Limited, 1925.

Ellis, W.D., ed. *Saga of the Cyclists in the Great War 1914–1918.* n.d., Canadian Corps Cyclist Battalion Association, 1965.

English, John. *Borden: His Life and World.* Toronto: McGraw-Hill Ryerson Limited, 1977.

Fetherstonhaugh, R.C. *The Royal Canadian Regiment 1883–1933.* Montreal: Gazette Printing, 1936.

– *The Thirteenth Battalion, Royal Highlanders of Canada, 1914–1919.* Montreal: The Thirteenth Battalion, Royal Highlanders of Canada, 1925.

Ford, Nancy Gentile. *Americans All! Foreign-Born Soldiers in World War I.* Texas A&M University Press, 2001.

French, General Sir John. *Report.* Ottawa: King's Printer, 1910.

Gibson, Captain W.L. *Records of the Fourth Canadian Infantry Battalion in the Great War 1914–1918.* Toronto: The MacLean Publishing Company Limited, 1924.

Gilner, Elias. *War and Hope: A History of the Jewish Legion.* New York: Herzl Press, 1969.

Gordon, Hampden. *The War Office.* London: Putnam, 1935.

Gould, L. McLeod. *From B.C. to Baisieux: Being the Narrative History of the 102nd Canadian Infantry Battalion.* Victoria, BC: Thos. R. Cusack Presses, 1919.

Grafton, Lieutenant-Colonel C.S. *The Canadian Emma Gees: A History of the Canadian Machine Gun Corps.* London, ON: Hunter Printing Company, c. 1938.

Granatstein, J.L., and J.M. Hitsman. *Broken Promises: A History of Conscription in Canada.* Toronto: Oxford University Press, 1977.

Granatstein, J.L. *The Greatest Victory: Canada's One Hundred Days, 1918.* Don Mills, Ontario: Oxford University Press, 2014.

Great Britain, House of Commons, The War Cabinet. *Report for the Year 1917.* London: HMSO, 1918.
Great Britain, Ministry of National Service. *Report.* Vol. 1. *Upon the physical examination of men of military age by National Service medical boards from November 1st 1917 – October 31st 1918.* London: HMSO, 1920.
Great Britain, War Office. *Field Service Regulations.* Part 2. *Organization and Administration, 1909.* London: HMSO, 1909.
– *Infantry Training 1914.* London: HMSO, 1914.
– *Manual of Military Law 1914.* London: HMSO, 1914.
– *Statistics of the Military Effort of the British Empire during the Great War.* London: HMSO, 1922.
– *War Establishments: 1915, Revised Establishments for Certain Reserve Units and Depots.* London: HMSO, 1915.
– *War Establishments.* Part 16. *Canadian Forces (France) 1919.* London: HMSO, 1919.
Greenhous, Brereton. *Semper Paratus: The History of the Royal Hamilton Light Infantry (Wentworth Regiment) 1862–1977.* Hamilton: RHLI Historical Association, 1977.
Griesbach, William Antrobus. *I Remember.* Toronto: The Ryerson Press, 1946.
Grieves, Keith. *The Politics of Manpower, 1914–1918.* Manchester: Manchester University Press, 1988.
Griffith, Paddy. *Battle Tactics of the Western Front: The British Army's Art of Attack 1916–1918.* London: Yale University Press, 1994.
Hamilton, General Sir Ian. *Report on the Military Institutions of Canada.* Ottawa: Government Printing Bureau, 1913.
Harris, Stephen J. *Canadian Brass: The Making of a Professional Army 1860–1939.* Toronto: University of Toronto Press, 1988.
Haycock, Ronald. *Sam Hughes: The Public Career of a Controversial Canadian 1885–1916.* Waterloo: Wilfrid Laurier University Press, 1986.
Hayes, Lieutenant-Colonel Joseph. *The Eighty-Fifth in France and Flanders.* Halifax: Royal Print & Litho Limited, 1920.
Hitsman, J. Mackey. *Attempts to Integrate Canada's Armed Forces before 1945: Report No 15.* Ottawa: Department of National Defence, Directorate of History, 1967.
Hodder-Williams, Ralph. *Princess Patricia's Canadian Light Infantry 1914–1919.* Vol. 2. London: Hodder & Stoughton, 1923.
Hopkins, J. Castell. *The Canadian Annual Review of Public Affairs: 1918.* Toronto: The Annual Review Publishing Company, 1916.
Hunt, Captain M.S. *Nova Scotia's Part in the Great War.* Halifax: The Nova Scotia Veteran Publishing Co. Limited, 1920.

Hunter, Captain A.T. *History of the 12th Regiment, York Rangers, with Some Account of the Different Raisings of the Militia.* Toronto: Murray Printing Company Limited, c. 1912.

Iarocci, Andrew. *Shoestring Soldiers: The 1st Canadian Division at War, 1914–1915.* Toronto: University of Toronto Press, 2008.

Jabotinsky, Vladimir. *The Story of the Jewish Legion.* New York: Bernard Ackerman, 1945.

James, Brigadier E.A. *British Regiments 1914–1918.* London: Samson Books, 1978.

Johnston, Lieutenant-Colonel G. Chalmers. *The 2nd Canadian Mounted Rifles (British Columbia Horse) in France and Flanders.* Vernon: Vernon News Printing & Publishing Company, c. 1931.

Keren, Michael, and Shlomit Keren. *We Are Coming, Unafraid: The Jewish Legions and the Promised Land in the First World War.* Plymouth: Rowman & Littlefield Publishers, 2010.

Kerry, Colonel A.J., and Major W.A. McDill. *The History of the Corps of Royal Canadian Engineers*, vol. 1, *1749–1939.* Ottawa: The Military Engineers Association of Canada, 1962.

Knight, Jill. *The Civil Service Rifles in the Great War: "All Bloody Gentlemen."* Barnsley, South Yorkshire: Pen & Sword Military, 2005.

Love, Major Albert G., and Major Charles B. Davenport. *Defects Found in Drafted Men: Statistical Information Compiled from the Draft Records, Showing the Physical Condition of the Men Registered and Examined in Pursuance of the Requirements of the Selective Service Act.* Washington: Government Printing Office, 1920.

Love, David W. *A Call to Arms: The Organization and Administration of Canada's Military in World War One.* Winnipeg & Calgary: Bunker to Bunker Books, 1999.

Lyddon, Colonel W.G. *British War Missions to the United States 1914–1918.* London: Oxford University Press, 1938.

Machin, Lieutenant-Colonel H.A.C. *Report of the Director of the Military Service Branch.* Ottawa: King's Printer, 1919.

MacLaren, Roy. *Canadians in Russia, 1918–1919.* Toronto: Macmillan of Canada, 1976.

Macphail, Sir Andrew. *Official History of the Canadian Forces in the Great War, 1914–1919: The Medical Services.* Ottawa: F.A. Acland, 1925.

Macpherson, Major-General Sir W.G. *History of the Great War Based on Official Documents: Medical Services General History.* Vol. 1. London: HMSO, 1921.

McEvoy, Bernard, and Captain A.H. Finlay. *History of the 72nd Canadian Infantry Battalion, Seaforth Highlanders of Canada.* Vancouver: Cowan & Brookhouse, 1920.

McLellan, Roy A. *Day to Day Experiences during World War I and World War II.* Privately printed, c. 1958.

McWilliams, James L., and R. James Steel. *The Suicide Battalion.* Edmonton: Hurtig Publishers, 1978.

Messenger, Charles. *Call to Arms: The British Army 1914–1918.* London: Weidenfeld & Nicolson, 2005.

Miller, Carman. *A Knight in Politics: A Biography of Sir Frederick Borden.* Montreal & Kingston: McGill-Queen's University Press, 2010.

Miller, Ian Hugh Maclean. *Our Glory and Our Grief: Torontonians and the Great War.* Toronto: University of Toronto Press, 2002.

Millman, Brock. *Polarity, Patriotism and Dissent in Great War Canada, 1914–1919.* Toronto: University of Toronto Press, 2016.

Moir, John S., ed. *History of the Royal Canadian Corps of Signals 1903–1961.* Ottawa: Corps Committee Royal Canadian Corps of Signals, 1962.

Morton, Desmond. *Canada and War: A Military and Political History.* Toronto: Butterworths, 1981.

– *The Canadian General: Sir William Otter.* Toronto: Hakkert, 1974.

– *A Military History of Canada.* Edmonton: Hurtig Publishers, 1985.

– *Ministers and Generals: Politics and the Canadian Militia 1868–1904.* Toronto: University of Toronto Press, 1970.

– *A Peculiar Kind of Politics.* Toronto: University of Toronto Press, 1982.

– *When Your Number's Up: The Canadian Soldier in the First World War.* Toronto: Random House of Canada Ltd., 1993.

Newman, Stephen K. *With the Patricia's in Flanders 1914–1918: Then & Now.* Saanichton, British Columbia: Bellewaerde House Publishing, 2000.

Nicholls, Lieutenant-Colonel T.B. *Organization, Strategy and Tactics of the Army Medical Services in War.* London: Bailliere, Tindall and Cox, 1937.

Nicholson, Colonel G.W.L. *The Gunners of Canada.* Toronto: McClelland and Stewart, 1967.

– *Official History of the Canadian Army in the First World War: The Canadian Expeditionary Force 1914–1919.* Ottawa: Queen's Printer, 1962.

Ontario, Province of. *Statutes of the Province of Ontario.* Toronto: King's Printer, 1909.

Osborne, John Morton. *Voluntary Recruiting Movement in Britain, 1914–1916.* New York: Garland Publishing, 1982.

Pariseau, Jean, and Serge Bernier. *French Canadians and Bilingualism in the Canadian Armed Forces.* Vol. 1, *1763–1969: The Fear of a Parallel Army.* Ottawa: Department of National Defence, Directorate of History, 1988.

Perry, Frederick William. *The Commonwealth Armies: Manpower and Organisation in Two World Wars*. Manchester: Manchester University Press, 1988.

Phillips, Roger F., Francis Dupuis, and John Chadwick. *The Ross Rifle Story*. Sydney, Nova Scotia: J.A. Chadwick, 1984.

– *A Technical Appraisal of the Ross Rifle*. Antigonish, NS: Casket Printing and Publishing, 1984.

Philpott, William. *War of Attrition: Fighting the First World War*. New York: The Overlook Press, 2014.

Pitsula, James M. *For All We Have and Are: Regina and the Experience of the Great War*. Winnipeg: University of Manitoba Press, 2008.

Radley, Kenneth. *We Lead, Others Follow: First Canadian Division 1914–1918*. St Catharines: Vanwell Publishing, 2006.

Rannie, William F., ed. *To the Thunderer His Arms: The Royal Canadian Ordnance Corps*. Lincoln, ON: W.F. Rannie Publisher, 1984.

Rawling, Bill. *Surviving Trench Warfare: Technology and the Canadian Corps, 1914–1918*. Toronto: University of Toronto Press, 1992.

Reville, F. Douglas. *History of the County of Brant*. Vol. 2. Brantford, ON: Hurley Printing Company, 1920.

Reynolds, Major E.G.B. *The Lee–Enfield Rifle*. New York: Arco Publishing Company, 1962.

Richardson, James D., ed. *Compilation of Messages and Papers of the Presidents*. Washington: Bureau of National Literature, n.d.

Roy, R.H. *Sinews of Steel: The History of the British Columbia Dragoons*. Brampton: Charters Publishing Company, 1965.

Ruck, Calvin W. *The Black Battalion: 1916–1920: Canada's Best Kept Military Secret*. Halifax: Nimbus Publishing, 1987.

Rutherdale, Robert Allen. *Hometown Horizons: Local Responses to Canada's Great War*. Vancouver: UBC Press, 2004.

Satzewich, Vic. *Racism in Canada*. Don Mills, ON: Oxford University Press, 2011.

Simkins, Peter. *Kitchener's Army: The Raising of the New Armies 1914–1916*. Manchester: Manchester University Press, 1988.

Stacey, C.P. *Canada and the Age of Conflict: A History of Canadian External Policies*. Vol. 1, *1867–1921*. Toronto: The Macmillan Company of Canada, 1977.

Starling, John, and Ivor Lee. *No Labour, No Battle: Military Labour during the First World War*. Stroud, Glos.: The History Press, 2009.

Steel, James R., and Captain John A. Gill. *The Battery: The History of the 10th (St Catharines) Field Battery Royal Canadian Artillery*. St Catharine's: 10th Field Battery Association, 1996.

Stewart, William F. *The Embattled General: Sir Richard Turner and the First World War.* Montreal and Kingston: McGill-Queen's University Press, 2015.

Summers, Jack L. and René Chartrand. *Military Uniforms in Canada.* Ottawa: Canadian War Museum, 1981.

Swettenham, John. *Allied Intervention in Russia 1918–1919 and the Part Played by Canada.* London: Allen & Unwin, 1967.

Tascona, Bruce. *From the Forks to Flanders Fields: The Story of the 27th City of Winnipeg Battalion, 1914–1919.* Winnipeg: Bunker to Bunker Books, 1995.

Theobald, Andrew. *The Bitter Harvest of War: New Brunswick and the Conscription Crisis of 1917.* Fredericton: Goose Lane Editions and the New Brunswick Heritage Project, 2008.

Thompson, John Herd. *The Harvests of War: The Prairie West, 1914–1918.* Toronto: McClelland and Stewart, 1981.

United States. *Statutes at Large of the United States of America.* Washington: Government Printing Office, 1909.

– *Treaties, Conventions, International Acts, Protocols and Agreements between the United States and Other Powers, 1910–1923.* Vol. 3. Washington: Government Printing Office, 1923.

United States, Bureau of the Census. *Historical Statistics of the United States, Colonial Times to 1970: Part I.* Washington: US Government Printing Office, 1975.

University of Western Ontario. *The Hour of Trial & Sorrow: The Great War Letters of the Leonard Family.* London, ON: University of Western Ontario, 2015.

Urquhart, Lieutenant-Colonel H.M. *The History of the 16th Battalion (The Canadian Scottish) in the Great War 1914–1919.* Toronto: The Macmillan Company of Canada Limited, 1932.

Wallace, O.C.S., ed. *From Montreal to Vimy Ridge and Beyond: The Correspondence of Lieut. Clifford Almon Wells, B.A. of the 8th Battalion, Canadians, B.E.F. November 1915–April 1917.* Toronto: McClelland, Goodchild & Stewart, 1917.

Ware, Colonel Francis B. *The Story of the Seventh Regiment Fusiliers.* London: Hunter Printing Company, 1946.

Warren, Arnold. *Wait for the Waggon: The Story of the Royal Canadian Army Service Corps.* Toronto: McClelland and Stewart Limited, 1961.

Watson, Lieutenant-Colonel W.S., ed. *The Brockville Rifles, Royal Canadian Infantry Corps (Allied with the King's Royal Rifle Corps): Semper Paratus, An Unofficial History.* Brockville: The Recorder Printing Company, 1966.

Watts, Martin. *The Jewish Legion and the First World War.* Basingstoke, Hants: Palgrave Macmillan, 2004.

Wheeler, Captain Owen. *The War Office, Past and Present*. London: Methuen & Co., 1914.
Wiktor, Christian L., ed. *Unperfected Treaties of the United States of America: 1776 1976*. Vol. 4. Dobbs Ferry, NY: Oceana Publications, 1979.
Willett, T.C. *A Heritage at Risk: The Canadian Militia as a Social Institution*. Boulder, CO: Westview Press, 1987.
Williams, Captain Basil. *Raising and Training the New Armies*. London: Constable and Company, 1918.
Wilson, Barbara M., ed. *Ontario and the First World War 1914–1918: A Collection of Documents*. Toronto: Champlain Society, 1977.
Winegard, Timothy. *For King and Kanata: Canadian Indians and the First World War*. Winnipeg: University of Manitoba Press, 2012.
Wise, S.F. *Canadian Airmen in the First World War: The Official History of the Royal Canadian Air Force*. Vol. 1. Toronto: University of Toronto Press, 1981.
Wong, Marjorie. *The Dragon and the Maple Leaf: Chinese-Canadians in World War II*. Toronto: Pirie Publishing, 1994.

ARTICLES AND BOOK CHAPTERS

Anstead, Christopher J. "Patriotism and Camaraderie in a Peacetime Militia Regiment 1907–1954." *Histoire Sociale–Social History* 26, no. 52 (November 1993).
Avery, Donald. "Ethnic and Class Relations in Western Canada during the First World War: A Case Study of European Immigrants and Anglo-Canadian Nativism." In *Canada and the First World War: Essays in Honour of Robert Craig Brown*, edited by David MacKenzie. Toronto: University of Toronto Press, 2005.
Bliss, Michael. "War Business as Usual: Canadian Munitions Production 1914–1918." In *Mobilization for Total War, The Canadian, American and British Experience 1914–1918, 1939–1945*, edited by N.F. Dreisziger. Waterloo, ON: Wilfrid Laurier Press, 1981.
Brown, Colonel J. Sutherland. "Military Policy of Canada, 1905–1924 and Suggestions for the Future." *Canadian Defence Quarterly* 1, no. 4 (July 1924).
Brown, Robert Craig and Donald Loveridge. "Unrequited Faith: Recruiting the CEF 1914–1918." *Revue Internationale d'Histoire Militaire*, no. 54 (1982).
Crerar, Adam. "Ontario and the Great War." In *Canada and the First World War: Essays in Honour of Robert Craig Brown*, edited by David MacKenzie. Toronto: University of Toronto Press, 2005.

Dennis, Patrick. "A Canadian Conscript Goes to War – August 1918: Old Myths Re-examined." *Canadian Military History* 18, no. 1 (2009).

Dutil, Patrice A. "Against Isolationism: Napoléon Belcourt, French Canada, and La grande guerre." In *Canada and the First World War: Essays in Honour of Robert Craig Brown*, edited by David MacKenzie. Toronto: University of Toronto Press, 2005.

Gagnon, Jean-Pierre. "Canadian Soldiers in Bermuda during World War One." *Histoire Sociale–Social History* 23, no. 45 (May 1990).

Gill, Douglas, and Gloden Dallas. "Mutiny at Etaples Base in 1917." *Past & Present*, no. 69 (November 1975).

Granatstein, J.L. "Conscription and My Politics." *Canadian Military History* 10, no. 4 (Autumn 2001).

– "Conscription in the Great War." In *Canada and the First World War: Essays in Honour of Robert Craig Brown*, edited by David MacKenzie. Toronto: University of Toronto Press, 2005.

Gwynne, Lieutenant-Colonel R.J. *Explanations and Details for Movements in Cavalry Training*. Winnipeg: Colonial Press, 1909.

Hamilton, Colonel C.F. "Lieutenant-General Sir Willoughby Gwatkin – An Appreciation." *Canadian Defence Quarterly* 2, no. 3 (April 1925).

Jackman, S.W. "The Victoria Pioneer Rifle Corps, British Columbia, 1860–1866." *Journal of the Society for Army Historical Research* 39 (1961).

Lackenbauer, P. Whitney. "Pay No Attention to Sero: The Mohawks of the Bay of Quinte and Imperial Flying Training during the Great War." *Ontario History* 96, no. 2 (Autumn 2004).

Maroney, Paul. "The Great Adventure: The Context and Ideology of Recruiting in Ontario, 1914–1917." *Canadian Historical Review* 77, no. 1 (March 1966).

Morton, Desmond. "The Short, Unhappy Life of the 41st Battalion, CEF." *Queen's Quarterly* 81, no. 1 (Spring 1974).

Murray, Captain W.W. "Canadians in Dunsterforce." *Canadian Defence Quarterly* 8, no. 2 (January 1931).

Sharpe, C.A. "Enlistment in the Canadian Expeditionary Force: A Regional Analysis." *Revue d'Études Canadiennes / Journal of Canadian Studies* 18, no. 4 (hiver/Winter 1983–1984).

– "Enlistment in the Canadian Expeditionary Force: A Re-evaluation." *Canadian Military History* 24, no. 1 (Winter/Spring 2015).

Sokolov, Hyman. "The Jewish Legion for Palestine." In *Jewish Life and Times: A Collection of Essays*. Winnipeg: Jewish Historical Society of Western Canada, 1983.

Vance, Jonathan F. "Research Note: Provincial Patterns of Enlistment in the Canadian Expeditionary Force." *Canadian Military History* 17, no. 2 (Spring 2008).

Walker, James W. St G. "Race and Recruitment in World War I: Enlistment of Visible Minorities in the Canadian Expeditionary Force." *Canadian Historical Review* 70, no. 1 (March 1989).

Willms, A.M. "Conscription, 1917: A Brief for the Defence." *Canadian Historical Review* 37, no. 4 (December 1956).

Winegard, Lieutenant T.C. "Dunsterforce: A Case Study of Coalition Warfare in the Middle East, 1918–1919." *Canadian Army Journal* 8(3): Fall 2005.

UNPUBLISHED SOURCES

Cameron, Captain L.R. "The Command of the Overseas Military Forces of Canada in the United Kingdom, 1914–1918." Ottawa: DHH Historical Report no. 98 (n.d., declassified 3 December 1986).

Campbell, David. "The Divisional Experience in the C.E.F.: A Social and Operational History of the 2nd Canadian Division 1915–1918." PhD diss., University of Calgary, 2003.

Foyn, Sean Flynn. "The Underside of Glory: AfriCanadian Enlistment in the Canadian Expeditionary Force, 1914–1917." Master's thesis, University of Ottawa, 1999.

Hapak, Joseph T. "Recruiting a Polish Army in the United States, 1917–1919." PhD diss., University of Kansas, 1972.

Ramsay, Michael Albert. "Tactics in Crisis: The Intellectual Origins of Modern Warfare in the British Army, 1870–1918." PhD diss., Queen's University, 1997.

Ruskoski, David T. "The Polish Army in France: Immigrants in America, World War I Volunteers in France, Defenders of the Recreated State in Poland." PhD diss., Georgia State University, 2006.

Ryan, Michael Patrick. "Supplying the Materiel Battle: Combined Logistics in the Canadian Corps, 1915–1918." Master's thesis, Carleton University, 2005.

Smylie, Eric. "Americans Who Would Not Wait: The American Legion of the Canadian Expeditionary Force." PhD diss., University of North Texas, 2002.

Walker, Richard J. "The Political Management of Army Leadership: The Evolution of Canadian Civil–Army Relationships 1898–1945." PhD diss., University of Western Ontario, 2003.

NEWSPAPERS AND PERIODICALS

Boston Daily Globe
Canadian Defence Quarterly
Canadian Observer
Canadian Railway and Marine World
Charlotte Daily Observer
Chatham Daily Planet
Edmonton Daily Bulletin
Edmonton Journal
Grain Growers' Guide
Hamilton Spectator
Labour Gazette
Lethbridge Daily Herald
London Advertiser
Medicine Hat News
Montreal Gazette
New York Times
Royal Gazette (Bermuda)
St Marys Argus
Stratford Daily Beacon
Stratford Daily Herald
Times of London
Toronto Globe
Toronto Star
Toronto World
Vancouver Sun
Wiarton Echo
Woodstock Daily Sentinel-Review

Index

Advanced Headquarters, 248–9
aliens: acceptance in CEF 1917, 68; barred from enlisting 1914–15, 67; enlistment of, 66–70; internship of, 37; *Military Service Act* and conscription 1918, 68
Army Service Corps (British): Canadian wartime recruits, 45, 46

bantam battalions, 59–61
black recruits, 73–4
Blake, Sergeant Maud, 102
British-Canadian Recruiting Mission, 88–91; and French Canadians, 90; recruiting in Canada for the Jewish Legion, 89–90
British flying services, Canadian manpower, 44–5

Canadian base depots, 1st Division 1915, 233–4
Canadian Casualty Assembly Centre (CCAC), 214–16; problems, 216–17
Canadian Casualty Training Battalion, 216
Canadian Command Depot (CCD), 26, 215–18

Canadian Corps Railhead Depot (CCRD), 248–9
Canadian Corps Reinforcement Camp (CCRC), 27, 139, 176, 210, 240, 243, 245–50, 246 fig. 9.1, 246 fig. 9.2; designed to meet Canadian needs, 250; locations, 248; organization, 246; staff responsibilities, 248
Canadian Defence Force (CDF) 1917, 122–4
Canadian Expeditionary Force (CEF): establishment, 11; histories of, 7; increase in numbers, 38, 113, 192
Canadian General Base Depot (CGBD): established, 234–5; handling of drafts, 238–9; isolated from CEF, 235–6; new organization and site, 239–40; and reinforcements, 242–4, 250; staffing and workload, 237
Canadian identity, 12; in British army, 46, 86
Canadian Infantry Base Depots: conditions in, 239; consolidation of, 241–2; reinforcements and, 241;

routine, 240–1; staffing and organization, 240
Canadian Training Division (CTD) Shorncliffe, 131
citizenship and enlistment. *See under* enlistment criteria
Command Depots, British prewar planning, 170–2
conscription. See *Military Service Act*
convicts, 92–4
corps depots, 186–7
corps training depots: established in England 1914, 210; problems, 210–11; PPCLI depot in England, 211–13

dentures, provision of, 61–2
depot batteries, establishment in 1915, 185–6
districts and divisions, organization as of March 1914, 19 table 1.1

England, command and control: creation of HQ Overseas Military Forces of Canada and effect on training, 160–2; effect on training, 158–62; lack of coordination between Shorncliffe and Bramshott, 160
enlistment: of aliens (*see* aliens); in prisons, 92–4; of skilled workers to specialist corps, 63
enlistment criteria: age, 56–9; citizenship, 66–70; dental, 61–2; exceptions, 63; height, 59–61; medical, 63–5; in prisons, 92–4; psychological and psychiatric, 65–6; vision, 62
entrenching battalions: Canadian, 242–3; established by BEF 1915, 173; phased out in 1917, 173

equipment: Pattern 1908 web, 162, 236; Pattern 1916 Oliver, 162
ethnicity and enlistment: ambivalence about, 243; ethnic groups deemed "safe," 70; First Nations, 75–7; visible minorities, 71–5
expatriate Canadians: in Montenegrin, Serbian, Czech, and Polish armies, 46–8
eyeglasses, provision of, 62

false statements on enrolment, 77–9
First Nations: in 1st Canadian Pioneer Battalion, 46; in 26th Middlesex Light Infantry, 24; enlistment, 75–7; as non-commissioned officers, 23, 24; supposed ban from enlistment in CEF, 23; tradition of militia service before the war, 23
furloughs: effect on training in Canada, 128, 152–3, 155

headquarters, militia and district: organization and difficulties, 17–18
Hughes, Sam, Minister of Militia and Defence 1911–16, xvii; and ammunition problems, 147; authority constricted by convention, 104–5; authorizes new battalions, 118, 192; creation of Canadian Corps and divisions, 49–50; emphasis on militia-style training, 27; formation of depots, 185–8; increases to CEF, 38, 113; indecisiveness, 115; and recruiting structure, 104–20, 125; recruiting outside of parent district, 114–15; and revised height criteria, 59; resignation, 220, 227, 155, 196; temperament, 16–17

Imperial Munitions Board: construction of airfields, 45; employment of Canadian labour, 42
Inland Water Transport (Royal Engineers): Canadian recruits, 45–6

Jewish Legion, 47, 89–90

labour: civilians and soldiers diverted to British industry, 36–7

machine gun training, 149–52; Colt machine gun, 149–50; Lewis gun training in Canada, 151; Savage Lewis guns and compatibility problems, 150–1; substitution of Lewis gun for Colt, 150
manpower management: and 5th Division, 50–1; determining fitness to serve at the front, 96–7; determining number of men fit and available to serve, 79–82; diversion of civilian workers to British firms, 36–7; government efforts to control enlistment, 38–40; increase in strength of infantry, machine gun, and engineer units, 50–3; medical categories, 95–6; national conference to mobilize manpower, 41; OMFC and new units, 232–3; shortage of civilian workers and effect on CEF, 38–40
medical screening of recruits: role of physicians, 63–6
Military Service Act (1917): and convicts, 93–4; discussion and historiography, 10–11; manpower policies, 40; movement overseas and contribution to Canadian Corps 1918, 206–7

militia: Active, Reserve, and Permanent Force, 14; role in mobilization, 107–10
militia, peacetime: characteristics and effect on CEF, 33; clothing and equipment, 29–31; demographic makeup, 21–2; francophones in, 19; local initiatives, 28–9; training and facilities, 24–5; questionable standards in 1914, 29; recruiting and training cycles, 20; summer camps, 25–8; visible minorities in, 22–4
Militia Council, structure and difficulties with Sam Hughes, 15–17
mobilization: of 2nd Division, 107–10; centres, 125–6; of First Contingent, 107; pre-war, 106–7
Muslims, 22

Overseas Military Forces of Canada (OFMC): creation and reforms 1917–18, 227–30

Permanent Force, peacetime units and shortcomings, 14–15
physicians. *See* medical screening of recruits

recruiting: in 1915 (*see* recruiting in 1915); of Americans (*see* recruitment of Americans and American residents); in Bermuda, 83–4; in Britain, 84–6; by CEF units, 113; centralization by district, 124–5; of convicts, 92–3; and deferred enlistment, 114; and development of district control, 117–18; in district mobilization centres, 125–6; in France and Belgium, 84; of immigrants (*see* recruitment of immigrants); issues in 1915–16, 115–16; outside of parent district, 114–15; return to militia-based methodology 1917, 196–9; requirement to be Canadian citizen, 85; unit-based approach ends, 119–20; wholesale creation of infantry battalions, 192–5; of women, 102

recruiting depots in Canada 1914, 185

recruiting in 1915: gradual demise of militia recruiting, 112; militia recruiting 1917, 120–2; use of civilian recruiters in Atlantic Canada, 111–12; use of militia units, 111. *See also* Canadian Defence Force

recruitment of Americans and American residents, 86–91; 7th Field Company recruiting agent in Detroit, 88; advertising in American newspapers, 87; Bohemian National Alliance (Canadian Branch), 88; modifications 1917, 88; U.S. laws, 87. *See also* British-Canadian Recruiting Mission

recruitment of immigrants: Canadian attitudes toward, 98; language issues, 100–1; from non-English-speaking countries, 97–9; Royal Canadian Regiment deserter born in Germany, 99–100; security concerns, 99

reinforcement demands: and Canadian Section, 175–6; drawbacks to system, 176–7; establishment of GHQ 3rd Echelon, 173–5

reinforcements: partly trained 1916–17, 243–4

reserve establishments in England, 223–5

reserve infantry battalions: in Canada, 188–9; problems in Canada, 189–90; problems in England, 191, 192; resistance by CEF units, 190–1

reservists: British, 43; recall of Canadian residents by other nations, 42–3

reserve units in England: command, coordination, and control, 226; organization, instructors, and problems 1915–16, 219–22; training camps, 225–6

Russian-Canadian soldiers: enlistment of, 68–70; at Shorncliffe, 100

statistics, problems with CEF, 8

territorial affiliations: units in England and France 1917–18, 230–2

territorial depot battalions: development, 199–201; difficulties forwarding reinforcements from Canada, 205–6; final form and establishment, 201–2; infantry arrivals in England 1917–18, 204–5; origins, 195–6

training, assessment standards including musketry, 139–40; base training school (Bull Ring), 140–1

training, British doctrine used by CEF: ACI 1103/1916 (fourteen weeks), 136–7; ACI 1968/1916 (fourteen weeks), 136–7; ACI 1230/1917 (fourteen weeks), 137; ACI field firing exercise, 136; AO

324/1914, 135; AO 388/1914, 135; replacement of British syllabi by Canadian nine-week emergency syllabus, 137–9; WO 156/1915, 135–136; WO 156 Canadian modification, 136

training, comments by British authorities, 131; comparison with British units, 131–2; First Contingent 1914-15, Valcartier 1914, 129; former service in First Contingent, 132–5; Salisbury Plain, England 1914–15, 130–1

training, coordination between Canada and England, 155–8; effect of fatigues in England, 164–7; effect of lack of winter clothing and facilities (*see* winter clothing and facilities); machine gun (*see* training, machine guns); training levels of battalions arriving in England, 156–7

training, machine guns, 149–52; Colt machine gun, 149–50; Lewis gun training in Canada, 151; substitution of Lewis gun for Colt, 150; Savage Lewis guns and compatibility problems, 150–1

training, rifles and ammunition, 142–6; ammunition, 146–8; charger loading, 143–4; redistribution of rifles, 145; rifle handling standards on arrival in England, 148

training and furloughs. *See* furloughs

unemployment and recruiting for CEF in 1914, shortages of skilled tradesmen, 34–6
units outside of the Canadian Corps, 53–4

wastage: causes and rates by corps, 178–81; effect on unit fighting strength, 181–2; pre-war estimates and revised rates in 1914, 177–8; revised rates, 178
weapons: obsolete rifles in peacetime militia, 31–3; standardization between Canadian troops in England and France, 163–4
winter clothing and facilities: effect on training, 153–5; limited issues of snowshoes, 154–5
women: Sergeant Maud Blake, Canada's only known female soldier, 102; Captain Julia Willmothe Henshaw, recruiting officer 1915–17, 125; proposed enrolment by 16th Light Horse 1907, 28; unsuccessful attempt in 1918 to raise Canadian Women's Army Auxiliary Corps, 102–3
wounded: held by Canadian Casualty Assembly Centre (*see* Canadian Casualty Assembly Centre); held by reserve battalions 1915, 213–14